Revolution as Development:
The Karen Self-Determination
Struggle against Ethnocracy
(1949-2004)

Revolution as Development: The Karen Self-Determination Struggle against Ethnocracy (1949-2004)

Jack Fong

Universal Publishers
Boca Raton, Florida

Revolution as Development: The Karen Self-Determination Struggle against Ethnocracy (1949-2004)

Universal Publishers
Boca Raton, Florida • USA
2008
REV 1

ISBN-10: 1-59942-994-2
ISBN-13: 978-1-59942-994-6

www.universal-publishers.com

Library of Congress Cataloging-in-Publication Data

Fong, Jack, 1970-
Revolution as development: the Karen self-determination struggle against ethnocracy (1949-2004) / Jack Fong. -- 1st ed.
    p. cm.
  Includes bibliographical references.
  ISBN-13: 978-1-59942-994-6 (pbk. : alk. paper)
  ISBN-10: 1-59942-994-2 (pbk. : alk. paper)
 1. Ethnic conflict--Burma. 2. Karen (Southeast Asian people)--Burma. 3. Conflict management--Burma. 4. Burma--Politics and government--1988- 5. Burma--Social conditions--1988- I. Title.
  HN670.7.S62F66 2008
  305.895--dc22

2008003104

Table of Contents

VI. Liberation Ethnodevelopment and Key KNU Institutions

VII. Myth of the "Internal Affair": Geo and Petropolitical Complicity

VIII. 2004 Ceasefire Concerns for the KNU

IX. Conclusion

Acknowledgements

Before we begin, I want to express my deepest gratitude to all the kind people abroad and at home that have supported this project. At the University of California, Santa Cruz, I begin by first thanking my mentors: historian of South Asia Dr. Dilip Basu, ethnic and indigenous scholar Dr. John Brown Childs, development scholar Dr. Ben Crow, jurisprudence scholar Dr. Hiroshi Fukurai, political sociologist Dr. Craig Reinarman and Dr. Guillermo Delgado from the Latin American and Latino Studies Department. They challenged me with very profound questions regarding the Karen—many of which I hope were answered in this work.

My gratitude also goes to Stephen McNeil, Regional Director of Peacebuilding and Relief Work for the *American Friends Service Committee* based out of San Francisco, California. Stephen was kind enough to take time from his busy schedule to meet with me as well as provide for me insight into the world of Karen refugees. I would also like to thank Dr. Rodolfo Stavenhagen, whose brief correspondence with me through email regarding ethnodevelopment has helped me immeasurably. My application and readjustment of Dr. Stavenhagen's ideas represent the core of my work.

In Thailand, I also cannot overemphasize my gratitude to my childhood friends, Jane Ritdejawong and Owen Silpachai. It is absolutely no exaggeration to say that this research would not have materialized were it not for Jane's assistance. As an accomplished television journalist and producer, Jane visited the Karen State of Kawthoolei after the 1995 fall of its capital, Manerplaw. She thus had first-hand experience with the suffering experienced by the Karen. Because of Jane, I see an important role journalists can play with field researchers conducting ethnographic research in the context of systemic crisis. Owen, also a childhood friend, was gracious enough to provide for me one of his dwellings in Bangkok's Silom District. Being situated in this part of the city allowed me to be close to important venues for publishing/printing, internet use, money exchange, and public transportation. I was able to finish the rudimentary sections of my research in his Silom condominium. Logistically, Owen's assistance was priceless.

In Kawthoolei, I have to thank Colonel San Htay (pseudonym) for taking time out from his extremely busy schedule to meet with me. From the day we crossed the Moei River to arrive at Mu Aye Pu, until my last meeting with him in Bangkok prior to my return to the United States, I have always felt a deep sense of respect for his courage in navigating an epic struggle against oppression. I am also very thankful for Col. San Htay's assistants, also pseudonymously referred to Tha Doh, Maung Baw, Hope, and Roni who were kind enough to assist me at Mu Aye Pu and beyond Mu Aye Pu. Much gratitude also goes to the KNLA's Captain "Tony" who, on leave from the frontlines, enthusiastically shared with me his views on the Karen struggle.

I also want to extend my thanks to the Mya brothers, as well as the late General Bo Mya, along with other KNU commanders who graciously allowed me hold dialog with them. I would also like to thank the Karen villagers, the bright and energized Karen youths, and the KNLA at Mu Aye Pu, who shall not be referred to by name due to the sensitivity of their standing. I am also extremely grateful to the visiting commanders from the 201 battalion, and commanders of the 202 battalion at Mu Aye Pu, that were kind enough to allow me into their world. I also want to thank the nurses at 202, one of whom spoke good English and helped me to connect to the non-English speaking Karen at the base. I also thank the two Thai intelligence officials by the name of "Peter" and Lieutenant "Wila" that were also kind enough to share with me Thai views on the Karen struggle at the 202.

Thank you to the many authors, writers, and journalists that, in the name of uncovering the truth, have risked their well-being to analyze and report on the conditions of the Karen in Burma from a local and global perspective. For readers interested in assisting the Karen cause, the many Karen non-governmental organizations cited in the text all have excellent websites and accept donations.

Finally, and without exception, I dedicate my research to the Karen people and all peoples of Burma engaged in their drive for democracy. I have been nothing more than an interloper in your epic and only hope that my work will be able to repay the lessons all of you have given me on life, hope, and freedom.

Author's Note

There are many political and non-political organizations in Burma. In the text, as is the customary practice, the full name of the organization will be listed upon first mention, followed by the acronym in parentheses; subsequent references to the organization will only be in acronym format. Should readers forget the meaning of the acronyms, refer to this page, derived from Martin Smith's 1999 work *Burma: Insurgency and the Politics of Ethnicity*.

ABSDF:	All Burma Students Democratic Front
ABFSU:	All Burma Federation of Students Union
AFPFL:	Anti-Fascist People's Freedom League
ALP:	Arakan Liberation Party
APC:	Armored personnel carrier
ASEAN:	Association of Southeast Asian Nations
BIA:	Burma Independence Army
BSPP:	Burma Socialist Programme Party
CBE:	Citizens for a Better Environment
CCP:	China Communist Party
CNF:	Chin National Front
CPB:	Communist Party of Burma
CPT:	Communist Party of Thailand
DAB:	Democratic Alliance of Burma
DKBA:	Democratic Karen Buddhist Army
DKBO:	Democratic Karen Buddhist Organization
DNUF:	Democratic Nationalities United Front
EGAT:	Electricity Generating Authority of Thailand
EIA:	Environmental Impact Assessment
ERI:	Earth Rights International
FAO:	Food and Agriculture Organization
FBR:	Free Burma Rangers
FPMA:	Five Party Military Alliance
FWI:	Fritz Werner Industries
HRW/A:	Human Rights Watch/Asia
ICG:	International Crisis Group
IDP:	Internally Displaced People
IMF:	International Monetary Fund
INGO:	International non-governmental organization
KAF:	Karen Armed Forces
KEF:	Kawthoolei Education Fund
KGB:	Karen Governing Body
KHRG:	Karen Human Rights Group

KIA:	Kachin Independence Army
KIO:	Kachin Independence Organization
KMT:	Kuomintang
KNA:	Karen National Association
KNDO:	Karen National Defence Organization
KNLC:	Karen National Liberation Council
KNLP:	Karen/Kayan New Land Party
KNPP:	Karenni National Progressive Party
KNUP:	Karen National United Party
KPLA:	Kawthoolei's Peoples Liberation Army
KRC:	Karen/Kawthoolei Revolutionary Council
KTWG:	Karen Teachers Working Group
KWO:	Karen Women's Organization
MIS:	Military Intelligence Services
MNLA:	Mon National Liberation Army
MOGE:	Myanma Oil and Gas Enterprise
MPF:	Mon People's Front
MTE:	Myanma Timber Enterprise
MTTT:	Mobile Teacher Training Team
NCGUB:	National Coalition Government Union of Burma
NCUB:	National Council of the Union of Burma
NDUF:	National Democratic United Front
NGO:	non-governmental organization
NLA:	Nationalities Liberation Alliance
NLC:	National Liberation Council
NLD:	National League for Democracy
NLD-LA:	National League for Democracy-Liberated Area
NMSP:	New Mon State Party
NULF:	National United Liberation Front
NUFA:	National Unity Front of Arakan
PA:	People's Army
PNO:	Pa-O National Organization
PDP:	Parliamentary Democracy Party
PLA:	Patriotic/People's Liberation Army
PSLP:	Palaung State Liberation Party
PTT:	Petroleum Authority of Thailand
PVO:	People's Volunteer Organization
RAN:	Rainforest Action Network
RC:	Revolutionary Council
RECOFTC:	Regional Community Forestry Training Center
SAIN:	Southeast Asian Information Network
SEATO:	Southeast Asia Treaty Organization
SHRF:	Shan Human Rights Foundation
SLORC:	State Law and Order Restoration Council

SPDC:	State Peace Development Council
SSA-S:	Shan State Army-South
SSIA:	Shan State Independence Army
SSNLO:	Shan State Nationalities Liberation Organization
SSPP:	Shan State Progress Party
STR:	Special Township Region
SWAN:	Shan Women's Action Network
UN:	United Nations
UNHCR:	UN High Commissions for Refugees
UNRISD:	UN Research Institute for Social Development
UPNO:	Union Pa-O National Organization

Names of Karen individuals I personally interacted with will be given pseudonyms to protect their identities. However, those individuals that have had public exposure, for example, in the press and/or in the televised media, will be referred to by their actual names.

Preface

Before exploring the epic Karen struggle for self-determination, I find it important to point out the date of September 27, 2007, during the Buddhist uprisings in Burma where tens of thousands of serried people, with hands adjoined, marched alongside the unarmed Buddhist clergy—the *Sangha*—shielding them from potential harm. On this date, in the eastern hills of what is in essence the descending flanks of the eastern Himalayas, hundreds of kilometers away from Burma's former capital at Rangoon, the Karen National Union (KNU), the political body of the Karen Revolution, urged all ethnic nationalities of Burma to support the predominantly Buddhist and Burman monks in their uprisings against military rule. In solidarity with the people of Rangoon and all of Burma the KNU communiqué stated:

> We...earnestly urge you, the armed forces, to stop shooting and killing the people and the Sanghas, and stand on the side of the people and the Sanghas by turning...against the...generals, who are making you commit heinous crimes so that they may remain in power (Irrawaddy.org, September 28, 2007).

Upon reading this communiqué, I was swept by very deep, powerful, and visceral emotions, for it was the KNU and the Karen National Liberation Army (KNLA) that granted me entrance to their free state of Kawthoolei between January 2004 and May 2004. At the KNU headquarters of Mu Aye Pu, base for the KNLA 202 battalion, I was introduced to themes of the Karen Revolution and Karen nation construction. Sadness overcame me, however, since I knew that the Karen armed struggle, along with struggles by other democratically aspiring ethnic nationality groups, is ignored precisely for the same reason that Aung San Suu Kyi's approach based on *satyagraha* is not.

My work thus focuses on the Karen self-determination struggle begun in 1949. The Karen struggle against military rule in Burma has often been overlooked by the international community when compared to the exploits of democratic activist Aung San Suu Kyi. The Karen have been fighting a fifty-nine year campaign of ethnic discrimination and cleansing directed against them by various pro-Burman governments. The ethnopolitical problems that have affected the Karen have thus predated for decades the democracy struggle that the world now sees in Burma. The Karen Revolution is rich with cues that point to how nationalist and democratic politics are ideologically harnessed to attain autonomy and development. It is within this complex world that those interested in Burma must begin since there are *many* regional players in its epic sociopolitical landscape.

Chapter I
The Karen Epic and the Journey

The Epic

At the time of this writing an uprising by Burmese monks in major cities of Burma[1], otherwise known as Myanmar by polities that recognize the current military regime, appears to have come to a temporary close. However, reports on the uprisings, presented on television for the world to see, and linked historically to the military crackdown upon the student uprisings of 1988 and the denial to Aung San Suu Kyi the prime ministership, have ignored the source of the country's problems: its labyrinthine and unresolved ethnopolitics. Indeed, for decades the region's ethnic minorities, or ethnic nationalities in the political parlance of the region, have challenged the hyper-nationalist militarists from the dominant Burman ethnic group.

By ignoring the region's ethnopolitics, world attention on Burma is highly myopic and exhibits numerous political blind spots. Specifically, world attention on Burma overlooks how the interior of the region, populated by fiercely independent non-Burman peoples in their respective nations, can be analyzed transnationally. It is within this context that I introduce the Karen ethnic nationality and their struggle for liberation against three atavisms and forty-six years of genocidal military rule. Indeed, the Karen struggle against Burman chauvinism, or *Burmanization*, has the dubious distinction of being the twentieth century's longest and most underreported civil war, begun in 1949 and continuing to this very moment.

The Karen struggle began in January 1949, when Burma's independence from colonial rule was beset by social breakdown. Burma, a country ruled by an *ethnocracy*[2] since 1948 and by three military regimes since 1962, has engaged in frequent military campaigns of ethnic cleansing against its ethnic nationalities. As Rangoon descended into various incarnations of military rule, Karen self-determination was employed in hopes of countering a totalitarian and racist regime. In the early years of the war the Karen aspired to fight for a separate state but have since shifted their platform toward fighting for a greater autonomy within a federalized Burma.

---

[1] As Heppner, founder of the Karen Human Rights Group, notes, "those who do not recognize the military junta as a legitimate government continue to use the name Burma" (Heppner 2000, 1). I will do so as well.

[2] A term utilized by Stavenhagen (1986, 1996) and David Brown (1994) to refer to the ethnic group with the most political power within a multiethnic or pluralistic setting. I shall expand on this in greater detail in Chapter 2.

The fighting between the Karen and Rangoon has the dubious distinction of being one of the longest civil wars of the twentieth century, lasting well into the twenty-first century. Yet the tensions between the Karen and Burman predate the post-colonial period. As a Karen village elder had told Major Abbey at the Karen village of Kya-in before the end of World War II, and at a time when inter-communal strife was increasing daily:

> As a minority, our political union with the Burman in the past...has not been a safe, satisfactory and happy one. History repeats itself. Centuries ago, before the advent of British rule, our ancestors had continuously suffered the persecution at the hands of the Burmans and no sooner had the British left this shore...the tell-tale temperament of the Burman made itself felt on the Karen masses... We strongly appeal...to the authorities concerned, that the Karen be allotted a certain part of Burma where we could...administer ourselves free from the Burman (Rogers 2004, 76).

For decades Rangoon's attempts at consolidating the country were based on forcefully persecuting ethnic nationalities like the Karen. The Karen have responded with a self-determination struggle against one of the world's most brutal military regimes. In this regard, the examination of how the Karen people aspire to develop themselves is simultaneously an examination of how the military polities of Burma and its construction of the nation-state have failed.

In 1962, after General Ne Win's coup that established the first military regime of Burma, the Burma Socialist Program Party (BSPP), Rangoon has been attempting to subdue not only the Karen but other ethnic nationalities through an ethnic cleansing policy known as the *Four Cuts* (*Pya Ley Pya* in Burmese). Karen activists are not the only group employing this designation, as international observers, pressure groups, and non-governmental organizations have also designated the events inside Burma as genocide/ethnic cleansing (Rogers 2004; International Crisis Group 2003; Karen Human Rights Group 2000; Smith 1999; Human Rights Watch 1995, 1997, 1998; Lintner 1994; Fredholm 1993; Falla 1991).

By the early 1990s, when the second military regime, the State Law and Order Restoration Council (SLORC) rejected democratic elections and reforms voted by the Burmese, as well as putting election winner Aung San Suu Kyi under house arrest, the *Tatmadaw*—generally used to refer to Burma's armed forces—has repeatedly been condemned by the United Nations, the International Labour Organisation, the European Union Parliament, the US State Department, and various human rights organizations for its rampant human rights abuses.[3] Yet still the Tatmadaw has remained intransigent in its treatment of the Karen, other ethnic nationalities, as well as pro-democracy Burmans.

Burman chauvinism can clearly be seen in the explicit behaviors of members of the Tatmadaw: in 1992, Tatmadaw General Ket Sein had publicly announced, "In ten years all the Karen will be dead. If you want to see a Karen, you will have to go to a museum in Rangoon" (Rogers 2004, 40). Yet Ket Sein was hardly the only Burman chauvinist at the time. In February 1996 on Myanmar TV, deputy chairman General Maung Aye, the current regime's number two man after General Than Shwe, was shown "stamping on a Karen flag" and forcing a recently surrendered Karen leader "to kneel before him and apologise for their rebellion" (Rogers 2004, 40). Indeed, the Tatmadaw's confidence in Burma's development was quite pronounced by the late 1990s: it had destroyed the very important Karen capital of Manerplaw in 1995—home to a variety of democratically aspiring ethnic coalitions as well as a base for the NLD. By 1997, it had immobilized Aung San Suu Kyi and her political party, the National League for Democracy (NLD). Thus, in 1997 SLORC renamed its polity to the State Peace and Development Council (SPDC).

The Karen have had little choice but to maintain their course toward self-determination. One of the principles of their revolution mandates unending resistance and no surrender. However, in 2004, an informal gentleman's ceasefire was declared by Rangoon and the KNU. Tatmadaw General Khin Nyunt wanted to negotiate with the KNU in hopes of attaining a lasting peace. The KNU responded, and General Bo Mya of the KNU, KNU congress members, and top KNLA commanders were invited to Rangoon for talks. It was during this window period that I first entered Kawthoolei, the name the Karen give their homeland.

However, despite a gentleman's ceasefire, the Tatmadaw had repeatedly betrayed this agreement by continuing their harassments and violations of Karen human rights in areas which should be free from the fighting. Moreover, hawks in Rangoon concerned that Khin Nyunt's political gestures were too concessionary, ousted him in a military coup in late 2004. Since then hardliners led by the SPDC's General Than Shwe have consolidated their hold on power.

Rangoon's continuing acquisition of weaponry from their main ally, China, means that the Karen continue to face frequent offensives and attacks by a modernizing military. The disparity in weapons between the two sides is even more shocking when we consider that despite Burma's military rule, the

---

[3] The Tatmadaw evolved from the Burma Independence Army (BIA) established by Japan during World War II to fight the British. Fredholm notes that the BIA "distinguished itself by slaughtering and massacring ethnic minorities to such an extent that even the Japanese had to step in" (Fredholm 1993, 75).

regime has not been invaded by another country since its 1948 independence from Britain; that is, Burma has no international enemies, its entire half-million troops and military apparatus exists solely by waging war against its ethnic nationalities and the pro-democracy Burman activists who struggle alongside them.

The fifty-nine year saga of the Karen resistance continues to this very day, with new issues, both local and global, that beset the KNU. The current older and younger generation of the KNU leadership are attending to a generational change in its rank and file as well as continuing to attend to multiple generations of war-fatigued Karen, many of whom have been relegated to being refugees and/or internally displaced peoples (IDPs). Regardless of which Karen one speaks to the vast majority are ready for a political and peaceful resolution to the conflict for since 1949 over 300,000 Karen lives have been lost, thousands of villages have been razed to the ground, over a million Karen have been internally displaced, over one hundred thousand Karen have been forced to flee as refugees into Thailand, and the fragile ecosystems on which their livelihood depends are being destroyed.

Although many Karen do not want a peace that would compromise the ideals of the Karen Revolution, some Karen are ready for peace at all costs. The KNU, on the other hand, have not been defeated by the Tatmadaw. In this complex ethnopolitical terrain, amid the dozen self-determination groups that are still challenging Rangoon's authority, the Karen—one of Burma largest ethnic nationalities after the Burmans—emerge as the ethnic nationality "that has fought the longest, suffered the most, and came closest to achieving their aims of self determination for a greater autonomy" (Peck 2004, Rogers 2004). At the time of this writing, ceasefire talks have all but evaporated and a formal peace agreement with conditions acceptable to both the KNU and the SPDC does not exist.

The staying power of the Karen struggle typifies how disadvantaged ethnic minority groups seeking to improve their human condition remain one of the most significant factors for social change (Gurr 1993). It is my hope to introduce the Karen struggle as an example of what Benedict Rogers describes as a "wider struggle that all the people of Burma are fighting for" (2004). Yet to effectively read how the Burman militarists violently deny the Karen development and how the Karen concomitantly respond by engaging in their own autonomous development requires us to employ a perspective contributed by Rodolfo Stavenhagen known as *ethnodevelopment* (1986, 1996).

As a development strategy ethnodevelopment positions the state to foster "development of ethnic groups within the framework of the larger society" (Stavenhagen 1986, 92). By virtue of this statement, Stavenhagen provides an honest picture of multiculturalism, namely that resources are skewed toward and by the dominant and/or largest ethnic/racial group, in our case, the Burmans. The CIA breaks down Burma's population as such: Burman - 68 percent, Shan - 9 percent, Karen - 7 percent, the Rakhines and Rohingyas of Arakan - 4 percent, Chinese - 3 percent, Indian - 2 percent, Mon - 2 percent, and other at 5 percent (CIA World Factbook 2005). The Karen population, depending on which source one refers to, ranges between 2.5 million to 7 million. The underestimated figure is what the SPDC claims, while the KNU claims the latter figure (Rogers 2004, 30). Accurate population figures are impossible to come by since the last formal census ever taken in Burma took place during the 1930s while it was under British rule.

Hardly a "Union" as claimed by Burman nationalists, the country contains over 130 ethnic nationalities and over 100 languages spoken. But more importantly, the Karen are not the only ethnic nationality engaged in a struggle for democracy. Following the Karen in 1949, the Shan, Mon, Karenni, Arakan, Chin, Kachin, and many other ethnic nationalities have all launched their own self-determination struggles against the Tatmadaw. Most have since signed ceasefires during the different amnesties offered by Rangoon, while a handful continue on alongside the KNU.

That ethnodevelopment emphasizes development policies need to be "sensitive to the needs of ethnic minorities and indigenous peoples and where possible controlled by them" is perhaps nowhere more exigently appropriate than in Burma, given the aforementioned diversity and autonomy demanded by many of its ethnic nationalities (Clarke 2001, 413). The most significant benefit of employing an ethnodevelopment perspective is the *a priori* acceptance that ethnicity has material consequences, and that somehow a multicultural configuration contains some form of resource asymmetry. In the case of Burma's political landscape, one that is fraught with acute ethnic inequalities and systemic crises, the asymmetry in material consequences and quality of life experienced by different ethnic nationalities invites scrutiny into the role that ethnicity plays in development.

Although the ethnodevelopment envisioned by Stavenhagen (1996, 1993, 1986), Hettne (1996), and Clark (2001) assumes the centralized polity can function as a conduit from which resources are then distributed toward ethnic minority development, this approach cannot fully illustrate what is actually occurring in Burma. Since Burma's independence in 1948, pro-Burman governments, flushed with power from acquiring larger territories, have preferred to use force and maldevelopment to consolidate peripheral areas where the majority of Burma's ethnic nationalities conceptualize as territories of their own nations. Moreover, since General Ne Win launched his coup to establish Burma as a militarized state in 1962, Rangoon has *institutionalized* a violent process of internal colonization upon Burma's ethnic nationalities. The Karen and their homeland of Kawthoolei have not been spared and have been subjected to the heaviest brunt of Burmanization throughout its fifty-nine year struggle.

Whatever articulation of ethnodevelopment that occurs for the Karen is based on being structurally opposed to what the Tatmadaw conceives of as development. For the Karen, their self-determination for a greater autonomy, designed to preserve heritage, culture, way of life, and a regional political economy is thus a *bottom-to-top* ethnodevelopment process. This is an important distinction to remember for it means that Karen development occurs not from the charity of the Burmese state, but from its own Karen-administered institutions. Indeed, I point out that the Karen ethnodevelopment trajectory *is* the revolution the KNU launched in 1949, and is a response to how frequently development strategies "based on a top-down design have failed to reach their explicitly stated objectives" (Sachs 1992, 7).

Karen ethnodevelopment harnesses its own social institutions and regional political economy that are structurally opposed to Rangoon to sustain their self-determination struggle. These they use to develop as much as possible the lives of the Karen people in Kawthoolei. At the peak of Karen nationalism and administrative efficacy, the KNU administered their own hospitals, various social departments, and schools that teach in the main Karen dialects. Although these institutions have suffered tremendously due to the fifty-nine years of protracted warfare, it is nevertheless important to identify the structures and assess their benefits upon civilian Karen. This is an important task because it is through these institutions that the KNU has constructed their nation as well as their own sense of legitimacy as an autonomous political entity.[4] Indeed, the Karen that manage their country's institutions and political economy exemplify a hitherto unexplored trajectory of ethnodevelopment as a liberation movement and revolutionary force. Thus Karen *liberation ethnodevelopment* is explicitly unlike Stavenhagen's ethnodevelopment.

Given the complexities of Karen and Burmese ethnopolitics, two questions drive my work. The first question asks: what are the distinguishing features that allow the Karen to sustain their struggle in spite of the adversities that have confronted their revolution? More specifically what KNU institutions reinforce Karen self-determination as a form of development? The second question is: what factors will affect the future of the Karen struggle and the Karen way of life as they continue to seek a greater autonomy through self-determination? To answer these two questions requires us to (1) fuse ethnopolitics with the material analyses of the Karen human condition as well as (2) make visible that ethnicity, apart from its intimate links to the cultural system, is also very much a development system comprised of political institutions and political relationships.

---

[4] My use of the term *state* implies a multicultural or relatively homogeneous country. I do not employ the term nation-state because it overlooks the contradictions of multiethnic or multicultural realities, which is characterized by many intra-state nations, not just one nation constructed by a dominant ethnic group.

In the process of exploring the Karen struggle and its ethnodevelopment, I attempt to counter two myths regarding the Karen struggle. The first myth is that British colonization and Christian indoctrination generated the clash of Karen and Burman identities. Although the United Kingdom was certainly a colonial power that ruled Burma as a province of India until a few years after World War II ended, and supremely versed in decolonizing machinations that would configure most of its former colonies to be in political disarray and sectarian strife, to argue that British colonials and Christian missionaries constructed the Karen identity—as suggested by Rajah (2002), Bryant (1997), and Keyes (1979)—overlooks how the cultural fault lines predate any systematic European colonial maneuverings to pit one group against another (Wee 2002). Indeed, Gurr reminds us that autonomy demands by indigenous groups should not be taken for granted as a recent phenomenon, as they only emanate from groups with "a tradition of political independence and sharp cultural differences from dominant groups" (1993, 316).

Moreover, attributing the beginning of the Karen Revolution as being instigated by the British is exactly the line continued to be held by the various military regimes. It is a trite position that has been regurgitated to justify its continuing enforcement of violently punitive measures against the Karen as colonial collaborators. Furthermore, adopting this stance overlooks the fact that after World War II Burman militarists also colluded with the British under the Attlee administration, which, after relinquishing Burma, began supplying Rangoon with arms to quell the first decade of the Karen Revolution. It also overlooks the fact that Burma has itself become an internally colonizing force implementing its own unique divide-and-rule formula for repressing its ethnic nationalities.

The second myth to be dispelled is that self-determination politics are the "internal affairs" of Burma, a claim repeatedly made by the Tatmadaw so as to ward off international scrutiny and condemnation. This line is still held by the SPDC, the current military regime now based out of Burma's new capital at Naypidaw.[5] The position of not interfering with the internal affairs of Burma is also subscribed, albeit nominally, by states such as China, India, Thailand, and the Association of Southeast Asian Nations economic bloc (ASEAN). In reality, there is nothing politically or materially "internal" regarding Rangoon's maneuverings against the Karen. Rangoon and its military juntas readily court and receive from many countries tacit support and funding for their internally colonizing policies.

Discrediting the second belief is important because it makes visible the different networks that have formed internationally to sustain the regimes. Yet, the panglossian international community continues to expect the regimes

---

[5] The scope of this book encompasses a time dimension when Rangoon was still the administrative capital. As such, the remainder of this text will employ Rangoon when discussions center on domestic policies supported or enforced by the Tatmadaw.

to be the catalysts for change. Burma's regimes have had many decades and numerous political opportunities to shift toward a genuine democracy and the development of its ethnic nationalities and regions, yet it has chosen to evolve under various atavisms of military rule. Even under Burma's first prime minister after independence, U Nu, the "democratic" period saw Burman chauvinism and Burmanization generate ethnic bloodshed.

This is why it is important for us to be conscious of the players that maintain dialog with Rangoon, as well as making visible the links Rangoon has with other governments that are complicit in the international participation of genocide. One cannot fully understand the dynamics of self-determination without exploring the geopolitical context that surrounds all players.

To accomplish these goals, the Karen struggle will first be situated historically so that changing ideological, political, geopolitical, and military anatomies of the Karen Revolution can be made visible. Here I am in line with scholars like Edmund Leach (1964) who emphasized that understanding a culture is a historical process based on ever-changing social structures, and Stefano Varese (2002) who criticized the "poverty" of an ahistorical ethnography. Yet I would like to add a corollary to Varese's advocacy on the importance of historical analyses: that historical dynamics should be viewed dialectically. Because the human condition of the Karen since Burma's independence has been within a context of protracted conflict, the evolving "spiral" of Karen revolutionary dynamics can only be understood against the policies and maneuverings of the Tatmadaw, where diametric tensions between the two break, evolve, and reform.

One of the most challenging aspects of writing about the Karen struggle is determining what social features to include in my analyses. To detail every factor that has shaped the Karen struggle would be a task too monumental for the scope of this book. Readers interested in an exclusive Karen civilian perspective, the Karen ethnogenesis and their exodus from Mongolia in two distinct waves before the Christian era, the Karen during the colonial period, the history of religion in Karen culture, and the ideas presented by the proto-Karen nationalist, Sir San C. Po, will have to engage in independent readings elsewhere. My examination begins during the charged nationalisms that emerged in Burma after World War II.

The Journey

The approach employed to create this work was significantly influenced by Michael Burawoy's important text, *Global Ethnography* (2000). I attempted to break out of the researcher's solitary confinement of being "bounded to a single place and time" and acquire information from more than one place and source (2000, 4). As such I followed my Karen contacts as they navigated their struggle transnationally, be it in Kawthoolei, Mae Sot, Doi Saket, Bangkok, and even California. I did not desire to be a lone and secluded researcher, an image made popular by Bronislaw Malinowski when he resided with the Trobriand islanders during the early part of the twentieth century.

My examination of Karen liberation ethnodevelopment is based on a synthesis of historical, critical, exploratory, and descriptive research. It is primarily *historical* in that I observe the evolving aspects of Karen self-determination as well as how Karen institutions and development have had to respond to them. It is *critical* in that I ultimately make the case that the military regimes' construction of a "Union" of Burma, due to its draconian policy of internal colonization and ethnic cleansing, qualifies the state of Burma as a failed nation-state project. It is *exploratory* in that I am trying to make visible how Karen self-determination and development of the Karen nation occurs within the context systemic crisis—a condition where social institutions of a society are unable to effectively provide welfare for its citizens due to war (and as we shall see in the next chapter, few development analyses or strategies factor in systemic crisis and its capacity to influence the parameters of an ethnic group striving to develop). And finally, it is *descriptive* in that I try to describe how key Karen social institutions attempt to sustain Karen liberation ethnodevelopment.

Information was derived from interviews, documents, and historical examinations of Karen 20th century development through KNU institutions. I was also mindful of Burawoy's caveat to not let analyses "disappear into the interiors of organizations and institutions" (Burawoy et al. 2000, 6). However, conducting research in the field forced me to factor in the circumstances of interacting with actors in a war zone. Thus, scheduled interviews, data collection, and interpersonal interactions frequently faced two main barriers.

First, gathering information in the context of war meant that the duration of my time spent interacting with pro-KNU Karen at various sites was subject to time constraints. My sample of participants was small. Sadly, much interview data were thrown out because some of these Karen later abandoned the struggle, a status I worried would jeopardize their safety were I to include their sentiments. Commanders and colonels I had the most interaction with since many of them spoke rudimentary Thai and/or English. My stay at the 202 was intermittent and dictated by ceasefire talks that either freed up or restricted contacts from holding dialog with me. Given these uncertain circumstances, KNU factions that had their own spin on the struggle, and the sensitivity of information during war, I did not have time to form the long-term bonds needed to be privy to more in-depth information.

Due to the volatility of ceasefire talks, arrangements for my stay were thus designed for me to get as much information as possible within the shortest possible time. I did not have the needed resources for a long-term trek into Kawthoolei like Karen experts such as Falla (1991), Smith (1999), Rogers (2004), or Lintner (1994). Thus, the information and insights drawn from the field were acquired from conversations and observations with Karen civilians, KNLA guerillas, and journalists at Mu Aye Pu, as well as from interactions with them at confidential areas dispersed within Thailand. Fortunately my "thickest" immersion in Karen nationalism began a few weeks after my arrival to the 202, when the rank and file of the KNU and KNLA arrived at Mu Aye Pu for festivities on January 31st, Karen Revolutionary Day.

Second was my inability to converse in the Karen dialects of Sgaw or Pwo. I lacked the financial means to employ professional interpreters that would have assisted me in activities related to my research. Up until Karen Revolutionary Day, this forced me to rely on Karen interpreters that were only rudimentary in Thai. Adding to the difficulty was my colloquial and conversational Thai, which was far from effective in communicating the abstract details related to self-determination and ethnodevelopment. This did not stop me from holding candlelight meetings with many young KNLA soldiers. The meetings were not interviews per say, but more of a question and answer interaction based on holding dialog.

I did not view reliance on dialog-based interactions as a total disadvantage. A very powerful realization that dawned on me was that the Karen, like the Peruvian Ashaninka that Varese studied (2002) or other threatened indigenous groups, are a people in survival mode. As a result the Karen were clear in their articulations regarding how they felt about their lives, and this could only be captured through the informality of talk. And it was in this mode where the Karen most appreciated my presence. This quality, I can only hope, cemented the relationship between my research and the Karen human condition. I hope that the outcome of my immersion—despite my status as an outsider working within a less than desirable time frame—will show the consistent links between how Karen liberation ethnodevelopment in times of war is intimately linked to how the Karen construct their nation.

Given these circumstances, an alternative designation would be that my approach is a result of *site work*, a term recommended by my colleague John Brown Childs. Indeed, the hyper-intense world of inconclusive ceasefire talks that could quickly revert to war, the intergenerational personalities engaged within this war, as well as the uncertainties involved in the daily maneuverings of the KNU and civilian Karen displaced by war, resulted in a *hyper*-time research context where as much information as possible needed to be gathered in the shortest possible time frame. Therefore, my work is far from a "pure" ethnography, if such a term exists, but a fusion of historical analyses and site work, with information drawn heavily from the former.

Determined to ground the Karen struggle in its local and temporal histories, I realized that recovering a painful past was not easy. This process was further exacerbated by the demands of war and poverty that affected the participants I interacted with. As aforementioned, I realized that much of my data contained too many one-sided and factional views regarding the Karen struggle, necessitating me to supplement my research with additional information from journalists, anthropologists, development strategists, and activists, as well as publications by pressure groups and international and local non-governmental organizations.

Although many scholars have written on the civil wars in Burma, my preferences were for those writers who possessed *experiential authority*, or the ability to "'feel' the foreign context" (Clifford 1983) by transferring knowledge derived from having experienced what is being examined. Burmese scholars' insights and exposures to the Karen human condition are needed to accent the realities of Burma, a region quite unfamiliar within the American sociological imagination of Southeast Asia. Certainly many notable academics and scholars deserve more mention, but in terms of grasping the Karen revolutionary experience so that the people's suffering can be communicated viscerally to readers, having experiential authority is a vital prerequisite for uncovering the complexities of Burma's ethnopolitics.

My first contact with a Karen occurred in Bakersfield, California in June 2003. I had the pleasure of meeting with an ex-KNU member at her home. Her husband was a commander of one of the KNLA brigades. The meeting was ostensibly about where and when to enter Kawthoolei. However, it turned out to be a long and in-depth dialog where I was given a condensed history of the Karen struggle. Moreover, I was advised on how to prepare logistically for the trip. During this period I also made a series of carefully scheduled phone calls to Colonel San Htay of the KNLA. Prior to my arrival in Mae Sot, Thailand, I thus already had the opportunity to speak with an important KNLA figure.

Over a period of five-and-a-half months between January and May 2004, I collected information with Karen and KNU members at four major sites. In chronological order, my first meetings with the KNU took place at Mae Sot, in Thailand's Tak province, directly east of Kawthoolei's Pa-an District. This first meeting was based on being introduced to Colonel San Htay. Over lunch we talked about the state of the Karen struggle. Dialog and discussion followed regarding how and when to schedule my eventual trek into Kawthoolei.

The second site for gathering information was at Mu Aye Pu, the KNU base for the KNLA 202 Battalion, in the 7th Brigade area which administers Pa-an District. Mu Aye Pu is separated from Thailand by the Moei River. I arrived at Mu Aye Pu in early January 2004. Setting foot on this patch of Karen soil, albeit within the orbit of Thailand (after all, one could, with strong arms, throw a stone to the Thai bank of the river) created an atmospheric state of surreal anxiety. I climbed a series of steps that led to the top of the base as the eyes of civilians and soldiers watched our entourage reorient ourselves to what was, in essence, a community engaged in rebellion within their jungle sanctuary. At Mu Aye Pu I held dialog with the KNLA, the nursing and medical staff, some villagers, as well as with base commanders.

My most important contacts at Mu Aye Pu were forged on the January 31st celebrations of Karen Revolutionary Day. Amidst powerful performances by Karen *Don* dancers and their drummers, hundreds of Karen villagers, a battalion of KNLA soldiers standing in formation, over a dozen large woks with frying meats and its concomitant white smoke from charcoal flames, and over two dozen KNU/KNLA commanders including General Bo Mya gathering for festivities, I ended up meeting key KNU/KNLA officers, Thai intelligence, and observers from international charity organizations. Moreover, many Karen I met on Karen Revolutionary Day were quite fluent English speakers. They had to be, since this contingent of Karen was in charge of linking the Karen struggle to an international audience sympathetic to human rights. This strategy attracted visitors representing humanitarian groups and many were frequently taken on tours to Karen refugee camps along the border. The key individual I met on this significant day was Pastor Lah Thaw, whose kindness, charisma, and forthright manner in holding dialog impressed me highly.

After departing Mu Aye Pu, I returned to Mae Sot with an entourage of KNU congress members, British charity representatives, and Thai intelligence officials. Dialog took place in Mae Sot during late February. The interactions took place in a variety of settings: at a hotel where KNU members frequently preferred to stay, at a barber shop where Pastor Lah Thaw, surrounded by his bodyguards, was getting a haircut, and inside a hotel room where KNU members reviewed taped footage of National Day celebrations. Important conversations also took place in the hotel dining area with Thai intelligence officers who discussed with me Thailand's role in the KNU struggle over breakfast, coffee, and cigarettes.

In a quiet scenic suburb not far from Chiang Mai, Thailand, was another site where I was able to hold dialog with key KNU members during March 2004. It was the location for the headquarters of a ministry headed by Pastor Lah Thaw. There I was able to converse with KNU members and Karen youths engaged in missionary work and humanitarian relief efforts. I also attended a Sunday church service in Chiang Mai, conducted by Pastor Lah Thaw. Most importantly, in Chiang Mai, reports, documents, statistics on the Karen situation, be it maps, refugee camp figures, and assessments of the Karen struggle from a KNU point of view, were provided for me. After returning to Bangkok, I made another visit to the outskirts of Chiang Mai to meet with KNU members and pro-KNU Karen. I was also able to join a contingent of Karen that welcomed visiting representatives from various international non-governmental organizations.

I was also able to intermittently hold dialog in Bangkok over many months. Pastor Lah Thaw, KNU members, as well as Colonel San Htay and his brothers often held high-level confidential meetings with Thai officials in the safer environs of the city. During their visits to the Thai capital I would be contacted to meet with them. However, I would never be able to anticipate their arrival as they only contacted me when they were already in Bangkok, and only if they had the time to spare for meetings. It would also be in Bangkok where I began writing in earnest. Five months transpired from when I first met Colonel San Htay in January 2004, until my last meeting with him in May 2004. Finally returning to the U.S., I was able to hold dialog with Pastor Lah Thaw in Norwalk, California, when he visited during summer 2004 to receive his Honorary Doctorate degree from a local Christian university.

Overview of Text

The product of my experiences with the Karen inside Kawthoolei, in northern and western Thailand, in Bangkok, as well as in the United States, has resulted in the following chapters: In Chapter 2 I briefly outline the twentieth century evolution of development theory and thinking. Given that I hope to conceptualize the Karen Revolution as a development trajectory, it is imperative that conventional models of development, especially the economistic models, be discussed historically since the end of Word War II. I will then explore important paradigm shifts by compartmentalizing them on a continuum divided by decades following World War II until the present.

In Chapter 3 I begin my exploration of Stavenhagen's ethnodevelopment by examining its main component, ethnicity, as well as the theoretical debates surrounding ethnicity and its relationship to nation construction. Without a deep understanding of ethnic dynamics a convincing argument for Karen liberation ethnodevelopment cannot be made. In spite of the lengthy discussion on theories related to ethnicity and ethnic conflict, my work is *not* an anthropological examination of Karen culture, of which many authors have already contributed excellent works, but how a politicized Karen ethnicity plays a role in their social development. I thus heed Gurr's reminder (1993) that ethnicity will always have multiple expressions *beyond* culture:

> It is a commonplace to say that the intangible quality of cultural identity gives special intensity to their demands. It is less often recognized that these peoples' historical experience of victimization and exploitation also strengthens group identity and contributes to their sense of collective injustice (1993, 36).

In the process, I also outline coalition politics of the KNU, many of which have been excluded from political representation by the military governments, and thus are also in structural opposition to it. I hope to demonstrate that in the Karen struggle against military dictatorship, ethnodevelopment is a revolutionary force that contests totalitarian rule.

In a politically condensed format, the fifty-nine year history of the Karen struggle will be explored in Chapter 4. The transcommunalities—coalitions that challenge a politics of conversion (Childs 2003)—formed and broken, the territories won and lost, as well as the KNU's experiences with leadership and ideological transitions will also be explored. Military and political developments throughout its fifty-nine years of struggle will be discussed. Chapter 4 describes how the Karen Revolution has evolved, and how changing political and military climates affected and continue to affect KNU maneuvers. The international links formed by the KNU since 1949 will also be explored.

In Chapter 5 I examine the implementation and consequences of the Four Cuts—the military regimes' internal colonization policy—upon the KNLA and the civilian Karen population. For the non-combatant Karen, the effects of the Four Cuts will be examined in six major areas: (1) villagers and villages, (2) forced labor, (3) women, (4) internally displaced peoples (IDPs), (5) refugees, and (6) the regional Karen political economy.

In Chapter 6 I describe key KNU institutions that have allowed for the administration of Kawthoolei as an autonomous state, and how these institutions at certain periods during fifty-nine years of the Karen struggle allowed the Karen to repel Burmanization and the Four Cuts. The institutions are: (1) the KNU, (2) the KNLA, (3) the Forestry Department, (4) the Health Department, and (5) the Education Department. I will then argue that these KNU-established institutions, structurally opposed to the military governments, represent the quintessential manifestation of a unique type of ethnodevelopment I designate as *liberation ethnodevelopment*. By fusing Karen self-determination politics with their liberation ethnodevelopment, we can then use Karen institutional frameworks to make visible the anatomy of a revolutionary state.

In Chapter 7 I discuss how geopolitical and petropolitical maneuvers by the international community reinforce military rule. The role of Thai and Chinese regional politics, along with the petropolitics of oil transnational corporations (TNCs) will receive much scrutiny. Other states indirectly complicit in genocide will also be discussed. In this chapter I debunk the Tatmadaw's defense that the Karen "problem" belongs in the country's "internal affairs" by showing the globalized links between the regimes and the international community. I also attempt to demonstrate the close links between genocide and the destruction of the Karen ecosystem, and how the severed links between the Karen relationships toward their environment have reinforced their destitution.

After exploring the above topics, I return to the twenty-first century of the Karen struggle in Chapter 8, specifically to the year 2004 when the KNU engaged in ceasefire talks with the SPDC. The talks were ultimately suspended when SPDC General Than Shwe purged the relatively moderate General Khin Nyunt, the latter of which supported some form of rudimentary compromise with democracy activists and ethnic nationalities. Important field interviews I witnessed and personally conducted will accent the exigency of events. The aim of this chapter is to describe issues important to the KNU as they navigated the ceasefire talks in an uncertain and precarious period of their struggle.

In Chapter 9, the concluding chapter of my work, the main focus will be on how the future of Karen liberation ethnodevelopment will be shaped. An assessment will also be made regarding why the international community has not been able to foster the establishment of democracy in Burma. Also I discuss whether the international community focuses too much on Aung San Suu Kyi and the NLD, at the expense of the KNU and Burma's other ethnic nationality polities, for bringing forth democracy to Burma.

Chapter II
Development and Karen Self-Determination

The main aim of this chapter is to "funnel" general development perspectives historically so that they will lead into more detailed discussions about ethnodevelopment. The discussion of the following perspectives, however, is purposely written as a brief historical account and not meant to be exhaustive. Development literature is far too large for such a task. I have structured the flow of the chapter in a manner that presents how conceptualizations of development have evolved over many decades, beginning with how development was understood as economic growth, to development as economic distribution, to development as the improvement of the human condition and the removal of socially limiting conditions. Thus, the historical sequencing of development perspectives has been designed to only introduce, not finalize, how development perspectives have evolved.

Development Perspectives in a Historical Context

The idea of development is a word that is almost "synonymous with progress" (Thomas 1992, 6). Yet a variety of ideas exist as to what "progress" actually means. Born from the context of the post-World War II period, progress was characterized by two major dynamics: (1) the decolonization of many parts of the world into a "Third World," that is, the countries "inhabited by non-Europeans that were poor and for the most part colonized by Europe" (McMichael 1996, 28), and (2) the polarization of certain parts of the world into the geopolitical orbits of the USSR and the US. Within this context, US President Truman generated interest in his mention of "development" during his 1949 inaugural address. The suggestion, however, was that the non-Western world was underdeveloped; Truman thus set the precedent where "global hegemony" was granted to a "purely western genealogy of history" and development (Sachs 1992, 9).

There are many ideas on what constitutes development. Cowen and Shenton (1996) in their important work *Doctrines of Development* divide development into two types: one that is intentional practice and the other an immanent historical process. As immanent process, development can historically be viewed as social change where societies are transformed over long periods, and as intentional practice "consisting of deliberate efforts aimed at progress on the part of various agencies, including governments, all kinds of organizations and social movements" (Cowen and Shenton 1996; Thomas 1992, 7).

Cowen and Shenton argue that development was born from nineteenth century intellectual thought that desired to find a way to fuse rapid and significant change (progress) with order through guided intent. Trusteeship, that is, the managers and technocrats who position themselves to determine the process of development for those who are deemed to be less developed, was the stratum that would realize this natural progress and change toward modernity (Storey 2000; Cowen and Shenton 1996, 4). Development doctrine, according to the authors, thus married development to trusteeship.

The initial purpose of development studies was intended to examine notions of progress in terms of improvements made toward people's quality of life, albeit from the perspective of the North. Yet in the decades following World War II scholars, development agencies, and development strategists from different parts of the world have contributed their own perspectives on development. The aim of this chapter demonstrates how many of these perspectives ended up compromising with or contesting against development trajectories prescribed by the North. Over time even definitions of development change in "extremely fast and in very uncertain ways" continuously clashing and evolving with various disciplines competing to contribute effective models toward human progress (Thomas 1992, 1). Although much of development thinking now focuses on the importance of free markets and global trade, new development approaches are emerging to resist or reject the premise that globalization functions as development (Stavenhagen 1993, Allen and Thomas 1992, Hettne 1990)

A. 1950s

During the post-World War II period, the preoccupation with development in a decolonizing world as a means to counter communism generated newer articulations of what development approaches should attend to (Bernstein 1971). The post-1945 period is significant because the disciplines of economics and sociology were yet unable to fully articulate the dimensions of global development in ways that would transcend Western growth models. In regard to development economics, "its neglect of culture, of disciplines such as history, sociology and anthropology, meant that it never produced a theory of economic development and of industrialization. The inability of economic theory to live up to this task was soon appreciated" (Bernstein 1971, 143).

In sociology the modernization paradigm attempted to map out "stages" where an "unproblematic transition from traditional to modern society" occurred based upon "Western individualism...or Western technology...or a mixture of these two factors" (Kiely 1995, 41). Modernization theory is a view of human progress influenced by post World War II reconstruction plans such as the Marshall Plan as well as the "twin sisters" of the international banking system established at Bretton Woods in 1944: the World Bank and the International Monetary Fund (IMF) (McMichael 1996, 49). The aim of arriving at modernity through modernization was nowhere more apparent than in the development strategies of the 1950s. Indeed, "modernization theory" was the development discourse from the 1950s to the late 1960s (Kiely 1995, 2).

Modernization was viewed as attainable when societies passed through a series of stages on their way toward modernity (Rostow 1960, Kiely 1995). Capitalist development was viewed as the model for other post-colonial nations to emulate. Insofar as they relate to the capitalist West, development strategies during the 1950s had mostly focused on economic growth through structural factors. Influenced by John Maynard Keynes' view that unemployment is a consequence of the absence of "certain key markets for... supplies of consumption goods," the burden was left to the government to create spending in these markets so as to help a faltering economy (Toye 1987, 34).[6]

The structuralist approach toward development was subscribed to by Latin American economists such as Raoul Prebisch. Development economics of the structuralist variety emphasized the need for (1) transformation of the economic and social structure, (2) the importance of ownership and control of resources, and (3) the key role of industrialization (Smith 1993, 281). There were also inputs from non-Latin American structuralists, such as British Dudley Seers who argued that development occurred if dependence upon primary exports for capital accumulation is halted. Seers argued that emphasis needed to be shifted toward domestic industrialization as generators of capital, conducted through the process establishing state and economic apparatuses that can further attempts at import substitution industrialization (ISI) (1983). In spite of their efforts, Hunt describes the structuralists as "intellectuals and bureaucrats who unlike the neo-Marxists accepted a philosophy of development through capitalism" (1989, 51).

Between the 1930s and 1970s, many countries of the Third World adopted ISI development strategies based on the (1) promotion of a domestic industrial base to serve the home market, (2) the reduction of dependence on imported (and often expensive) manufactured goods along with export of relatively cheap unprocessed goods, and (3) the protection of domestic industries via tariffs/import controls. Kiely asserts: "Although such a strategy did not preclude export promotion...it is only a slight exaggeration to claim that ISI was the development strategy from the 1950s to the 1970s" (1998, 83).

---

[6] This was the approach adopted by Franklin D. Roosevelt in the New Deal that led the United States out of the Depression. Roosevelt created programs to give relief, create jobs, and stimulate economic recovery for the U.S.

As an ideological perspective, ISI strategies can be viewed as a form of economic nationalism. As a development policy, economic nationalism protected a country's domestic economy from international economic forces—especially market forces that disadvantaged the home country. Seers argues:

> To the internationalists who claim...the world is...increasingly "interdependent"... I would reply that this interdependence is highly asymmetrical, involving those overseas in accepting not merely the cultural values which the superpowers press on them, but also the arms and other products and associated political programmes (Seers 1983, 122, cited in Toye 1987, 37).

For structuralists like Prebisch and Toye, the object of development is "the structural transformation of underdeveloped economies in such a way as to permit a process of self-sustained economic growth...along the lines of...industrially advanced countries" (Hunt 1989, 50). Thus, when one thinks of structuralist development, one needs to juxtapose the tensions between a domestic approach toward development and an internationalist approach toward development, the latter of which argued for "expanding rich-poor links through trade, capital aid and technical assistance" (Toye 1987, 40).

B. 1960s

During the 1960s growth strategies based simply on increasing economic growth were criticized as being too narrow and economistically oriented (Sen 1999, McMichael 1996, Hettne 1990). Indeed, even the United Nations redefined development in its 1962 publication *Proposals for Action* as a move beyond an economistic approach toward development:

> The problem of underdeveloped countries is not just growth, but development... Development is growth plus change. Change, in turn, is social and cultural as well as economic, and qualitative as well as quantitative... The key concept must be improved quality of people's lives (Sachs 1992, 13).

Efforts at promoting development in the 1960s were also enhanced by the United Nations' 1962 establishment of the Economic and Social Council of the United Nations (ECOSCO). ECOSOC aimed to balance the "social" and "economic" concerns of development. From this orientation emerged alternative UN views toward development, as in the 1963 establishment of the United Nations Research Institute for Social Development (UNRISD). The UNRISD, for example, would utilize scholars like Rodolfo Stavenhagen to examine the material consequences of ethnicity and culture in development.

Despite attempts at promoting development during the 1960s, there were significant problems. First, many Third World nations outside the orbit of USSR and US geopolitical influence rightly argued that development aid was most generous to the allies of the pair. As a result, the world developed unevenly, and many decolonized countries not in the orbits of the USSR/US received relatively less aid. For example, US aid to Iran (which during the 1960s still had Shah Pahlavi on the throne), Turkey, Israel, India, Pakistan, South Vietnam, South Korea, the Philippines, Thailand, Laos, and Taiwan "matched the total aid disbursement to all other Third World countries" (McMichael 1996, 55).

Second, criticisms against development strategies emerged from newly decolonized nations. In 1955, at the invitation of leaders from Burma (which at the time was led by U Nu), Sri Lanka, India, Pakistan and Indonesia, 29 countries eventually met in Bandung, Indonesia to form the Non-Aligned Movement (NAM). The NAM represented the interests and priorities of developing countries by addressing common concerns as well as developing joint policies in international relations. More importantly for the discussion of development, it stressed the importance of resisting the pressures of the major powers, maintaining their independence and opposing neo-colonialism and Western domination (McMichael 1996). By the 1960s, NAM members had begun to suspiciously view development strategies from the major powers as a "postwar international project" manipulated by the West for their own interests (Hart 2001, 650). By the end of the 1960s, the belief that development was constituted by various stages toward modernization was no longer accepted because the model was derived from the "achievements of advanced countries" (Brohman 1995a, 125).

C. 1970s

During the 1970s, attempts were made to establish a unified approach toward development. The emphasis was not on the development of "things" but the development of man. As such, development during this period was understood as "economic and social transformation" (McMichael 1996, 109). In the 1974 Declaration of Cocoyoc, development was conceptualized to mean "fulfillment" of the human actor by "pursuing many different roads to development based on self-reliance" (Sachs 1992, 15), while by 1976, the Basic Needs Approach promoted by many experts, governments, and even the World Bank, was adopted as a means of attaining for underdeveloped regions a "specific minimum standard of living before the end of the century" (ibid., 15).

During this period Seers conceptualized development to mean fulfilling the potential of the "human personality" (Seers 1979). Seers argued that although "economic growth is for a poor country a necessary condition of reducing poverty," it is far from being a sufficient condition (ibid., 12). For Seers development theory and strategy necessitated three conditions for the fulfillment of the human personality: (1) the capacity to obtain physical necessities (particularly food), (2) a job (not necessarily paid employment, but including studying, or working on a farm), and most importantly (3) *equality*, which should be considered an objective in its own right (Thomas and Potter 1992, 120).

With the onset of neoliberal doctrine during the late 1970s development was rearticulated by the World Bank's *World Development Report 1980* as successful "participation in the world market" (McMichael 1996, 109). Third World countries would now emulate not necessarily the West, but newly industrializing countries (NICs) via export oriented industrialization (EOI) based on (1) industrial production oriented toward the world market rather than a protected domestic market, (2) industrial production taking place in a context of (more or less) free trade, and (3) industrial production situated in a competitive global arena to drive innovation (Kiely 1998).

During the 1970s, transnational banks (TNBs), with deposits beyond the jurisdiction and control of any government, began to make massive loans to Third World governments. The World Bank, the International Monetary Fund, and the U.S. Federal Reserve Bank functioned as neoliberal mechanisms that circulated American dollars internationally (McMichael 1996, 114). As a result of this process, some Third World countries began to pursue development programs with some predictability (1996, 115). Smith is correct to argue that modernization development viewpoints of the late 1960s were never really discarded but instead had morphed into yet another atavism, a "geographical euphemism of globalization" (Smith 1997, 174). Indeed globalization would proliferate around the globe by the 1980s, linking many countries into a common world market and economic system (Thomas and Potter 1992).

Also during this period, three alternative development doctrines would attempt to enhance our understanding of an international and increasingly neoliberal world economy. On such doctrine, known as underdevelopment theory and made popular by Paul Baran in his 1957 work *Political Economy of Growth* blames the global world economy for the plight of the Third World. As Kiely elucidates in *Sociology of Development* (1995), the general philosophy of underdevelopment is that the international economy operates systematically to sustain and distort the economies of less developed countries. As such, development cannot occur in the periphery since wealth from the periphery was transferred back to the developed countries. McMichael (1996) and Kiely (1995) attribute underdevelopment to be a result of the consequences of colonialism or modern imperialism since development in the poorer economies was far from positive (McMichael 1996, Kiely 1995).

Dependency theory emerged from underdevelopment theory in that it depicted the structural linkages, "embedded in class, productive, and market relations," between metropolitan and peripheral states that stifled development possibilities in the Third World (McMichael 1996). Its main proponent, most notably Andre Gunder Frank (1969a, 1969b), along with Latin American scholars and activists, argued that low levels of development in less economically developed countries were caused by their reliance and *dependence* on more economically developed countries. Kiely notes that the inconclusive outcome of ISI strategies (for example, the newly industrialized countries did quite well when compared to Latin American countries), especially when countries were still "importing more than they were exporting," reflected the "subordinate position of the Third World in the international economic order" (1995, 86; also in Kiely 1998). For those subscribing to the dependence school, one way to counter the international economy is to engage in some form of protectionism or active withdrawal, sometimes referred to as delinking.

Evolving out of the dependency school is world systems theory, made popular by Immanuel Wallerstein (1980a, 1980b, 1988). Wallerstein argued that a world capitalist economy was already established by the sixteenth century with the onset of colonialism. According to world systems theory, the global economy had divided up the globe into four different categories: core, semi-periphery, periphery, and external, into which all regions of the world could be situated. All non-core countries advanced the core in one way or another, and differed in the degree of exploitation meted out to them by the core. Unlike Frank's use of the binary in the metropole vs. satellite configuration, Wallerstein accommodated a sort of global middle class—a buffer zone—exemplified by countries in semi-periphery.

D. The 1980s and 1990s: Neoliberal Development

One general assessment that can be made about neoliberal strategies employed in the Third World during the 1980s and 1990s is that it has not resulted in even development. Selected countries from the three global regions of Africa, Latin America, and Asia will be touched upon. Although only general data will be drawn from a few countries in each region, one will be able to see that the negative consequences of neoliberal development are international in scope.

In the 1980s and 1990s, neoliberalism took hold in twenty-nine sub-Saharan countries. After over a decade of structural adjustment programs (SAPs), the prognosis is not favorable. Indeed, upon the realization of the international financial institutions' (IFIs) inability to develop the countries, political leaders such as South Africa's Mandela declared, "We are convinced, left to its own devices, the South African business community will not rise to the challenges that face us" (Hanson and Hentz 1999, 497). Claims of neo-colonialism, especially by South Africa's labor groups, are used to attack the structural adjustment policies mandated by IFIs. According to Desai (2002), during the 1990s the consequences of neoliberal policies in South Africa have generated: (1) spiraling unemployment, (2) increases in the "ubiquity of a relatively unstable and non-unionized workforce" (2002, 17), and finally (3) increases in the gap between the rich and poor. Desai notes that in 1996, "40 percent of the population got less than 3 percent of the national income while the richest 10 percent enjoyed over 50 percent" (2002, 18). In Zambia, IFIs also encountered much resistance. Zambian president Kenneth Kaunda vociferously condemned neoliberal doctrine and IFIs as organs of neo-colonialism and broke his relationship with them in May 1987 (Hanson and Hentz 1999, 482-483).

In 1981, the Organization of African Unity (OAU) proclaimed that the 1980s would be Africa's "decade of industrialization." However, the consequences of neoliberal approaches toward industrialization and development have been gloomy. Moreover, attempts by the IFIs such as the World Bank and IMF to usher in SAPs have only resulted in Africa being relegated to "newly emergent free zone playgrounds for Northern Atlantic 'casino' investors" (Klak and Myers 1997, 146). Billet (1993) is more cynical, arguing that the OAU's claim about African development during the 1980s and 1990s is comical in hindsight.

The case of Latin America is no better. Although neoliberals would cheer the 1990s as a "triumph of neoliberal economic policies and globalisation in Latin America," this claim only accounts for short-term assessments of development in the region (Amann and Baer 2002, 945). Even though SAPs by IFIs did help minimize inflation in the 1980s and 1990s, as well as stabilize macroeconomic performance, they also exacerbated "inequalities and heightened poverty levels in most of the region" (Roberts and Arce 1998, 217). This characterized Fujimori's Peru where he implemented an "economic shock treatment" that had less than desirable consequences: by the time Fujimori's term concluded there was a virtual collapse of state revenues and expenditures (Roberts and Arce 1998).

Brazil did attain some "notable" growth as it was able to attain price stability (Amann and Baer 2002). It was also able to raise its Human Development Index (HDI), which improved consistently between 1990 and 1998. However, Amann and Baer caution that the figure (in 1998) of .747 was still "substantially below not only the advanced industrial countries but most...larger Latin American countries as well" (2002, 954). Between the mid-1990s until the end of the twentieth century, Brazil's growth performance was described as anemic. In fact, annual growth rate in the 1990s averaged only 1.82 percent as compared to the 1980s average of 3.03

percent (Amann and Baer 2002, 950). Moreover, Brazil's traditional problem of its distribution of income was not resolved. Amann and Baer note that "no matter what policy regime, the distributional problem has always haunted the country" (2002, 951). In fact, Brazil continues to have one of the "world's most uneven distribution of income" (2002, 952-953).

EOI development strategies implemented by the "four tigers" NICs of Hong Kong (not a country per se, but since 1997, a component in one of China's many special economic zones that implement free market policies), Singapore, South Korea, and Taiwan allowed these regions to experience "annual average growth rates of around 8 percent, compared with 7 percent for Japan, and 3 percent for the United States and the European Community" (Kiely 1998, 97). It is important to note that few developing countries up until the 1980s adopted this form of development policy because it entailed much risk (since markets are overseas). Neoliberals attribute East Asian successes to their adoption of EOI, but are less able to explain away the beneficial outcomes that government management of the economy had upon their respective East Asian economies.

Wade (1990) cautions readers about attributing the aforementioned East Asian successes entirely to neoliberal strategies. Wade argues cogently in *Governing the Market* that state intervention was a standard practice during East Asia's period of development. Indeed, the states of South Korea, Taiwan, Japan, and Singapore explicitly engaged in financing key industrial sectors of their economies. Even neoliberals, through the *East Asian Miracle* report of 1993, were forced to concede to this reality. However, neoliberals claimed that state intervention successes were due to "market friendly" strategies.

On the other hand, in the late 1990s Thailand, South Korea, Indonesia, and Malaysia experienced financial crises. Hart notes that "Wall Street was...directly implicated in the financial meltdown following the devaluation of the Thai baht in mid-1997" (Hart 2001, 652). Yet for Thailand between 1960 and 1990, its GDP expanded "more than eighteen fold, with a...7.5 percent average annual growth rate throughout that period" (Smith 1992, 293). Between 1980 and the early 1990s, Thailand experienced an annual average growth rate in exports "of 30 percent, and GDP grew by 9.2 percent a year" (Kiely 1998, 123). In addition, poverty levels were reduced.

However, because Thailand accommodated structural economic reforms encouraged by the World Bank, the wealth generated was spent on debt repayments and as "profits to the transnational corporations" (Smith 1992, 293). Kiely counters with the argument that Thailand's structural adjustment policies were "limited in their implementation, or not carried out until well after the boom was under way" (1998, 122). Thailand's "severe imbalances in the distribution of wealth" has negatively affected its natural resources and infrastructures. Moreover, consequences of a population boom in Bangkok have created one of the world's most polluted cities. The consumption of water pumped from underground aquifers is making Bangkok sink up to 100 mm annually (Smith 1992).

Scholars like DeMartino (1999) propose that Third World countries currently engaged in free trade should reinstate some form of policy to insulate them from the global economy, as well as establish high tariffs and capital controls. Although this policy would hark back to the era of "inefficient" ISI and Keynesian-influenced economics, De Martino cites the realities of the Asian financial crisis and the continuing lackluster performance of neoliberal policies as reasons to reconsider the strategy (1999, 334). DeMartino argues that "global neoliberalism undermines policy autonomy and thereby threatens the ability of domestic social democratic regimes to ensure economic security and equality" (1999, 344).

Due to the continued uneven nature of global development Sachs designated the 1980s as the "lost decade for development" (1992, 16). Even though there was high growth in the East Asian economies of the "four tigers," that is, Taiwan, Singapore, Hong Kong, and South Korea, pessimism prevailed. Sachs noted that the pessimism resulted from the aggressive implementation of SAPs that meant for many countries "abandoning or dismantling, in the name of development, most of their previous achievements" (1992, 16). Moreover, the "new vision" and corresponding SAPs espoused by the World Bank's 1985 report (World Bank 1985, 1), where "markets and incentives can work in developing countries," actually led to an even greater dependency upon richer nations, especially from sub-Saharan African countries (Kiely 1995, 129; George 1990, 143; Hunt 1989). By the end of the 1980s many parts of the South set about dismantling the failed adjustment programs where "leftovers from the North (atomic waste, obsolete or polluting manufacturing plants, unsellable or prohibited commodities)" were attended to in the name of sustainable development (Smith 1997, 174).

E. Criticisms of the Neoliberal Model

Scholars and practitioners of development studies have had close to three decades of hindsight to evaluate neoliberal approaches toward development. So far much of the criticism directed at neoliberal models have been based on the disappointing results that neoliberal development continues to have in the South. For example, although growth is experienced it is experienced only for the short-term. Overall long-term growth in the South through neoliberal development is not conclusive. Instead, neoliberal development policies have "brought devastating results to most developing countries, particularly to their poorest, most vulnerable and disadvantaged classes and social groups in sub-Saharan Africa, certain parts of Asia, and Latin America" (Brohman 1995a, 131).

The neoliberal approach is problematic because "individuals and social groups are treated like atomistic facts or things that are devoid of any social content or meaning" and presumed to "follow universal laws which determine their behavior" (Brohman 1995a, 305). The model also unfairly assumes that "producers in the Third World can compete on a relatively equal basis with established producers in the First World" (Kiely 1998, 127). This tendency to not take into account the differences in *global* entitlements between "early" as opposed to "late" developers reproduces a contradiction that heralded the demise of modernization theory (Brohman 1995a).

As aforementioned, the neoliberal model does not explicitly acknowledge the benefits or authority of state intervention on its own terms, but rather, subsumes state imperatives to "market friendly" interventions (See Kiely 1995, 1998; Hewitt 1992, Hart 2001, Toye 1987). There is also the example of how organs of neoliberal development, the transnational banks and corporations (TNBs and TNCs, respectively), ignore state environmental regulations with grave consequences: "The chemical leak from a Union Carbide pesticides factory in Bhopal, India, which killed 2,000 people and maimed an estimated 200,000 is the most telling example" (Kiely 1998, 74). This suggests then, that TNC development of the Third World is not uniformly positive, and that they "vary in time and place" (1998, 75).

A theoretical view of neoliberalism fails to fully capture *real* processes of neoliberalization, which entails a "historically specific, ongoing, and internally contradictory process or market driven sociospatial transformation, rather than as a fully actualized policy regime, ideological form, or regulatory framework" (Brenner and Theodore 2002, 353). For Brohman, the variety, creativity, and diversity of development attempts in many different parts of the world cannot be understood by "any other simple mechanistic framework and different strategies need to be conceived for different countries and different time periods" (1995a, 124).

Brohman critiques neoliberal doctrine for its complicity in bolstering the interests of only the powerful classes. Brohman argues that neoliberal development has also polarized class divisions within Third World countries. Moreover, this polarization is often linked to authoritarian governments in which "the vested interests of the elite monopolize state access to the exclusion of the popular sectors" (1995b, 300-301). As a result, the political power relations that have been established by neoliberal development are often accompanied by "restrictions on market participation by some classes and social groups" as well as "limitations on aggregate demand rooted in societal polarization" (Brohman 1995b, 301).

One of the strongest criticisms directed at the neoliberal model is its Eurocentrism and insensitivity to indigenous voices. But what does Eurocentrism mean, exactly? Hettne defines Eurocentric development strategies as those that rely on "development theories and models rooted in Western economic history and consequently structured by that unique, although historically important, experience" (Hettne 1990, 36). Joseph, Reddy and Searle-Chatterjee (1990) make the distinction that Eurocentrism is a special case of ethnocentrism, defined as "the tendency to view one's own ethnic group and its social standards as the basis for evaluative judgments concerning the practices of others...with the implication that one views one's own standards as superior" (1990, 1). Hettne reminds readers that the formative conditions in regard to European nation-state building are undoubtedly different than the rest of the world. The criticism directed against Eurocentrism, especially by scholars sympathetic to the development conditions of the Third World, is thus a reaction to a perceived continuation of infringement and imposition of European values regarding issues related to quality of life and progress.

The Eurocentrism in development economics at the beginning of the Cold War has, unfortunately, transformed development discourse of the period into prescriptions for geopolitical foreign policy agendas. Here, I share my views with Hunt who indicates that after the Second World War there was "a growing sense of political urgency concerning the promotion of economic development in the underdeveloped regions in order to maintain international stability and to contain the expansion of communism" (Hunt 1989, 45).

Eurocentrism within development studies has often been associated with the neglect of geographical, cultural, and ethnic diversity as well as incorrect readings of the social and historical experiences of individual countries and regions (see Allen's 1992 discussion on Halliday). For example, neoliberals like Balassa assert that economists who favor inclusion of non-economic factors in development analyses exemplify "faulty or inadequate economic reasoning" akin to our ancestors who tried to find the "causes of lightning and thunder in the supernatural" (Balassa 1988, 274). Thus, Eurocentrism has affected ideas and generated conflicting viewpoints about development trajectories between the advanced industrial countries and the Third World (Hettne 1990, Brohman 1995a). The consequences for development studies are not desirable:

> In the North, it has impoverished development studies and related disciplines by blocking access to alternative concepts and indigenous sources of knowledge...In the South, it has perpetuated intellectual dependence on a restricted group of prestigious Western academic institutions that determine the subject matter and methods of research (Brohman 1995a, 128).

According to Hettne one radical solution to the problem of discourse imperialism was for Southern scholars to abandon Western concepts such as neoliberalism in favor of ideas drawn from "national schools" (Hettne 1990,

99). Many of the national schools that embraced notions of indigenized development were from the African continent:

1. Afro-Marxists emphasized Marxist-Leninist ideas of economic development and political structure. Major examples were Kwame Nkrumah and Sekou Touré during the first half of the 1960s.

2. The moderate socialists, including Kenyatta of Kenya and Kaunda of Zambia, favored a state controlled "socialist" economy but were at the same time anxious to attract foreign investment capital.

3. The social democrats were closely connected with European socialism and frequently pro-Western in outlook, for example Leopold Senghor of Senegal and Tom Mboya of Kenya.

4. The agrarian socialists were associated with Nyerere's *Ujamaa* philosophy based on extended family kinship socialism. For Nyerere, rather than looking for foreign models of socialism development models could be derived from traditional African society (Hettne 1990, 109; Klinghoffer 1969, 16; Nyerere 1968).

Beyond Neoliberal Development: Alternative Development

Apart from just economic growth there is still a global and dynamic interaction between actors from differing cultures, societies, and geopolitical orientations that compete to define what development means. The issues that surround such interactions are complex and include ozone depletion, debt, AIDs, drugs, terrorism, currency crises, hunger, and human rights (Thomas and Potter 1992, 263). Because neoliberal development has generated many contradictions on the global arena critics are considering development strategies that counter what many see as a crisis in development and global capitalism (Storey 2000, Korten 1990, Mander and Goldsmith 1996). Moreover, by the 1970s interdisciplinary efforts by "social psychologists, historians, anthropologists and political scientists" all attempted to articulate newer development approaches that could make visible the conditions of poor nations (Bernstein 1971, 143).

Actors engaged in activism and seeking agency in these spheres of life have relied on identity politics in hopes of countering the anticipated and unanticipated effects of globalization (Basch, Glick, Schiller and Blanc 1994, Thomas and Potter 1992). The growing demand made by actors engaging in such a trajectory has been designated by Stavenhagen and Hettne as belonging to the "Alternative Development" paradigm (Stavenhagen 1986,

1996; Hettne 1990). Alternative development steers away from the "perils of globalisation" and situates development in the local (Mander and Goldsmith 1996). Alternative development emphasizes freedom and democratic principles (Clarke 1991), focuses on environmental justice (Sharp 1995), and attempts to empower and grant agency to actors by emphasizing voluntary action (Chambers 1983, Korten 1990).

Korten goes as far as designating alternative development as generating a paradigm shift with regard to theory; alternative development thus represents a "third paradigm" and claims to redefine the means and ends to development (Korten 1990). Stavenhagen and Hettne also believe that alternative development represents a break with mainstream development thinking and practice, generating a distinct shift in the way development is theorized and implemented. As such alternative development is about the "content" and not the "form" of development (Hettne 1990, 153). It also signifies a shift from a top-to-bottom bureaucratic mass development toward "creating development appropriate for the needs and interests of the popular majority in Third World countries" (Brohman 1996, 324). Indeed, Stavenhagen and Hettne note that alternative development strategies have been most embraced by Third World governments, social movements of various kinds, and small groups of researchers and planners from the South (Stavenhagen 1986, 1996; Hettne 1990).

As such alternative development is development that is people-centered and empowering, emanating from the institutions of civil society. Brohman states that alternative development seeks "relatively equitable income distribution, basic-needs provisions, human resource development, popular participation and democratization, socially and spatially balanced growth, and cultural and environmental sustainability" (Brohman 1996, 334). However, countering enthusiastic supporters of alternative development, I prefer to read alternative development as a reformist rather than a rejectionist position *vis-à-vis* mainstream development. The alternative development paradigm is reform-oriented in that alternative developmentalists still see a role for state institutions and external expertise with the conditions that intervention must be made more "relevant," inclusive, and based upon people as subjects rather than objects (Edwards, 1989). This reformist relevance is even more significant should alternative development policies be utilized to attend to the consequences of war where the human condition is acutely different than the abject poverty experienced by peoples in non-conflict situations.

The conceptualization of alternative development as a reformist rather than a break from mainstream development is also important for another reason: its ideas and principles are not necessarily new. Indeed Gavin Kitching, a proponent of industrialization (1982), examined (and criticized) nineteenth century "populists" who advocated a more communal means of production to counter the technocratic excesses of large-scale production-based economies. At the risk of oversimplification, populism thus reflected the sentiment that "small is beautiful" because it focused on the feasibility and desirability of small-scale distribution (Kiely 1998, 13).

In his important 1982 work *Development and Underdevelopment in Historical Perspective* Kitching presented many populist parallels to alternative development. For example, nineteenth century populists like socialist Robert Owen and anarchist-philosopher Pierre-Joseph Proudhon lamented on the dehumanization of a modern industrialized way of life and its negative effects on property relations. Both desired a return to small-scale peasant production that focused on issues related to distribution rather than just productivity. The productive forces would ideally be the farms that would trade with one another in a laissez-faire type of perfect competition (Kitching 1982, 26-35). According to Kiely in his 1998 work *Industrialization and Development*, nineteenth century Russia contained some of these agrarian communes that represented the basis for "both a more organic community and a more humane modernizing process which avoided the excess of British industrialization" (Kiely 1998, 13).

Yet one need not go as far back as the nineteenth century to espouse an atavism of alternative development. As recently as the 1970s the International Labour Organization (ILO) also made their case for labor intensive industrialization and development of the informal sector. According to Kitching, the ILO "was not against large scale industry per se, but rejected the widespread commitment to such industries, particularly when they were often high-cost and inefficient and did not increase output" (cited in Kiely 1998, 13).

Kitching notes the ILO also reemphasizes the importance of agricultural reform in a manner that would benefit peasant farming, but with the added benefit of labor enhancing technologies through improvements of irrigation systems, better seed selection, and better use of fertilizer as opposed to "large tractors and mechanized harvesting" (ibid., 14). As such the ILO reaffirmed its continuity with the populists of yesteryear because it also emphasized the importance of "small-scale industry and agriculture, combined with a focus on greater equality of distribution" (ibid., 14).

However, to argue that alternative development represents a twenty-first century populism is an oversimplification. Kitching was an industrialist who believed that the economies of scale were more efficient than small-scale production, and was a proponent of industrialization as a means to development. As such, Kitching's critique of populism should be juxtaposed to his preferences for industrialism. To extrapolate that Kitching's critique of populism will also suffice as a critique against alternative development overlooks the historical evolution of industrialized capitalism into its supra-incarnation: globalization. Analyses of alternative development should thus be juxtaposed to globalization and not to industrialism. The twenty-first century has seen the rise and potential decline of the efficacy of globalization, which include the industrialization element, but also the geopolitical, geopostcolonial, and transnational dimensions in globalization dynamics that generate its own non-class contradictions.

In his analyses, Kitching also neglects the non-class contradictions inherent in globalization. What I am referring to by non-class contradictions is that the presupposed conflict between an internationalized working class and a global bourgeois, will inherently be entangled in a web of social relationships that emanates from a myriad of localized cultural and environmental contexts. It is at this crucial juncture that alternative development embarks from. It is also at this crucial juncture that I believe alternative development can withstand Kitching's critique. Kitching's argument that industrialization is development sounds much like a cause and effect proposition that is too narrow and apolitical. Thus, Kiely is correct to acknowledge that Kitching's technocratic approach toward development overlooks social factors (Kiely 1998, 7). Kiely also notes that "others have argued that the meaning of development is wider than simply economic growth, and have thus criticized industrialization on this basis" (1998, 9). The "others" that Kiely refers to are, I believe, the advocates of the alternative development paradigm.

Alternative development also adopts a basic-needs strategy "designed to satisfy the fundamental necessities of the largest number of people rather than economic growth for growth's sake" (Stavenhagen 1986, 75). In the alternative development approach there is "no universal path to development" (Hettne 1990, 154). Instead it focuses on bringing ecological, feminist/eco-feminist, indigenous, and ethnic issues of particular regions into more locally-specific development analyses. It is also an approach that wishes to be "participatory rather than technocratic" and builds upon "existing cultural traditions rather than reject them off-hand as obstacles to development" (1986, 75). Stavenhagen explains:

> This shift in emphasis is due to the permanent questioning of formerly adopted paradigms. This approach competes currently with the other approaches, not because it has already empirically proven to be more successful, but because it addresses itself to issues and concepts which have hitherto been ignored by the other approaches, yet which are of basic concern to millions of people around the world (1986, 75).

Stavenhagen includes other components that he believes constitute the alternative development category: (1) agricultural development (as compared to industrial development) and (2) domestic or household development (as opposed to a focus on labor, capital, technology and nationally-oriented dimensions of development). On the latter point, Stavenhagen argues that extended or joint families provide the basic framework for the rural economy in many regions of the South. Stavenhagen argues "but not only there; the

48

'submerged' economy of Italy or the parallel economies of socialist countries such as Poland, turn to household strategies for survival…and is linked to the reappraisal of the role of women in social and economic dynamics" (Stavenhagen 1986, 77).

Although one cannot for certain know whether the venerable economist Amartya Sen (1999) is a strong subscriber of ethnodevelopment, Sen proposes development ideas that certainly resonate well with the alternative development paradigm. In *Development as Freedom*, Sen (who describes himself as a Smithian), explains that development should be directed toward enhancing human freedoms as opposed to unfreedoms. Here we see Sen tap into the normative aspects of development; instead of what development "is" Sen discusses what development "ought" to be; instead of emphasizing the form of development, content is emphasized instead. Sen provides a dual understanding of freedom by distinguishing it as a "*process* that allow freedom of actions and decisions" and as "actual *opportunities* that people have, given their personal and social circumstances" (1999, 17). Sen argues that an "adequate conception of development must go beyond the accumulation of wealth and the growth of gross national product and other income related variables. Without ignoring the importance of economic growth, we must look well beyond it" (1999, 14). Similarly, Toye reminds readers that quantifiable economic growth does not equal development:

> For example, output can be produced by the severe exploitation of labour—the payment of mere subsistence wages, bad health and safety conditions and the unfair treatment of workers—with…profits being channeled to private banks… This would be the kind of development that few people would vote for…so would growth…accompanied by environmental pollution and gross overcrowding (Toye 1987, 3-4).

Sen argues that development approaches should be based on the processes of "expanding the real freedoms that people enjoy" (1999, 3). Sen departs from an economistic development discourse and proceeds to explore how the qualitative value of freedom can be translated into notions of development. By arguing for a more evaluative approach based on how "relative weights of different types of freedoms" affect social progress, Sen intellectually traverses into the realm of sociology and anthropology. Sen's emphasis on the need for development to usher in freedoms extends the concerns expressed by Toye, namely that development studies should not be just the examination of "output of goods and services," but instead, should be represented and articulated by a host of interdisciplinary indicators of development (1987, 3).

Sen argues that people participation can also determine what constitutes development. Sen makes it clear that in democracies where political leaders are more readily held accountable for their actions, people power can generate the dynamics that lead to the removal of unfreedoms (defined as the lack of freedoms). Sen explicitly acknowledges that a freedom-centered perspective has a "generic similarity to the common concern with 'quality of life', which too concentrates on the way human life goes...and not just on the resources or income that a person has" (1999, 24). Sen concedes:

> The focusing on the quality of life and on substantive freedoms, rather than just on income or wealth, may look like something of a departure from the established traditions of economics, and in a sense it is (especially if comparisons are made with some of the more austere income-centered analysis that can be found in contemporary economics) (1999, 24).

The central concept in Sen's development approach is based on achieving full human capabilities, not unlike what Seers (1979) advocated in terms of fulfilling the human personality. Sen defines *human capability* as "the ability— the substantive freedom—of people to lead the lives they have reason to value and to enhance the real choices they have" (1999, 293). When there is poverty, famine, and various crises human capability is denied and the capacity for freedoms to, say, convert "primary goods into the person's ability to promote her end" does not occur (1999, 74-75). In this situation Sen notes that people experience *unfreedoms*.

Interestingly, although Sen attempts to analyze sources of unfreedoms (e.g., crises, famine, and oppression of women), Sen does not directly address in *Development* ethnically generated forms of unfreedoms. Why does Sen neglect ethnic-related aspects of development, a condition that Stavenhagen (1986) describes as a "paradigmatic blind spot" in conventional development studies? Fishman (1980) provides a rudimentary answer in that Sen, despite his innovative contribution to development discourse, still displays the tendency to "ascribe [ethnicity] to disruptive and disadvantaged peoples" (Fishman 1980, 95). But I speculate there is a deeper reason for Sen's avoidance of the ethnic issue and the reason can only be made clear after exploring the implications of Stavenhagen's ethnodevelopment in Chapter 3. Indeed Stavenhagen's concern about the "ethnic question" and its integration into development studies' analytical framework is absolutely crucial for understanding how development can address the Karen struggle for self-determination (1986, 77).

The United Nations Development Program (UNDP) would lead the way in adopting the alternative development paradigm. During the 1990s, the UNDP development strategy came to be understood as a process based on the "enlargement of relevant human choices" (Sachs 1992, 17). By 1994 and 1999, the UNDP would publish two important reports under the heading *Pacific Human Development: Putting People First* (1994) and *Pacific Human*

Development: Creating Opportunities (1999). Both embraced the essence of the alternative development paradigm for implementation in the Pacific region.

In both reports there is a focus on advocating people-centered development. Emphasis is placed on creating a sustainable human development which places people at the center of development while balancing "the coping capacities of societies and the carrying capacities of nature" (UNDP 1994, iii). It also emphasized that its regional policy expressed "concern for people's welfare and the continued strength of indigenous communities" (ibid., 6) as a means to counter a "development path that leads to widespread human deprivation, which is now the prevalent condition of many developing countries" (ibid., 6).

Both reports claim that this is the "ultimate objective of development," although this was more explicit in the 1994 publication (UNDP 1999, 5). Both reports critique an economic-growth approach and focus on creating greater capabilities for populations in which human development is both an ends and a means. The 1994 report claims that there is a natural affinity between people-centered development and the Pacific communities (UNDP 1994, iii). More importantly, alternative development can be secured through redefining partnerships between institutions, away from conventional or mainstream policies of economic growth. The key strategies for achieving alternative development are increased participation and empowerment, closer collaboration between governments, intra-state institutions, and communities (Storey 2000). Additionally, attention and importance are placed on NGOs and people-centered organizations that can realize such goals (ibid., 1).

In both reports a central place is given to organized participation at the communal level. In 1994 the UNDP stressed: "another key step towards ensuring sustainable human development is increased participation by communities and individuals" (ibid., 3). The report discusses NGO involvement in the Pacific as a more people-centered development and notes its "maximum use of rural-based and urban community organizations to allow for more effective participation" (ibid., 3). Both UNDP *Pacific Human Development* reports clearly reveal that alternative development has emerged as a broad collection of ideas *and* ideals linked by the objective of pursuing participatory, sustainable, and justice-oriented development (Storey 2000).

Other important organizations such as the International Foundation for Development Alternatives, based out of Switzerland (IFDA), the Institute for World Order (New York), and the Center for the Study of Developing Societies (Delhi) have also adopted the alternative development approach. However, it would be the Dag Hammarskjöld Foundation, via Marc Nerfin of the IFDA, which explicitly defined the aims of alternative development as[7]:

---

[7] The Dag Hammarskjöld Foundation based out of Uppsala, Sweden, is an autonomous development think tank that publishes *Development Dialogue*. Indeed at the time of this writing

- Need-oriented (being geared to meeting human needs, both material and non-material).
- Endogenous (stemming from the heart of each society, which defines in sovereignty its values and vision of its future).
- Self-reliant (implying that each society relies primarily on its own strength and resources in terms of its members' energies and its natural and cultural environment).
- Ecologically sound (utilizing rationally the resources of the biosphere in full awareness of the potential of local ecosystems as well as the global and local outer limits imposed on present and future generations).
- Based on structural transformation (so as to realize the conditions of self-management and participation in decision-making by all those affected by it, from the rural or urban community to the world as a whole, without which the goals above could not be achieved) (Nerfin 1977, 10).

The aforementioned discussion on how various advocates of alternative development conceptualize the development project is intended to funnels us to an important discussion to follow, ethnodevelopment. As I hope to demonstrate in Chapter 3, ethnodevelopment represents a dimension of the alternative development paradigm that will be most useful for understanding Karen self-determination.

---

in July 2005, the foundation actually was engaged in a seminar project titled "Another Development for Burma."

Chapter III
Ethnicity and Ethnodevelopment

One of the more ambitious models of the alternative development paradigm is ethnodevelopment. The model is based on Stavenhagen's 1986 publication "Ethnodevelopment: a neglected dimension in development thinking" and his ambitious 1996 publication *Ethnic Conflicts and the Nation-State*, which resulted from a 1990 research project sponsored by the United Nations Research Institute for Social Development (UNRISD). Stavenhagen defines ethnodevelopment as development programs that foster "the development of ethnic groups within the framework of the larger society" (1986, 92). Stavenhagen's ethnodevelopment aimed to study "the nature and characteristics of conflict between ethnic groups in the process of development" (Stavenhagen 1996, ix).

Stavenhagen's ethnodevelopment thus represents but one of a variety of post-Truman development strategies where the South is given the role of defining the arrangements, features, and forms of their social development. Stavenhagen's ethnodevelopment approach can be conceptualized as a critique of the modernist project, a critique shared by Prebisch, Baran, and Hettne, all of whom are critical of development approaches that fall under a Western or American world view of reality (Stavenhagen 1986, 1996).

To understand why ethnodevelopment is such an important strategy for understanding Karen self-determination, I will first explore the definitions of ethnicity that enhance our understanding of Rodolfo Stavenhagen's ethnodevelopment. Then I will discuss key theoretical foundations that aid our understanding of ethnicity as well as the complex relationship it has with nation construction and nationalism. The function of ethnicity will then be explored in the context of systemic crisis. Finally, I critique Stavenhagen's approach.

Definitions of Ethnicity

Understanding the role of ethnicity is crucial for understanding the role and function ethnodevelopment. There is not one overarching definition for ethnicity (Stavenhagen 1986, 1996; Clarke 2001). Glazer and Moynihan identified the first appearance of "ethnicity" in the 1972 edition of the *Oxford English Dictionary* and noted "ethnicity seems to be a new term" (Glazer and Moynihan 1975, 1). The term "ethnic," however, goes back to antiquity and is derived from the Greek term *ethnos*.

The ancient Greeks used the term *ethnos* in a variety of ways. In Homer we hear of *ethnos hetairon*, a band of friends, *ethnos Lukion*, a tribe of Lycians, and *ethnos melisson* or *ortnithon*, a swarm of bees or birds. Aeschylus calls the Persians an *ethnos*, Pindar speaks of the *ethnos aneron* or *gunaikon*, a race of men or women, Herodotus of *Medikon ethnos*, the Median people, and Plato of *ethnos kerukikon*, a caste of heralds (Hutchinson and Smith 1996, 4).

The term "ethnic" made its appearance in the English language during the Middle Ages when it evolved to denote non-Christian and non-Jewish pagans (Hutchinson and Smith 1996, Eriksen 1996). By the time European colonialism had established administrative institutions in annexed territories the concept began to point to racial characteristics. The reason for this was simple enough—the understanding of race at the time was tied to biological evolution as argued by eighteenth century physiologist and comparative anatomist such as Johan Blumenbach (Gould 1994, 65).[8] When colonizers arrived on distant shores and encountered its indigenous populations, the phenotypical differences in what Geertz (1963) identifies as skin color, facial form, stature, and hair type, were immediately and explicitly apparent. Over the centuries the subsequent subjugation of indigenous peoples established and reinforced a hierarchical dimension to emergent social relationships. Race was constructed, understood, and exploited on a cultural continuum where the subjugated peoples were understood as inferior *vis-à-vis* the colonizer (Gould 1994). By the first-half of the twentieth century:

> In the United States, "ethnics" came to be used around the Second World War as a polite term referring to Jews, Italians, Irish and other people considered inferior to the dominant group of largely British descent (Eriksen 1993, 3).

The French language, however, would adopt the concept of ethnos and assign it a corresponding community via the term *ethnie*. Stavenhagen frequently employs this term, as will I. For the purposes of my work, I will treat the ethnie as *a group and its corresponding community, where at its widest expanse, constitutes a nation based on the belief of a common ancestry, a shared society, and memories of a shared historical past*. This definition is a result of combining Hutchinson and Smith's material definition of ethnie as an "ethnic community which possesses a permanent physically bounded territory, over

---

[8] It was Blumenbach, writing 80 years before Darwin, who assigned the term "Caucasian" to refer to Europeans. He justified this act due to a Georgian female skull he examined and which prompted him to remark that it was "the most beautiful…primeval type…the others diverge by most easy gradations. Besides, it is white in color, which we may fairly assume to have been the primitive color of mankind, since…it was very easy for that to degenerate into brown, but very much more difficult for dark to become white" (Gould 1994, 69).

and above its political organizations," with their symbolic definition of the ethnie as "a named human population with myths of common ancestry, shared historical memories, one or more elements of common culture, a link with a homeland and a sense of solidarity among at least some of its members" (Hutchinson and Smith 1996, 6).

But what about the term "ethnicity"? According to Hutchinson and Smith, the English language has no "concrete noun for *ethnos* or *ethnie*" even though the French language retained its proper noun usage (1996, 4). The English language instead prefers to treat *ethnicity* as primarily cultural phenomenon. This understanding of ethnicity employed by cultural anthropologists up until the period following World War II would eventually evolve. By the 1970s, the understanding of ethnicity as a static category that contained culture (or was itself culture) transitioned toward an understanding that ethnicity was instead a dynamic phenomenon, highly fluid in its reproduction of codified symbols, language, myths and memories (Andersen and Collins 2000, Anderson 1991). Anti-essentialist/postmodern thinkers such as Hall (1992), Chapman, Tonkin and McDonald (1989) subscribed to this tradition. Other scholars, however, have warned that underscoring ethnicity as a primarily symbolic or cultural phenomenon leads to a distorted understanding of how an ethnie develops (Barth 1969, Keyes 1979, Brass 1991, Gurr 1993).

As early as 1954, Leach, then Barth in 1969, and Keyes in 1979, have redefined ethnicity to refer to sociopolitical entities that contain what Barth terms "cultural stuff." Leach introduced to us how these sociopolitical entities compete with one another in a structurally opposed manner via Kachin and Shan relationships in Burma, while Barth argues that group competition is only made possible by socially organized boundaries that define the ethnies apart from one another. Keyes would fuse Leach and Barth's ideas and apply them in his examination of the Karen, noting "there must be structural oppositions between groups for ethnic boundaries to exist" (Keyes 1979, 5).

I have opted for definitions of ethnicity that deemphasize the function of culture (although I do not claim that this approach will minimize the ambiguity of the term ethnicity[9]). Nevertheless, I am aware that ethnicity and culture are intimately linked experiences. A neglect of an ethnie's symbolic and material culture can also lead to a distorted understanding of how an ethnie develops, as committed by Halliday (1979) when he prematurely downplayed the capacity of Iran's Shia population to depose the US-sponsored Shah. Although Halliday had much to offer readers in his discussion of how the mullahs and ayatollahs shaped Iranian politics, his

---

[9] Fortunately, Stavenhagen resolves the confusing deployment of terminology for identifying the diacritica of ethnies and concludes, "whether ethnic groups are called communities, nations, nationalities, peoples, minorities, or tribes is a matter of convention" (1996, 4).

political economy background resulted in only a partial perspective on the importance of religious culture.

In the interest of this work, I favor definitions that treat ethnicity as a sociopolitical phenomenon whose momentum generates material consequences. And because it is through the cultural reproduction of the ethnie that "the basic norms which structure the life of the group are defined" (Stavenhagen 1996, 20), I plan to read ethnicity holistically as the total symbolic (consciousness) and material output (development) of a given people. Nationalism, then, represents the most intense and holistic articulation of ethnicity. Here, I agree with nationalism and ethnicity scholars such as Smith (1998), Connor (1994), Horowitz (1985) and Armstrong (1982) that nationalism—the love of one's nation—is a consciousness resulting from an actor's connection to his/her largest *felt* descent and kinship group. Indeed, Armstrong (1982) and Horowitz (1985) both argue that the nation is but a modern equivalent of a pre-modern ethnic identity and thus, a *more developed* form of the ethnic group. In a contribution that will have great relevance to my work Patterson (1983) adds that ethnic consciousness regarding nation is further strengthened by an "awareness of a threatened or real crisis and the need which this crisis both stimulates and by which it is resolved" (1983, 27).

Two symbiotic forces that generate the consciousness of ethnicity are ethnic identity and ethnic identification. Ethnic *identity* is "introversive, a self definition and a search for personal uniqueness that occurs within the minds of individuals" (Kumekawa 1993, 206) and influenced and internalized by a people's shared sets of meanings and experiences (Castells 1997). Ethnic identity is a result of the process of ethnic *identification,* an "extroversive...self-comparison with others and a search for shared cultural traits that places an individual in a public social context" (Kumekawa 1993, 206). Thus ethnicity is to the ethnie what class consciousness is to class (Brass 1991). From the perspective of my work ethnicity becomes one of several forms of association "through which individuals pursue their interests relating to economic and political advantage" (Brown 1994, xii). Karen ethnicity and Karen nationalism, then, will refer to the liberation consciousness associated with the Karen ethnie.

Theories and Debates on Ethnicity

Whether one treats ethnicity as material, cultural, racial, religious, or a combination of each feature, ethnies can be understood by "their persistence over time and their capacity for biological and cultural reproduction" (Stavenhagen 1996, 4). This qualification is extremely important for two reasons.

First, by injecting a temporal dimension into the understanding of ethnies, it allows us to take our observation of ethnies out of a symbolic realm and situate it within a historical and material context. Barth asserts in his important work, *Ethnic Groups and Boundaries* (1969) that the capacity for an ethnie to remain a coherent social group is due not to its ability to isolate itself in ecological or cultural niches, but precisely in the opposite condition where the ethnie, over time, utilizes other groups to imply "marked difference in behavior" from their own. For Barth the social organization of ethnic boundaries over time, its ability to include as well as exclude actors, and not the "cultural stuff" within it, defines the ethnie. Barth notes that time strengthens ethnic boundaries to a point where even if there is interethnic interaction the social organization of cultural boundaries can still effectively maintain the ethnie's sense of coherence and identity. Conversely Barth notes:

> Nor can it be claimed that every...diversification within a group represents a first step in the direction of subdivision and multiplication of units. We have well-known documented cases of one ethnic group, also at a relatively simple level of economic organization, occupying several different ecologic niches and yet retaining basic cultural and ethnic unity over long periods (Barth 1969, 13).

Barth's ideas on boundaries have great implications for understanding why ethnic conflicts are so frequently a protracted phenomenon. Joshua Fishman in his 1989 work *Language and Ethnicity in Minority Sociolinguistic Perspective* notes that "once ethnic boundaries have been heavily invested with interpretations and enactments, these acquire a logic and dynamic of their own, and can become...exceedingly difficult to alter" (1989, 26). The staying power of ethnic boundaries needs to be remembered as one reads about the Karen ethnie and its struggle for self-determination. For over half a century, the Karen Revolution via the KNU has transformed itself ideologically, diplomatically, and militarily, yet it remains—even to its staunchest critics— the key organization that represents the Karen people by fighting for that elusive boundary that can realize their state of Kawthoolei.

Second, Stavenhagen's provocative description of an ethnie's staying power serves introduce us into the rich debate on how ethnicity functions. At first reading, Stavenhagen's emphasis on an ethnie's ability to "persist over time" sounds very much like the provocative *primordialist* argument for ethnicity.

A. Ethnicity as a Primordial Entity

Edward Shils first introduced the term *primordialism* in 1957 to explain how certain social bonds between members of societies persist over time. When used to describe ethnicity, primordialism refers to how actors of an ethnic group link themselves to ancestry and history. Daniel Bell (1975) grounds ethnicity in its primordialized context by noting its *pre-industrial* basis that, with the rise of industry, became intersected by economic and class interests. It is important to note that Shils' use of the term did not denote what *is* about the ethnie, but what it *appears* to be. Geertz further contributes to an understanding of primordialism by designating it as an abnormal articulation of state formation, while simultaneously remarking on its "overpowering" and "ineffable quality" to maintain bonds within the ethnie, from which its actors view ties to blood, race, language, locality, religion and/or tradition as "given" (Geertz 1963).

Grosby (1996) treats primordialism as a particular pattern of social orientation that human beings attribute to relations of descent. The relations of descent are framed by beliefs in objects such as kinship and ancestry, tradition, and territory. In this regard, he is reinvoking the rich insights given by Max Weber's observation of ethnicity, especially on the strengthening of kinship via blood relationships and shared political memories. Weber viewed ethnicity as a non-rational (not irrational) issue and was fully aware that there need not be an objective basis to such ties. But Weber also noted that when "these ties are lacking, or once they cease to exist, the sense of ethnic group membership is absent, regardless of how close the kinship may be" (Weber 1996, 36).

Grosby and Brass argues that a child is not just raised by the family, but by a larger cultural collectivity in which the family immerses the child for socialization. This larger collectivity progresses from the clan to the tribe and ultimately to the nation, with nation representing a politicized ethnie with articulated aspirations *and* administrative apparatuses that further their group rights (Grosby 1996, Brass 1991). For Grosby ethnic groups and nationalities exist "because there are traditions of belief and action towards primordial objects such as biological features and especially territorial location" (1994, 168). The individual is primordial in that he/she participates in the larger society by learning about its heritable objects: language, non-material and material culture, and collective consciousness, all of which incite emotions and powerful feelings within the ethnie.

> One's parents give one life. The locality in which one is born and in which one lives nurtures one; it provides the food necessary for one's life. The larger collectivity in which one is born and in which

one lives protects one's life from the potentially threatening chaos of the external world (Grosby 1996, 55).

Grosby's view on primordialism can be juxtaposed to the simplistic reductionism made by Eller and Coughlan: that primordiality and the solidarity of a collective is primarily a matter of emotion (Eller and Coughlan 1993). In a direct response to Eller and Coughlan, Grosby counters that "emotions are aroused by the cognition of the object" (1996, 53). Grosby then proceeds to render the social constructionist view increasingly more inadequate: because the aforementioned objects allow actors in an ethnie to develop attachments and ties that are meaningful to one another, the emotive dimensions of a collective serve to reinforce cohesion and stability among members of the ethnie. With these ties the individual is able to participate in bounded patterns within the ethnie. These ties are in turn historically evolving patterns, constituting the legacy of history, of tradition. Grosby explains:

> Herein lies a part of the reason for the significance that human beings attribute to primordial relations...the family, the locality, and one's own "people" bear, transmit and protect life. This is why human beings have always attributed and continue to attribute sacredness to primordial objects and the attachments they form to them. This is one of the reasons why human beings have sacrificed their lives and continue to sacrifice their lives for their own family and for their own nation (ibid., 56).

This is not to say that there aren't radical primordialists who try to draw a direct link between biological drives and the formation of groups. Pierre Van Den Berghe (1978, 1996) is one such scholar who adopts a sociobiological view to argue that all humans—indeed, all organisms—are "programmed" to be "nepotistic" so as to generate an "inclusive fitness" within the collective. Indeed, for Van Den Berghe, ethnic groups are the "in-breeding super families" of human history that delineate their uniqueness by maintaining clear social and territorial boundaries with other ethnic groups (Van Den Berghe 1978). The concept of nations, then, is based on the widest expanse of kin selection and so "nations are to be treated as descent groups in the same manner as ethnic groups" (Smith 1998, 147). Although Van Den Berghe's assertions do not enhance the understanding of Karen self-determination as much as Grosby's more moderate primordialism, an assessment of the former's arguments is enlightening.

In his 1996 article "Does race matter?" Van Den Berghe carefully responds to two main postmodern and anti-essentialist criticisms directed against sociobiological accounts of race and ethnicity. The first criticism is that an ethnie's claim to common ancestry is a myth and the second is that this myth is substantiated by the fact that ethnies stress cultural markers of membership over inherited biological traits. Although these criticisms are extremely formidable, Van Den Berghe provides some interesting and provocative responses.

The "myth" of ethnicity and its claim to a common ancestry, according to Van Den Berghe, is not necessarily a myth "if members of an ethnic group are sufficiently alike in physical appearance and culture, and having lived together and intermarried for a sufficient period" (1996, 58). Van Den Berghe estimates this "sufficient period" as spanning three to four generations. Yet even he concedes that ethnicity and race are not immutable, and that their mutability can be caused by several generations of exogamy that include about 25 percent of the ethnie's population. Yet when this generational exogamy is minimized or non-existent the myth develops a "substantial measure of biological truth," which in turn generates the Barthian boundaries that define and reinforce the ethnie's staying power. He convincingly argues:

> The Emperor of Japan can effectively claim to be the father of the Japanese nation in a way that Queen Victoria could never validate her claim as mother of India. Ethnicity or race…must correlate with a pre-existing population bound by preferential endogamy and a common historical experience (1996, 58).

Van Den Berghe also responds to the trite claim that frequent usage of cultural markers by ethnic groups must, therefore, render ethnicity a symbolic phenomenon. Here Van Den Berghe notes that such a situation only occurs when ethnies that live in regional proximity with one another, over time, dilute the genetic and phenotypical markers to set themselves apart. Van Den Berghe concedes that if there are long periods of interethnic intermarriage, conquest or the condition of being conquered, the resulting populations in neighboring ethnies will "look…much alike" (1996, 58). As such they will naturally have to rely on cultural markers. Yet he insightfully notes that even when people rely on cultural markers, the markers will center on constructions of kinship that point to biological descent.

Van Den Berghe emphasizes that when phenotypical markers "do a reliable job" of differentiating between groups, the use of these markers is virtually guaranteed. European colonization of the world is an example where the great distances involved in territorial acquisition inevitably activated this phenotypical awareness. In other words, phenotypical discernment will only "work" between groups that are physically different, as between the Zulus and Boers of Africa: "you could shoot at 500 meters and never make a mistake" (1996, 61).

> Facial features (notably eye, lip and nose shape), hair texture and physical stature are also used where they are diacritic… In Rwanda

and Burundi where the Hutu-Tutsi-Twa distinction is marked by large group differences in height, stature is widely used as a criterion. It works better in Rwanda where a rigid caste system hindered interbreeding, than in the more fluid social structure of Burundi, but in both cases, the physical distinction was used as a quick and dirty basis for sweeping genocidal action... A particularly gruesome atrocity against the Tutsi in Rwanda was to amputate them at the knee to cut them down to size (Van Den Berghe 1996, 61).

As radical as this assertion is, Van Den Berghe concedes that if ethnies do physically look alike, then cultural markers such as language are more effective than genetic or phenotypical traits for differentiating between ethnies:

> Norwegians and Swedes...could never be racists toward one another, even if they wanted to. They have to listen to one another before they can tell who is who. The Nazis tried to be racists with the Jews but their biological markers worked with perhaps 10 to 15 percent reliability. In practice, they used mostly cultural markers: circumcision, synagogue attendance, the Star of David, denunciations, surnames, etc. They actually had a very difficult time picking out the Jews from their Gentile neighbors, especially in the assimilated Jewry of Western Europe (1996, 61).

Van Den Berghe's assertions can be extrapolated to Burma where phenotypical differences between Burman and other ethnic nationalities are to a certain extent existent but not significantly activated. For the Karen the use of cultural markers such as preference for endogamy within the ethnie and pride in their moral behavior as documented by Keyes (1979), Moerman (1968), and the fourteen year research on the hill populations in the region of the Thai/Burmese border by Kunstadter (1965-1979), function as Barthian boundaries that distinguish the Karen, for example, from the Thai:

> Although accepting a structurally subordinate position to the dominant lowlanders, at least some Karen hold the belief that they are morally superior, pointing specifically to lax sexual behavior on the part of the Thai as compared with the Karen. In this the Karen echo the Lue...who use their ethnic identity as a mechanism for avoiding class considerations and for asserting a pride in their moral behavior (Keyes 1979, 12).

Father Sangermano, who wrote of the Karen at the end of the eighteenth century, similarly identifies the Karen through cultural markers:

It is worthy of observation that, although residing in the midst of the Burmese and the Peguans, they not only retain their own language, but even in their dress, houses, and everything else are distinguished from them; and what is more remarkable, they have a different religion (Keyes 1979, 1).

B. *The Social Construction of Ethnicity*

Primordialism has been severely criticized, especially by the postmodern discourse or those scholars that employ its vocabulary, for essentializing the "essence" of the ethnie and for reducing cultural and social behavior to biological drives. As such cultural studies and postmodern anthropology prefer to read ethnicity as primarily a symbolic, cultural, and socially constructed phenomenon. In this realm, postmodernist scholars such as Said (1979) and Hall (1992) argue the malleability of ethnicity and the negation of any inherently biological aspect about the ethnie, that is, ethnies are not "immemorial, discrete, persisting units" (Hutchinson and Smith 1996, 8). From this perspective ethnicity exists in a constant state of flux as its members come and go due to a variety of reasons such as migration, conquest, and/or intermarriage.

It is via this anti-essentializing approach that ethnicity and culture are "deconstructed" to finer and finer levels of aesthetic discernment. Unfortunately, one outcome of such a treatment is that in the hands of postmodern scholars the examination of ethnicity has been relegated to a fad. As a fad, it has also become popular for scholars like Anderson (1991) and Hall (1992) to view ethnicity as "imagined" and socially constructed. Yet for Grosby, the sloganeering of clichés such as "social construction" has been nothing more than an excuse for "ignorance pretending to be knowledge" (1996, 53). No paradigm has done more damage to the treatment and understanding of ethnicity than the postmodern approach.

Anderson, who comes from a Marxist tradition, justifies his claim that all ethnies are "imagined communities" simply because "even members of the smallest nation will never know most of their fellow-members, meet them, or even hear of them, yet in the minds of each lives the image of their communion" (Anderson 1983, 6). Hobsbawm and Ranger (1983) similarly point out the invented nature of tradition, although they do concede that the invented aspects of tradition are based on trying to establish continuity with a historic past. Nevertheless, Hobsbawm and Ranger's efforts to deconstruct tradition fails the moment they attempt to discern between "tradition" and "custom" (1983, 1). Their desire to split hairs has resulted in a convoluted passage, highly typical of many writings by social constructionists, in the second page of their otherwise important work *Invention of Tradition*:

'Tradition' in this sense must be distinguished clearly from 'custom' which dominates so called 'traditional' societies. The object and characteristics of 'traditions', including invented ones, is invariance. The past, real or invented, to which they refer imposes fixed (normally formalized) practices, such as repetition. 'Custom' in traditional societies has the double function of motor and fly-wheel. It does not preclude innovation and change up to a point, though evidently the requirement that it must appear compatible or even identical with precedent imposes substantial limitations on it (Hobsbawm and Ranger 1983, 2).

Unlike the primordialists, Hobsbawm, who is also from a Marxist tradition, discounts the effects of ethnicity and its purported link to ancestry and heritage. In another important work *Nations and Nationalisms since 1780*, Hobsbawm (1990) is especially critical in assigning ethnicity as a prerequisite to the construction of the nation-state. Hobsbawm speaks in the language of instrumentalism by noting that the nation-state is a phenomenon of the modern age, where rapid transformations of society compelled capitalist elites to utilize any political means to harness the emotions of the masses. Traditions based on ethno-symbolism such as flags, anthems, attire, and rituals, thus become a means for a people to remain cohesive. He notes:

A rapid transformation of a society weakens or destroys the social patterns for which 'old traditions' has been designed, producing new ones to which they were not applicable, or when such old traditions and their institutional carriers and promulgators no longer prove sufficiently adaptable (Hobsbawm 1990, 4-5).

Smith notes that Hobsbawm is not impressed with ethnicity and possesses a "hatred for nationalism...yet is prepared to concede its historical significance" (Smith 1998, 125). However, Hobsbawm's predictions on ethnicity, like Halliday on religion, were incorrect. The new nationalisms that emerged during the post-Soviet era in Central Asia, spanning all the way to Eastern Europe, would render much of his downplay of ethnicity's role in the formation of the nation-state as premature (he assigns their emergence to "economic difficulties" of the failing Soviet system). Moreover, Smith notes that Hobsbawm employment of the term ethnic is "unclear," and as a result Hobsbawm treats ethnicity in a way that conflates it with language, which is further confused "with actual descent" (Smith 1998, 127). Perhaps the most important critique Smith makes against Hobsbawm is that the former "fails to consider the importance of myths, memories, traditions and symbols" (Smith 1998, 127). Nevertheless Hobsbawm remained dismissive of ethnicity and its role in a globalized community:

The call of ethnicity or language provides no guidance to the future at all. It is merely a protest against the status quo or, more precisely, against the 'others' who threaten the ethnically defined group (1990, 168).

For Hobsbawm nationalism is a substitute for lost dreams and:

> ...is historically less important. It is no longer, as it were, a global political programme...it is at most a complicating factor...a catalyst for other developments... Nation states and nations will be seen as retreating before, resisting, adapting to, being absorbed or dislocated by, the new supranational restructuring of the globe. Nations and nationalism will be present in history, but in subordinate, and often rather minor roles (Hobsbawm 1990, 181-182).

Where Hobsbawm and Hobsbawm and Ranger succeed and Anderson fails is that the former attribute the invention of tradition, and ultimately of nation, to rapid systemic transformation. The authors note that this change weakens the social fabric where "old" social traditions were designed to function. The sociocultural dislocations that result from rapid systemic transformation necessitated a reconnection with a past that represents the ethnie's center of gravity. This observation is highly relevant for our understanding of the variations in Karen nationalist and ethnodevelopment trajectories. As you will read in Chapter 4, the Bo Mya-reinvigorated Karen nationalism that reemerged in the 1970s to challenge leftist Karen ideology resulted from a relinking with earlier ideals of the Karen Revolution, as articulated by its elite during the waning days of British colonialism. In this regard, I doubt Hobsbawm and Ranger would disagree that Bo Mya was able to successfully utilize "history as a legitimator of action and cement of group cohesion" (Hobsbawm and Ranger 1983, 12). Without Hobsbawm and Ranger being conscious of it, they have indirectly lent credence to the notion of primordialism.

Nevertheless Hobsbawm and Ranger, and especially Anderson, never explicitly acknowledged an important feature about the ethnie and its nation—a point brought home decades earlier by Shils, and more recently by Connor (1994): it isn't what the nation *is* (which I concede is a "construction"), but *what people perceive it to be* in the present as well as throughout, or even beyond time. In this regard anti-essentialists and postmodernists fail to appreciate the notion that nations and traditions are constituted and reproduced by people who believe their historical link. Moreover, this perception often commands a person's loyalty—an important feature earlier emphasized to us by Grosby.

Although postmodernist "contributions" to ethnicity are many, I choose not to devote much time immersed in their unhelpful ramblings. Here I share the same sentiments as Childs (2003) who reminded his readers not to fall into the "aimless ever-splintering relativism of postmodern perceptions of diversity and multiculturalism" (2003, 21). The postmodernist tendency to atmospherically deconstruct ethnicity and its cultural objects to the nth degree is actually a highly condescending prism if it is used to assess the Karen ethnie in survival mode. Karen nationalism, self-determination, and ethnodevelopment should not be treated as cultural aesthetics relegated to unceasing deconstructions and critiques. Furthermore, the postmodern approach is ineffective for solving problems related to development and the human condition. Its tendency to deconstruct and relativize normative approaches that characterize development strategies, to incessantly question or "contest" the motives of development without seeing the diversity contained within its approaches, and to view life and death issues as Western constructed binaries, renders it a discourse of denial:

> If we accept the argument...that the "binary opposition" between life and death is a Western one, then we have no way of effectively criticizing the massacres carried out by the colonial powers. Neither do we have any grounds for complaining when food is exported from one impoverished country to another, richer area, because starvation is a concept based on the Western binary opposition between life and death... Need I really go on citing such absurdities (Kiely 1995, 160)?

The postmodern approach is also debilitating because the methodology of deconstruction is usually adopted by scholars with much social capital but little praxian will. To be able to engage in deconstruction entails stable social conditions that grant time to the deconstructing thinker. The Karen and their elites in Kawthoolei are too intimately tied to the brutal realities of their struggle for such a luxury. Not one Karen engaged in their struggle that I had the privilege of meeting in Kawthoolei "deconstructed" their struggle.

Moreover, the postmodern discourse repeatedly obsesses itself with superficial critiques and "contestations" of cultural aesthetics such as "narratives" and "memories," a process that is elusive, lacks closure, and detrimental for organizational praxis and social movements. The problem with grounding ethnicity in a purely cultural space is brought home by Patterson:

> The point is that all human beings have some kind of culture. Merely to show that a given group has a distinctive culture or subculture, that this culture is meaningful to them, and that they are aware of it tells us little what generations of cultural anthropologists have not already informed us and nothing about ethnicity (Patterson 1983, 26).

The inability of the postmodern discourse to view ethnicity as containing multiple expressions beyond a purely cultural phenomenon renders it an ineffective approach toward understanding ethnicity; that is, how many times must thinkers of ethnicity be told of what is already self-evident, that ethnicity, tradition, community, nation, and nationalism are constructions? Even grounded development thinkers such as Hettne concede and acknowledge the obvious: if people do not belong to an ethnic group "ethnicity can, if necessary, easily be manipulated and even invented for political purposes" (Hettne 1990, 191). The point is how we can move *beyond* Anderson, Said, Hall, and Hobsbawm's eloquent yet superficial examinations of the *obvious* to observe the material and territorial consequences of ethnicity.

To move ethnicity beyond an aesthetic and subjectivist realm requires us to situate it within the dynamics of development. From the perspective of development, the point then becomes what do we do with the material consequences of "imagined communities" and "invented traditions" when there is rape, abject poverty, environmental destruction, genocide, and internal colonialism? Insofar as development can be conceptualized to improve the human condition through the elimination of socially limiting conditions, the postmodernist discourse is neither compatible nor helpful with its assessment of how ethnicity functions in development dynamics.

Another popular postmodernist tendency is the view that nationalism is:

> A pathology of modern developmental history, as inescapable as "neurosis" in the individual, with much the same essential ambiguity attaching to it, [with] a similar built-in capacity for descent into dementia (Nairn 1977, 359).

To assess nationalism in such a manner only points to the fact that postmodernists have themselves essentialized nationalism into a monolithic category. This prejudice is also shared by "Marxists and conventional Anglo-Saxon economists... [who] belittle the influence of nationalism and...treat it as evil" (Seers 1983, 30). Yet one of my most important contentions regarding the process of nationalism is that it contains its own contradiction that has rarely been addressed dialectically. Van Den Berghe clearly points to the paradox of nationalism in his 1990 work, *State Violence and Ethnicity*:

> The great paradox of nationalism is that in every multinational state that claims legitimacy by pretending to be a nation state, any manifestation of genuine nationalism (that is, one based on a preexisting ethnic community) must almost automatically be perceived by the ruling class as a destabilizing threat and thus can quickly lead to an escalation of repressive state violence. If a state is not a nation, as 85 percent or so of states are not, the very ideology of nationalism contains prescription for the suppression of the

genuine article as soon as it becomes the basis of political action (1990, 8-9).

I wholeheartedly concede that the nationalism derided by those concerned about its fascistic tendencies is not incorrect, but this criticism is directed toward a *top-to-bottom* nationalism. Within this trajectory we have the nation-states created by Adolf Hitler, Augusto Pinochet, Slobidan Milosevic, and Saddam Hussein, to name but a few. Yet by assuming that all nationalisms exhibit this trajectory, we ignore how ethnies invoke their own nationalisms to challenge fascistically-generated utopias. Due to this "blind spot," Marxists and postmodernists fail to see that fascism generates its opposite: a *bottom-to-top* nationalism I designate as *agency nationalism*.

Agency nationalism is diametrically opposed to fascism. Agency nationalism is a consciousness and lived experience where oppressed ethnies seek to acquire the agency to liberate themselves from their oppressors. The Karen struggle for Kawthoolei exemplifies this trajectory because it challenges the ethnic cleansing meted out to them by various pro-Burman military regimes. The Karen do so by constructing an ideology, a nation, and administrative apparatuses that are in structural opposition to Rangoon. In other words, Marxists and postmodernists are concerned with but one articulation of nationalism, built on the assumption that all nationalisms are prototypically fascistic. As we shall see in my work regarding the case of the Karen, nothing could be further from this presupposition.

Now that the contradiction of nationalism has been made visible, I reintroduce the ideas of Dudley Seers (1983). Rather than obsessing on the normativity of nationalism, Seers' *Political Economy of Nationalism* discusses how a nationalized political economy functions by noting its local, regional and geopolitical capacity to promote ethnic group cohesion. In coherence with the instrumentalist model to be discussed, Seers' view of a nationalist political economy includes activities that "promote the presumed interests of a group with cultural coherence showing at least a degree of linguistic and ethnic homogeneity" (1983, 9). Seers' also notes that this qualification extends to ethnies "submerged within one or more nation-states" (1983, 9). Here we see how Seers' nationalism can further inform the Karen political economy engaged in struggle. The implication of Seers' qualification means that Karen agency nationalism is as much an economic process as it is a political ideology. The arguments contained within Seers' *Political Economy* thus point to the syllogistic relationship between Karen self-determination, its agency-based nationalism, and its liberation ethnodevelopment.[10]

As Barth reminded us, an ethnie is reinforced and reproduced by the social institutions that delineate the ethnic boundaries of the particular group.

---

[10] Karen self-determination, agency nationalism, and its liberation ethnodevelopment are interchangeably used throughout this text.

These boundaries include the interplay of the material, such as territory, and symbolic aspects, such as cultural behavior and language. We can now utilize Seers' ideas to include a distinctive political economy as part and parcel of the ethnie. In this regard, the political economy of an ethnie has real material consequences for development because it forms the basis for conflicts over the distribution of resources, often "with grave regional and geopolitical consequences" (Hutchinson and Smith 1996, 13). I believe there is an urgency to resolve the contradictions in different nationalisms: when situated within the context of Asia or Africa ethnic disputes over autonomy, self-determination, or secession, "are among the most destructive, complicated and protracted" forms of conflict in the Third World (Khosla 1999, 1154).

C. Ethnicity as Political Instrument

The significance of Karen nationalism, then, steer us toward how the Karen ethnie functions as an instrument for attainment of their political goals. As such, the *instrumentalist* model is quite effective in illuminating the Karen struggle for Kawthoolei. Instrumentalism is a perspective that treats ethnicity as a social or political "instrument" for acquiring resources for the ethnie. Moreover, it identifies the ethnie elite as the stratum that mobilizes the support of the masses toward acquiring these resources. The elites thus construct nation via a range of symbols and cultural traditions that serve to "unite their communities and mobilize them for social and political advantage" (Smith 1998, 155). The resources circulate around power, status, and wealth. Achieving these goals require "influencing the state or, in certain situations, through secession" (Hutchinson and Smith 1996, 9).

> Hence we may infer that it is the competition between elites within a community, and between the elites of different communities, using multiple symbol selection, that mobilizes the members of communities and forms them into cohesive nationalities (Smith 1998, 155).

Instrumentalists such as Brass (1991) and Cohen (1969) concede that although actors form historical and emotive attachments to their ethnie, primordial attachments should be viewed as a variable. Indeed, many actors are bilingual, their religions subject to change, and the emotional ties formed toward their ethnie may lose significance. Cohen and Brass argue that at the macro level an ethnie's aspiration for nation is characterized by their mobilization to acquire social, economic and political rights, depending on the perceived needs of the ethnie. At the localized level this process includes day-to-day administrative issues such as places of employment, taxation, and funds for development. Ethnies also emphasize and seek control of "education in their areas of concentration so that they can teach the history, language, and culture of their group to their own children" (Brass 1991, 19). Cohen drawing from his examination of Africa's tribal politics argues that ethnicity is "essentially a political phenomenon" (1969, 199).

Instrumentalists point out that to the extent the ethnie has demonstrated results in their attempts at acquiring political rights, it moves toward establishing itself as a nation (Brass 1991). In this regard the instrumentalist approach suggests, more so than any theory on ethnicity, that the ambitions of an ethnie's elite may ultimately lead to the formation of administrative and institutional apparatuses of a prototypical state. It also activates different articulations of primordialism, an idea alluded to by Van Den Berghe when he argued that "ethnicity is *both* primordial *and* instrumental" (1996, 58).

> At this point, matters of descent, birth, and a sense of kinship may become important to ethnic group members, for the methods of inclusion and exclusion into the group often involve the explicit or tacit adoption of rules of endogamy and exogamy (Brass 1991, 18-19).

The strength of the instrumentalist position is, simultaneously, its weakness. Although it identifies the elite stratum as mobilizers of the masses and bearers of change, it does not resolve the question as to whether or not ethnie elites keep interethnic tensions simmering so that they can maintain their grip on power. Without an answer to this dilemma, critics have exploited this problem to condemn the elites not as some altruistic stratum that desire social change for the betterment of its constituency, but as a stratum that desires to keep tensions simmering so that they can justify and maintain their grip on power.

For scholars analyzing conflict, this view is based on *group mobilization theory*, a classic political science view emphasizing that leaders/elites calculate, utilize, and mobilize group resources and the group itself in response to changing political opportunities (Gurr 1993); it is a top-down view of how mobilization occurs. Natan Sharansky and Ron Dermer are proponents of this view in *The Case for Democracy: the Power of Freedom to Overcome Tyranny and Terror* (2004). The authors argue that Palestinian rage is an artificial construction of Arab elites so that they can maintain their hold on power. Only democracy can eliminate this machination. No wonder George W. Bush has developed what the February 5, 2005 *Economist* described as an "intellectual love affair" with Sharansky as the former imposes American "democracy" around the world.

Sharansky's argument flies in the face of history. As Gurr has empirically shown in his seminal work *Minorities at Risk: a Global View of Ethnopolitical Conflict* (Gurr 1993), even if resurgent nationalisms are led by modern political entrepreneurs, the success of their leadership is still dependent on being legitimated by the persistence of deep-rooted sentiments and experiences of a people that were "never completely extinguished by the modern state's policies of national integration" (Gurr 1993, 91). And given that the Karen have been exposed to repeated and "intrusive demands...by Burmans," the identities and historical grievances of the Karen are shared not only by the Karen elite, but by the vast majority of Karen living under oppression and in abject poverty (1993, 90).

Moreover applying a Sharanskian rationale to the Karen elite would distort the picture of the Karen struggle. First, the authors are extrapolating from a Palestinian and Jewish situation and applying their assertions in a geopolitically overarching manner. Second, a Sharanskian view supports a trickle down democracy that purportedly eliminates tyranny, but overlooks the fact that often time the oppressed is a democratic force. Indeed, the fifty-nine years of the Karen struggle have included elections at the local level and political elections and congresses within the KNU at the state level—all of which have taken place when war was and still is imminent in destroying the Karen way of life. It is myopic to focus on the merits of a trickle down democracy without considering the gate-keeping capacities of paranoid pro-Burman military regimes to render impossible a Sharanskian trajectory.

D. Ethnicity as Rational Choice

Rational choice theory closes the political distance between elites and its individual constituents. Whereas instrumentalists argue that ethnic *elites* harness ethnicity for political advantage, rational choice theorists such as Michael Hechter, author of the important work *Internal Colonialism* (1975), and Michael Banton (1994), treat ethnicity as a medium for *individuals* to acquire *personal* advantage. Overlapping the trajectory of instrumentalism, Banton and Hechter argue that participation in collective action must yield some sort of rewards to entice the individual. Ethnicity provides these rewards in cultural terms by allowing the individual the capacity to acquire status through ethnicity. Ethnic organizations then act as the nexus between collective aims and individual desires by monitoring resources and controlling information; that is, there are bridgeable links between the goals of the elite and its constituents.

Hechter's careful treatment of the relationship between individual preferences (which he believes are mostly idiosyncratic) and collective preferences, allows him to make the very important argument that not all individual preferences are in conflict with collective preferences. This argument challenges the classic assertion that individual rights and group rights are diametrically opposed and incompatible. For Hechter, although an ethnie desires wealth, honor and power, these cultural objects can similarly be desired by most individuals. Indeed, they "impel everyone in the group to act similarly" and "so long as the common preferences are known…then the idiosyncratic ones will cancel one another out" (Hechter 1986, 268). Here, rational choice theory and instrumentalism fuse into a process where self-maximization synchronizes with collective maximization.

The link between individual and collective interests can be quite logical: individuals agree to collective rewards for wealth, honor and power because they ultimately grant the individuals the capacity to attain their idiosyncratic preferences. Thus the individual complies with group norms to avoid negatives sanctions that would hinder his/her pursuit of personal interests.

On the ground, however, rational choice theory does not unfold as neatly. Social order does not rest on the basis of rewards and sanctions alone, yet rational choice proponents seem to suggest that rewards and sanctions from the ethnie are "necessary *and* sufficient" for social order (Hechter 1986, 271). Even Hechter concedes to the sociological argument that social order is more than just rewards and sanctions, but includes intangible factors such as upholding legitimacy and supporting a charismatic leader. Hechter additionally argues that many of the rewards and sanctions that affect an ethnie's stability come not from within the ethnie, but from external boundaries that "channel group members into distinctive positions in a cultural division of labor" (1986, 277). This is a powerful observation in that it points directly to the circumstances of the Karen ethnie and its relationship to a militaristic Burmanizing polity.

Banton is a more realistic proponent of rational choice theory: individuals seek to optimize personal rewards not only through ethnic identification, but also through other socially organized channels that compete with the collective demands of ethnicity. These include religion, class, nation or even friendships. For Banton, ethnicity is not a "living-force" as is often touted in much of the discourse on ethnicity. His examination of different interethnic predicaments is noteworthy in its implications.

To substantiate this point Banton and Mansor (1992) asked their readers to consider the predicament of a hypothetical Kuala Lumpur resident, the Malaysian Husin Ali. The scenario centers on Ali's patronage of a grocery store owned by a friend, a Chinese Malay by the name of Mr. Kow. An extraneous factor is introduced: a new grocery store is opened by a fellow Malay named Ahmad, in the same neighborhood.[11] A sample of respondents was asked whether Ali would transfer his patronage to Ahmad's new shop. The results indicated that respondents were split on their predictions as to whether Ali would choose his ethnic affiliation and thus patronize Ahmad's store. Banton and Mansor concluded that:

---

[11] It should be noted that anti-Chinese sentiment in Malaysia is a common articulation of its nationalism.

Our finding that self-interest in saving money or gaining social status, and sentiments of obligation to a friend, neighbor or fellow worker, were often more influential than ethnic identification (Banton 1994, 3).

Banton is not entirely reductionistic, however, given the ahistorical tendencies of rational choice theory. Banton notes that rational choice allows us to select roles, but these roles are arrayed on a scale proceeding from "basic" roles (e.g. gender) to "independent roles" based on other social relationships. Banton situates ethnicity at the middle of the scale and as such, ethnicity is not a primary identity of the actor in many social circumstances. But the important point to be made is Banton's acknowledgement that different social circumstances activate ethnic roles over others. He cites the former Yugoslavia as a prime example where the ethnic tensions have repositioned ethnic roles at the basic end.

The strength of Banton's analysis is his treatment of rational choice behavior as contingent with changing sociopolitical contexts. The important question that needs to be asked is what if anti-Chinese sentiments have taken on a protracted dimension? Will respondents' prediction of Ali's patronage change? Certainly. Banton wisely qualifies rational choice actions not as an *a priori* engagement with ethnicity, but where it is subsumed under the systemic stability of the social system.

What theory on ethnicity best elucidates Karen liberation ethnodevelopment? Because of the long duration and continuation of the Karen struggle, Karen ethnicity exhibits many of the diacritica discussed in the aforementioned theories. However, the aforementioned theories could have been further enhanced if they explicitly qualified when ethnicity is *most* activated, when it is *most* instrumental, when it is *most* primordial, and/or when it is *most* synchronized with individual preferences. Although Van Den Berghe's assertion that "ethnicity is *both* primordial *and* instrumental" is a good start, it similarly fails to discern the sociological contexts that "activate" or privilege certain modes of ethnie orientations (1996, 58). Banton, Brass and Cohen's instrumentalism come close, but nonetheless, fail to note the apparent "freezing" of ethnicity in certain social circumstances.

The Function of Ethnicity and Systemic Crisis in Ethnodevelopment

My response is to combine Banton and Mansor's (1992) ethnic roles as contingent with changing sociopolitical contexts with Patterson's (1983) emphasis on crisis functioning as a glue for ethnie cohesion, to argue that high levels of Karen instrumentalism, primordialism, and self-maximizing behavior are a function of *systemic crisis*. A good discussion on how undesirable systemic crisis reinforces the salience of ethnicity can be found in Willem Van Schendel's 1992 examination of nation construction underway with the *Jummas*[12] of Bangladesh's Chittagong Hill Tracts, a construction born from and reinforced by their historically conflictive relationship with the Bengalis.

The role of crisis in generating group cohesion was already implied upon as early as 1964, in Gordon's *Assimilation in American Life*. Although extrapolations from a 1960s American context to Burma should only be done cautiously, Gordon did highlight a unique feature that he believed explained two types of social participation: ethnic identity and cohesion, according to Gordon, is activated through the "function of the unfolding of past and current historic events" (1964, 53). The social relationships formed from the "unfolding of past and current historic events" where the "ethnic group is the locus" Gordon designated as *historical identification*. This is very different from social relationships that are formed by people who engage in cross-cultural relationships based on behavioral similarities, a process Gordon designated as *participational identification*.

Historical identification based on the construction of the Karen nation relies on the unfolding of past and current events, but with the added factor that these events are usually intensified by systemic crisis generated by Rangoon. That is, protracted crisis generates historical identification and solidifies it. Not only has the KNU succeeded in generating a coherent sense of nationhood among the diverse Karen nation during crisis, it should be remembered that ordinary Karen civilians dealing with and overcoming suffering and misery from the crisis have also emotively constructed a Karen nation. These two reinforcing Karen trajectories the Burmese military regimes would like to disrupt.

From the lived experiences of the Karen, systemic crisis manifests itself in three interrelated ways. First, it results when institutions of the state of Burma do not develop the Karen ethnie due to the former's internal colonizing campaigns (and when it does, it does so only through Burman chauvinism, e.g., supporting the construction of Buddhist churches instead of Christian ones or mandating the teaching of the Burman language). Second, it also refers to the consequences resulting from ethnocratic attempts to destroy the Karen ethnie's administrative institutions, as exemplified by the Four Cuts campaigns.

The third contribution to systemic crisis revolves around the effects of globalization. Rangoon's desperation for capital investment has meant that it readily welcomes foreign enterprises that tap into Burma's natural resources. As we shall see in Chapter 5, reports of forced labor drawn from Karen

---

[12] The Jummas represent a transcommunality of hill tribes in Bangladesh that have, in essence, coalesced into a nation to counter economic and cultural forays made into their lands by the Bengalis.

populations to support corporate enterprises exploiting natural resources in Kawthoolei abound. This scenario is very much in line with scholars who argue that the state and its "politics of nation-building" are being subverted by globalization dynamics (Gurr 1993, McMichael 1996, Yagcioglu 1996, Castells 1997, Sassen 1998). Yet dialectically, globalization dynamics reinforce indigenous resistances to these forces since it is in their areas where natural resources are relatively untapped.

> The global process of economic development and state building and the communications revolution have created a multiplicity of pressures on communal groups everywhere. Increased social interaction means that groups that once occupied isolated social niches are subject to differential treatment and stigmatization by advantaged groups. Members of the increasingly disadvantaged group react with resentment and a sharpened sense of communal identity and common interest (Gurr 1993, 90).

Since the military regimes have been unable to completely quell all the insurgencies in the Karen areas TNCs have co-dictated military policies with Rangoon to safeguard their interests. Corporate interests, in the form of logging and natural gas pipeline construction in Karen areas, further activate the Karen need to make visible the distinctiveness of their identity "as they are trying to separate themselves from the larger national unit of which they constitute a component" (Yagcioglu 1996, 7). The enterprises of the TNCs have opened up a new front in the Karen struggle, as they now have to disrupt the operations of the TNCs. That systemic crisis augments the salience of ethnicity because it makes visible the relative deprivation of the disadvantaged group to the "other" points to a conflict perspective known as *relative deprivation theory*. In relative deprivation theory conflict is a result of: (1) the perceived severity of the communal group's disadvantages in relation to other groups, (2) the extent of cultural differences between a communal group and others with which it interacts, and (3) the intensity of conflict with other groups and the state (Gurr 1993, 126).

The rationale for the Karen struggle via a relative deprivation approach would be that since the Burmans were granted a state after British decolonization, why weren't the Karen (or the Shan, the Kachin, the Mon, for that matter) granted their own state? Indeed, multiple expressions of resistance to crisis in the Karen narrative were born from feeling betrayed by the British who harnessed the Karen as allies during World War II, only to later hand over the issue of Karen statehood to a Burman polity during the decolonization of Burma.[13]

---

[13] An excellent BBC-produced documentary, *Forgotten Allies* (1997) taps into the Karen-British alliance during World War II. During the closing days of World War II, the Karen, fighting

If we ignore how systemic crisis freezes social relationships and ethnic boundaries we reinforce outdated social system models that are biased toward the fiction of systemic equilibrium. I find it important to remind readers, however, my assertion that systemic crisis can freeze ethnic boundaries and reinforce in-group cohesion should not be equated with the notion that an ethnie will remain a perennially static and discrete sociopolitical and sociocultural entity. Instead my point is that the nature of war limits harmonious interethnic migration, exchange, and cultural osmosis. Nations cannot at *all times* be viewed as "fluid and malleable," yet it is the fluidity and malleability of the nation that Van Schendel (2002) argues is emphasized by much of the "new literature" on the nation.

Employing systemic crisis as a prism for observing ethnicity unites three key theoretical models on ethnicity: systemic crisis activates a group's historical dimension as a means of generating cohesion (primordialism), it activates a people's capacity to utilize ethnicity as an instrument for collective mobilization and action (instrumentalism), and because systemic crisis can descend "upon the individual as a shared crisis" with a group (Patterson 1983, 27), it sets itself up to be a rationally chosen path of alignment for the individual to the ethnie, without the chosen path being idiosyncratic and incompatible toward collective aims. Thus when systemic crisis is applied in viewing Rangoon's maldevelopment of the Karen ethnie, one will see that the Karen have responded by harnessing their history, heritage[14], a highly educated elite stratum, and the commitment and sacrifice of Karen individuals to fight for a Karen nation.

Van Schendel (2002) points out that a perspective cementing the correspondence between nation and state is no longer useful. For Van Schendel a perspective that captures the ubiquity of systemic disequilibria is more relevant for assessing "nations without states, new nations that are invented before our eyes while older ones disintegrate, and older diasporic nations that are being joined" (2002, 115). In a remarkable display of foresight, the acknowledgement of systemic instability inherent in social systems was already a concern to scholars like Edmund Leach in the 1950s. In his seminal work *Political Systems of Highland Burma: a Study of Kachin Social Structure* (1954), Leach begins by critiquing anthropological and sociological tendencies to treat social systems as "naturally endowed with an equilibrium" (1954, x). Leach disagrees and argues that "real societies can never be in equilibrium" and that they are "a constantly changing environment" (1954, 4-5).

---

with their British allies, were able to ambush thousands of Japanese troops fleeing Burma. Countless thousands of Karen perished in this forgotten episode of World War II.

[14] A good source for being introduced to the ethnogenesis of the Karen can be found in D. M. Smeaton's *The Loyal Karens of Burma* (1887) and Harry I. Marshall's *The Karen People of Burma: a Study in Anthropology and Ethnology* (1980).

For Leach, societies are processes in time and its examination should be conducted within a clearly defined time period. Assumptions of societies in equilibrium negate this important temporal consideration and potentially render analyses ahistorical. He forcefully emphasizes that social equilibrium is an "illusion." Leach delineates his scope conditions clearly at the beginning of his work:

> Real societies exist in time and space... Every real society is a process in time... The essence of my argument is that the process by which the small units grow into larger ones and the large units break into smaller ones is not simply part of the process of structural continuity; it is not merely a process of segmentation and accretion, it is a process involving structural change (1954, 5-6).

Leach's methodological realism effectively captures the changes the Karen have gone through in their revolutionary struggle. As such, the Karen have had to construct their nation through two levels of systemic disequilibria: one from a failed construction of the Union of Burma, the other from the differing ideological tensions and changing military fortunes within the Karen liberation ethnodevelopment process.

Moreover, a protracted systemic crisis has significantly altered the interethnic relationship between the Karen and the Burman (as well as the relationship between Burma's other ethnic nationalities and the Burmans). Most of the aforementioned theories, save Patterson, Leach, Banton and Mansor, have explicitly overlooked how systemic crisis reconfigures interethnic relationships and alters the construction of the ethnie and the nation. A society with instability and concomitant reconfigurations of social relationships, infrastructure, and institutions, will have a different sociological diacritica than a stable one.

What is most important to reflect on, however, is not whether scholars view these theoretical assertions and critiques as clearly definitive of the Karen struggle, but how the Karen view their own destiny. As will be shown in Chapter 4, the diacritica of the Karen Revolution reveals a plurality of ideologies and worldviews, all of which served at times to strengthen, at times to weaken, the trajectory of their liberation ethnodevelopment. The reality on the ground is that for Karen engaged with their struggle, the lived experiences of their ethnicity is symbiotic with socioeconomic and sociopolitical maneuverings from their past toward the present, and from their present toward the future.

Ethnodevelopment

In my work I argue that Karen liberation ethnodevelopment is synonymous with agency nationalism. By synthesizing Hettne, Seers and Stavenhagen's ideas within a context of systemic crisis, ethnodevelopment can also be understood as the political economy of agency nationalism. Clarke (2001) notes the applicability of ethnodevelopment in the Southeast Asia, where since the 1990s, its strategies have been enacted through international donors concerned about the plight of ethnic minorities not only in Burma, but in Laos, Vietnam and Indonesia, with significant successes in promoting the liberation of East Timor in 1999.

The mere presence of an ethnodevelopment argument already implies the international acknowledgement that there are unequal cultural, social and economic relationships between ethnies in multicultural settings. Indeed, many scholars have consistently noted during the 1970s, when modernization and industrialization were accepted trajectories for state development, how multiethnic societies transforming under industrialization tended to develop and proceed unevenly (Bates 1974, Hah and Martin 1975, Hechter 1971, Hechter 1973, Melson and Wolpe 1970). What results from this asymmetrical trajectory is that one ethnie will tend to acquire more benefits and resources than others. Stavenhagen identifies this group as the *ethnocracy*.

Stavenhagen's concept of ethnocracy argues that the ethnie with the most political, economic and cultural power will attempt to dominate other ethnies in the image of its own and "impose its own particular ethnic interests on the whole of national society" (Stavenhagen 1996, 197). From the perspective of the Karen and the other ethnic nationalities fighting the military regime, these processes constitute *Burmanization* toward a Burman cultural model:

- The Burman language is made mandatory for government business from 1952 onward. The Burman language is the sole language taught from the 4th standard upward (Brown 1994, 48-49).

  > It was necessary to become fluent in Burman in order to progress up the educational ladder; further [a student] had to leave his local home area to advance his education because secondary schools were located in the cities and larger towns and the universities were situated in Burma proper... By moving to Rangoon or Mandalay for his higher education, a student became part of Burman culture, and in order not to stand out or be treated as a rustic, he tended to modify his dress, speech, and living pattern so that he fit in (Silverstein 1980, 221).

- Burma's history was taught from the perspective of Burman nationalism; according to Smith, the military tradition that Ne Win and the coup leaders celebrated was only a current atavism "dating back across the centuries from the founder of the modern Tatmadaw, Aung San, to the all-conquering Burman monarchs, Alaungpaya in the 18th century and Anawratha in the 11th" (1999, 197).

- The Ministry of Culture and Mass Education Movement promoted and reinforced the hegemony of Burman history (Brown 1994, 49).

- The religion of Buddhism was proselytized in the Karen hills under the auspices of the Ministry of Religious Affairs and the Buddha Sasana Organization (Brown 1994, 49).

Burmanization, along with its violent corollary the Four Cuts strategy to be examined later, exemplifies how Burma is an *ethnocratic state* (Brown 1994). Brown defines the ethnocratic state as "where the state acts as the agency of the dominant ethnic community in terms of ideologies, its policies and its resource distribution" (1994, 36). But Brown was not the only one to notice this ubiquitous pattern of multicultural asymmetry. In 1987, Weiner identified some characteristic features of multicultural societies:

> In country after country, a single ethnic group has taken control over the state and used its powers to exercise control over others... In retrospect there has been far less 'nation-building' than many analysts had expected or hoped, for the process of state building has rendered many ethnic groups devoid of power or influence (Weiner 1987, 36-37).

Brown lists three main tendencies of the ethnocratic state (1994, 36-38): First, the majority ethnie is disproportionately and overwhelmingly granted access to state elite positions, the civil service, and armed forces; when "recruitment...from other ethnic origins does occur, it is conditional upon their assimilation into the dominant ethnic culture."

> Moreover, the state elites use these positions to promote their ethnic interests, rather than acting as either an 'autonomous' state bureaucracy or as representatives of the socio-economic class strata from which they originate (Brown 1994, 36-38).

Second, the ethnocratic state positions its own values at the top of a vertical multicultural scale, and constructs its history in a hegemonic fashion. Although ethnocratic states may claim a sort of universalism, the ethnocentric assumptions underlying their domestic policies render the state neither "ethnically neutral nor multi-ethnic, but...mono-ethnic." Finally, ethnocratic states utilize their institutions, "its constitutions, its laws and its political structures" to reinforce a monopoly on power for the ethnocratic polity. Overall, politics in an ethnocratic state is based on the "introduction of values and institutions of the ethnic group into the peripheral communities" (ibid., 36-38).

The various military regimes and governments that have ruled Burma since its independence have all been ethnocratic, and the one in power currently is also ethnocratic. Even when Burma had its experience with democracy under U Nu, Rangoon was still ethnocratic in its domestic policy toward the Karen self-determination. But not only is Burma an ethnocratic state, it evolved into a totalitarian state after the ouster of U Nu in 1962. Currently, the Karen State of Kawthoolei is maldeveloped and suffering from genocide at the hands of the current military regime of Burma, the State Peace and Development Council (SPDC). As a result Steinburg (1990) notes:

> All the systems in Burma that allow growth, development and mobility are those dominated by the Burman cultural tradition... Minority languages are relegated to one's home and cannot be used other than for local purposes. Education is in Burman; the symbols of the state and the deployment of power are Burman... The 'Burmese Way to Socialism' might more accurately be termed the 'Burman Way to Socialism' because it reflects Burman cultural, political, and nationalistic norms (1990, 75).

The highly asymmetrical relationship between Burma's military ethnocracy and its ethnic nationalities constitute the most important dimension for ethnodevelopment analyses. Statistics clearly reveal ethnocratic hoarding of resources: In 1995, the military regime only allocated 12 percent of its budget for education, while 4 percent was spent on health (Brunner, Talbott and Elkin 1998). On the other hand 35 percent to 45 percent of Rangoon's budget was channeled toward defense expenditures (Ashton 2004). Moreover, since 1988, defense expenditures have been ambitious and based on modernization. Ashton notes "while an increasing proportion of Burma's annual defense expenditure is now used to pay for recurring personnel and maintenance costs, a high percentage is still devoted to the acquisition of new arms and equipment from abroad" (Ashton 2004).

Yet the Karen are not the only ones to suffer, as all peoples of Burma—including the Burmans—have suffered under military rule. It is well known that the failure of Ne Win's Burmese Way to Socialism prompted the United Nations to declare in 1987 Burma's status as a least developed country (LDC). A less known fact is that the United Nations Development Programme (UNDP) and its Human Development Index has also scored Burma as a "low human development" country. It ranks 133 out of the 174 countries surveyed by the UNDP—81 places behind Thailand, 12 places below Vietnam, and just 5 places above Laos (Brunner et al. 1998). This is a far cry from when Burma was perceived, at the time of independence in 1948, as Southeast Asia's prime candidate for economic prosperity. Furthermore, global finance institutions such as the World Bank, the Asian Development Bank, and the International Monetary Fund stay clear of assisting Burma due to its "excessive military expenditures, lack of macroeconomic transparency, and human rights abuses" (Brunner et al. 1998).

Yet one can certainly speculate that these low indicators for Burma could be even lower if observers were to ascertain the ethnic nationality regions. The military regimes' internal colonization and maldevelopment of the periphery, along with decades of protracted war, mean that destitution is asymmetrically worse off for the ethnic nationalities. Unfortunately, accurate statistics that measure quantitative aspects of Karen maldevelopment by Rangoon are impossible to come by. The qualitative dimensions of Karen maldevelopment detailed in Chapter 5, however, are plentiful. The qualitative indicators of how Rangoon asymmetrically distributes resources to its periphery should remind us how difficult it is for countries with ethnic diversity like Burma to unify as a state (Seers 1983). Moreover, Seers argues:

> A majority has no inherent right to impose national unity on the minority (or minorities), that wants to cut itself off from a culture it feels alien, especially if it is also exploited economically (1983, 74).

Seers then traverses into ethnodevelopment thinking when he further notes:

> But in some circumstances allowing secession may be preferable. An unappeased minority disrupts national unity; to suppress it is expensive... Norway and Sweden live amicably after their separation, and Ireland could hardly have been accommodated for long within Britain, especially since we were losing the room to make big concessions, as the colonial system disintegrated (1983, 74).

By employing an ethnodevelopment perspective to outline how the Karen engage in their own development, I am responding to what Seers, Stavenhagen, and Hettne describe as an inbuilt bias by conventional development thinkers who are "against ethnic identification and in favour of national identification, regardless of how unrealistic a particular nation-state project may be" (Hettne 1990, 193). This bias results from the assumption in much of development discourse that assumes away ethnic antagonisms and tensions as development occurs. Enloe argues that the opposite has happened—that "development does not automatically herald the demise of ethnicity" (1973, 34). According to Enloe the staying power of ethnicity is a response to the tendency of the ethnocracy to idealize assimilation and integration toward an ethnocratic ideal, often against the wishes of its ethnic nationalities (Enloe 1973, Ryan 1995; Stavenhagen 1986, 1996). Indeed, Enloe's observations capture the terrain of Burma's ethnopolitics.

When we examine Karen liberation ethnodevelopment in the coming chapters, it will be helpful to remember Thompson and Ronen's proposition that an ethnodevelopment perspective no longer perceives ethnicity to be an obstacle to modernization (Thompson and Ronen 1986, 1). This is because ethnodevelopment departs from conventional development theory in its emphasis that people are divided into territorial cultural groups as well as being individual consumers and producers, buyers and sellers, employees, and employers (Stavenhagen 1986, 1996).

A strong case for the relevancy and significance of ethnodevelopment praxis can be made. Stavenhagen reminds us that although there are over 150 countries officially recognized by the United Nations, "three to six thousand" ethnies exist "depending on the criteria used to define them" (1986, 84). Connor found that only 12 out of the 132 countries he examined were "essentially homogeneous from an ethnic viewpoint" (1972) while Nielsson (1985) found that only 45 out of the 164 countries examined could be considered as single nation-states, defined as where between 95 to 100 percent of the population are from a consciously agreed upon national identity. In a rather epic disclosure, Nielsson concluded that "the conventional concept of the nation-state fits only one-quarter of the members of the global state system" (1985, 33). Moreover, Gurr (1993) expands our understanding of ethnic tensions even further when he identifies 292 "ethnocultural" groups that are in conflict with 120 nation-states.

The inconsistent relationship between ethnies and the ethnocracy is indicative of flaws inherent in the processes of nation-state construction. Even though the nation-state emerged as a political concept during the French Revolution, it is still "considered to be the main building block of the world system" (Stavenhagen 1996, 2). As a political ideal, the nation-state would resolve the distances between the idea of a unified togetherness and actual political boundaries of its territory. In reality, however, many nation-states that emerged during twentieth century decolonization lumped multiethnic groups together into a superficial and overarching notion of a union. Policies were then constructed to encourage its constituents to conform to an ethnocratic ideal, often ignoring the variation and tensions of identities inherent within the nation-state.

For example, the Kurdish ethnie in Turkey's far east were referred to by the Turkish polity as "mountain Turks" rather than acknowledging their Kurdish identity. Turkish policies denied the Kurds a territorial and symbolic identity in hopes of subsuming the Kurds into a Turkish ideal. Currently, the Turkish ethnocracy is attempting to increase control in Kurdish areas because of the perceived potential liberation of the Iraqi Kurds—even though Iraqi Kurds have maintained that they have adopted a non-separatist platform. As

Ryan and Stavenhagen point out that intrastate multiethnic collectives, confined within their "new" countries, do not necessarily feel "nationhood" at the nation-state level. Stavenhagen notes that "even in multiethnic states strong pressures exist to make the state conform to…one homogeneous nation, hence the traditional and powerful notion of the nation-state and its attendant political principal, nationalism" (Ryan 1995; Stavenhagen 1996, 3).

Consider the implications for development: If only a few countries in the world can claim a homogeneous nation-state (assuming this provides societal stability for development to occur) then development policy in the remaining three quarters of the world may be highly ineffective. This is especially true if ethnic conflict is experienced as a "continuous form of collective action between ethnic groups over ethnic issues, and involves a certain degree of organization" (Stavenhagen 1996, 136). Indeed, Ryan makes visible a compelling point:

> Just…a generation ago Hannah Arendt claimed that revolutionary war would replace interstate war as the dominant form of… political violence. Clearly this has not been the case. Instead, if…one form of violence has been more prevalent than any other, it seems to be ethnic conflict (Ryan 1995, 1).

Development discourse that continues to ignore the historical and contemporary dynamics of ethnic conflict in unsuccessful nation-states is therefore ignoring one of the most important forces that affect development prospects in the Third World. Yet Stavenhagen is correct to argue that current development discourse is still focused on the task of "nation-state building" (1986, 82).

Stavenhagen's observation is accurate: in *Development* Sen expresses his concerns about ethnicity as being too "narrow" an identity. Sen's bias against ethnicity means that like most development scholars Sen is still working within a mainstream development paradigm where the unit of analysis is *still* the nation-state. Stavenhagen suggests that scholars like Sen "prefer to ignore the issue precisely because it may *question the premises of the nation-state* [italics added]" (1986, 91). For those who share Sen's view, to focus on development of ethnic nationalities would mean an entirely different unit of analysis for development thinkers, one that would have potentially drastic consequences for the stability of the nation-state.

Neither can Marxist analyses explain the contradictions within a multiethnic nation-state. As such, Fishman (1980) correctly noted that even Marx recognized that "ethnicity is a disruptive rival." In Marxist doctrine, ethnicity, as part of the superstructure, is the false consciousness that will be shed in a workers' revolution based on class consciousness. Stavenhagen disagrees and reminds us how "cluttered" class-consciousness actually is with ethnicity:

It will be remembered...that the French Communist party did not at first support the Algerian national liberation struggle. In the United States, the American Communist party in the 1930s proposed a national liberation strategy for American blacks, which was later withdrawn. Jewish Marxists were anti-Zionists in the nineteenth century. Later, however, Zionism included a militant Marxist wing (1986, 81).

Another example can be drawn from the Second International, when during World War I it dissolved as many of Europe's Social Democratic parties swung toward nationalism and threw their support behind their own national ruling classes. We have also seen this pattern with the former Yugoslavia, where upon Tito's death an unraveling of Yugoslavia's socialist order was inversely linked to the rise in ethnic consciousness, irredentism, and secessionary dynamics that emerged alongside a hegemonizing Serbian ethnocracy under Slobidan Milosevic. In the case of Burma, the many decades of struggle by ethnic nationalities have also persevered over communism, exemplified by the dramatic implosion of the Communist Party of Burma (CPB) in 1989 after which its constituents returned to their ethnic affiliations. It is no wonder that Tom Nairn, author of *The Break-up of Britain*, (1977) remarked "the theory of nationalism represents Marxism's great historical failure" (Nairn 1975, 3).

Critique of Stavenhagen's Ethnodevelopment

Stavenhagen concedes to some shortcomings of the ethnodevelopment approach. In his assessment of Nigeria's civil war where 30 new states, closely related to ethnic "homelands" were created within its borders, Stavenhagen noted that "the creation of states has also contributed to the proliferation of tertiary activities through the expansion of public administration and new state bureaucracy. These activities have not furthered healthy economic development" (1996, 154). Although this is an honest assessment, Stavenhagen did not give himself credit for his ethnodevelopment legacy—namely that the new Nigerian states are coexisting because of autonomy and without the bloody internal strife that characterizes Burma. In the case of Nigeria, we can use Clarke to reinforce the merits of ethnodevelopment by pointing to his view that ethnodevelopment is but a response to how mainstream development strategies tend to "generate conflicts between states and ethnic minorities and that such strategies are, at times, 'ethnocidal' in their destructive effects on the latter" (Clarke 2001, 415).

However, I do critique Stavenhagen on one aspect of his ethnodevelopment approach: although Stavenhagen does address ethnies that aspire toward self-determination when national development fails them, he does not explicitly address nor encourage ethnies that aspire toward self-determination in the context of systemic crisis or totalitarianism. This is problematic, for if an ethnocracy is brutally oppressive and maldevelops its peripheral regions, then the ethnodevelopment perspective should encourage liberation as part of its strategy for development, the premise being that ethnic groups once liberated can finally implement development policies that bolster their own notions of progress. For example, in his essay "Self-determination: right or demon," Stavenhagen makes an important distinction between separatism and self-determination:

> "Separatism" and "secession," as well as related concepts...relate to the political organization of states. Self-determination...involves the needs, aspirations, values and goals of the social and cultural communities we refer to as "peoples"... If self-determination is to be considered...as a type of collective existence, rather than a one-time political happening, then it ought to break out of the harness that its earlier identification with secession or political separatism imposes upon it (Stavenhagen 1993, 6-7).

Stavenhagen's ethnodevelopment is a pro-autonomizing but not pro-separatist ethnodevelopment:

> I am not arguing that every ethnic group in the world should have its own state. On the contrary, my critique of the nation-state or the ethnocratic state leads precisely in the opposite direction; that is, to the multinational, multicultural, multiethnic state...in which ethnic communities may find equal opportunity for social, economic and cultural development within the larger framework (1986, 92).

I do not share Stavenhagen's optimism regarding multiculturalism because it fails to explicitly address the contradictions inherent within the construction of the nation-state. Moreover, multiculturalism is a political euphemism that hides the failure of integrationist and assimilationist policies constructed by the ethnocracy. Indeed, when we observe multiculturalism as lived experiences, it is actually voluntary segregation conducted by people below who exercise their agency to live apart from one another. That is, how else can one explain the persistence of ethnic enclaves, for example? Multiculturalism is "visible" because of different groups' voluntary segregation at the level of social configuration, but is never addressed as such.

My argument differs from Stavenhagen, albeit still ethnodevelopment-based: if an ethnie already has established autonomous institutions and a political economy, and if the people of this nationality are fighting to maintain their way of life from ethnic cleansing, then it is already a

84

prototypical state, and that ethnodevelopment should explicitly encourage a complete evolution of this state toward liberation, whether it be self-determination or beyond. An internationalized ethnodevelopment approach toward the Karen should embrace a social configuration that grants ethnic nationalities as much autonomy as possible within a federal Burma, the current line held by self-determination groups like the Karen.

It is important to consider that international appraisals of federalism, insofar as it pertains to Burma's labyrinthine ethnopolitics, could alternatively view Karen self-determination as a "stopping point" between a Burmese union and Karen national independence (Walzer 1983, 223), rather than as two discrete dynamics as viewed by Stavenhagen. As Gurr pointed out in 1993, autonomy agreements did help dampen rebellions by the Muslim Moros in the Philippines, the Miskitos in Nicaragua, the Nagas and Tripuras in India, and the Afars in Ethiopia. Thereafter, should federalism fail, then what Gurr terms as an "exit" strategy, should be considered. McGarry and O'Leary (1993) echo Gurr's sentiments, both of whom agree that partition and/or secession often resolve ethnic conflict:

> Partition, self-determination, and secession are compatible with liberal democratic institutions (universal, periodic and competitive elections, alternations in power, and civic freedoms of expression, assembly and organisation), in that such states can, in principle, permit secessions and preserve democratic institutions.

One can also critique Stavenhagen's ethnodevelopment as being focused on a top-to-bottom development trajectory. In the case of the Karen, their ethnodevelopment has never occurred from the charitable views of the militarists in Rangoon, but from their own self-determination struggle that has been sustained and administered by their own institutions and political economy. Karen-established institutions exist in structural opposition to the institutions established by the military regimes of Burma. It is in this regard that the Karen struggle represents another variant of ethnodevelopment I have termed throughout this work as *liberation ethnodevelopment*.

Liberation ethnodevelopment is a preferred reading that emphasizes a freedom-based bottom-to-top ethnodevelopment strategy, as opposed to the more conventional top-to-bottom ethnodevelopment strategy proposed by Stavenhagen. Liberation ethnodevelopment is thus about how a self-determination group's political economy and social institutions function as it aims to become, in the context of a protracted genocidal war, an autonomous state. Indeed, liberation ethnodevelopment is the study of how an ethnopolitical economy contributes to the prototypical formation of new states.

Liberation ethnodevelopment is a normative perspective based on social justice in that it rejects development if it comes from an oppressive ethnocracy that is exploitative of its periphery. My decision to adopt this perspective should be seen in the context where Rangoon has used "development" as political camouflage to build Burmanization-friendly infrastructure that would allow genocidal policies to be carried out quickly in any self-determination territory (as in allowing private sector tyranny via oil TNCs such as Total and UNOCAL). This distinction is important because it allows us to view the ethnodevelopment process as one based on self-development of an ethnie as it attempts to delink itself from an exploitative ethnocracy.

Liberation ethnodevelopment is a response to the arguments put forth by the *group dominance model*, which argues that most "multiethnic states come into existence as a result of conquest by one group over other groups" (Dowley and Silver 1999; Sidanius, Feshbach and Pratto 1997). However, the group dominance model has little utility in explaining how Karen nationalism resists military rule and genocide. That is, if we utilize the group dominance model to explain ethnic conflict in Burma, it would mean that we would have to make an *a priori* assumption that the current state of Burma was "born" through the subjugation of ethnic nationalities like the Karen. By doing this we reinforce two erroneous assumptions: (1) that the Union of Myanmar is a state—which it has failed to be due to the oppression it has meted out to even its own Burman population, let alone the Karen, and (2) that the Karen have already been subjugated by Burmanization and conquest—which it has not in spite of the tendency for international observers, throughout the years, to speak of the Karen struggle in apocalyptic terms (Falla 1991).

This is an important difference between the explanatory power of liberation ethnodevelopment and the group dominance model. My employment of liberation ethnodevelopment takes the premise that the Karen and their territories in the mountains and hills have always had some sort of autonomy that predates Burman hegemony. From this perspective, I argue that influences of colonialism did not so much as construct a Karen nation as pitched by Keyes (1979) and Rajah (2002), but only reinvigorated Karen in-group sentiments that already predated British colonialism. What colonialism did do, however, was generate for the oppressed Karen a politicized elite that articulated their hopes and aspirations for freedom, leading to the launching of the Karen Revolution in 1949.

By making visible the trajectory of liberation ethnodevelopment, I question the premise of the Burman chauvinist state ruled by brutal military juntas. I will attempt to demonstrate in the remainder of my work that the state of Burma is an incomplete project so as to shift attention back to ethnic nationalities like the Karen who exhibit their own aspirations for nation in light of Burma's failure to form a union.

In the case of the Karen, liberation ethnodevelopment treats Karen self-determination not as an anomalous trajectory within the state of Burma, but as normal process where the oppressed seek cultural, economic, and political freedom. Yet to support this proposition the deployment of liberation ethnodevelopment will need to be situated within the context of systemic crisis. Only analyses within the context of systemic crisis can liberation ethnodevelopment be discerned from the dynamics of a non-revolutionary ethnodevelopment.

A final critique regarding Stavenhagen's ethnodevelopment is its neglect of anti-ethnocratic alliances as constituting a form of horizontal ethnodevelopment. In the context of Burma, the Karen are not the only people engaged in liberation ethnodevelopments as there have also been localized coalitions that involve grassroots and indigenous participation (Smith 1999). Throughout their epic struggles against Rangoon, ethnic nationalities such as the Shan, Mon, Karenni, Chin, and pro-democracy Burmans have, at one time or another, formed alliances (not officially recognized by Rangoon) that have linked up with the KNU. The interethnic links have included arrangements with constituents that were communists and Burman democracy activists, all united on an anti-Tatmadaw platform.

My preference is not to treat these links as mere coalitions lest these alliances end up being confused with interethnic coalitions formed by the Tatmadaw for their pro-Tatmadaw stance. Instead, I have decided to employ the term *transcommunality* to distinguish freedom-based coalitions from puppet coalitions established by Rangoon. The term transcommunality, introduced by Childs (2003) in *Transcommunality: from the Politics of Conversion to the Ethics of Respect*, is defined as "the constructive and developmental interaction occurring among distinct autonomy-oriented communities and organizations, each with its own particular history, outlook, and agenda" (2003, 10). The key feature of transcommunal politics is how it is rooted in communities and organizations that "address substantial, albeit often varied corrosive dilemmas" (2003, 10), and that their political aim "asserts distinctive and essential community/organizational allegiances that can serve as multiple bases for common action with others" (2003, 11).

Because a large number of Karen in Kawthoolei live a rural existence with the village as the center of social life, transcommunality will be a helpful concept for reading how the Karen and the KNU have, throughout their fifty-nine year struggle, formed alliances with other self-determination groups in the hills to survive genocide and Burman expansionism. My use of transcommunality in assessing Burma should be seen as employing a term that captures the plurality of alliance formations, created in the midst of crisis, that are diametrically opposed to the politics of conversion meted out by a Burmanizing ethnocracy.

The KNU administration of their self-determination struggle could not have lasted this long without the adroit transcommunal maneuverings conducted with potential allies. For example, one of the more powerful transcommunalities today is the Democratic Alliance of Burma (DAB), which includes Karen and pro-democracy Burmans, as well as a host of other self-determination groups, working side-by-side for a common goal of liberation, but with their cultural uniqueness intact and not blinded with only an "inward focused identity politics...that consciously cuts off its participants from contact with others in the name of racial, ethnic, or ideological claims of purity" (Childs 2003, 11). Indeed, Childs' formulation of transcommunality, that is, *heterogeneity + cooperation = resistance and freedom*, suggests how transcommunality can also function as a revolutionary force that enhances the trajectories of Karen self-determination (ibid., 8).

Stavenhagen acknowledges the difficulties in employing the concept of self-determination. He concedes that "'self-determination' means different things to different persons" and notes that it is "one of those unexceptionable goals that can be neither defined nor opposed" (1993, 3). In addition, Stavenhagen is prescient to see the contradictory tensions within ethnodevelopment: "It would seem that for some people self-determination is somewhat akin to an exclusive club: you fight hard to gain access...but once you are in, you would rather not see any new upstarts come along" (Stavenhagen 1993, 1). The importance of identifying the transcommunalities in Burma's civil wars, then, is due to its utility in pointing out that self-determination/liberation ethnodevelopment in Burma is not based on a politics of exclusion or a politics of conversion.

I plan to employ liberation ethnodevelopment and transcommunality in order to make visible the political economy, institutions, alliances, and political processes that have sustained Karen self-determination. As such, liberation ethnodevelopment and transcommunality will be explored as unfettered from its link to a violent militarist ethnocracy. Liberation ethnodevelopment and transcommunality highlight trajectories where disadvantaged peoples become agents of vertical and horizontal social change, and where this change emanates from what Guha calls the "politics of the people" (1983).

The momentum driving my arguments for liberation ethnodevelopment is explicitly normative. The arguments in my work support the KNU, ethnic nationalities, and pro-democracy activists' aims of establishing a federal Burma, a social arrangement that is quite visionary and politically advanced when compared to the highly regressive nature of Tatmadaw rule. By pitching a federal Burma where ultimately a policy of recognizing differences constitutes an ethnic democracy, I am reinvoking some of the ideals pitched by Johann Gottfried Herder, described by Dimostenis Yagcioglu as a "proto-nationalist German historian and philosopher" (1996, 8). The idea based on "recognition of differences" was introduced by Herder in the late 18th century to reinforce some profoundly insightful observations he had about being human. Yagcioglu summarizes some of Herder's arguments (1996, 8):

1. All humans have a distinct way of actualizing themselves. As a result, "we should not imitate, [nor] be forced to imitate others."

2. Humans need to find their own "original" way toward self-actualization, and "should not give up until we are sure we have found it. If we give up and choose someone else's way, we miss the point of our lives; we miss what being human is for us."

3. According to Yagcioglu, Herder believed that groups should also have their own means toward group self-actualization through their culture, and "only through its own culture can an ethnic group actualize itself."

4. Herder compelled Germans to "not try or should not be compelled to try to imitate the French" for if they do, they "become second-rate French."

5. Most importantly, and in much contradiction to the colonial and expansionist sentiment of the European powers of the time, Herder argues that "European colonialism should be rolled back to give colonized people the chance to be themselves without any impediment."

This ideal would be revisited again within the historical specificities of different anti-colonial struggles observed and participated by Fannon, Nyerere, Gandhi, and Xanana Gusmao.[15] In the case of the Karen who have been fighting internal colonization such as San C. Po, Ba U Gyi and other early KNU leaders whose legacies have significantly influenced the trajectory of the KNU to this day, the main theme is clear: that oppressed peoples must "purge themselves of the image colonizers imposed on them. Subjugated peoples...should develop their own self image relying on their own culture" (Yagcioglu 1993, 8).

In this regard, I frame my criticism of the various atavisms of Rangoon's military regimes with the ideals provided primarily by the Universal Declaration of Human Rights. My decision to adopt this normative stance was, once again, inspired by Yagcioglu (1996). Yagcioglu argues that since the defeat of Nazism, Fascism, and Japanese militarism, principles of non-discrimination and concepts of minority rights and cultural rights have gained widespread international attention. As a result, Yagcioglu optimistically argues that it has become "significantly more difficult for the nation-state governments to implement violent and brutal policies of oppression against minorities" (1996, 6). Yagcioglu notes:

> Since the eighties, and especially since the end of the Cold War, democracy based on liberal values and principles has gained an unprecedented popularity. Today more countries enjoy a democratic regime than ever before. Although not impossible, it is certainly

---

[15] Gusmao was a "poet-warrior" and leader of the East Timorese resistance against Indonesian occupation. Having fought Jakarta from the mountains of East Timor, and imprisoned in an Indonesian prison as well as serving under house arrest for more than six years, he liberated the country and became its first president, serving between 1999 and 2001.

more difficult and less acceptable to violate minority rights in a democratic regime.

Yet Yagcioglu is realistic:

> This does not mean, of course, that these rights and principles are not or cannot be violated. They are, but the governments that violate human rights or minority rights feel the need and the pressure to present excuses; and if they are not persuasive, they often have to face sanctions. That was not possible in the 19th or in the first part of the 20th century (Yagcioglu 1993, 6).

I have introduced what I hope are sufficient concepts and debates for those interested in the Karen struggle to effectively read and assess their liberation ethnodevelopment. In the following chapters, one should be able to see the salience of the aforementioned diacritica manifest in the Karen Revolution.

Chapter IV
The Karen Revolution: 1947 – 2004

The influences of various political ideologies upon the KNU are central to understanding the evolution of the organization, especially in regard to the forces emanating from the left and right that "tugged" at the organization. The KNU's history is also centered on four influential leaders who all had quite different positions along the ideological spectrum. Moreover, describing how the KNU navigated the political and military terrain cannot be discussed without accommodating the impact leftist ideology had on the organization at one time.

When reading this section that underscores the political developments of the KNU, it is important to remember that military events such as battles, skirmishes, surrenders, and attempts at ceasefires between Rangoon, CPB and KNU, as well as between other ethnic self-determination groups, characterize its organizational history. As a result, some paragraphs will discuss political issues while others are assessments of military events. I have tried my best to keep the account of events linear, but have taken the liberty of directing readers to important topics that have further been analyzed in other chapters.

I begin my discussion by exploring the two Panglong conferences held in the Shan State during pre-Independence Burma that framed the foundations for Karen self-determination. The first Panglong Conference was held during March 1946 while the second Panglong Conference was held during the early weeks of February 1947. Although the second conference is given much more scrutiny by Burma scholars, I hope to note the significance of the first conference as well.

In this section, I also hope to describe three evolutionary phases of the KNU. The years prior to the formation of the KNU in 1947 and up until the 1953 formation of the Karen National United Party (KNUP: 1953-1975), especially in regard to the delta region, is described by Mahn Ba Zan as the "First Phase" of the Karen Revolution. The categorization based on phases was employed by Zan to describe the Karen struggle in hindsight. The phases schema, however, I find to be particularly helpful in distinguishing the unique changes undertaken by the KNU throughout its historical development.

Within the phases schema, I hope to discuss the political events of the KNU in regard to the maneuverings conducted by Ba U Gyi[16], Hunter Tha Hmwe, Mahn Ba Zan, and Bo Mya, along with the KNU's relationship with

---

[16] The first chairman of the KNU, Ba U Gyi was educated at Magdalen College, Cambridge. In 1929, he qualified as a barrister at Middle Temple, London. He was fluent in English, versed in Latin, and married an English woman (Rogers 2004, 100).

Rangoon and other self-determination groups. Although other key players as well as the Karen population were involved in shaping the KNU, the aforementioned four provided the organization with its trajectory and identities. Moreover, each of the leaders forged links with supporters internationally and adapted ideologies from elsewhere to inform their revolution, making visible the overlooked point that the self-determination politics of the KNU has frequently been international in nature. Indeed, Colonel Nerdah Mya—son of Bo Mya—formulates the question best: "How can genocide, the killing of innocent civilians, rape, looting, destruction and involvement in the drug trade be an 'internal matter'" (Rogers 2004, 244)?

The period up until the beginning of the Karen Revolution is one of social instability and breakdown. Prior to the declaration of Burma's independence outside of the commonwealth in 1948, serious fighting had already broken out in virtually all areas of the country. During 1942, for example, the Burmese Independence Army (BIA)[17] had massacred Karen perceived to be pro-British collaborators in the Salween District. According to Brown, this "heightened" the Karen elite's consciousness about resisting Burman domination, leading to a preoccupation with "how to form a Karen state which could be autonomous of Burman domination" (1994, 61). Smith's description of the period as characterized by spontaneous uprisings, communal clashes, local rivalries, and warlordism captures the volatility of the time. Burma had begun her independence with no external enemies, but in a state of acute sectarian strife with its ethnic nationalities (Smith 1999).

During this period, the Karen and Mon populations in the delta and eastern as well as southern part of the country, along with the Burmans and Rakhines of the delta and Arakan State, the Was, Kachins and Shans of the north and northeast, as well as the Burmese communists, who were immersed in fighting in all the aforementioned areas, were all trying to define their new destinies. One should also bear in mind that over time as more Karen "liberated areas" were annexed by Rangoon, its revolutionary experiences also slowly shifted east from the delta to the rugged mountains and hills surrounding the Salween and Moei rivers.[18]

---

[17] During the early 1940s, the Burma Independence Army (BIA) was set up by Japan to train Aung San and his comrades. During this part of the Burmese struggle, Burman leaders allied themselves with the Japanese to fight the colonial British, supporting the Japanese invasion of Burma as a means toward liberation from the British. However, during this same period, the Karen were fighting with the British against Japan and the BIA. Toward the end of WWII, when Japan's fate was sealed, the Burmans switched alliances to fight with the British.

[18] It is important to note that not all encounters between the government and ethnic self-determination groups were in large conventional battles. Smith notes that since Burma's independence, in a typical year there are usually "one or two large-scale Tatmadaw operations…and occasional battles involving several thousand troops (with the CPB, KIO, and KNU)." However, "most of the fighting has long been characterized by small skirmishes and guerilla strikes" (Smith 1999, 100). The large-scale displacement of civilians, however, is dramatically more pronounced even though skirmishes may be localized.

First Phase: Ba U Gyi and the Four Principles of the Karen Revolution

The first Panglong Conference held during March 1946 included delegates from Rangoon along with Shan, Kachin, and Chin chiefs. Their discussions revolved around the future of autonomy for the ethnic nationalities. Shan leaders voiced their case for an autonomous state. Representatives of the Chin and Kachin also articulated their sentiments and cynicism regarding their relationships with the Burmans. The Karen did not formally participate during the first or second Panglong conferences, preferring to field Karen representatives that were present only as observers. Without a formal Karen self-determination platform for participation, the first conference nevertheless still painted a future Burma comprised of autonomous ethnic states for some of its ethnic groups. Lintner describes the conference as one where a "common plan for rebuilding the war-devastated frontier areas" was also discussed (1994, 68). There was also political venting as the future Burman prime minister, U Nu, attacked British occupation with much vitriol. In turn, Kachin leaders responded by summing up the ambivalence of how the ethnic nationalities felt toward the Burmans.

> What have the Burmese public done towards the hill peoples to win their love and faith? It was through the influence of a section of the Burmese public who, while saying that we all belong to the same race, blood, and home, called in our enemies, the Japanese, that the hill people have suffered miserably during those dark years that followed.

> For the hill peoples the safeguarding of their hereditary rights, customs and religions are the most important factors. When the Burmese leaders are ready to see this is done and can prove that they genuinely regard the hill peoples as real brothers equal in every respect to themselves shall we be ready to consider the question of our entry into close relations with Burma as a free dominion (Smith 1999, 74).

The two absences of formal Karen participation in the Panglong conferences are telling. Indeed, Karen elites had other objectives in mind. In August 1946, a four-man "Goodwill Mission" contingent of English-trained Karen professionals, a pan-Karen elite, had decided to go to London to negotiate directly with the British Labour government of Clement Attlee. The members of the Goodwill Mission were: (1) Sydney Loo-Nee, a former member of the House of Representatives before the Japanese invasion, (2) Pho Chit, former member of member of parliament and Minister of

Education in 1939, (3) Thra Din, president of the Karen Central Organisation, and (4) Ba U Gyi, the Oxford-educated lawyer, a "dynamic 42-year-old barrister who had worked together with Aung San for reconciliation with the Burmese during the Japanese occupation" (Lintner 1994, 81). Members of the mission first thanked the British Government for "their deliverance from the Japanese" (ibid., 69). For the next five months the Karen also shared their visions on how they wanted an equal footing in determining the destiny of Burma's future, a vision not shared by the British.

Moreover, the British had already thrown in their lot with Aung San and the Anti-Fascist People's Freedom League (AFPFL) as the sole political party to represent an independent Burma. Although the AFPFL did contain ethnic nationality members such as Karen, Shan, Kachin, Chin and Arakanese, there emerged mutual distrust among its members during the post World War II period. Since the British recruited mostly hill ethnic nationalities while the Japanese allied themselves with the Burmans during the war, there was mistrust and a lack of interethnic cohesion within the organization. By 1946, Burman nationalists had seized most of the organization's power and thus comprised the contingent of politicians who secured deals with the British.

Clement Attlee had desired to distance his administration from any vestige of Britain's colonial legacy by dismantling reminders of the British empire. The alliance the British previously had with the Karen had thus become a liability. Moreover, the Viceroy of India, Lord Mountbatten, had already sided with Aung San before World War II ended. At the time, however, no matter how much the conservative sector of Parliament had desired to distance itself from its old Karen allies, it stipulated that the Karen had a right to negotiate its status with the Burmans. By proposing the formation of a Frontier Areas that included Kawthoolei, it stipulated that the Karen "should not form part of the proposed Burmese dominion until such time as they clearly express a desire to join it" (Rogers 2004, 83).[19] Moreover, Labour Members of Parliament followed with its own prescription that advocated keeping British government control over the Frontier Areas "until such time as their inhabitants signify their desire for some suitable form of amalgamation with Burma proper" (ibid., 82).

By the end of World War II, British foreign policy toward the Karen had changed substantially. During September 1945, the Karen took the initiative and drafted a plan detailing the self-administration of a "United Frontier State." There was no response from London, prompting the Karen to re-draft yet another proposal reiterating Karen desires for, at the very least, a federation of Autonomous National States in Burma. Furthermore, the Goodwill Mission that was traveling about London in 1946 received no

---

[19] British colonialism never directly administered the Karen areas in the hills, hence the designation of Frontier Areas. The Burman population in the Irrawaddy plains, however, was by 1886, under direct British administration.

formal backing for a free Karen State lest the proposal would upset Aung San and delegates of the AFPFL. Hugh Tinker,[20] a pro-U Nu British professor at the University of Lancaster, provides insight into British sentiments in a 1946 letter written between two British delegates, P.G.E. Nash and Sir Gilbert Laithwaite:

> The Secretary of State [for Burma] did not wish to get entangled with Karen political demands which might prove embarrassing and would prefer that the object of the visit of this mission to the UK should be a private nature to thank HMG [His Majesty's Government] for its assistance (Lintner 1994, 69).

On the other hand, there were British sympathizers for the Karen cause. H.N.C. Stevenson,[21] one of the few British officials who took the Goodwill Mission delegates seriously, had already predicted months earlier that unless Karen demands were addressed the Karen will rebel. During his stay in Burma Stevenson was director of the Frontier Areas Administration (FAA)[22], and had called for a census of the Karen so that their population and its political implications for territory could be addressed. Moreover, his close relationship with the Karen meant that Stevenson's assessment was more accurate than those made by London. In a remarkable display of prescience Stevenson correctly anticipated the maneuvers of the Karen:

> ...knowledge gained in four years of guerilla war...if they go all out for their demands they have the guts, the skill, and the allies (the northern tribes) necessary to wrest them from the Burmese by force, if other means will not prevail. The only thing that restrains them is the belief that we will repay their loyalty by giving them a homeland. I have come to the regrettable conclusion that the present Karen quiescence means simply that they refuse to quarrel with us. But when we go, if go we do, the war for the Karen State will start (Smith 1999, 75).

[20] Tinker was never sympathetic to the Karen to the degree that he could have affected British policy to support them. In 1982, he had written a colleague that "the regime in Burma is not the oppressive dictatorship you believe it to be... I believe there is more freedom in Burma than in India" (Rogers 2004, 90).

[21] During World War II, H.N.C. Stevenson served many years with Burma's different ethnic nationalities in what the British designated as the Frontier Areas.

[22] Burma during British colonization was divided into Ministerial Burma (which included much of the Irrawaddy from Rangoon to Mandalay) and the Frontier Areas where the ethnic nationalities like the Karen, Shan, Karenni and Kachins lived. The FAA oversaw the administration of the Frontier areas, and as Fredholm 1993 notes: "The Frontier Areas were also economically neglected, a fact that remained true also in the post independence years" (Fredholm 1993, 25).

Yet realizing that he was "talking to deaf ears," Stevenson resigns his post at the FAA. The reception of the Goodwill Mission was also discouraging, even patronizing. Lintner's 1981 interview of Thra Din, one of the members of the mission, is revealing:

> The delegation remained in London throughout the cold, rainy English autumn without accomplishing anything...the most exciting event the British hosts arranged for their Karen visitors appears to have been a visit to the Sunlight Soap Factory outside London (Lintner 1994, 69).

Later in 1946, Sir Hubert Rance's cable to Lord Pethwick-Lawrence disclosed no changes in the British position:

> We should start with the premise that there is only one Burma and that the part known as Ministerial Burma and that known as the Frontier Areas are merely part of the whole. They have been one in the past and they must remain one in the future so that our ultimate aim is always a united Burma in the shortest possible time (Smith 1999, 77).

There were, however, many British World War II veterans that had "fought with the Karen against the Japanese and the BIA—who felt that the British should not let their erstwhile, loyal allies down" (Lintner 1994, 69). Some prominent British soldiers indeed remained loyal to the Karen in return. Moreover, many pro-Karen British sympathizers felt that since the Karen revolutionaries had engaged in preemptive diplomacy even before the first Panglong Conference, this justified the need to address the Karen cause first. Indeed, Ba U Gyi and his contingent in 1945 had already petitioned to the British government for assistance by noting: "The last three and a half years have shown us what can and most inevitably will happen to a small race or nation in the absence of a protecting power" (ibid., 72). The implication was clear: the Karen needed British or Commonwealth protection. An important feature of Karen political maneuverings, thus setting it apart from other ethnic self-determination groups, is that the Karen leadership often engaged with preemptive international diplomacy when conducting its self-determination politics.

On January 27, 1947, Aung San of the AFPFL and British Prime Minister Clement Attlee formalized the Attlee-Aung San agreement in London. The agreement grants Burma an "interim government...in preparation for independence 'with or without the British Commonwealth'" (Lintner 1994, 339). London, however, still expected the AFPFL government to achieve unification aims "with the free consent of the inhabitants" in the "Frontier

Areas," even though ultimately neither the Burmans nor British honored the stipulation (Rogers 2004, 83).

Political controversy followed shortly thereafter. Two members of Aung San's delegation did not sign the agreement. Moreover, because no ethnic nationalities had delegates at the signing in London, there were protests from larger nations such as the Karen while the Shan and Kachin leadership similarly did not view the signing as legitimate. Neither did the CPB back in Burma believe that it was a legitimate agreement. Most damaging to the Karen experience was that the agreement did not contain any references to an independent Karen State.

The second Panglong Conference was held during early February 1947. This time the AFPFL delegation included Aung San's personal participation. Part of his negotiations included a trek he made up to the Shan areas to negotiate "with the hill peoples whose delegates had at last decided to join Burma and ask for independence from Britain" (Lintner 1994, 71). Aung San assured the various ethnic nationality groups that there would be "no unequal treatment in the future Union of Burma" (Fredholm 1993, 39). Once again, Karen revolutionaries did not participate in the second Panglong Conference although the Karen had four observers present. The Karen also boycotted the Executive Council and the Constituent Assembly elections, bodies that were to draft Burma's new Constitution. Rogers argues that this was a strategic mistake. As a result, the 1947 Constitution did not have any provisions for a Karen State and the "entire question of the Karen's future was left to be decided after independence" (Rogers 2004, 84).

A more charitable view is provided by Lintner, who argues that the main reason the Karen boycotted the elections was because their demands for self-determination were growing stronger while concomitantly the constitutional processes leading up to the second Panglong Conference again made no provisions for a Karen state. The conference which included twenty three representatives of the Shan, Kachin and the Chin, along with Aung San, resulted in the signing of the second Panglong Agreement on February 12, 1947 whereby the three groups recognized the Burmese interim government and would cooperate with it, thus setting the foundations for a federalized Burma. In any case, the Karen saved themselves from the embarrassment of being duped by the AFPFL since the ethnic nationality groups that did participate would never receive what they had asked for anyway.

The main achievement of the second Panglong Conference was Burma's adoption of a new constitution on September 24, 1947. The constitution contained provisions for certain nations to secede in the future as well as guaranteeing a democratic system and limited federalism. The Shan and Karenni states get the right to secede from the proposed Union of Burma after a ten-year period of independence. A Kachin State with no right to secede is established. There were no provisions made for the other large nations such as the Mons, Chins, Pa-os, Was and Arakanese. Similarly, no provision was provided for a Karen state and the right of secession "was expressedly ruled out for the Karen" even though informal negotiations had been taking place in Rangoon between the Karen leadership and the AFPFL (Smith 1999, 82).

The Karen distrust of the AFPFL meant that the Karen leaders were engaging in political developments far away from Panglong. The Karen already had all their delegates ready to attend a separate event planned for their own political destiny. On February 5, 1947, at the All Karen Congress held in Rangoon, seven hundred Karen delegates from various Karen political groups converged and merged to form the Karen National Union (KNU). It was formed by combining the "KNA, the Baptist KNA, the Buddhist KNA, the KCO, and its youth wing, the KYO" (Smith 1999, 83). Ba U Gyi becomes its first chairman.

In spite of this political development, no clear understanding or demarcation of the Karen state was made by Rangoon and the future of a Karen state would have to be decided after Burma's independence. Moreover the KNU boycott of the April 1947 Rangoon Constituent Assembly meant that there was no true voice to represent Karen demands and aspirations.[23] Thus, Rangoon's asymmetrical approach toward democracy, designed as a divide and conquer tactic, along with the KNU's unflinching stance, would have drastic consequences for the next fifty-nine years.

The newly formed KNU continued to make repeated demands for an independent Karen State outside the Union of Burma but still a member of the Commonwealth, in contrast to what the Burman nationalists desired.[24] The first resolution of the newly formed organization was an assessment of the Karen political situation:

> The Karen have through their Goodwill Mission, made known in unmistakable terms to the British Administration their aspiration for a separate Karen State formed out of Tenasserim Division, Nyaunglebin Sub-Division in Pegu District, [and] including the Salween District in the present Frontier Area. His Majesty's Government completely ignored altogether the Memorial submitted since 15 January 1946. The Congress is, therefore, aggrieved at the silence observed on this matter in the [Aung San-Attlee] Agreement, and now fervently requests that due recognition be given to the Karen legitimate aspirations (Lintner 1994, 71).

---

[23] During the April 9, 1947 Constituent Assembly elections, the AFPFL, wins 60 percent of the seats. Even the CPB had seven members elected. The KNU, however, did not trust nor negotiate with Rangoon regarding its demands (Lintner 1993, 339).

[24] Karen desires to remain inside the commonwealth was unacceptable to Rangoon, which wanted a complete delinking from their British colonizers.

Ba U Gyi's Four Principles of the Karen Revolution is also adopted during this period and soon becomes the *raison d'etre* of the KNU and Karen struggle, defining its stance to this very day:

1. There shall be no surrender.
2. The recognition of the Karen State must be completed.
3. We shall retain our own arms.
4. We shall decide our own political destiny.

The Karen National Defense Organization (KNDO) is also established as the KNU's village militia on July 17, 1947. During the early 1950s the KNU under Ba U Gyi would attempt to organize the delta Karen. In August of 1947, elsewhere at the western edge of Burma, the *Mujahid* Party, Burma's first Muslim resistance organization, is formed in Arakan State and led by Jafar Kawwal. By December of 1947, Kawwal launches his self-determination struggle for an Islamic State and begins their struggle by taking on the Buddhist Arakans led by U Seinda as well as the CPB and Rangoon. Within a year the CPB begin their armed struggle and instigate heavy fighting against government forces. The CPB gain and lose ground in a series of engagements with government forces.

Tragic political developments also occurred during this period. On July 19, 1947, Aung San and six of his cabinet ministers are assassinated in Rangoon. Lintner's detailed account, of which I will rely much on throughout my work, is vivid and worth noting in full:

> On the morning of 19 July 1947 a green-painted army jeep came speeding through the streets of Rangoon. Its occupants were dressed in military fatigues and were brandishing tommy-guns and other semi-automatic weapons. No one paid much attention to them; World War II had just ended and military-looking people were no strange sight in the Burmese capital.
>
> The jeep stopped outside the Secretariat...in central Rangoon. Security was tight, as the Governor's Executive Council, the pre-independence de facto Burmese cabinet led by Aung San, was in session. Aung San...had been warned that his life might be in danger, but somehow the gunmen aroused no suspicion as they drove through the central porchway and entered the Secretariat complex.
>
> The hitmen, guns in hand, jumped out of the jeep and half-ran towards the main building. They hurried upstairs and on reaching the room where the cabinet was meeting, they pointed their guns at the assembled ministers, shouting: "Remain seated! Don't move!" Aung

San rose to his feet—and the men opened fire. The shooting continued for about thirty seconds, and the uniformed men left the building, jumped into their jeep outside and accelerated away... Nine bullet-ridden bodies lay on the floor: Aung San; his close friend and erstwhile student leader Thakin Mya; Ba Choe, the former editor of the nationalist Deedok journal and now a prominent statesman; Razak, a Muslim school principal and politician; Aung San's elder brother Ba Win; Mahn Ba Khaing, one of the few ethnic Karen to have participated in mainstream Burmese politics; and Sao Sam Htun, the *saopha*, or prince of the Shan State of Mong Pawn... There was also Ohn Maung, a deputy secretary of the Ministry of Transport, who had entered the conference room to submit a report when the assassins struck, and Ko Htwe, Razak's eighteen-year-old bodyguard (Lintner 1994, xiii).

Aung San had left behind his wife Khin Kyi, two boys, and a two-year old daughter named Suu Kyi. U Saw, Aung San's political rival that had contested for the premiership of independent Burma was arrested, convicted, and hanged in May 1948. Aung San Suu Kyi, in her own words, describes U Saw as "a man of large ambitions who had not been able to accept the rise to national leadership of Aung San, whom he was wont to describe as a 'mere boy'" (Suu Kyi 1995, 35).

With a diverse contingent of Burma's most capable leaders eliminated, U Nu thus emerges as the new AFPFL leader, chief of the cabinet, and Prime Minister. It was also U Nu that stated during the transfer of power from Britain to an independent Burma, "I am a hundred percent against the creation of Autonomous States for the Karen, Mons and Arakanese." It is within this political context that Ba U Gyi had attempted to organize the Karen nation.

In October 1947, KNU delegates from all of Burma meet at Moulmein and continue to voice their demands for an independent Karen State that would include the Tenasserim Division, Irrawaddy Division, Insein and Hanthawaddy districts, and Nyaunglebin subdivision of Pegu District. The KNU had even sent Prime Minister Attlee and the British parliament a communiqué that prophetically warned:

It is a dream that Karen and Burman can ever evolve a common nationality, and this misconception of one homogenous Burmese nation has gone far beyond the limits and is the cause of most of the troubles and will lead Burma to destruction... Karen and Burman belong to two different racial origins [and] to two different civilizations. To yoke together two such nations under a single state, one in numerical minority and the other as a majority, must lead to growing discontent and final destruction (Smith 1999, 87).

In a House of Commons debate on November 5, 1947, Winston Churchill, now leader of the opposition and frustrated by Attlee and his administration's lack of recognition for the Karen cause, declared to Parliament: "All loyalties have been discarded and rebuffed; all faithful services have been forgotten and brushed aside…We stand on the threshold of another scene of misery and ruin…which should ever haunt the consciences of the principal actors in this tragedy" (Rogers 2004, 88).

On January 4, 1948, Burma declared its independence from Britain, with U Nu established as its first prime minister. On February 11, the KNU organized Karen in dozens of towns and villages to further their demands for a separate Karen State. According to Karen activists roughly 400,000 were involved in the demonstration, prompting the KNU and AFPFL to engage in negotiations. The negotiations take place on March 10, 1948, but are unsuccessful. Finally by October 1948, Rangoon implements its belated Regional Autonomy Enquiry Program, which is designed to assess Karen claims for a free state. Once again Karen delegates repeated their claims for an independent state that would include much of the Irrawaddy Delta, as well as the mountainous and hilly border areas adjacent to Thailand.

As early as 1948 in the delta, the KNU, Arakan mujahids, AFPFL and CPB forces were already fighting one another (in the north for example, Karen forces, along with soldiers from the Kachin ethnic nationality, were systematically defeating CPB units). However, the Tatmadaw and KNU were still the key players in this region because:

> The Tatmadaw and KNU…recognized that the delta would be the…battleground for the long-term success of the Karen… Unlike the sparsely populated mountains in the east, there were large villages, abundant food supplies and a constant stream of new recruits… And while by December 1950…the government had retaken…major towns under KAF control, through 1951 the situation was one of stalemate…towns remained under KNDO control and KAF units roved freely from Henzada to Pyapon in the Lower delta…further confirmation of the scale and spread of the Karen population (Smith 1999, 148).

During this period the boundaries of Kawthoolei contained less than 25 percent of the Karen population of Burma. With their focus already on the delta Karen the KNU also simultaneously looked southward along the Tenasserim for allies.

In the politically precarious period after independence the Burmese army was plagued with mutinies and defections. During the summer of 1948 thirty-one soldiers at Abya Buda, Pegu District, kill their officer and defect to the CPB (Lintner 1994, 341). By August over 300 Burmese soldiers defect with thirty-two army trucks and form the Revolutionary Burma Army (RBA), ultimately allying themselves to the CPB. Assassinations are not just directed against the government or KNU delegates: in the northeast region of Burma, the Karenni leader, Bee Tu Reh, is arrested by government forces and extra-judicially executed on August 9, 1948. Bee Tu Reh argued that the Karenni did not need to answer to Burma because they have always been independent. His murder causes the Karenni to break out in rebellion. Karen and Mons also break out in rebellion in the southeast, along the Tenasserim division. By the end of August 1948, KNDO units closer to the Gulf of Martaban seize Thaton and Moulmein.

To add to the anxieties of Rangoon, the KNU continues its preemptive diplomacy: toward the southeastern hill areas of the Tenasserim Division bordering Thailand, the Karen and Mons form an alliance to have a joint Mon-Karen administration which would allow the Karen crucial access to seaports on the Andaman Sea. Smith notes that this alliance was possible because "ties between Karen and Mon leaders in the Moulmein area grew closer"; moreover, "it was the first clear statement of KNU recognition that the territories they were claiming were not racially exclusive" (Smith 1999, 115).

By this time, many leaders of the AFPFL were convinced that a postcolonial conspiracy, namely that British, Americans, as well as the Burman-dominated CPB, would be harnessing KNDO/KNU resistance as a vehicle to destabilize the entire country. Yet it is important to remember that the KNU's main objective was not based on an explicit overthrow of the government in Rangoon, as the CPB and other leftist groups attempted to do. The Karen Revolution was based on self-determination, with the aim of establishing a state where Karen are able to, in the words of a Rangoon report from the Regional Autonomy Enquiry Commission, "develop socially, politically, educationally, and economically on their own lines" (ibid., 114). This assessment by Rangoon is still referred to by KNU activists today as they often point out that only the Karen and the AFPFL really knew what the Karen truly desired, implying that much of the international community had failed to understand the historical and ethnopolitical depth of the region.

An American missionary sympathetic to the Karen struggle, Dr. Gordon Seagrave, who was imprisoned in 1951 by Rangoon, noted that "the trouble was…the Karen demanded just too much" (ibid., 148). General Smith Dun, an ethnic Karen who distinguished himself militarily under the British, also commented that the KNU had desired the best part of Burma. Yet from the perspective of the KNU, they were logically asking for a constituency that was representative of where most of the Karen population lived.

One may speculate, however, how a map of Kawthoolei would appear if the KNU were to have achieved its aims. Since the delta population of the Karen are physically separated by plains that lead up to the eastern hills where the hill Karen resided, any territorial demarcation between the two regions would have to cut across Rangoon—either through the north, which would mean that Karen territory would effectively surround Rangoon, or it would include Rangoon itself, a scenario the AFPFL as well as the Burman population would unlikely accept.

A relatively more plausible scenario would be Karen territory that skirts the coastal regions where the Irrawaddy River fans out toward the Andaman Sea, south of Rangoon. This too would be problematic since it would mean that Rangoon would not direct have access to the sea. One possibility is if the AFPFL were to move its administration back to Mandalay. Although this move would immediately situate the AFPFL in the historical heartland that provides a historical link with its dynastic Burman past, abandoning cultural symbols such as the Shwedagon Pagoda to the Karen would be out of the question. Unfortunately, a political agreement was never reached regarding demarcation of Karen territory. Violent circumstances created by Burmans, with hatred built up during World War II when the Karen fought alongside the British, would ultimately drive Rangoon and the Karen toward war.

Between December 23-25, 1948, government forces throw hand grenades into a Karen church, killing eighty unarmed Karen villagers celebrating Christmas in Palaw, Tavoy District. Two hundred more Karen are killed in nearby villages in the following days. Early in 1949, Burmans seized one hundred Karen men, women and children and locked them inside a Christian church in a Rangoon suburb. Prime Minister U Nu received a "curt telephone message" from the Rangoon police: "The mob intends to pour petrol on the building and set it ablaze" (Lintner 1994, 11). U Nu personally arrives at the scene to diffuse the crisis. The KNDO responds by raiding a Burman village seventy-five kilometers south of Rangoon and executing six men in front of the appalled villagers. During this same period the Attlee administration approves shipments of arms to the AFPFL intended solely for suppressing the Karen uprising. Politics does make strange bedfellows.

At this time the armed struggle had yet to begin in earnest, but events were pushing Karen politics to the point of revolution. Significantly, it is important to note that during the years leading to the beginning of the Karen struggle, the majority of Karen troops were still "loyal" to U Nu and Rangoon, despite the various aforementioned ethnic communal clashes. The early victories achieved by the KNDO and Kachins against the CPB were done under the auspices of Rangoon. Indeed, Ba U Gyi and U Nu were still engaging in political dialog literally until the eve of the Karen Revolution. Yet in spite of the political maneuverings by the KNU and AFPFL, the Karen fight for freedom and self-determination would soon begin.

For safety reasons, Ba U Gyi, the KNU, and hundreds of KNDO militiamen had moved their headquarters to a building in Insein, a township with a Karen majority twelve kilometers north of Rangoon. Ba U Gyi orders the KNDO to protect the majority Karen population from a series of bloody anti-Karen uprisings. They begin disarming government officials in the township as well as adjacent townships of Gyogon and Thamaing. On

January 30, Rangoon outlaws the KNDO. During the early hours of the morning troops are sent to order the KNDO to capitulate. On January 31, 1949, Ba U Gyi orders KNDO units to intercept and halt advancing government troops. The Karen Revolution begins with clashes at Ywathit Road junction leading to Gyogon (Lintner 1994).

A series of Karen defections from the Burmese Army followed, with the 1st and 2nd Karen Rifles defecting from the Burma Army and pledging their allegiance to the revolution, bolstering the KNDO and KNU with an expanding army. U Nu responds by ordering the 1st Kachin Rifles to attack the KNDO. The Kachin Naw Seng, a decorated World War II hero, and one who also had "fought more intensely against the CPB than any other unit" as well as being one of the most able commanders of the Burma Army, blatantly refused (ibid., 13).

In hindsight, the Seng's rejection of U Nu's order shouldn't be too surprising: Naw Seng was a Christian like many Karen and "he had no desire to fight them on behalf of the Burmans, whom he in any case never fully trusted" (ibid., 13). As a result, on February 21st, Naw Seng took his entire battalion to join forces with the 1st Karen Rifles under another able commander, the Karen Lieut. Colonel Min Maung. With already over 10,000 Karen soldiers mobilized all over the country and with many of them on their trek south to converge on Insein, KNDO forces already at Insein came as close to four miles from Rangoon, seizing Mingaladon Airport and removing the guns from abandoned British Spitfires planes. By February 2, 1949, the entire town of Insein falls under KNDO control.

The nascent AFPFL General Ne Win responds by sending his troops to encircle Insein. A 112-day siege was underway. Shelling and massive fighting around Insein and Rangoon signaled that the Karen struggle had begun in earnest, and according to Fredholm "it was no longer possible to turn back" (Fredholm 1993, 101). Over two thousand KNDO troops are positioned around Insein inside trenches, bunkers, and behind roadblocks.

> Housewives prepared packets of cooked rice and fish paste...for the troops, and girls drove jeeps to deliver the rations to the boys in the trenches along the outer defence lines. Food was never a problem; Insein was the site of several rice mills, and the godowns were quickly taken over by the KNDO (Lintner 1994, 12).

Running short on supplies and ammunition, the logistics ultimately was disadvantaged toward the KNDO protecting Insein. Although other Karen forces had mobilized their Karen comrades by converging on Rangoon, many were intercepted by government troops and were repulsed or surrendered. Developments up north were relatively more favorable as Karen forces in alliance with other ethnic self-determination groups managed to seize Mandalay on March 13, 1949. Because of the lightning advances made by combined Karen forces during early 1949, as well as large defections of Karen units toward the KNU, Rangoon decides to engage in talks.

The British and Commonwealth ambassadors arrange a ceasefire. During early April 1949, Ba U Gyi arrives in Rangoon for negotiations with U Nu and Ne Win. Bo Mya recounted how U Nu was alleged to have told Ba U Gyi, "I won't relinquish even an inch of Karen State. If you want it, fight for it." Moreover, U Nu and Ne Win had exploited the temporary calm of the ceasefire to resupply their troops. In addition, Burman office workers during the brief truce were invited to "take potshots at the Karen…for the price of one rupee each" (Fredholm 1993, 102). Within a few days the talks failed and government troops, resupplied and repositioned, seize the initiative by resuming the fight on April 9, 1949. This time the Burmese Air Force participated in bombing runs in the city. On May 22, 1949, after 112 days of siege, the KNDO was forced to relinquish Insein. There were over 500 KNDO fatalities and an estimated 500 government fatalities, an unknown number of civilians also perished. Fredholm comments:

> The battle of Insein should not be dismissed in importance. If the KNU had been able to hold Insein and to push on toward Rangoon, the history of Burma would have been completely different. Now, with Rangoon still in Burman hands, the KNU never managed to establish a large, independent Karen State. They came close, though, and this very real threat to the Burman state may…be one reason…many Burman nationalists even today feel a special hatred toward the KNU (ibid., 103).

The KNU, unlike any self-determination group at the time, was not only on the brink of seizing Burma's capital: had it succeeded a large population of delta Karen would have been added to the KNU administration. The battle for Insein, along with its accompanying ethnic nationalities warfare all over the country, resulted in over sixty thousand killed and over one million homeless (Fredholm 1993, Smith 1999).

The fall of Insein shifted Karen forces closer to the eastern hills near the town of Toungoo. By June of 1949 the Karen establish their "Government for Kawthoolei" in Toungoo approximately 130 miles northeast of Rangoon. At Toungoo all Karen military units are reorganized under the unified Kawthoolei Armed Forces (KAF), the precursor to the KNLA.

The KNU proclaims an independent Karen state on May 20, 1949 with Ba U Gyi appointed the country's first prime minister. "Kawthoolei,"[25] or "the

---

[25] "There is some uncertainty over the exact origins of the name Kawthoolei. The term first surfaced after the war and is a world-play with several possible meanings. Veteran nationalists usually explain it as the 'country burnt black', that is, the country which must be fought for (Kaw=country, thoo=black, lei=bare), but it is also often described as 'flowery' or 'green' land. The 'thoolei' is a green, orchid-like plant common in the eastern hills" (Smith 1999, 141). The

country without evil," was designated and Toungoo was designated its capital. However, government offensives succeeded in capturing Toungoo on March 19, 1950 forcing the Karen to reestablish new headquarters at Mawchi. Lucrative mines were built in Mawchi to exploit its natural resources and provide revenue for the KNU. In July of the same year the new capital of Papun is established southeast near the Thai border.

The KNU via Ba U Gyi then organizes a congress at its new Karen headquarters in Papun on July 15, 1950. The KNU contingent is impressive, comprised of many veterans of Force 136[26] such as Saw Sankey, Hunter Tha Hmwe and Mahn Ba Zan. The proclamation of Ba U Gyi's Four Principals of the Karen Revolution takes place along with the establishment of the Kawthoolei Governing Body (KGB), designed to manage the administration of KNU-held areas.

However, Ba U Gyi's ability to lead the KNU was cut short on August 12, 1950, when he and his comrade Saw Sankey, the latter also a lawyer-turned-commander that participated in the earliest delta Karen uprisings, along with "one or possibly two British officers" (their identities have never been confirmed), were caught in a government ambush and slain (Fredholm 1993, 105; Lintner 1994). Lintner identifies as least one of the British officers as a "Mr. Baker," but not more is known about him or his colleague. Lintner, through interviews with KNU veterans, pieces together Ba U Gyi's last hours:

> On 11 August, the party reached the small village of Taw Kaw Koe near the Thai border, northwest of Mae Sot. Given the secret nature of their mission, they decided to spend the night under the trees of a betel nut plantation on the outskirts of the village, near Ler Pu Klo River. But the party had been spotted by a Burma Army informer in Taw Kaw Koe, who promptly reported to the nearest garrison... Troops led by Maj. Sein Lwin...surrounded their bivouac at three in the morning of the 12th. An army officer shouted in the dark for the rebels to surrender. When no response was forthcoming, the troops opened fire. Saw Ba U Gyi, Saw Sankey, Mr. Baker and their bodyguards all died in a hail of bullets (Lintner 1994, 87).

What was Ba U Gyi doing near Mae Sot? Smith and Lintner note that the minutes from Ba U Gyi's final attendance at the KNU congress recorded his words as "I am now going to pull a political stunt" (Lintner 1994, 86; Smith

---

KNU certainly has the last word on this, translating it as "the land of light" or the "country without evil."

[26] Force 136 was an elite unit of the anti-Japanese resistance during World War II. Symbolized by a spider and its spider web, it engaged in guerilla tactics to ensnare and sabotage the enemy. Force 136 also gathered intelligence. General Bo Mya was a veteran of Force 136 (Rogers 2004, Smith 1999).

1999, 143). Although the passage is cryptic, speculation suggests that Ba U Gyi was at the very least expanding the international scope of the revolution, "presumably en route to Bangkok and into contact with the outside world" (Smith 1999, 143). Fredholm reinforces this view:

> It is possible, although by no means certain, that Ba U Gyi at the time was one his way to Thailand, in that case most probably to ask for help abroad. This will probably never be known...as no witnesses remain who were privy to his plans (Fredholm 1993, 105).

During the early 1950s the Tatmadaw, invigorated by the effects of Ba U Gyi's death upon the rank and file of the KNU, took the initiative and launched offensives in the delta region. The KNU leadership, as well as the Tatmadaw, understood the significance of the delta: it had a large Karen population, the Karen had access to the sea, and many urban infrastructures were already in place to promote a strong local economy. Fredholm notes that the 1950-1951 period produced the fiercest fighting in the Irrawaddy Delta region because many of the pro-KNU Karen population during this period lived there (Fredholm 1993, 105). By the end of 1950 KNDO-administered delta towns of Einme and Pantanaw fall to government forces. Unable to repulse the larger and better-equipped Tatmadaw, Karen forces and a sizeable part of the population withdraw and head to the eastern hills. Many of the Karen fighters that remained in the delta communities were beginning to surrender to the government.

On January 19, 1951, Hunter Tha Hmwe is elected the new KNU chairman. However, Tha Hmwe is bogged down by political and military activities in the delta and cannot take his post in the hills until three years later. Thus, Skaw Ler Taw represented Tha Hmwe until the latter's arrival in the eastern hills in December 1954. Due to the death of Ba U Gyi as well as intense fighting around the delta regions, the first half of the 1950s was, according to Skaw Ler Taw, "one of the most difficult the KNU ever faced" (Smith 1999, 144).

Nevertheless, the Burmese Parliament in Rangoon formally establishes a Karen State in September of 1952 that encompassed only eastern Burma's mountains and hills, but not before dividing up the Karen population even further the year before: on October 5, 1951, the Burmese parliament successfully "remedied" the Karenni independence movement (a subgroup culturally close to the Karen) as well as dividing the pan-Karen consciousness by renaming the Karenni State the Kayah State, thus eliminating any reference or notion of Karenni claims to their former independence.[27]

---

[27] Because the Karenni people are related to the Karen, they receive KNU support. For KNU visionaries, a pan-Karen state includes the Karenni areas, without objection from the Karenni. Fredholm notes that the Karenni have fought for the KNU and Karen have fought for the

The new Karen State, minus the Karenni areas, was created by combining the Kawkareik, Hlaingbwe, Pa-an, and Thandung districts with that of the Salween district. Most of the area was already under KNU control, and the 11,600 square mile "backwater" of rugged and malarial mountains and hills lacked a seaport (Smith 1999). The new Karen State also did not include the crucial area of the delta, prompting Fredholm to argue that the AFPFL "gave away only what was already lost" (Fredholm 1993, 105). Noted Burma scholar Josef Silverstein summarizes the situation:

> While the Karen were promised a state of their own, the territories in the plains area, where a majority lived, were not included in their state because that would have brought a large number of Burmans under Karen rule. The territory allotted to the Karen was seen as underdeveloped, isolated from the cities and other points of contact with the outside world (Silverstein 1981, 52).

Rangoon's actions convinced the Karen leadership that the creation of the Karen State was designed to "squeeze out the Karen cause all along" (Smith 1999, 146). Furthermore, only roughly 600,000 Karen were in the area in 1956 while about 80 percent of the Karen were estimated to reside outside the government-designated Karen State (Smith 1999). The KNU thus rejects Rangoon's construction of the Karen State because the key delta Karen populations were excluded. Immediately, critics argue for an expanded Karen State to include more towns such as Toungoo, Thaton and Amherst, the latter two being crucial coastal towns. Even the pro-U Nu, Hugh Tinker, was forced to condemn the proposed additions:

> There is room for a more generous policy towards the Karen... An expanded Karen State would still leave over half of the Karen community outside its territory in the Delta districts, but such a move would provide unmistakable evidence that the central government intended to give the Karen their full share in the national life (Smith 1999, 147).

There were some positive developments on the KNU's political front. In November of 1952, the CPB and the KNU formed a precarious alliance via the Zin-Zan Agreement, named after the CPB's Thakin Zin and the leader of the delta Karen, the leftist Mahn Ba Zan. The CPB and KNU had been familiar enemies and have clashed frequently, but both organizations finally decided to coordinate their activities against the Tatmadaw. During the early

Karenni (Fredholm 1993). The Kayah, on the other hand, are only the largest of the dozen or so ethnic sub-groups within the state, and thus, "there is no ethnic basis whatsoever for the continued usage of the name Kayah as a term of regional ethnic identity" (Smith 1999, 145).

1950s the KNU partnership with the CPB resulted in the KNU's adoption of Maoist tactics and communist themes to accent the Karen struggle, even though the KNU "never designated itself as a communist organization and never in fact can be said to have been one" (Fredholm 1993, 107).

Second Phase: Ideological Strain between Mahn Ba Zan and Hunter Tha Hmwe

In November of 1953, the KNU's First National Congress takes place in Papun. The discussion mostly focused on the disintegrating relationship with the KMT, the details of which will be discussed further in this section. During the congress KNU members also approved the establishment of the Karen National United Party (KNUP: 1953-1974), the KNU leftist wing based on supporting the population of delta Karen, with Mahn Ba Zan elected its leader. In essence the KNUP is a leftist organization relatively autonomous from the right-wing Karen contingent concentrated along the Thai border and it cooperated closely with the CPB. The KNUP constructed itself as the KNU's vanguard party based on the perception that the KNU's foundations "were still not firm and did not reach all levels of society" (Smith 1999).

The conclusion of the congress included a memorandum release to the Thai government and other ethnic self-determination groups announcing the formation of the Kawthoolei Governing Body (KGB) and that the KNU would be "seeking recognition from the United Nations for a Kawthoolei Free State adjoining the Thai border" (ibid., 1999). Once again, the Karen engage with international diplomacy as they conduct their revolution.

This new political trajectory meant that KNUP members had to align the organization to the more conservative KNU leadership. This happened at the first National Congress in November 1953 as KNUP leaders from the delta made their way to Papun to meet with KNU leaders. Nevertheless, it would be three years before the KNU would entertain the political concerns of the KNUP as other developments were also occurring at the Congress.

The formation of the KNUP can be credited with a new and revolutionary shift in Karen nationalist thought through its "Second Phase" Program. Although this ideological shift to the left is often attributed to Mahn Ba Zan, it was Ba U Gyi who, in 1949, brought copies of Mao Zedong's *On Guerilla Warfare* and *On Protracted War* and Liu Shao-Chi's *On Inner Party Struggle* to Toungoo. The turn toward the left meant that even pro-British Karen leaders were familiar with leftist literature. Under Mahn Ba Zan, it would be Mao Zedong's ideas that contributed greatly to the KNU's philosophical and political structure, especially in the organization's approach toward class analyses and social arrangements.

Mao Zedong's emphasis on the revolutionary potential of the peasantry was adopted by the second phase KNU during the early 1950s. By now the educated Karen in the delta, ex-civil servants, and career military officers began to surrender to the AFPFL. As a result the KNU had to identify another section of the population they could harness to continue the revolution effectively. Many of Mahn Ba Zan's cadres such as Tin Oo, Skaw Ler Taw and Maung Maung believed that the continuation of the revolution would have to depend on rural farmers and forestry workers "who are not only feeding and sheltering KAF units but also had to bear the brunt of the fighting" (Smith 1999, 150).

For many KNUP members, class analyses conducted on the conditions of rural farmers and forest workers were brought into the discourse. Already dismissed is the class of vacillating intellectuals who could not be depended upon, exemplified by the 1950s defeatism of many middle class Karen in the delta. Mao effectively argues this point in his *Five Essays on Philosophy*, reminding his readers not to count on the middle class as a revolutionary force because they would splinter, with one faction joining the revolution and the other faction defending the interests of the bourgeois, the class status they hoped to attain. In a 1988 interview with Smith, Skaw Ler Taw discusses the KNUP orientation at the time:

> Through our revolutionary experience we had found that the class characteristics laid down by Mao Zedong were to a certain extent true. Intellectuals waver very easily. Many of those who had joined surrendered within two years. Peasants, too, have some possessions and are not always reliable. Only the workers, who have nothing, could be relied upon (ibid., 151).

Mao also influenced the military structure of the Karen armed forces. It was arranged in a manner where its armed forces were assigned three roles: regular forces, guerilla forces, and the village militia. The last two roles were almost exclusively deployed by the KAF and KNDO, respectively, with guerilla warfare tactics effectively utilized in challenging the Tatmadaw. It is important to remember that as the Karen resistance was slowly pushed toward the eastern mountains and hills, guerilla warfare became the main method for struggle. By effectively synthesizing quasi-Maoist social arrangements with the exigencies of the Karen struggle, the influence of the KNUP upon other ethnic self-determination groups cannot be underestimated. Fredholm notes:

> Eventually all ethnic movements made this change, resulting in what today is a large number of ethnic insurgent movements with thoroughly Maoist organization and tactics, but a strict nationalist ideology (1993, 106).

Not all KNU policies were influenced by the KNUP's leftist ideology. Further complicating the revolutionary experience was that the US-backed KMT remnants of the Chinese civil war had entered the Shan State to regroup with plans to launch offensives back into communist China. As a result the KMT was able to control its border with Thailand as well as coordinate its strategy from northern Thailand. The KMT spillover had grown to about 12,000 soldiers by the end of 1951, with the Thai city of Chiang Mai described as the KMT's rear base. Seeing the utility of allying itself with an organization that receives direct US military support the KNU leadership and the KMT form an alliance, albeit a precarious and ineffective one. Few joint campaigns were conducted between the KNU and the KMT. Fredholm notes "in most cases the KMT forces made big but empty promises, both about arms deliveries and about keeping pressure on the pro-government forces" (Fredholm 1993, 106). Smith notes that:

> Not only were few of the promised weapons ever handed over, but the KMT failed to defend positions and never paid for supplies. Whenever the enemy attacked, they would withdraw without telling anybody. We lost a lot of good positions that way (Smith 1999, 154).

However, Lintner provides an alternative account revealing a more sincere gesture from the KMT to link with the Karen and the Mons. In his interview of Francis Yap, a KMT operative in Burma during the 1950s, Yap presented a picture of political alliances undone by logistical problems. With 900 military "instructors" and roughly 4,500 tons of ammunition:

> The ships were unable to get close to the shore because the place where they were supposed to dock, Ko Lagut, an island off the coast near Ye town, had already been occupied by the Burma Army. But if these ships had reached us, the outcome of Burma's civil war would have been different. The weapons were meant for the KMT, the Mons and even the Karen, if they were willing to join us (Lintner 1994, 110).

The KNU-KMT alliance was formed because at the time it was believed that the latter would be able to provide weaponry for the KNU. Politically, allying itself with another anti-communist platform may have allowed the KNU to repulse the growing influence of the CPB as well as establish a political link to the United States. Although large-scale military equipment never reached the Karen resistance, the situation did not significantly alter KNU sources of revenue as it could rely on the lucrative Thai informal economy, corrupt Thai generals, and "whatever they could buy from corrupt Burma Army personnel" (ibid., 110).

Although the KNU was fighting the CPB up until the Zin-Zan truce, both organizations were, however, still fighting the hated Tatmadaw. Within this context, China backed the CPB while the US/KMT backed the KNU. Further complicating the politics, the strong leftist KNUP prevented a more intimate partnership between the KNU and the US/KMT. Although joint operations occurred between the KMT and the KNU, the KNU never received significant military support from the US/KMT because of the leftist aspirations of the KNUP. On the other hand, China did not militarily assist the CPB in any significant way until the late 1960s when its support of the CPB became much more pronounced. Indeed, the lack of Chinese influence in the late 1950s according to Smith "contradicts...many Western counter insurgency analysts that, by establishing ethnic minority 'autonomous regions', the CCP was trying to annex South-East Asia by more subtle means" (Smith 1999, 158).

By February 1953, joint KNU/KMT offensives were launched against Karenni cities of Loikaw, Loipuk, Bawlake and Name Hpe. The Tatmadaw responded with more offensives, this time switching its focus away from the delta region toward the hills. By May 1953 Hlaingbwe had fallen and by November the Tatmadaw had captured the mines at Mawchi that provided the KNU with a profitable income. The activities by the alliance convince Rangoon to increase Tatmadaw offensives into the mountains where KNU/KMT activities were taking place. From the perspective of Rangoon it was unacceptable that yet another imperial power, now represented by the United States, was trying to influence its sovereign affairs.

Later during the year, amid international protest against the KMT encroachment on Burmese soil and the role the United States had played in the process, the KMT decide to formally withdraw from Burma. By mid-May 1954, the withdrawal resulted in the departure of 5,329 KMT soldiers. There were still, however, 12,000 KMT stationed in the Shan hills of Burma (Lintner 1994, 123).

During March 1954, Karen and Mon delegates arrive in Bangkok for a meeting with the Thai military in hopes of acquiring assistance against Rangoon. The Thai military grants approval for the Karen and Mon to build military camps at the Thai border as well as purchase supplies from Thailand, namely through border towns such as Mae Sot. The Thai military also begins to implicitly support Ba U Gyi's successor, the powerful KNDO military commander Tha Hmwe, who finally arrives in the eastern hills from the delta to lead the KNU in December 1954. He immediately replaces the Karen Governing Body (KGB) with the more pro-right Karen Revolutionary Council (KRC: 1954-1964). The KRC was comprised of delta and eastern division representatives from all the KNU's military brigade districts. It would also emerge as a pro-right faction within the KNU organization to challenge what at the time was the much stronger KNUP.

Not willing to tolerate residual KMT forces still fighting in a "localized" nature and alarmed at renewed Karen and Mon resistances Rangoon launches more offensives during the 1954-1955 dry season.[28] Rangoon's military response finally culminated with the defeat of the KMT at Doi Tung in May, breaking the "back of the KMT" (Linter 1994, 125). KAF forces, now without its partnership with the KMT—if there ever was an earnest one— was forced to repel further Rangoon offensives into their areas. In March 1955, under Operation *Aungtheikdi* (final victory) Tatmadaw forces "pushed up the narrow jungle road...to Papun which, after six years in KNU hands, was abandoned without resistance" (Smith 1999, 154). The KAF strike elsewhere when 200 troops launch an offensive against Khalaukchaik, a town near Rangoon.

As for the CPB, the People's Army found a brief respite and was more than capable at repulsing smaller government forces that were diverted from its campaigns against the KNU. Karen guerillas continue to attack the Tatmadaw via ambushes on patrols, trains, and buses as well as remote government outposts. In most towns across the country government forces "rarely ventured beyond the town gates after dark" (Smith 1999, 160). Yet the fortunes of the CPB cannot be considered promising. There were factions developing in its political leadership. The alliance the CPB had tried to form with other left-oriented nationality groups was weak and more nominal in nature. This superficial configuration would ultimately unravel the organization in the future.

By May 1955 CPB leaders adopted its revisionist "Programme for Cessation of Civil War and Peace within the Country," which aimed to implement a "peaceful communist evolution" and allow for the "possibility of peace talks with the AFPFL" (Smith 1999, 162). CPB members fielded candidates for elections under the National United Front and the Burma Workers and Peasants Party which competed against the AFPFL, giving the latter a "surprisingly close run in the 1956 election despite widespread allegations of AFPFL ballot rigging" (ibid., 162).

Contemporaneously, KNU activities during this period were based on fanning out and linking up with other resistance groups as well as redefining its ideological foundations. During April 1956 in the hills near Papun the Democratic Nationalities United Front (DNUF: 1956-1958) is formed and chaired by Mahn Ba Zan. Paradoxically, the KNU's first attempt at transcommunality excludes the CPB, even though the KNU via the KNUP was inspired by its ideology and had declared a truce with the CPB via the Zin-Zan Agreement of 1952.

The DNUF was comprised of Karen, Karenni, Mon, and Pa-O. The transcommunal group's aim was to organize ethnic self-determination group

---

[28] In weather patterns of Southeast Asia, the dry season does not necessarily mean dry air. It is "dry" to the extent that there is no rain, but the thick humidity remains perennially consistent.

members to form an anti-Rangoon military front in the coming future. However, to make attendance more convenient for other emergent nationalist groups as well as expanding its membership base, a second conference was held in 1957 further west in the Pegu Yomas. The second conference was meant to accommodate groups such as the Intha, the Kadu-Danu, and delegates from the Arakan State; many members of these groups were unable to make the arduous journey to the first conference.

Also in the hills near Papun, the Second National Congress was held between June 26 and July 11, 1956, resulting in the Kawthoolei Armed Forces (KAF) being given a new incarnation as the Kawthoolei People's Liberation Army (KPLA). The second phase line pitched by the KNUP since 1953 is finally formally introduced to the KNU leadership during the congress. In order to consolidate more support from the Mon, Indian, and Muslim ethnic nationalities in Karen territory "the political name 'Kawthoolei' replaced the ethnic name 'Karen' in most official titles" (Smith 1999, 171). The KPLA and CPB launch operations against the Tatmadaw, resulting in their capture of Pegu and Pyuntza in January 1957.

Watching attempts to establish peace unfold under the auspices of the CPB, U Nu realized that to establish peace by negotiating with the CPB would result in the partitioning of the country that would mirror Korea and Vietnam. Moreover, U Nu was concerned that negotiating with the CPB would grant the organization too much legitimacy. U Nu responded with a shrewd political maneuver by offering a general amnesty under the Arms for Democracy program in 1958. The outcome was stunning: by the end of 1958, the CPB's Arakan ally under U Sein Da, the Arakan People's Liberation Party (APLP), surrenders with over 1,000 soldiers. The Pa-O Union under U Hla Pe also surrenders with 1,300 troops and over 5,000 volunteers.[29] Four hundred members of the Shan State Communist Party (SSCP) under Moh Heng also surrender while 1,111 members of the Mon People's Front (MPF) under Nai Aung Tun follow.[30] Eight hundred CPB members also surrender as well as over 2,000 soldiers from the People's Volunteer Organization (PVO), a pro-communist remnant of Aung San loyalists.

> The terms of individual peace agreements may have differed, but during 1958 over 5,500 armed insurgents officially "entered the light" to be greeted at lavish welcoming ceremonies by government officials. Probably as many more simply returned home to their villages without first informing anyone (Smith 1999, 168).

---

[29] U Hla Pe was cozy with Rangoon only until 1972, when he again went underground to renew the armed struggle under the Pa-O National Liberation Organization.

[30] On July 20, 1958, immediately after the MPF yielded to U Nu, Nai Shwe Kyin and Mons rejecting U Nu's Arms for Democracy form the New Mon State Party (NMSP) and the Mon National Liberation Army (MNLA). Both groups go underground to fight the AFPFL.

The exact number of those who submitted to the 1958 amnesty is unknown. The CPB, assessing in hindsight during its 1985 Third Party Congress and accounting for those who deserted claimed that over 11,650 soldiers from various ethnic self-determination groups surrendered (Smith 1999, 169). As a result, U Nu's 1958 amnesty literally dismantled the first united ethnic self-determination front, the DNUF, when its Mon and Pa-O constituency surrendered.

Despite the numerous surrenders of many ethnic self-determination armies, the KNU is the sole organization that rejects U Nu's 1958 Arms for Democracy program. Neither was it significantly affected by the failure of its first attempt at transcommunal self-determination politics via the DNUF. In contrast to the declining fortunes of the aforementioned ethnic self-determination groups, the KNU experiences a major political revival during the mid-1950s and a stronger sense of unity than at anytime previous. By 1950, the KNU claimed to have 24,000 dedicated fighters as well as 4,000 MPF allies that rejected U Nu's amnesty. It was also during the 1950s that a local hill Karen commander of the 7th Brigade, Bo Mya, would begin his climb to KNU prominence in the eastern mountains and hills along the Thai border. By the end of the 1950s the resilience of the KNU was enough to qualify it as the Tatmadaw's most formidable foe.

Logistically unaffected by the mass surrender of U Nu's 1958 Arms for Democracy program, the early 1960s represented one of the most active periods for the KNU. It launches various offensives based on "train ambushes in the delta, naval raids off Mergui, and the sacking of government outposts in the eastern hills" (ibid., 189). Karen troops also launch offensives during March 1961, resulting in the seizure of major towns along the Mandalay-Rangoon line. However on April 13, 1961, the KNU lost one of its most able commanders, General Min Maung, a contemporary of Ba U Gyi, to an ambush during combat in the Karen hills. Moreover, the KRC headquarter at Mewaing and Karen strongholds at Kyeikdon and Leke, west of the Dawna Range, were captured. Local Karen units and villagers sympathetic to the Karen cause move deeper into the rugged hills and forests to continue their revolution.

Rangoon faced another unanticipated consequence: with many resistance fighters having surrendered to the regime, they now formed legitimate coalitions able to challenge the regime in the political arena. General Ne Win and his supporters worried about the destabilization of the country by ethnic groups using the ballot box to further their nationalist causes. In the months following the general amnesty it was difficult for pro-Rangoon Burmans to distinguish between the ideologies of the ex-resistance and the new political opposition that was emerging. Indeed, over 40,000 amnestied ethnic and ex-CPB members transformed themselves into powerful and "legal" voting blocs. Moreover, the KNU having rejected U Nu's Arms for Democracy moves its underground delta headquarters to within 10 miles of Rangoon.

Other factors such as a bad economy and continuing lawlessness in many parts of rural Burma compelled Ne Win to seize power in a bloodless coup at the end of September 1958.

On October 28, 1958, U Nu formally resigns. Ne Win replaces U Nu and forms a new "Caretaker Government" (1958-1960) to attend to the political and social chaos that characterized much of the country. During the Caretaker Government, Rangoon presents grossly inaccurate "official" statistics regarding the wars against the ethnic nationalities.

> In the first week the Caretaker Government was in power, the military estimated that there were about 9,000 insurgents in the country, less than a third the number of 1949. By 1960, the government claimed that out of these, 1872 had been killed in action during operations since 1958, 1,959 had been wounded during the same period, 1,238 captured alive and 3,618 had surrendered. If these figures were correct, there would have been only 300 rebels left in the country by 1960 (Lintner 1994, 146).

Following Ne Win's coup, KNU/CPB units struck railway lines leading to Paungdawthi and Payagyi, as well as railroad stations and lines at Daiku and Nyaunglebin. Two hundred Karen troops also ambush a train north of Moulmein resulting in seventeen casualties, including the deaths of several police officers and government officials.

The Caretaker Government did not represent the end of Burma's "democracy" per se, as Ne Win still deferred to a legalistic approach and "frequently appeared in parliament to answer questions and had even petitioned it to allow him to rule for more than six months" (Lintner 1994, 170). Ne Win, however, firmly emphasized a strong militarist central government. Moreover, within two years, he would respect the vote and return power to U Nu when the 1960 election results required him to do so. Nevertheless, during the Caretaker Government Ne Win's policies still aimed at Burmanizing many of the ethnic nationalities in Burma, for example, by applying "pressure on the hereditary leaders in the Shan and Kayah States to surrender their rights in exchange for financial payment" (Silverstein 1981, 53).

In the wake of U Nu's Arms for Democracy program, the adroit statesmanship of Mahn Ba Zan's KNUP results in the formation of the National Democratic United Front (NDUF: 1959-1975), established during May 1959. It is a Communist-inspired front, organized by the CPB to include the KNUP (not the KNU) and the NMSP as well as soldiers from other ethnic armies that rejected U Nu's mass amnesty. It also formally represents a full alliance between one faction of the KNU toward Communism and class struggle. The NDUF would ultimately consist of the Chin National Vanguard Party (CNVP), the Karenni National Progressive Party (KNPP) and Pa-O resistance fighters. Although the CPB and the KNUP were the key participants in military operations, it was nevertheless an alliance that yielded beneficial gains across Lower Burma and the delta until the 1970s.

The formation of the NDUF did not occur without objections from the more conservative constituency of the KNU. Protest was most vocal from the Christian base of the Karen leadership and its accompanying anti-Communist stance. Another problematic issue was how class and ethnic identities competed as ideals, that is, class aspirations of the KNUP encouraged partnerships with the predominantly Burman leadership of the CPB, while ethnic aspirations of the KNU represented the focus of nationalists that aimed for self-determination.

For the Karen, Karenni, and Pa-O who emphasized self-determination, the KNUP's alliance with the predominantly Burman CPB was perceived to be too closely linked to Burman interests. For the pro-right Karen leadership, the class aspirations of the KNUP—insofar as they prompted alliances with Burmans—was perceived to conflict with the KNU's guiding principal of establishing a "liberated" Karen state first, to be achieved before agreeing to discuss territory with any party or government in Rangoon, be it the AFPFL or CPB.

The KNUP was exerting its own sense of political autonomy by supporting the NDUF. The leadership of the KNUP was also frustrated by the need to get final approval from the KNU for their operations and decided that through the KNUP it could at least proactively engage with the Karen politics of the delta. The three year delay it took for the KNU to accept the KNUP's second phase line must have left a deep negative impression on Mahn Ba Zan and his colleagues' view of the KNU leadership; thus, the formation of the NDUF by bypassing formal KNU control signaled the growing rift within the rank and file.

By the 1960s, the KNUP had matured and become a highly influential movement within the KNU. It gained such prominence as a vanguard party that "the name KNU was eclipsed and did not surface in common usage until the 1970s" (Smith 1999, 172). In an interview with Smith in 1985, Skaw Ler Taw describes the second phase as "more or less a communist strategy"; similarly, Marshall Shwin, a veteran of the KNA, the predecessor to the KNU, describes the second phase ideology as being "more than socialism, less than communism" (ibid., 171). Even Mahn Ba Zan "described himself as a socialist and…was an admirer of Robert Owen" (Smith 1999, 171). Smith possesses documents from the Record of the Second National Congress that reveals how the KNUP approached its politics in socialist terms:

- To set up a sovereign Karen State;
- To permit other nationalities to set up their own sovereign states;

- To set up a People's Democracy Federal Union based on the right of self-determination for every minority;
- To set up a socialist state (Smith 1999, 171).

The KNUP further identifies its areas of focus:

- Main Enemy: imperialism, feudalism and Burman chauvinism;
- Immediate Target: the AFPFL which represents those interests;
- Strength: the leadership of the working class, but the main strength will be the peasants, the backbone of the revolution, under the workers' leadership;
- Alliances: intellectuals, government employees, businessmen;
- Temporary Alliances: national bourgeois;
- Strategy: armed struggle as the main tool, agrarian revolution as the second;
- Military Strategy: protracted warfare;
- Agrarian Strategy: abolition of landlordism;
- Foreign Policy: peaceful coexistence.

The KNUP distinguished its constituency from the KNU by emphasizing its connection to the constituency of delta Karen. The delta region, "with its maze of rivers, islands, rich rice lands, fruit orchards, jungles and mangrove swamps," contained terrain highly conducive to guerilla warfare (Lintner 1994, 16). The KNUP military and political terrain of the delta "diamond," with Henzada to the north, Bassein to the west, Rangoon to the east, and Pyapon to the south, meant that KNUP, KAF, and KNDO activities coexisted simultaneously with the AFPFL, the CPB, and Muslim mujahids. The political and social effects from this complicated tapestry of ideologies cannot be underestimated. Yet as a political force emanating from the delta, KNUP ideology was still able to influence Karen political resolve up toward the eastern hills. Moreover, Smith notes:

> Many of the administrative and military reforms the Karen National United Party...now introduced in its ten-year helmsman ship of the KNU movement became a standard model for ethnic nationalists fronts elsewhere in the country...the political language of the KNUP was still setting the tone for many ethnic insurgent debates (Smith 1999, 170).

Through its synthesis of Maoist and nationalist ideologies, the KNUP subscription to communist ideology resulted in the centralization of all aspects of the Karen struggle. By October of 1969, the KNUP officially proclaims its adherence to Marxism-Leninism and Maoism. This included the modeling of the KAF along Maoist lines: regular forces were designated for conventional warfare, guerilla tactics would be used to engage a stronger enemy, and village militias would protect rural areas. Secondly, there was an expressed desire to improve relations with farmers and workers from other nationalities in Karen areas. The process was implemented through land reform programs based on agricultural cooperatives and a "foreign affairs policy based on the principles of peaceful coexistence" (Smith 1999, 151).

As a result of KNUP prominence, the KNU at this time was not without its political contradictions. Leaders of the KNU were concerned by the KNUP's excessive Marxian critiques of religion. The KNUP had already generated tensions in the delta between the Buddhist and Christian political constituencies, as well as within Karen towns and villages. Indeed, in 1956 a KNUP representative lecturing on agrarian policy "alienated Buddhist and Christian representatives by describing Kyaikitiyo monastery in Thaton in derogatory terms" (Smith 1999, 173). Bo Soe, an ex-Buddhist monk and Karen commander of the Fifth Brigade then based out of Thaton—the strongest of the KNU's eastern brigade with over 1,200 soldiers—refused to attend any remaining classes.[31]

In 1960, the pro-right frustrations against the leftist trajectory of the KNUP prompts Ba U Gyi's successor, Hunter Tha Hmwe to form the National Liberation Alliance (NLA: 1960-1963). The formation of the NLA occurs after Tha Hmwe personally holds talks with the Southeast Asia Treaty Organization (SEATO), Thailand, the CIA, and the KMT. They inform him of their rejection of the KNU's leftist stance even though few second phase policies were ever implemented in the eastern hills.

Cold war concerns were justifiably starting to dictate political action in Thailand. As a result the KNU was allowed to open an underground embassy in Bangkok in hopes of winning Western aid for the Karen struggle. From the perspective of Bangkok, it appeared that communism was enveloping Thailand: Vietnam, Laos, Cambodia, and Burma all had powerful communist parties and armies that were becoming powerful forces to contend with. There were still misunderstandings:

> American analysts had the somewhat bizarre idea that the KNU's declaration of a Free State of Kawthoolei fitted into a grand communist strategy, orchestrated by China, to overrun South-East Asia by declaring "autonomous nationality regions" across the mainland peninsula (Smith 1999, 213).

---

[31] Bo Soe's 5th Brigade was also notorious for its poor discipline: his own soldiers later assassinated him. Another 5th Brigade commander, Bo Lin Htin, would also capitulate to Rangoon in 1964 (Smith 1999, 173).

In Smith's interview with KNU veteran Skaw Ler Taw, the latter commented on the rationale of the period: "Unless we change our line we will get no help. The quickest way to get help will be to drive out the left leaders" (ibid., 213). In this regard, Tha Hmwe's NLA can be contrasted with the NDUF in that the former was nationalist-based and the latter class-based, with both organizations existing in a tense relationship.

Frustrated with Mahn Ba Zan and the highly influential KNUP cadres who rarely consulted with him regarding KNUP initiatives, Tha Hmwe excludes the CPB in the NLA transcommunality. Instead the NLA includes the Kachin Independence Organization (KIO), a Shan underground resistance group by the name of *Noom Suik Harn* (Young Warriors), the KRC, as well as an NDUF member, the KNPP. The original aim of the NLA was to organize simultaneous Karen, Karenni, Shan, Mon and Kachin uprisings across eastern Burma while at the same time appealing for international support.

It even sent three NLA columns to the Shan State to forge diplomatic and military ties with Shan, Palaung, and Kachin leaders. The NLA organization would last only three years, however. Tha Hmwe, who by now disillusioned with the KNUP's influence upon the KNU, had developed sentiments that would eventually result in a complete rift within the KNU. However, despite the growing problems within the organization, the KNU was by that time, in control of one of Burma's largest ethnic nationality armies.

Sensing the rift within the KNU organization as well as concerned about its ability to recruit more Karen to the KNU's expanding military, Tatmadaw army commanders invite the KNU leadership for peace talks in early 1960. The talks fail to produce any agreements. On April 4 1960, General Ne Win's Caretaker Government is dissolved and peacefully returns power to U Nu and Burma's parliamentary democracy. Although international observers have argued that the Caretaker Government was the "best-run government since independence," the populace decided in favor of U Nu, a major critic of the Caretaker Government, awarding him 52 percent of the votes and 157 seats in the Chamber of Deputies. Ne Win's coalition managed to garner only 30 percent of the votes cast and 42 seats (Smith 1999, 186).

U Nu, however, did not immediately address the growing rift within the Karen struggle as he now had to attend to a series of new crises: the Shans via the *Noom Suik Harn*, the Shan State Independence Army (SSIA) and the Kachins via the KIO, had broken out in rebellion. The Shan rebellion resulted from its rank-and-file that insisted on holding Rangoon accountable for the terms of the 1947 Constitution derived from the second Panglong Conference, which guaranteed the right of Shan secession by the end of ten years. The tensions between Rangoon and the Shan State were reaching a critical point.

Khun Kya Nu, the Shan leader from Rangoon University, estimated that over 40,000 fighters could have been mobilized had weapons been available for everyone. Similarly, the KIO was also restive and fast becoming one of the most formidable and best organized ethnic self-determination groups in Burma. The emergence of the KIO during 1961 was a reactive nationalism based on U Nu's pledge to make Buddhism Burma's official state religion under the State Religion Act. This was viewed by the predominantly Christian Kachins and many Christian Karen as continued centralization and Burmanization by Rangoon. Moreover, against the protest of Kachins, Rangoon cedes three Kachin villages to China during this period, undermining the credibility of the AFPFL.

Another important factor that caused great anxiety between Ne Win and his cadres was U Nu's attempt to solve the ethnic issue in one "grand gesture." The famed Federal Seminar was borne from ideas proposed in 1960 by Shan leaders who argued that ethnic minorities needed to have a conference where they could continue to pursue their goals for a federalist Burma (Silverstein 1981, 53). The movement desired to replace Burma's highly centralized system of government with a federal system. Its principles in one form or another are still demanded by ethnic self-determination groups like the KNU to this very day.

On February 24, 1962, the Federal Seminar convened under the auspices of U Nu. Ethnic nationalist leaders congregated in Rangoon in hopes that the Federal Seminar would pave a way toward a peaceful solution to Burma's civil wars (Silverstein 1981, 53). The return of U Nu and his support of the Federal Seminar meant that for the first time since the Panglong conferences a political solution to Burma's ethnic civil wars appeared likely.

U Nu organized the Federal Seminar to ascertain the feasibility of a federalist Burma based on a form of constitution "with powers shared equally between the minority states and the Burman-majority areas...these, they proposed, would now have to be reconstituted as one: a single 'Burma' state with powers no different from any of the minority states" (Smith 1999, 195). This arrangement would ensure that there is autonomy and self-government for each ethnic group, thus preventing Rangoon from monopolizing political and economic power. In essence, a federal Burma, with a united fiscal monetary system within an interlinking system of autonomous states, is the antithesis of a centralized Burma, the latter with Rangoon as its nucleus. It would parallel the European Union of today, but on a much smaller territorial scale.

Ne Win was watching from the sidelines and viewed the seminar as superficial diplomacy for increasingly aggressive separatist-oriented demands by the ethnic nationalists. Fearing that a federal Burma would fragment and disintegrate the country, Ne Win launches a historical coup and suspends the constitution to prevent what he believed would be Burma's unraveling. The coup of 1962 would set a precedent by entrenching military rule in the country that has lasted to this very day. The events leading to Ne Win's return are worth recounting. During the evening of March 1, 1962, while U Nu was concluding his Federal Seminar conference with Shan and Karenni leaders at his residence, and just before he was about to make his formal speech on the issue:

> A visiting Chinese ballet troupe staged a performance in Rangoon. It attracted a large audience, among whom could be seen the increasingly powerful General Ne Win. The show went on until late in the evening. When it was over, the general shook hands with the leading Chinese ballerina, and then quietly left. The audience assumed that he too was going home to sleep after watching the show... The armed forces had other plans, however. In the early hours of 2 March, troops moved in to take over strategic positions in the capital. At about two o'clock in the morning, U Nu was arrested at his home... Five other ministers, the chief justice and over thirty Shan and Karenni leaders were also taken into custody. Among them was ex-president Sao Shwe Thaike, who was led away by armed guards, never to be seen again (Lintner 1994, 169).

Ne Win's coup had apprehended all the key representatives attending the Federal Seminar, decisively putting an end to political dialog regarding the issue of Burmese federalism (Silverstein 1981, 53). Later that morning at 8:50 A.M., Ne Win went on the air and announced: "I have to inform you, citizens of the Union, that the armed forces have taken over responsibility and the task of keeping the country's safety, owing to the greatly deteriorating conditions of the Union" (ibid., 169).

U Nu's desire to entertain the possibility of a federal Burma, along with Ne Win's view that U Nu was not up to the task of maintaining order in the Union, led to the coup of 1962 that brought Ne Win back to power. It further entrenched him in Burmese politics until the pro-democracy crackdown of 1988. Unlike the Caretaker Government where Ne Win ruled through a relatively democratic process, the 1962 return of Ne Win meant the end of a parliamentary democracy based on Burma's 1947 constitution and signaled the beginning of a sinister era where the military ruled by decree.

It would first start with the process of deculturalization of ethnic national identities. By first nationalizing the schools, the main Karen languages of Pwo and Sgaw could no longer be taught in previously state-managed schools. Prior to nationalization, the KNU had administered their schools up to the tenth standard. Ne Win had also nationalized religious schools, "which meant that missionary schools for the Karen qualified for closure" (Tharckabaw and Watson 2003). Yet although Ne Win's 1962 coup abolished any attempts at a federalized Burma, an unanticipated consequence was the upsurge of new recruits for the ethnic armies:

Hundreds of young Kachin students filtered into the hills of the north, where a formidable rebel army was being organized…Karen students went to the eastern hills, and even among the Muslims along the East Pakistan border in the western Arakan area, a new rebel movement sprang up. Many Burmans joined the almost depleted ranks of the Communists in the Pegu Yoma Mountains north of Rangoon (Lintner 1994, 173).

The 1962 coup resulted in a military that "introduced its own set of laws to formalise, rather than legalise, its omnipotence" (Lintner 1994, 170). On July 4, 1962, Ne Win announced the formation of the Burma Socialist Program Party (BSPP) that put into practice the ideology and policies of the new regime via the "Burmese Way to Socialism." By early 1963 Ne Win promulgates the "state take-over of production, distribution, import and export of commodities… No new private enterprises would be allowed and on 23 February all banks were nationalized" (ibid., 178).

Militarily the BSPP soon began operations against the CPB, which by now had full Chinese support, and soon against all of Burma's ethnic self-determination groups. Under Ne Win's BSPP, the resolve of the KNU and ordinary Karen would be tested to its very core for the next twenty years, especially with the Ne Win-sanctioned Four Cuts Policy Program. However, during 1963 there was some hope as Ne Win organizes peace talks with major resistance groups in the country.

In 1963 peace talks resume again, this time with a Ne Win-sponsored general amnesty that lasts from April 1, 1963 until the failure of talks on November 14, 1963. Talks began with the Communist Party of Arakan, the Shan State Independence Army (SSIA), Shan National United Front (SNUF), *Noom Suik Harn*, the Tailand[32] National Army (TNA), KIO, CPB and the NDUF allies, the KNUP, the KNPP, NMSP, and the Chin National Vanguard Party. For the majority of all parties involved in talks with Rangoon, the basic feeling was that Ne Win's peace talks clearly implied that resistance forces had to end their rebellion and surrender unconditionally. The main conditions were: (1) all troops must be concentrated in designated areas, (2) troops must not leave these areas without permission, (3) organizational work must stop, and (4) fund-raising must stop. The talks fail miserably. The KNU did not engage in these talks. Smith provides a KNUP summary report which provides the rationale for not engaging in talks with Rangoon:

---

[32] Not to be confused with Thailand. The Tai National Army operated in Shan areas.

As the RC[33] keeps on demanding our unconditional surrender we cannot accept it. If we follow the RC's demands to stop all our organizational work it means that we must abolish our Party. If we follow the RC's demand to stop our administration it will mean that we must hand over all our territory to them. And if we follow the demand to gather all our troops in one place it will mean they can crush us any time (Smith 1999, 210).

The failures of the 1963 peace talks generate more fighting. Ne Win's next move would reveal his tendency renege on his pledges. On November 15, 1963, after the failure of the talks and "written into the terms of the ceasefire agreement," it was agreed that there would be a three-day pause before "either side recommenced military actions" (Smith 1999, 212). But only two days after the failure of talks KNUP and KNPP teams barely escaped an attack by three Tatmadaw army regiments. One must recall that during the siege of Insein, Ne Win similarly utilizes a ceasefire with Karen forces to reinforce his troops for further attacks.[34]

Although offensives are launched against many ethnic self-determination groups after the failure of the '63 talks, Ne Win refrains from launching any attacks on the KNU during the late dry season of April and May. Informed by intelligence of the developing chasm within the KNU and carefully observing the developing situation during the period of the Third Kawthoolei National Congress during April, Ne Win and the Tatmadaw were anticipating the coming split within the Karen struggle. The Third Kawthoolei National Congress of 1963, held north of Papun, was the first gathering since Mahn Ba Zan's Second National Congress had met in 1956. Tha Hmwe, president of the pro-right KRC, organized the meeting with the intention of rejecting the left-oriented ideologies of the Second Phase Program. At the Congress Tha Hmwe urged:

1. The KNU abandon its anti-imperialist stance and seek aid and military assistance from the West.
2. A definition of the enemy along racial lines; thus the "Burman" was the "enemy" of the Karen people. The KNUP opted for "Burman chauvinism."

---

[33] The Revolutionary Council is a Tatmadaw body.
[34] Ne Win's character was suspect even to Aung San. Bo Kyaw Zaw, one of the Thirty Comrades of which Aung San and Ne Win was part of noted how "Aung San and Ne Win quarreled quite often... Aung San was always very straightforward, Ne Win much more cunning and calculating. But Aung San's main objection to Ne Win was his immoral character. He was a gambler and a womaniser, which the strict moralist Aung San—and the rest of us as well—despised" (Lintner 1994, 36).

Finding no support for his concerns, Tha Hmwe and the KRC grow increasingly distant from the aspirations of the Third Congress. The antagonisms between the pro-left and pro-right factions would be capitalized upon by Rangoon. The split finally occurs on April 24, 1963, when Tha Hmwe refuses to return to the Congress despite pleas from delegates of the KNU and KNUP to do so. Instead, Tha Hmwe and 11 KRC members depart and move their contingent to the Thaton area to join the commanders of the KNU's Fifth Brigade, Bo Lin Htin and Bo Soe.

Tha Hmwe had actually asked Bo Mya to join him, knowing full well that Mya was a staunch anti-communist like himself. Mya told Tha Hmwe that he needed to consult with Zan prior to making a decision. Mya had to straddle the ideological divide carefully; Rogers interviewed Bo Mya regarding this episode:

> When Mya asked Zan if he was a communist, Zan replied, "I believe in God and I am praying every day." Mya, a new and devoted convert to Christianity in turn reminded Zan: "If that is the case I will follow you. But if you are a communist, I'll depart from you" (Rogers 2004, 102).

Returning to Hmwe, Mya also discloses his reasons for remaining behind: "I know you are patriotic and a nationalist, but your subordinates are doing things I do not like, raping and killing people." Mya then continues, "Today I may not follow you. But one day, if I know you are going the right way, I may do so. But please do not go back and surrender to the Burmans." Hmwe replied to Mya that he simply wanted to "go home and become a farmer" (ibid., 103).

Because Tha Hmwe and much of his KRC contingent left the Third Congress before it concluded, the KNUP was able to take control over much of the KNU movement. Without a vociferous pro-right Karen contingent, the KNUP unabashedly embraces its leftist/nationalist stance:

> For the progress and development of the Karen people we accept Marxist-Leninism as our guiding principles. But we do not accept the KNUP as a workers' party but as a nationalist party for the progress and development of the Karen people (Smith 1999).

Ne Win exploited Tha Hmwe's departure to his advantage. A delegation from Rangoon arrived at Lin Htin's camp with gifts, supplies, two elephants, as well as a personal invitation for Tha Hmwe to travel to Rangoon. Tha Hmwe, the KRC, as well as the KNUP arrive in Rangoon for talks. The KNUP would reject its negotiations with Rangoon within three months while the KRC continues to maintain dialog for another six months. Hunter Tha Hmwe, the KRC, and roughly 400 soldiers surrendered to the BSPP in 1964.

Moreover, in February 1964 soldiers loyal to the KRC launched an attack on the KNUP base at Kaypu village, north of Papun. Smith notes that the Bo Lin Htin-led raid was coordinated with the Tatmadaw as well as Tha Hmwe. Seventeen KNUP supporters were killed, prompting Bo Mya—by now a KNU military strongman with few rivals challenging him since Min Maung's death—along with KNUP and KPLA troops, to attack and burn down a number of villages under Lin Htin's jurisdiction.

By March of 1964 Tha Hmwe had surrendered to the BSPP and would live out his remaining years under virtual house arrest in Rangoon. However, at the time of Tha Hmwe's surrender Ne Win had promised the KRC conditional political concessions that Rangoon had never promised to any other Burmese insurgent organization: (1) The KRC must drop any demand for the right of secession. In return, the BSPP would agree to rename the Karen State by the nationalist name of "Kawthoolei," (2) The BSPP would consider introducing public policy to "enlarge Kawthoolei to include Karen-majority areas of the Irrawaddy and Tenasserim Divisions," (3) KRC officials would be appointed to sit on the security and administrative committees in each district and the KRC would be part and parcel in the drafting of Burma's new Constitution (Smith 1999, 217).

Not surprisingly Ne Win would not honor any of the pledges made to Tha Hmwe. According to Smith's interview of KNDO veteran and underground organizer Mika Rolly, Tha Hmwe regrets his mistake within a year of his surrender and actually attempts to reconcile with the KNU, the SSIA, the KIO and other political allies.

The numerical outcome of the Tha Hmwe's surrender was actually small. Although the exact numbers are hard to come by, the roughly 400 that joined Tha Hmwe were from Bo Lin Htin's Fifth Brigade in Thaton, the 3rd Battalion of Bo Truman's No. 3 Nyaunglebin Brigade, as well as a handful of soldiers from the KRC. Smith estimates the number of soldiers retiring constituted "probably less than 10 percent of all Karen forces at the time...[and] virtually all were from the Eastern Division; very few Karen surrendered in the Pegu Yomas or Delta Division" (Smith 1999, 218; Lintner 1994, 181). Nevertheless, the symbolic implications were profound: despite over a dozen formidable resistance groups that participated in Ne Win's 1963 peace talks, Tha Hmwe and the KRC were the only group to lay down arms and surrender to Rangoon, an ironic shift when compared to U Nu's 1958 Arms for Democracy call where numerous armed groups had surrendered while the KNU held out.

Tha Hmwe's associate, the Fifth Brigade commander Bo Lin Htin, also "cooperated" with Rangoon, but in a manner that was hardly deferential. By the mid-1950s, Lin Htin's Fifth Brigade had already gone underground and continued to operate out of the Thaton area. The contradictions in Lin Htin's character, described by Lintner as a "warlord type" and by Smith as "ebullient and well-read," revealed itself when he sent a company of troops into the

Thai town of Mae Sot to sack its only police station. Lin Htin believed that Thai arms merchants and local officials had cheated him during a transaction (Smith 1999, 221; Lintner 1994, 181). Lin Htin had also married Ne Win's ex-mistress, Naw Louisa Benson, a famous Karen-Jewish actress and "twice crowned" Miss Burma. Karen sources speculate that Lin Htin had hoped to use Naw Louisa "to get close to the strongman and have him assassinated" (Lintner 1994, 181).

Lin Htin also attempted to form a network with SEATO, the CIA, and the KMT for contacting several Western embassies in Rangoon to perhaps garner support for a coup against Ne Win. In Rangoon, Lin Htin even formed the short-lived underground National Liberation Council in 1965 through which he held secret talks with disillusioned Tatmadaw officers in hopes of winning them over. To KNU leaders, Lin Htin's plan was to "establish a new base area in the remote Tavoy-Mergui districts of the southern Tenasserim Division, which, unlike the mountains along the Thai border, could easily be supplied by land and sea" (Smith 1999, 221). Whatever his exact agenda, Lin Htin's exciting plans were uncovered. Lin Htin was ambushed outside a theater in Thaton on September 30, 1965, by what Lintner describes as "unknown assassins" and Smith describes as "government troops" (Smith 1999, 221; Lintner 1994, 181). Following his death, rumors swept Rangoon and Moulmein,

> ...of unmarked submarines surfacing in the Gulf of Martaban and, though there is no evidence that Lin Htin ever received any official encouragement, few Karen leaders today believe it is entirely coincidental that within four years this very plan resurfaced with the NLC's successor, Un Nu's CIA-backed Parliamentary Democracy Party (Smith 1999, 221).

Observers of Tha Hmwe cite two main reasons for his surrender. First, in an interview with Smith, Mika Rolly notes that Tha Hmwe "was simply tired. He did not think we could win without foreign aid. He had tried everything possible but never succeeded" (Smith 1999, 213). Smith and Lintner note that Tha Hmwe already realized the need for non-communist western aid since the mid-1950s even though he initially backed some of the land reform policies introduced by Mahn Ba Zan. Second, Tha Hmwe was often excluded from dialog with KNUP members, who acted without consulting him. He was also, along with the more conservative Buddhist and Christian constituency, growing increasingly weary of the ideology of the Second Phase Program. One consequence of this meant that a rift had also formed between Tha Hmwe and his comrade, Mahn Ba Zan.

> In many ways the two men, both devout Christians, cut a striking contrast: the Sgaw Karen, Tha Hmwe, an impassioned orator and

populist leader, who described himself as a "capitalist" as against the Pwo Karen "socialist," Ba Zan, a stoic, cautious politician who relied on the importance of party organization (Smith 1999, 214).

What were the major factors that steered the KNU toward a leftist trajectory? The main geopolitical factors centered on what some in the KNU leadership perceived as the betrayal by the "democratic west," thus causing disillusionment among some members within KNU ranks. One could argue that fortunes of international diplomacy, at the time, were disadvantaged toward the KNU. Despite initial international sympathizers such as the US, the KMT, Australia, and Thailand, with the onset of KNUP influence upon the KNU, Western aid—nominal and logistic, slowly evaporated.[35] Thus, the role and influence of the KNUP within the KNU had severe consequences. By being perceived as leftist by the West, the KNU, at least from the perspective of the KNU rank and file, was prevented from receiving heavy and direct military support from the US and its international allies.

The surrender of Tha Hmwe did not result in a chaotic period where bloody succession struggles ensued. By now, Bo Mya, was beginning to eclipse his "elderly Marxist predecessor Mahn Ba Zan" through his leadership in the eastern hills and "no one has seriously challenged Bo Mya since" (Falla 1991, 44). By filling the vacuum left by Tha Hmwe within a decade's time the "Third Phase" of the Karen Revolution under Bo Mya would be characterized by the KNU's return to a more nationalistic platform. However, the difficult period of redefining the KNU's identity did not end with the conclusion of the Second Phase. Indeed, the departure of the KRC and Hunter Tha Hmwe was only the first major ideological split within the KNU. During the third phase, the KNU would see a second split that would result in the removal of many KNUP cadres and a further streamlining of its ideological foundations.

Third Phase: Bo Mya and the Nationalist KNU in the 1980s

Bo Mya's shadow…looms large over the Karen nationalist movement; in Burmese society today he enjoys an almost mythological reputation which, depending on one's perspective, lies somewhere between a modern day Robin Hood, Billy the Kid, [or] Che Guevara (Smith 1999, 281).

---

[35] The role of Thailand is quite extensive that a special section will be devoted to its positive and negative role in the Karen struggle.

Bo Mya was born in 1927 in the hills near Papun and was introduced to armed struggle during World War II.[36] As a police constable under Japanese administration when it occupied Burma he quietly relayed information and intelligence to British and Allied Forces. During World War II Bo Mya joined Force 136, a British-organized undercover unit designed to penetrate behind Japanese lines. Force 136 would later wreak havoc upon Japanese soldiers. Thousands of retreating Japanese soldiers attempting to flee out of Burma as World War II drew to a close had to traverse through Karen territory. While the British were celebrating their recapture of Rangoon, the Karen resistance in the mountains and hills eliminated over 12,000 Japanese soldiers—the vast majority of them ambushed as they tried crossing rivers.

Throughout his tenure as a soldier and eventual leader of the KNU, General Bo Mya was able to command the admiration, respect and fear from Karen and Tatmadaw soldiers alike. Although many Karen soldiers are Buddhists and/or animists, their loyalty to Mya is based on their identification with him as a Karen hills man that was "one of them," an honor not necessarily bestowed upon the more educated Karen leaders from the delta (Falla 1991).

Smith notes that Bo Mya attributes World War II as generating the experiences that would be the turning point of his life: during the period Mya frequently witnesses BIA atrocities in the Papun hills. Mya's membership with Force 136 also presented itself favorably, for he was mentored by one of its commanders Saw Butler, "who had swiftly risen during the war to become one of the highest ranking Karen officers in the British Army" (Smith 1999, 282). Under Butler, Bo Mya had become "more of an adopted son" and a protégé as he accompanied the former "on government service around the country" (ibid., 282). However, as the 1950s signaled a protracted period of warfare for the KNU, Bo Mya established himself in the eastern hills and rose up the ranks of the organization. By 1960, he had attained the rank of Colonel and commanded the 7th Brigade of the Eastern Division.

A year later, the animist-born Mya converted to Christianity under the Seventh Day Adventist Church by marrying Thra Mu Lah Poh, a Seventh Day Adventist Karen. Even though Ne Win's peace talks had successfully courted Hunter Tha Hmwe and the KRC into defection and surrender, by mid-1965, Bo Mya, under a renewed and reinvigorated Karen nationalism, solidified his power in the eastern hills near the Thai border. A year earlier Mya had already established a military reorganization of the Eastern Division by appointing old comrades who had served and remained loyal to him since the 1950s.

---

[36] Like many other Animist Karen, Mya's birth date was never recorded. January 20, 1927 was chosen by the KNU for his birthday celebrations which are treated with great pomp and ceremony in Kawthoolei each year (Smith 1999, 497).

The KNU under Bo Mya returned to its nationalist roots by reinvoking Ba U Gyi's Four Principles of the Karen Revolution. In Smith's interview of Saw Ba Lone of the KNU's Education Department, the latter reflects:

> After 20 years we found we had to use the simplest system to approach our people. If the political discussion was too complex, our people could not always understand. Especially we found the CPB-KNUP discussions had not worked. The traditions and culture of the Karen people are very simple. Saw Ba U Gyi recognized this. His four principles are based upon the concept of national unity (Smith 1999, 286).

During the late 1960s, the KNU under Bo Mya accelerated the end of KNUP influence which was further augmented by Tatmadaw successes in the delta region. Mya's first major political move resulted in the 1966 expulsion of pro-leftist members of the KNUP, which included a request for KNUP leader Mahn Ba Zan and Skaw Ler Taw—two KNUP leaders to whom he was most close to—to leave the organization willingly and peacefully. For Mya, the KNUP was viewed as too left-leaning for the conservative factions of the KNU.

> By this action Bo Mya had effectively staged a coup d'etat and the entire Eastern Division fell under his control. For the moment the abrupt departure of the KNUP leaders left a large vacuum in the political administration of the eastern hills which needed to be filled (ibid., 285).

Along with the rejection of the KNUP in 1966, Bo Mya forms the short-lived emergency military administration called the Karen National Liberation Council (KNLC) and consolidates the KNU military wing as the Karen National Liberation Army (KNLA). Mya establishes himself as commander of its forces, eventually becoming the KNLA Chief-of-Staff. Mya had hoped that the anti-communist KNLC would usher in Western support, but hope again failed to materialize. Nevertheless, Mya reinforces the KNLC by consolidating brigade jurisdictions: all areas under KNU control are divided into seven KNLA brigades, protecting each of the seven districts of Kawthoolei.

The departure of the Mahn Ba Zan and his cadres was not permanent, however. In mid-1967, sensing the political prowess and prescience of Mya, Mahn Ba Zan and four ex-KNUP representatives: Ba Thin, Than Aung, Tha Byit and Maung Maung, return to rejoin the KNU. By 1968, Bo Mya, Mahn Ba Zan and other KNUP returnees would form an emergency KNU institution to streamline the transition of the KNU toward a nationalist platform. The Karen National United Front (KNUF: 1968-1970) was the outcome of their discussions, which Smith describes as a "halfway house on the road to the reformation of the KNU" (1999, 286). When it was disbanded in 1970, the KNU once again reemerged as an uncluttered organization focused on the goals of self-determination.

By 1968, the KNUP was no longer an effective organization to resist Tatmadaw polices. At the Ninth KNU Congress in 1974 its members voted to dissolve the KNUP and close ranks with the KNU. In 1975, the reunited KNU emerges without its vestigial KNLC or KNUP. Mahn Ba Zan then becomes KNU president until Bo Mya replaces him in 1976. At the time, Smith notes that "Mahn Ba Zan quite likely believed he could win Bo Mya over, but instead there was a long battle of wills between the two men which Bo Mya eventually won in 1976 when he replaced Ba Zan as president of the KNU" (Smith 1999, 285).

The third phase KNU under Bo Mya would also redefine their self-determination goals. By 1968 the federalist aspirations repressed by Ne Win's 1962 coup once again became an important theme within the KNU movement. In contrast to a "people's democracy" espoused by the KNUP, the third phase KNU proclaimed its idea of a "national democracy" to be based on a "federal parliamentary system of government that allows national minorities political, economic, and cultural rights as distinctive as those enjoyed by the French or Italians in the cantons of Switzerland or the Lahu and the Kachins in the autonomous regions of China" (ibid., 286). Since 1968, the idea of a national democracy has been embraced by virtually every self-determination group as a means toward extensive autonomy, but still within a "Union" of Burma.

To further the aims of a national ethnic minorities front aimed at federalism, the third phase KNU also includes its transcommunality with the Mons and the Chins, ultimately establishing alliances with them as well as with U Nu and his Parliamentary Democracy Party (PDP: 1970-1974). U Nu had fled Ne Win's regime and was desperately trying to rebuild his political base by siding with the ethnic minorities. In Bangkok on May 25, 1970, the National United Liberation Front (NULF: 1970-1974) was signed into existence.

The political constituents of NULF were the KNU, the Chin Democratic Party (CDP), the New Mon State Party (NMSP) and the PDP. With Bangkok's role in cementing this new alliance the KNU was able to receive international recognition for its role in fighting the BSPP regime. Karen leaders were even given a "liaison office" in Bangkok and a KNUF team during the 1970-1973 worked freely in the city. The new transcommunality also benefited the KNU financially for "though the exact amounts were never revealed, KNU leaders say they received a down payment of four million baht from the PDP...while the NMSP gained two million baht" (ibid., 288).

NULF thus becomes an important political platform to further the aims of a federalist Burma. NULF promoted two main goals: (1) the overthrow of Ne Win's "sovereign government," and (2) the establishment of a Federal Union Republic to be based on "the principles of equality and justice and would include all nationalities in the Union" (Smith 1999, 288). According to Smith, NULF's platform if successful would eventually mean:

> ...national boundaries between the different races, including the Burmans, would have to be re-examined and new Mon, Arakan and Chin states created with full powers of local autonomy. As a result, this would bring the total number of states in Burma to eight: Arakan, Chin, Kachin, Karen, Karenni, Mon, Shan and, for the first time, Burman. Inside Burma the NULF's main tactic would be "armed struggle," but in the international arena it would remain strictly "non-aligned" (Smith 1999, 288).

Within two year's time, NULF would experience the factionalism that has frequently plagued Burma's self-determination groups. Although Karen and Mon soldiers assisted the PDP in their armed struggle against Ne Win's regime, many resented the presence of hundreds of Burman soldiers on minority territory. As a result of the differing sentiments, there was asymmetrical cooperation between different ethnic armies and their support for the PDP.

> The strongest protests were from the KNU 1st brigade officers in Thaton...who had refused to obey Bo Mya's order to work with the PDP. Particularly notorious was one battalion commander, Bo Din Gha whose men had once attacked a KNUP column in which Mahn Ba Zan had been traveling. Ba Zan never forgot this. Matters finally came to a head in 1970 when the brigade commander, Kyaw Hoe, came to tell Bo Mya of his difficulty getting his officers to obey orders. Mya responded by inviting eight company commanders to his general headquarters for talks. When they arrived on 22 February 1971, all eight were arrested and summarily executed (Smith 1999, 290).

Moreover, the predicted mass defections from the Tatmadaw never occurred even though U Nu and the PDP had set up a radio station to broadcast their goal to overthrow Ne Win. His dramatic message did incite student protests in Rangoon that were put down by the military. Moreover, the military exploits of the PDP's military wing, the Peoples' Liberation Army (PLA), did not make a significant impact against Tatmadaw forces even though it claimed to have killed 925 government troops in over 77 battles between 1970-1973 (ibid., 289).

Ideological disagreements would also test the Karen and Mon constituencies, prompting a split in their support for the NULF. Some KNU leaders disagreed with the emphasis of a Karen State within a federalized Burma, arguing that this ideological trajectory contradicted their revolutionary aims for self-determination set forth by Ba U Gyi in 1947. Voicing their concerns to other members of NULF eventually prompted the organization to grant the Karen and Mon the right of secession. The pro-union U Nu, believing that federalism would invite foreign interference into Burma, would have none of this and quickly resigned from NULF in April of 1972. Nevertheless about 1,500 KNU with NULF forces attack and seize the town of Myawaddy on March 18, 1974. Fighting was so intense that "the Burmese Army was only saved by its air force" (Falla 1991, 28).

The KNU holds its Ninth KNU Congress in September of 1974 and formally proclaims its tenets for the third phase. It also departs from the NULF transcommunality. Mahn Ba Zan, Maung Maung, Than Aung, Bo Mya and Pu Ler Wah drafted the new KNU Constitution that shifted its political ideology to the right, thus redefining and reaffirming the Karen struggle in a new ideological stance that holds to this day. In its "Ten Articles of the aims and objectives of the KNU," the need for a vanguard party such as the KNUP is eliminated. As such, the KNU became "the sole organ for the development of the Karen national cause, the elite of the Karen national revolution. The KNU is the highest organ for all Karen people and represents all Karen people" (Smith 1999, 295).

The third phase KNU also "resolved" the class question by noting in Article 3 that no class divisions exist among the Karen because "every farmer, worker, intellectual, petty and national bourgeois are the strength of the KNU." It further emphasized its desires to "have a good relationship with every class and organization from the outside world." Article 4 states: "Patriotism is our sole ideology. We will never accept dogmatism." Also, in response to the errors of its history, Articles 6-8 warn of the need to guard against warlordism, as well as "leftist and rightist divisions or adventurism and opportunism" by engaging in "self-criticism" (Smith 1999, 295).

By now, any pretense suggesting that the KNU could relive an era influenced by the Zin-Zan Agreement of 1952 was dead, despite the fact that through the 1970s the Chinese-backed CPB fanning out of Burma's north was winning an impressive series of "battles of annihilation" against government troops (even though much of the CPB in the delta and the Pegu Yomas had surrendered to Rangoon by 1975) (Lintner 1994, 216). Yet Smith notes that "since the military coup of 1962 the CPB has never been able to regain any real foothold in the cities" while Fredholm adds "the last ones were hunted down and killed or captured in 1975" (Smith 1999, 128; Fredholm 1993).

The mid-seventies, however, presented the KNU with geopolitical dilemmas. The organization, in need of Western "capitalist" aid, also had to attend to Western foreign policy concerns. Within this context, Bo Mya often described Kawthoolei as a "Foreign Legion" for Thailand, guarding its borders and preventing "links between the Burmese communists and Thai communists" (Smith 1999, 297). "If the West would help us with money and recognition, they would not regret it," proclaimed Mya (Smith 1999, 297). By 1975, one main thorn remained in the KNU organization, Mahn Ba Zan. A year later a pivotal event that would secure Bo Mya's authority over the KNU centered on the final ideological clash between the two giants.

For many inside Thai and US military circles Mahn Ba Zan was perceived as a leftist sympathizer. At the time, both Thai and US governments were anxiously anticipating and trying to prevent a communist link-up between the CPB and the Communist Party of Thailand (CPT). Communism had consolidated much of Southeast Asia as Vietnam, Cambodia and Laos fell under the influence of Beijing and Moscow. Moreover, the CPT was at the peak of its power during the mid-1970s. Anxiety had developed inside the Thai government over attempts by the CPT to link up with the CPB via the Shan State. CPT units from across the border were already indirectly assisting the campaigns of the CPB. Even up until the late 1980s, CPT cadres were active at the Kawthoolei/Thai border, from Thailand's Prachuap Khiri Khan province in the South all the way to the southern regions of Mae Hong Son province in Thailand's northwest. Often the CPT was able to supply the CPB based out of Tenasserim with medicine, M16s, RPGs and M79 grenade launchers.

> The CPB had maintained large warehouses...in base areas dotted along the Yunnan border. Wide eyed visitors were amazed to see that many of the boxes had never been opened; in fact these stockpiles were so great that the CPB itself became a major arms broker to other ethnic insurgent forces in north east Burma well into the 1980s (Smith 1999, 302).

With CPT and the Chinese Communist Party's assistance between 1975 until its 1989 collapse, the CPB had made many attempts to fan out from the Shan State to reinvade central Burma. In a context where the Vietnamese Communists had united their country and the Khmer Rouge was in the process of implementing its own agrarian communism under Pol Pot, Bo Mya was compelled to purge Mahn Ba Zan so that significant Western aid and international recognition could be granted to the Karen struggle, as well as to their attempts to prevent the CPB and the CPT from linking up.

In this volatile context, it did not help that prior his ouster Mahn Ba Zan proclaimed his support for the Chinese government and praised it for its emphasis on supporting minority rights. According to Smith, Mahn Ba Zan perceived the internecine warfare within Burma to be a triangular conflict that pitted the CPB, Rangoon, and ethnic self-determination groups against one another. Thus, when still president of the KNU, Mahn Ba Zan proclaimed that he would ally the KNU with any group that supported the aims of the KNU. To placate potential Western organizations in charge of disseminating aid, Bo Mya reacted to Mahn Ba Zan's assertion by categorically discerning that the KNU would "accept aid *only from capitalist* nations" and not from any indiscriminate alliance as proclaimed by Mahn Ba Zan. On August 10, 1976, Mahn Ba Zan, the president of a reunited KNU borne from KNUP dissolution, resigned as president of the KNU and was relegated to the role of being the organization's "honorary adviser" (the CIA was purportedly complicit in Mahn Ba Zan's ouster). After briefly serving his office between 1975 and 1976, Mahn Ba Zan's removal thus paved the way for Bo Mya to have uncontested control of the KNU.

> The KNU's long experience of relations with the CPB came to an end in 1975 and Bo Mya, despite a number of contacts in the 1980s, never really relented on his anti-communist line. It is noteworthy that, despite these long years of contact, very few Karen actually joined the CPB and in very few Karen communities has the CPB ever been able to establish base areas (Smith 1999, 329).

With Mahn Ba Zan standing down, Mya consolidates his power by becoming the KNU's President, Minister of Foreign Affairs, Minister of Defense, as well as the Chief of Staff for the KNLA. Mya imbues the KNU with what Rogers describes as "quasi-Old Testament" penalties where adultery results in imprisonment, alcohol is banned, and the death penalty is enacted for those possessing, consuming, and dealing drugs—especially opium (Rogers 2004, 105).

The significant aid package promised by the US and Thailand never materialized. As a result, the KNU did not militarily engage with the CPT while "local KNU and CPT forces continued to simply ignore each other's existence" (Fredholm 1993, 112). The failure of receiving aid did not deter KNU resolve, however. With a renewed fighting vigor, Tatmadaw offensives on the 101 Special Battalion headquarters at Kawmoorah were repulsed by the KNLA in 1977. In 1980 a Tatmadaw offensive launched against the 6th Brigade at Three Pagoda Pass was similarly unsuccessful.

With Bo Mya now at the helm of the organization, the KNU was indispensable in assisting the Thai government's attempts to halt the communist threat at its border regions. Smith notes that the "Thai Army owes a debt of deep gratitude to the KNU…which might explain why senior Thai officers were reluctant to turn their backs on the KNU, despite the closening [sic] of Rangoon-Bangkok ties in the late 1980s" (Smith 1999, 299). Even today, with the legacy of friendlier ties with the Tatmadaw established by Thailand's former Prime Minister Chaovalit Yongchaiyudh that has lasted for over a decade, I was still able witness many Thai intelligence officers holding warm and politically strategic dialogs with Bo Mya and his advisors before and after National Day celebrations during my January 2004 stay at Mu Aye Pu.[37] Smith's assessment still reflects the state of Thai/KNU relationships today, correctly noting that many Thai officials continue to acknowledge that the KNU is "the *de facto* government along most of Thailand's western border" (Smith 1999, 299).

> Because of its support, no serious restrictions were placed until the 1990s on the cross border trade out of which it and several other...members have financed their struggles. KNU...leaders have remained on close personal terms with senior Thai intelligence, police and army...officers. Karen casualties have been treated in Thai hospitals and KNLA commanders allowed into the 1990s access to Thailand and the region's thriving arms black market (ibid., 299).

There were also transcommunal maneuverings by the KNU during the mid-1970s. Disappointed with the outcome of its NULF membership and its inclusion of U Nu's Burman PDP, the KNU explores transcommunality formations that would exclude Burman political groups. During this period, KNU commanders were already hosting and training other armed ethnic self-determination groups at its many bases. The establishment of federalism was still being pitched in one form or another, and in a political incarnation that would later lead to the establishment of the National Democratic Front transcommunality (NDF: 1976-present), the formation of the Revolutionary Nationalities Alliance (which according to Smith "largely existed on paper"), aimed to overthrow Ne Win's regime and proclaim "a federal union of independent national states based on the principle of equality and national self-determination" (ibid., 294).

On May 19, 1976, the National Democratic Front was established as a non-Burman, ethnic nationalities front that continued to aim for self-determination for its member groups. With nine members at its formal 1976 inception, and over 20,000 volunteer troops "from the Himalayan foothills on the India-China border to the dense rain forests of Tenasserim," the NDF by its peak in 1991 had twelve self-determination groups representing the formidable transcommunality (ibid., 386).

Although six NDF self-determination groups have since signed formal ceasefires with Rangoon or resigned from the transcommunality, the remaining NDF self-determination groups are either still in a non-ceasefire

---

[37] In 1989, Chaovalit was the first Thai Army Commander in Chief to recognize the SLORC despite loud protests from within Thailand.

mode or informal ceasefire talks.[38] The NDF would come to represent the one transcommunal front that would have significant influence on the political terrain of Burma's civil wars. Indeed, the inauguration of the NDF in 1976, despite initial factionalism, drew the "largest meetings of insurgent leaders ever held in Burma" (Fredholm 1993, 115). Moreover, as a political force the NDF would represent a viable "alternative to the totalitarian Burman rule of Ne Win" (ibid., 115). Not all KNLA soldiers shared the nationalist sentiments espoused by the NDF. A setback did occur when ex-KNUP soldiers from the 14th Battalion, disenchanted with the KNU leadership, defected from the KNLA in 1978 and joined up with the CPB.

The NDF was a successful transcommunality due to four important reasons. First, the NDF had a realistic goal: within a decade the KNU, along with other ethnic self-determination group members of various transcommunalities, would explicitly depart from its aggressive demands for secession. According to Fredholm, a shift toward a federalist line "especially for the KNU, but also to some extent for veterans of the other parties, was a considerable backing-down from their earlier, separatist demands" (Fredholm 1993, 115). How extremely difficult it must have been for its leaders to come to this decision is difficult to imagine. It was hoped that the decision would garner support from the Burman population. In October 1984, at its Third Plenary Central Presidium, the NDF stated:

> The NDF does not want racial hatred. It is struggling for liberty, equality and social progress of all indigenous races of Burma because Burma is a multi-national state inhabited and owned by all. In the so-called Burma of today, the National Democratic Front intends to establish a unified Federal Union with all the ethnic races including the Burmese (Smith 1999, 386).

Smith describes how difficult the transition must have been for the KNU: "For the KNU, the decision to seek a 'Federal Union' represented a considerable compromise. Just two months earlier Bo Mya had issued a declaration announcing 'to the world the independence' of the 'Republic of Kawthoolei'" (ibid., 506). The federalist position would still be based on self-determination through the creation of new nationalities states to include a Burman state, along with a system of designating autonomous regions for minorities within each of the states. Smith continues, "Veteran Kachin, Karen, Karenni, Mon and Shan leaders may still dream in their hearts of independent nations, but...all NDF members have stuck by this 'federalist'

---

[38] The Tatmadaw utilizes ceasefires as a means to divide up anti-government groups. As we shall see throughout the history of Burma's various wars, some ceasefires are with prominent groups, while other are with smaller battalions or factions of certain groups. In any case, most anti-government united fronts are slowly "chipped" away by this tactic.

line through the hard years since" (Smith 1999, 386). Moreover, the KNU under Bo Mya and the KIO under Brang Seng, two respected nationalist leaders, would dominate the NDF movement in the 1980s.

The second factor was the NDF transcommunal political organization and military arrangement. During 1986, in a move designed to foster closer military cooperation and enhance logistics between the armed forces of different self-determination groups, the NDF was divided into three regional command areas. The northern command was represented by Kachin, Palaung and Shan troops and their political leadership, the central command included Wa, Pa-O and Karenni troops and their political leadership, while the southern command was constituted by Mon, Arakan, and Karen troops and their political leadership (Lintner 1994, 269). The conviction of the NDF, in spite of its internal differences, would mean that the aforementioned armies would now be a unified military force. On paper, the jurisdictions of the three regional fronts literally covered all of Burma.

Third, despite Mya's contempt for the CPB, the KNU's precarious acceptance of the NDF's alliance with the CPB was, nevertheless, a pragmatic decision that succeeded in enlarging a military front against Rangoon. With larger territories neutralized by the NDF's alliance with the CPB, guerrillas from all member organizations had more territorial mobility. Smith notes, "for the first time in nearly 40 years of insurgency all the main opposition groups and well over 30,000 rebel troops were allied against the 190,000-strong Tatmadaw" (Smith 1999, 357). Lastly, the NDF also gained international attention through their delegates' 1987 visits to the United Kingdom, West Germany, Switzerland and Japan. During their visits, the NDF transcommunality asked the international community to end Burma's civil war.

Bo Mya's successful maneuvering of KNU participation in the pro-federalist NDF and the removal of Mahn Ba Zan and any residual support for left-wing factions contributed to the KNU's organizational consolidation. Appointed the first chairman of the NDF, a post Mya would hold until 1987, Mya increases his nationalist influence across the transcommunality of self-determination groups. However, following the period after Bo Mya's political consolidation of the KNU, the Karen struggle would be beset by political and military challenges that would again test its newly established ideological foundations.

During the 1980s, Bo Mya, the KNU, and the NDF would be significantly tested by three factors:

1. The Four Cuts campaigns first launched by the Tatmadaw and directed in the delta during the 1950s, would by the mid 1980s, reach KNU and NDF territories in the hills;
2. The pro-democracy crackdown of 1988 would create a new political and military arena for the KNU to further its transcommunal politics as well

as prompting the Tatmadaw to launch sustained military operations against the KNU, KNLA, and its allies;

3. The KNU's relationship with the CPB would become more precarious.

After exploring these three factors, we will return to the Third Phase KNU in the 1990s. The last decade of the twentieth century would simultaneously provide political opportunities and further military setbacks for the KNU. KNU and NDF support for Aung San Suu Kyi's NLD through yet another coalition, the Democratic Alliance of Burma (DAB), and her reciprocity in acknowledging the political legitimacy of DAB, would signify a new momentum in the politics of Burma. The continuing Four Cuts campaigns, however, would push the KNU and the Karen way of life to the periphery of Kawthoolei.

A. Internal Colonization through the Four Cuts

After Ne Win solidified his power in 1962, a counter-insurgency strategy was developed known as the Four Cuts (*Pya Ley Pya*). Its main aim was to sever "four main links between the insurgents, their families, and the local population" (Fredholm 1993, 91). The four main links to be cut were food supplies, financial flow, intelligence gathering, and capacity to recruit new soldiers. Karen are understandingly more cynical, describing the Four Cuts in more forthright terms as a means to cut off the rebels from their own people, from access to the outside world, from supply lines, and to cut off their heads (Smith 1999; Fredholm 1993, 91; Falla 1991, 28).

Fredholm notes that the Four Cuts strategy was modeled after the British during their subjugation of the southern African Boers during the Boer Wars of the previous century (Fredholm 1993). Smith additionally notes:

> The strategy...owes much to the 'new village' tactics developed by British forces under Sir Robert Thompson in defeating the CPM [Communist Party of Malaysia] insurgency in Malaysia; it was also similar to the 'strategic hamlet' programme the United States employed, with Thompson's advice, in Indo-China. Both were criticized for their gross abuses of human rights (Smith 1999, 259).

Indeed during the Vietnam War, the strategic hamlet program was implemented in Laos and Vietnam to forcibly relocate millions of peasants, rural villagers and hill peoples. The Tatmadaw also began to "rehearse" their Four Cuts during 1966 against the Kachins and the KIO. It was, according to Smith, a "drastic scorched earth policy" employed in the Myitkyina, Hukawng Valley, the Naga hills and the Kanmaing region where thousands died unreported to the world outside (Smith 1999, 220). Its application against the delta insurgents, primarily the delta Karen when the region was still very much under KNU influence, occurred in its rudimentary form even as early as the pre-Ne Win 1950s. Its effects during the 1950s were limited:

> While effective in denying guerrillas food and territory, such operations usually did little more than push insurgent forces deeper into Burma's great mountains and forests. Rebel commanders and their followers invariably escaped, emerging again later to fight another day (Smith 1999, 258).

Interestingly, the main difference between the scorched earth campaigns prior to Ne Win's coup and the campaigns launched after his seizure of power lay not in its tactics (although variations in the implementation Four Cuts were later refined). It had more to do with the new and more denigrating status accorded the ethnic nationalities. After the overall failure of the 1963 peace talks, rebels no longer had any political status. No longer "Burmese," they were relegated to the designations of saboteurs, bandits, smugglers, and racists bent on destroying the Burmese approach toward socialism as well as dividing the union. As a result of these designations, the Tatmadaw had given itself *carte blanche* in their dealings with the self-determination groups.

However, it would be too convenient and a mistake to view the Four Cuts strategy as purely a British or Western import. The emotions and sentiments which characterize the Four Cuts strategy is historically rooted in Burman ambitions and aspirations for empire dating back centuries, beginning with the conquering Burman monarchs from the "three strong Burman kingdoms of Anawratha of the Pagan Dynasty (1044-1287), Bayinnaung of the Toungoo Dynasty (1486-1752), and Alaungpaya of the Konbaung Dynasty (1753-1885)" and leading up to Aung San, founder of the Tatmadaw (Smith 1999; Fredholm 1993, 21). Falla provides a reflective journal entry by Dr. John Crawfurd, based upon the latter's 1827 visit to the Royal Burmese Court of Ava. Crawfurd noted:

> The conduct of the Burmans on their predatory excursions is cruel and ferocious to the last degree... 'You see us here', said some of the Chiefs to Mr. Judson, 'a mild people living under regular laws. Such is not the case when we invade foreign countries. We are then under no restraints, we give way to all our passions, we plunder and murder without compunction or control. Foreigners should beware how they provoke us when they know these things' (Falla 1991, 361).

Smith describes how General Saw Maung, Ne Win's successor after the latter resigned following the 1988 pro-democracy crackdown, reproduces this chauvinism in a 1990 radio broadcast: "In a...defence of his own Buddhism and Burman ancestry, he looked back over 900 years to the country's first Buddhist ruler at Pagan who had embarked on an era of military conquest to impose his own religious solution on the people" (Smith 1999, 419). Not surprisingly, ethnic nationalists claim that there was an "undeniably racial element in planning and carrying out these attacks" (ibid., 258). Indeed, the Four Cuts attacks were undertaken "by predominantly Burman officers against Karen, Karenni and Mon villagers" (ibid., 397). Burman nationalists also fused international themes of struggle to frame the country's struggle with its insurgents. Myint-U observes:

> The young politicians of the independence movement looked to Sinn Fein, the Fabian Society, the Indian National Congress and the rise of Japan for their inspiration, and not [only] to the last remnants of the House of Alaungpaya and the lost world which they represented (Myint-U 2001, 246).

Little has changed since then: Rangoon still continues to use the Four Cuts to underscore Burman hegemony by emphasizing the "primacy of the nation over its parts" (Silverstein 1981, 54). It is but only the most recent atavism of how Burman chauvinism has attempted to reproduce its hegemony through internal colonization. Colonel Aung Thein of the Tatmadaw remarked in the late 1980s that the Four Cuts shall be used to "fight the insurgents until they are eliminated" (Lintner 1990). In 1997, the Tatmadaw general Maung Aye was quoted as saying "the Burmese vow to pursue offensives against rebels indefinitely" (HRW/A July 1997, 13).

Ne Win's early implementation of the Four Cuts campaigns took place in the delta during the 1950s while its campaigns in the hills would intensify in the following decades. There were successes in the delta as it succeeded in driving out the Karen (as well as the CPB). The Karen would migrate eastward to the Pegu Yomas to entrench themselves there, followed by the Tatmadaw. However, Tatmadaw successes were pyrrhic when the fight was taken to the eastern hills. [39]

The Four Cuts campaigns against Burma's ethnic nationalities were never implemented in one given period. Instead, Burma's profile of diverse terrains and ethnic territories, the differing capacities of its ethnic armies, as well as their differing periods of military engagements, were all factors that compelled Ne Win to fight the war "on several fronts in a systematically seesaw fashion according to the relative strengths and merits of different rebel forces" (Smith 1999, 307-308).

---

[39] There have also been numerous attacks on smaller villages throughout various districts. For detailed listings of these villages, refer to *Suffering in Silence: the Human Rights Nightmare of the Karen People of Burma*, published by the Karen Human Rights Group, 2000 (ed. Claudio Delang).

During lulls in the fighting the KNLA made two unsuccessful attempts to penetrate back to the delta and renew their revolution. In September 1982 an underground KNU cell in Rangoon was uncovered, and its plans to attack a government radio station resulted in the deaths of two policemen and two guerillas. The Four Cuts is employed during January of 1983 as government forces begin offensives against Karen bases near the Moei River and Thai border.

The KNLA responded during mid-February. A heavily armed column of 200-300 KNLA troops with elephants attempts to infiltrate westward into the Pegu Yoma range. Tatmadaw forces intercept them near Nyaunglebin soon after KNLA soldiers crossed the Rangoon-Mandalay railway line. According to Lintner, "six government battalions supported by armour pursue the...column, which is wiped out" (Lintner 1994, 370).

Despite these setbacks, during mid-1983 the KNLA was able to down three government Bell helicopters used by the Tatmadaw and initially donated by the US to combat drug trafficking operating out of the Shan hills. During the same year in mid-June Tatmadaw forces capture the important 6,000 feet Nawtaya mountain peak after fierce fighting (Nawtaya peak provides a panorama of key KNU bases along the Moei River).

Smith notes "the Four Cuts campaign in south-east Burma in the years 1984-1990 was without doubt, one of the most brutal military operations since independence" (Smith 1999, 397). In January 1984 large Four Cuts offensives are concentrated against KNU bases at the Dawna Range along the Thai border. Sustained operations against the NMSP and KNPP along the Thai border are also commenced. Between January until March of 1984 and with their strategic vantage point atop the 6,000 feet Nawtaya peak, the Tatmadaw carry out a series of large offensives against KNU 7th Brigade strongholds: Mae Tah Waw on the northern Moei River falls, but KNLA forces at Maw Po Kay put up a fierce resistance. In March, then Thai Army commander-in-chief General Chaovalit allows the Tatmadaw to attempt attacks on Maw Po Kay from the rear through Thai territory. During the same year, even though the KNU was still engaged in heavy fighting against the Tatmadaw in the hills it also dispatched a KNU mortar team to assist allies of the NDF in their battle with the Tailand Revolutionary Council (TRC)[40] at Mae Aw in March 1985. Between May 29 and June 16, 1985, KNLA forces again shell the town of Myawaddy.

Between 1986 and 1987, the Tatmadaw shifted their offensives toward the KNU's First, Second, and Third brigade bases at Thaton, Toungoo, and Nyaunglebin, respectively, creating a massive exodus of thousands of refugees fleeing into Thailand, as well as creating many more thousands of internally displaced persons (IDPs). The timber mills at Wale, one of many sources of revenue for the KNU, were torched in March 1987. The KNU did

---

[40] This Shan separatist front included drug warlord Khun Sa and his Shan United Army.

have some important successes in repulsing Four Cuts attacks. In February of 1987, the KNLA was able to defeat the Tatmadaw's No. 84 light infantry battalion and seize its supply base in Kadaingti, west of the Salween River. Over 150,000 rounds of ammunition and 30 weapons were acquired.

From the perspective of any given self-determination group, the Four Cuts campaigns would come in spurts—albeit deadly ones—against their peoples, towns and villages, as well as the military. Thus, it is important to remember that the Four Cuts campaigns were not only directed solely against the Karen and the KNU, but against all other self-determination groups. Virtually all ethnic self-determination groups and the Burmanized CPB, at one time or another, would suffer under the hammer of the Four Cuts. When it arrived wanton destruction of lives, along with villages and farmland literally cleared from the mountains and valleys would follow.

That said, the Karen in KNU territory can be argued to have suffered the most from the Four Cuts campaigns. During the 1970s until the surge of pro-democracy activities in 1988, the populations between Mandalay and Rangoon were living relatively peaceful lives, virtually ignorant of what was happening in the hilly and mountainous frontiers. Not until the military started shooting its own citizens during the 1988 pro-democracy crackdown, coupled with what fleeing democracy activists were able to witness as they fled into the hills did central and lower Burma citizens realize how extreme their government could be. For the Karen by 1988, villages along the 70-mile stretch from north to south along the Dawna Range were in a state of devastation.

> Dozens of villages had been burnt down, crops confiscated and fields destroyed. Several thousand villagers had moved into new 'strategic villages' on the plains to the west, while over 20,000 Karen refugees had crossed into Thailand (Smith 1999, 398).

Moreover, Rangoon desperately had to sustain their Four Cuts campaigns after the 1988 pro-democracy crackdown: five thousand democracy activists, the majority of them Burman, had fled to KNU territory. There and with KNU support the All Burma Students Democratic Front (ABSDF) was formed. In other ethnic areas 2,000 activists and students found safe haven in KIO territory while another 1,300 individuals found safety in areas controlled by the NMSP (ibid., 371).

The consequences of the Four Cuts have been devastating to the Karen as well as other ethnic nationalities. Yet because the Karen struggle continues onward while over a dozen ethnic self-determination groups have signed ceasefires with Rangoon, the Karen and the KNU continue to feel a redirected and intensification of the Four Cuts as the Tatmadaw face an increasingly smaller number of rivals. The maldevelopment and Burmanizing campaigns have degraded the human condition of the Karen in all spheres of life. Psychologically many Karen have been traumatized. Materially and culturally the Karen are experiencing genocide. The swidden economy of the Karen has virtually been destroyed forcing an increasing reliance upon the informal economy. Four Cuts military offensives against the KNLA continue to erode more liberated areas from Kawthoolei.

> Today, although the KNU have claimed that 2-3 million Karen live in Kawthoolei, the reality is a fraction of that and the territory that the Karen National Liberation Army can to any degree defend consists of little more than a strip of forested hill country stretching for hundreds of miles down the border. There is no front...the 5,000 KNLA soldiers would have to be spaced one every hundred yards to achieve that. Instead, there is a game of cat-and-mouse (with the roles alternating), and points of contact on the main routes through the forest...these the Karen defend ferociously (Falla 1991, 29).

Yet it is important to note that even by 1988, years after the first wave of Four Cuts offensives and despite the government's far superior manpower and resources Mae Tah Waw was "the only important KNLA base to have fallen in years of non-stop fighting" (Smith 1999, 399). Moreover, by October 1988, when intense pro-democracy activities prompted the Tatmadaw to concentrate its troops nearer to Rangoon, the KNLA recapture Mae Tah Waw after a month long assault, aided by a small and newly indoctrinated group of "freedom fighters" consisting of fifty pro-democracy students that had fled Rangoon.

The year 1988 was a fierce year not just for the Karen and the KNU but also for all of Burma's self-determination groups. In October of 1988, battles were reported in the Tenasserim, Sagaing, and Pegu areas. The CPB fought three large battles against the Tatmadaw in the eastern Shan State while the KIO had captured the important Myitkyina-Bhamo road from the Tatmadaw. Every group was "jockeying for position at the end of the rainy season...a near annual, though largely unreported event" (ibid., 19).

By the late 1980s most villages in the plains and in Pa-an and Hlaingbwe districts had succumbed to Tatmadaw forces. As a response, the KNLA, along with about 300 NDF troops comprised of Mon, Arakan, Pa-O, and Wa soldiers increased their defenses at other regional positions such as Klerday, Maw Po Kay, Mae La, and Kawmoorah. Tatmadaw operations into these areas were successfully repulsed and government troops suffer heavy losses. Nevertheless, unlike typical hit-and-run offensives often employed by the Tatmadaw and even though the Tatmadaw were unable to achieve their aims against bases at Klerday, Maw Po Kay, Mae La, and Kawmoorah they "did not retreat but instead remained in the region...a new move in the eastern hills...directly inspired by the successful Four Cuts operations in the Irrawaddy delta" (Fredholm 1993, 113).

The Tatmadaw policy of holding captured territory characterized the four-year fight with the KNLA at Maw Po Kay. Between 1984 and 1989, KNLA and Tatmadaw soldiers often engaged in close-range trench warfare with artillery and sniper fire resulting in hundreds of fatalities on both sides. Furthermore, with the demise of the CPB in 1989, the Tatmadaw was able to shift its focus back toward the ethnic armies. It seizes the KNU/DAB/ABSDF headquarters at Klerday on January 19, 1989. By March of 1989, and after four years of fighting, the KNU base at Maw Po Kay is captured after intense fighting. Phalu and Three Pagoda Pass fall to the Tatmadaw during the same year.

Due to the epic scope of how the Four Cuts campaigns unfolded, I have only discussed Rangoon's logic and rationale for its implementation. The internally colonizing processes and its effects upon the KNU, the KNLA, and civilian Karen—especially the flight, plight and suffering experienced by Karen refugees and IDPs—require us to revisit the Four Cuts in Chapter 3.

B. The 1988 Democracy Crackdown: Effects on the KNU

The 1988 pro-democracy protests and its bloody crackdown on August 8 by the junta have forever been etched into the late twentieth century history of Burma. During this period, democracy activist Aung San Suu Kyi emerges as a formidable political symbol. The events of 1988 also influenced the trajectories of the KNU and the NDF transcommunality, particularly in regard to the generals who succeeded General Ne Win after his resignation from the BSPP. To understand the events of August 8, 1988, we need to depart from the politics of Kawthoolei and begin a year earlier in Rangoon, Burma's former capital.

It is generally agreed that three main factors contributed to the emergence of national democracy sentiments: (1) the September 1987 demonetization of the kyat,[41] (2) the relegation of Burma to Least Developed Country status by the United Nations in December of 1987, and (3) the symbolism of Phone Maw's death.

On Friday, September 5, 1987, Burma's official radio broadcast announced a brief, but for many, a detrimental message:

> The State Council proclaims the following ordinance to have the same force as law. Ordinance No. 1 of 1987: the 25, 35 and 75 Kyat currency notes issued by the Union of Burma Bank will cease to be legal tender as of 11 A.M. on Saturday, September 1987, the 13th day of the waxing moon of Tawthalin, year 1349 of the Burmese calendar (Lintner 1994, 273).

---

[41] Due to inflation, US$ 1.00 was worth 310 kyats in December 1997.

According to Lintner, no reason was given. Yet in one gesture "60 to 80 percent of all money in circulation in Burma had become worthless" (Lintner 1994, 274). The demonetizations of the 25, 35, and 75 kyat notes meant that people's savings were wiped out instantaneously (Fink 2001).[42] The timing could not have been worse:

> Final exams were approaching for the students in Rangoon. This was also when they had to pay their yearly fees and, suddenly, they found that most of their money was valueless (Lintner 1994, 273).

In a portent of events to come, over three hundred Rangoon Institute of Technology students rampaged from their campus to Insein Road where they "smashed traffic lights and burnt government vehicles" (ibid., 273). The students undoubtedly felt trapped and disillusioned under Ne Win's Regime. Perhaps many of their parents or elders reminded them that the kyat had been demonetized before (two years after Ne Win's 1962 coup, the 50 and 100 kyats were demonetized). The reason for demonetization during Ne Win's coup was based on the intention of "removing wealth from foreign hands" (Fink 2001, 32). In 1987, the main reason for demonetization was that it would shrink the profit margin and hopefully bankrupt black marketers. The latter excuse held little validity insofar as they pertained to Burma's insurgents since most of their funds were chiefly in Thai or Chinese currency (Lintner 1994, 274). Insofar as it pertained to the KNU, the demonetization had little, if any effect, on the financial base of the organization's already lucrative liberation ethnodevelopment, derived from its border trading posts.

In December 1987, the United Nations declared Burma as a "Least Developed Country," a distinction shared by impoverished nations such as Chad, Ethiopia, and Nepal. The BSPP regime, embarrassed by this dubious distinction, announced the UN's disclosure to the Burmese population four months later. When the announcement was made "many proud Burmese perceived" the status "as a national insult and a final confirmation of the total failure of twenty-six years of the Burmese Way to Socialism" (ibid., 274). Lintner sums up the overall feelings of the angry Burmese:

---

[42] A rare insight into Ne Win's psychology can be glimpsed here. The awkward numerical scheme for the currency was based on Ne Win's obsession with the astrological significance of numbers, which he "permitted to overshadow national government planning" (Lintner 1994, 274). For example, the 75 kyat note was introduced in Ne Win's 75th year (Smith 1999, 26). Although the 35 and 75 kyat note was introduced in 1985 and 1986 to replace the more logical 100 kyat note, more changes were around the corner. Later in the month of September, two more denominations were issued, the 45 and 90 kyat. The number 45, comprised of 4 and 5, add up to 9, while 90 was a numerologically significant outcome of 9 + 0. The number 9 was Ne Win's lucky number according to Ne Win's chief astrologer (Smith 1999, Lintner 1994).

> Burma was a potentially rich country, not a basket-case like Bangladesh, or a tiny island nation like the Republic of Kiribati—other nations in the region who had won the dubious distinction of being an LDC (Lintner 1994, 274).

Yet by being considered an LDC, Burma qualified to receive aid from international charity—and most likely from "imperialist" nations, a diplomatic irony the autarkic BSPP regime had hoped to avoid. At the time, Burma had an annual per capita income of only $200, debt exceeding $4 billion, and a foreign exchange of less than $20 million.

Due to the protracted civil war in the country, Burma's development was highly asymmetrical: defense spending consumed 40 to 50 percent of the national budget and "equally importantly, the widespread insurgencies continued to deny the government access to many of the areas richest in timber and mineral resources in the entire country" (Smith 1999, 24). By the late 1980s, it was clear that Ne Win's Burmese Way to Socialism was a dismal and total failure. This further reinforced the necessity to plunder through internal colonization the ethnic nationalities' areas, further sustaining a protracted period of internal maldevelopment. Indeed, the Burmese Way to Socialism had caused Burma to "rot in tropical isolation" (Hom 2002).

In the tense months that followed another factor contributed to the instigation of anti-regime protests. It started in, of all places, a Rangoon teashop named after Ne Win's daughter, Sanda Win, and frequented by Rangoon Institute of Technology students (RIT). On March 12, 1988, a brawl over bad music was the catalyst between Rangoon Institute of Technology students and a local drunken youth and his friends. Apparently, the drunken local would not relinquish the teashop's tape that played his preferred tunes to the RIT students, who had a tape ready and were waiting for it to be played. When the drunken local saw the three RIT complain to the store manager, a brawl ensued. The police was informed and the culprit arrested with his friends. The instigator of the brawl was the son of a BSPP official and was thus quickly released the next day.

The news infuriated the RIT students and a political dimension to the event quickly framed their frustrations. More students join the developing furor that soon reaches a crescendo outside the local police station. Five hundred riot police were mobilized. In the ensuing mayhem shots were fired and injured students fell to the ground. One of the demonstrators, Phone Maw, was severely injured and died shortly after. The regime blamed students for inciting the unrest, an accusation that ignited the massive pro-democracy movement across the country.

Within days, students from the RIT and Rangoon University united and organized even larger protests demanding an end to one-party rule. On March 16, at Inya Lake where students were marching soldiers at the front and riot police at the rear stormed the crowd. Unknown numbers of male and female students were clubbed to death, "forty-one suffocated to death in an over-crowded prison van," and "some of the arrested female students were gang raped."

> Some fleeing students made it down alleys and over walls into people's yards. Others ran into the lake with soldiers following them. Some students drowned because they couldn't swim or because they were beaten unconscious by soldiers. Witnesses recalled being horrified to hear the soldiers shouting, 'Don't let them escape!' and 'Kill them!' as they beat the unarmed students (Fink 2001, 51).

Authorities responded by closing the universities for months. By June of 1988, protests including thousands to the tens of thousands of students and sympathizers were already a common sight, as were trigger-happy and tear-gas wielding riot police. Students, civilians, and riot police regularly lost their lives: protests on June 21, 1988, resulted in eighty civilian and twenty riot police deaths, while on June 23 there were seventy deaths in Burma's historic city of Pegu, an hour's drive from Rangoon (ibid., 53). The scope of the protest would fan out from Rangoon, reaching Mandalay, Moulmein, Tavoy, Mergui, Toungoo, Sittwe, Minbu, Pakokku, and Myitkyina (Smith 1999). The main theme of protest and still the main political objective for the vast majority of anti-regime activists to this day, centered on removing Burma's one-party military rule and establishing a multi-party democratic system.

Other emergent political themes revolved around advancing Burma's development. This stance was most candidly expressed by the retired BSPP general Aung Gyi as early as July of 1987 through a series of public letters written to Ne Win. Aung Gyi had finally traveled abroad for the first time in over twenty-five years and was "stunned by the level of economic progress in other South East Asian countries" (ibid., 54). Upon his return, Aung Gyi described Burma's place in the international community as "almost a joke," quickly prompting his arrest by authorities (ibid., 24-25).

General Ne Win, unable to contain the political and economic developments of his country, resigns from power on July 23, 1988. Citing the numerous demonstrations as indicative of people's disapproval of his government, Ne Win suggested a referendum that would allow voters to choose between a one-party and multi-party Burma. The referendum never took place and there were few policy reforms. Instead, General Sein Lwin, a Ne Win loyalist, was chosen to be his successor. Students, and by now, civilians and even Buddhist monks sensing they had achieved at least some positive gains with the resignation of Ne Win, grew more adamant and confident.

University students knew Sein Lwin was Ne Win's protégé. Many Burmans remember Sein Lwin as the "Butcher of Rangoon": in 1962, to quell demonstrations against Ne Win's coup, he ordered troops to fire into university student protestors, killing dozens. He then ordered his troops to blow up the Union building at Rangoon University. For the Karen revolutionaries, however, Sein Lwin's legacy enters the Karen chronology at an earlier period: on August 12, 1950, it was the 27 year-old Maj. Sein Lwin who commanded the coterie that ambushed Ba U Gyi and his party at the outskirts of Taw Kaw Koe village, across the border from the Thai town of Mae Sot. In March 1988, Sein Lwin would reemploy his infamous *modus operandi* that instilled order through bloody crackdowns of protestors. Sein Lwin would again implement this method by August.

Students soon planned for a nationwide protest to take place on August 8, 1988, an auspicious date based on its numerological significance: 8-8-88. The excitement had even trickled down to the rural areas of Burma. By August 4, students all over the country were already denouncing Sein Lwin's regime. Tatmadaw troops were mobilized. By August 8, dock workers, high school students, monks, and virtually all demographics from all areas of Burma had walked out to join the many thousands that had taken to the streets. Later that evening in Rangoon, Tatmadaw troops began their suppression.

The demonstrations would last four days. In the aftermath, close to 3,000 demonstrators were killed in Rangoon, although exact figures will never be known. In other areas across the country killings also took place: in Sagaing 327 protestors lost their lives, in Bassein 30 civilians were killed as police and troops broke up over 5,000 demonstrators. Unable to contain the uprising Sein Lwin quits on August 12, 1988, having been in power for only 18 days.

On August 19, power was handed over to Dr. Maung Maung, a legal scholar and the only non-military official to serve in the BSPP (Fink 2001, Smith 1999). Maung Maung's appointment stopped the shooting temporarily. In a television address, Maung noted, "the fire of anger can be extinguished with the cool waters of love and compassion" (Smith 1999, 5). He proposed an eleven-man commission be established to assess the feasibility of a multi-party democracy, with its representatives touring the country to gauge people's assessment of the prevailing political, economic, and public climate.

On August 22, perhaps sensing a new democratic revival, demonstrations resumed all over the country. This time tens of thousands of demonstrators in Rangoon resumed their nationwide protests for the establishment of a multi-party democracy as well as calling for a nationwide general strike. In the historic northern city of Mandalay over 100,000 demonstrators, including Buddhist monks, took to the streets. Large marches also occurred in Prome, Taunggyi and Moulmein. In Sittwe, 50,000 protestors marched with red banners, the symbolic color for democracy. In distant ethnic states, demonstrators took to the streets by the thousands. In the Shan state over a two-week period "tens of thousands of villagers descended on a small market town which usually contained only a few thousand residents" (Fink 2001, 58). Moreover, in Pa-an, Karen State, Karen and Burmans congregated and marched together. Fink reminds us,

Like villagers in the Shan State, they had been victims of military campaigns and faced far greater difficulties than people living near or in the urban centres of Rangoon and Mandalay (Fink 2001, 58).

By August 24, doctors, lawyers, writers, musicians, actors, army veterans and even government office workers had joined the nationwide protests. In this exciting and celebratory atmosphere, Maung Maung lifted martial law. He set a referendum date of September 12 for voters to decide whether Burma's future government would remain a one-party or multi-party system. The BSPP appeared to be folding, as people power would be displayed all over the country in the following three weeks. Democratic organizations were set up, such as the All Burma Federation of Students Union (ABFSU), which would include up to 50,000 members. Fink describes the summer of 1988 as a period where "civil society emerges" (Fink 2001, 58). Most significantly, during what Smith describes as "democracy summer" various figures of Burma's democracy movement would appear.

The most dramatic emergence was Aung San Suu Kyi, daughter of Aung San. Oxford-educated Suu Kyi had returned to Burma to visit her ailing mother, Daw Khin Kyi, when the former was immersed in its protests. Suu Kyi had emigrated to India in 1960 when her mother was appointed Burma's ambassador to India. Later moving to England, she eventually married an Englishman, Michael Aris, whom she had written to "saying that if her country ever needed her, she would have to go, but that such a scenario had appeared unlikely" (ibid., 60). Although only two years old when her father was assassinated, the political capital from her father's name and through the urging of others, compelled Suu Kyi to emerge from her home and "put out a statement calling for the establishment of an independent committee to oversee multi-party elections" (ibid., 60).

By August 26, 1988, on the gentle slopes beneath the stunning Shwedagon Pagoda, Aung San Suu Kyi would give a speech to over half a million people ecstatically waiting to finally see the daughter of their beloved Aung San. Suu Kyi would become "the instant darling of the crowds and the immediate focus of the Western media's attention" (Smith 1999, 9). Fink notes that Suu Kyi's "eloquence and poise captivated the audience as she urged people not to turn on the army but to seek democracy in a peaceful and unified way" (Fink 2001, 60).

Suu Kyi would soon come to symbolize Burma's longing for democracy through her philosophy of using non-violent means to achieve the goals of the National League for Democracy (NLD), founded by ex-BSPP general U Tin Oo. For many Burmese, Aung San Suu Kyi was the female "reincarnation of Burma's independence hero," Aung San. Moreover, it was her father who had signed the Panglong Agreement with Burma's ethnic nationalities and "he had been one of the few Burman politicians they had ever trusted" (Lintner 1994, 303).

Aung San Suu Kyi was not the only anti-militarist leader that emerged during democracy summer. The 81 year-old U Nu also reemerged on the political scene, along with retired BSPP Brig. General Aung Gyi, the famous critic of Ne Win. However, it is important to note that despite the almost revolutionary gains made by democracy supporters and leaders, Ne Win was still in the background while Maung Maung and the BSPP had yet to relinquish their powers.

With the old guards of the BSPP having retreated to the safety of their homes around the heavily protected Inya Lake suburb, it appeared as though Ne Win's BSPP era had come to an end. Finally, during the September Congress of 1988, 75 percent of party delegates (968 out of 1080) voted for a multi-party system of government. The BSPP appeared to concede and noted that they would be organizing the election. The opposition, on the other hand, demanded the immediate resignation of the BSPP from Burma's government and called for the formation of an interim government to facilitate elections. The BSPP rejected both demands and protestors take to the streets again on September 12.

The warning signs were beginning to be visible. It would be, as Smith correctly noted, the "calm before the storm" (Smith 1999, 14). Little did Burma's population realize that the BSPP was to embark on another incarnation of its militarism: on September 18, 1988, General Saw Maung took control of government and established the State Law and Order Restoration Council (SLORC). By November, in hopes of transitioning from a "socialist centrally-planned to a free market economy" SLORC announces its desires to open more of Burma's market to foreign investment, a line that would be continued under the next atavism of military rule under the State Peace and Development Council (SPDC) (Smith 1994, Chapter 3).

SLORC then began to implement "more draconian measures than Ne Win had ever imposed" (Delang 2000, 12). Saw Maung was a Ne Win and Sein Lwin loyalist and many believed that Saw Maung was being maneuvered politically by Ne Win. With yet another military man in charge, protestors took to the streets en masse. The following days would result in more carnage for democracy supporters. The United Kingdom, the United States, Germany, and Japan denounced the actions of the regime and promptly cut aid to the country.

According to Smith, during the first week following the securing of power by Saw Maung, over 1,000 university students, monks, even schoolgirls, were reportedly killed. Tatmadaw troops even shot into a crowd of 1,000 students peacefully organized outside the United States Embassy, where an amateur cameraman caught the footage and distributed it around the world. Saw Maung described the 500 fatal casualties as looters. There was hand-to-hand combat between student/civilian coalitions and Tatmadaw/government sympathizers. By the end of 1988, estimates place over 10,000 fatalities. Some government troops and agents were also killed. It is unknown how many countless numbers—perhaps hundreds, perhaps thousands—of people went missing. By 1989, the 6,000 NLD supporters and democracy activists who did not flee were already under custody. But students that did make it to the liberated areas of Kawthoolei and other ethnic territories would form a crucial nexus for future democracy activists to finally link with self-determination groups in the hills.

After the Tatmadaw's pro-democracy crackdown of 1988, a new generation of Burmans would go underground to join with self-determination groups fighting the military regime. Those that remained behind would continue to launch sporadic anti-government protests, most of which resulted in bloody crackdowns. In the aftermath of the 1988 pro-democracy crackdown over "10,000 students and civilian activists fled underground into the insurgent-controlled mountains" (Smith 1999, 371). Over 6,000 democracy supporters—many of them Burman, were granted shelter by the KNU in the liberated areas of the Dawna Range, over 2,000 fled to KIO areas while 1,300 were granted refuge by the NMSP.

> After their own brutal treatment by the security forces and the wanton destruction of ethnic minority villages they witnessed on their way, many said they now understood for the first time the die-hard attitudes of veteran insurgent leaders like Bo Mya, Brang Seng, Saw Maw Reh and Nai Shwe Kyin (ibid., 385).

One can only imagine the impression that emerged among the student activists as their epic trek ended in the jungles, mountains, and hills of the liberated areas. Born with BSPP propaganda that described the ethnic nationalists in the mountains as "'bandits', 'renegades' and anti-Burman 'separatists,'" the arrival of the "bedraggled groups" must have been stunned to find "schools, hospitals and the machinery of well-run governments and armies functioning around the ethnic borderlands" (Smith 1999, 383). Indeed, many admitted to being ignorant of the carnage that had befallen the country around them for decades:

> Stunned by the contrast between the brutality of the army in the cities and the unexpected generosity of the 'bandit' rebels in the hills, many young students, including those who had relatives in the army, pledged themselves to work for the betterment of life in the war-torn ethnic minority regions of the country (ibid., 411).

Similarly, the influx of predominantly Burman IDPs to Karen territory must have evoked among the Karen a sense of tragic continuity regarding the misery of those challenging military rule.

Almost immediately, many began to train as soldiers. The new recruits impressed even the most "battle hardened of KNU veterans" (Smith 1999, 17). Skaw Ler Taw notes that "they are really keen to fight...to them there is no other way to destroy military rule and achieve true democracy and peace in the country" (ibid., 17). With NDF backing, a small but determined army was created from democracy students and activists at the KNU base of Kawmoorah on November 5, 1988. The military transcommunality, the All Burma Students Democratic Front (ABSDF: 1988-present) was at the time of its establishment comprised of fifty representatives from 18 student groups. Many of the young cadres would receive intensive military training from the KNU. Almost immediately, ABSDF units were indoctrinated into the fighting. In 1989 Kawmoorah was again attacked by the Tatmadaw, vividly recounted by ABSDF fighter Htun Aung Gyaw:

> We intercepted the enemy transmission line and found out that about 300 Burmese troops were crossing the Moei River to the Thai side and planned to attack from the front line and from the Thai side... KNU commandos and the students crossed the river and guarded the Thai side to prevent this two-pronged attack. Unfortunately, the Thai border guards arrived and told us that we have no right to use Thai soil... They promised us if SLORC used their soil they would not hesitate to force them out of Thailand, initially using an air attack to bomb the intruders... But at dawn our camp was attacked from both the front line and the Thai side. The enemy was taking a position from the Thai market opposite from Kawmoorah. We were waiting for the Thai army to attack the SLORC but in reality the Thai army retreated two kilometers away and watched. One Thai army plane circled around our camp but there was no air attack as they had promised us. The KNU sent the best commandos without hesitation and attacked SLORC troops who were stationed at the Thai market place. Luckily we won the battle, killing 70 enemy soldiers while on our side we lost our 3 best commandos. The colonel who led the Burmese troops fled to the Thai Army and begged for help. He was later escorted by the Thai Army back to Myawaddy (BurmaNet News, February 18, 1995).

By January 1990, over 5,000 ABSDF soldiers had enlisted, divided over 18 battalions. Ten of the battalions, the 201st to the 211th, were in KNU territory.[43]

---

[43] The 101st and 102nd battalions were in NMSP territory, the 303rd battalion in KNPP territory, the 601st was in PNO territory, the 701st and 702nd was in KIO territory in Burma's northeast, the 801st was with the SSNLO, and the 901st was with the NUFA in northwest Burma (Smith 1999, 410).

The students who fled the cities found sanctuary in the ethnic 'liberated zones'... Amidst the hardships of malaria, jungle life and Tatmadaw attacks, students claimed they felt more at liberty in their new home in the hills than they had ever felt in Rangoon and the towns (Smith 1999, 407).[44]

Not all activities with the new arrivals were based on military indoctrination, however. The subsequent meetings held by political dissidents with their hosts revolved around forming an alliance with the ethnic nationalities transcommunality, the NDF. Perhaps the most ambitious project resulting from their dialog was the formation of a parallel government that would compete against Rangoon for legitimacy. At the KNU/NDF headquarters at Klerday on November 18, 1988, the KNU's next transcommunal experiment results in the birth of the Democratic Alliance of Burma, with Bo Mya elected its chairman (DAB: 1988-present). The declared principles of DAB, which includes both Burman and non-Burman representatives are:

1. The removal of the military dictators;
2. The establishment of democratic government;
3. The cessation of civil war and the establishment
   of internal peace;
4. The establishment of national unity and a
   genuine federal union.

Borne from the federalist principles of the NDF and united with democracy activists' calls for the establishment of a multi-party government for Burma, DAB now included Burman and Muslim political constituencies as well politically exiled groups from abroad. The DAB is a result of a political compromise where ethnic nationalists dropped their separatist demands and in return, democracy activists agreed to work toward a federal Burma with autonomy granted to ethnic states. The significance of DAB cannot be underestimated

The forging of ties between ethnic self-determination groups and Burman opposition groups generated a synergistic response against military rule. From this new bond emerged a new political situation where a 'tri-partite' dialogue could be pursued. Lawyers for DAB also designed several drafts of a new federal constitution for Burma.[45] A good example of institutions structurally

---

[44] In January 1989 alone, 80 percent of the 1,000 students at Three Pagoda Pass had malaria. Over a dozen perished and "on any given day, up to a quarter were too ill to train" (Smith 1999, 407-408).

[45] Tri-partite politics in Burma refer to the interaction of the military regime, pro-democracy forces, and ethnic groups.

opposed to each other DAB and SLORC became "two declared governments in the country, each committed to the annihilation of the other" (Smith 1999, 22). Yet more importantly for General Bo Mya and the KNU the formation of DAB and ABSDF (both of which were established in KNU territory), finally succeeded in making the Karen "rebel state" of Kawthoolei the base for the entire pro-democracy and ethnic resistance movements against Rangoon.

C. Problems with the CPB

In March 1986, KNU representative U Soe Aung traveled with eight other NDF delegation members to renew a military alliance with the CPB. Over half a year of trekking through the mountains and engaging in many unnamed battles with the Tatmadaw, the NDF delegation arrived in northern Burma to cement their relationship with the CPB. The NDF delegation would eventually sign a joint military accord with the CPB. Bo Mya rejected this treaty outright in August of 1986. Mya was angered by these developments for two main reasons:

First, Mya had since the 1970s, staunchly maintained his anti-communist stance. Mya was concerned that the hard political, diplomatic, and military gains made against communism in the 1970s was now jeopardized. After all, Mya's rise to power was based on rejecting much of the second phase line held by the KNUP and its alliance with the CPB through the Zin-Zan Agreement of 1952. His concerns were also more than ideological, as it was believed at the time that arms shipment from the West was contingent on the KNU's severing of ties with the CPB and other leftist groups. Second, there was apprehension within the KNU toward any alliances with the Burman-led CPB, the latter which had convinced many ethnic minority soldiers to give their lives to fight Rangoon "racialists" in their name. Moreover, Bo Mya had correctly identified certain CPB units as being involved in "drug-trafficking and 'chauvinism towards the indigenous peoples'" (Smith 1999, 389).

Many facets of Burman chauvinism revolted Bo Mya: despite the diversified ethnic constituency of its People's Army (PA), the CPB leadership was predominantly Burman and its leadership was perceived to carry the same hubris as the militarists in Rangoon. Mya and other nationalist leaders also did not agree with the CPB's dogmatic class analyses that made little room for self-determination politics. Indeed, the CPB leadership still believed that "the national question in Burma is in essence a question of the peasantry" (ibid., 329). Most controversial of the CPB stance, especially as expressed by its leader Thakin Ba Thein Tin and his comrades, was their belief that "there could be no question of a federal union" and that they were "opposed to narrow bourgeois nationalism" despite conceding that Burma's minorities have suffered greatly under Burmese chauvinism (Smith 1999, 328, 363).

Bo Mya and KNU representatives like Skaw Ler Taw, the latter in an interview given to Smith, knew all along that:

> The CPB had a standing order to split nationalist parties. Mao said that in any organization there are three groups: the progressives, the neutrals or moderates, and the conservatives. Like Mao, the CPB's policy was to join with the progressives, win over the neutrals and expel the die hards. We soon realized that this was what the CPB had been trying on us ever since our first meetings in 1952 (Smith 1999, 329).

KNU and NDF members weren't the only group with this insight, however. The slowly emerging nationalist sentiments within the CPB acknowledged what self-determination groups had known all along: the CPB had for decades recruited from local ethnic minorities and adeptly divided these nationalities, forcing them to choose a pro-left (communist) or pro-right (nationalist) path. Those who chose the latter path were either purged or expelled. By 1989, the overriding sentiment by ethnic nationalities fighting for the CPB's People's Army was that they were "being used merely as cannon-fodder in the CPB's unending war with Rangoon" (ibid., 375).

> The CPB had used disastrous, Chinese-inspired human-wave tactics, resulting in huge numbers of deaths. The readiness of the almost exclusively Burman leadership of the CPB to sacrifice its hill-tribe cannon fodder without hesitation reflected its long-standing insensitivity towards the ethnic minorities... Resentment of the old leadership became even more intense than before (Lintner 1994, 294).

As a result, the political move by the NDF during the mid-1980s to accommodate the CPB nearly caused the KNU to leave the NDF. The KNU remained part of the NDF transcommunality, however, despite the remaining ideological split. Nevertheless the tensions did create a political casualty: a frustrated Bo Mya left the presidency of the NDF when his two terms expired in 1987. Saw Maw Reh, president of the KNPP, replaced him.

Bo Mya and other NDF leaders did not have wait long to witness nationalist sentiments burst out of the CPB. Indeed, Mya and other nationalist leaders had for quite some time been anticipating the break-up of the CPB due to its unresolved ethnic problems. Moreover, many CPB members must have been swept up by the democracy movement of 1988, which made the ethnic leadership in the People's Army confront the CPB's own ineffective and ageing leadership, as well as their inability, like Rangoon, to resolve the ethnic, military, economic, and political problems of Burma.

In this regard the CPB was not unlike the various military regimes out of Rangoon: regardless of ideology, Burman-led polities have never been able to gain complete ethnic minority support throughout Burma. Moreover, Rangoon was again offering ceasefire talks with resistance groups and many of the CPB's ethnic recruits began to consider the alternatives.

A series of ceasefires began to take place beginning in 1989. The SLORC, frightened by the resolve of democracy activists as well as feeling for the first time international condemnations for its killing of democracy students and activists, decided to make offers of ceasefires to various NDF members. It, once again, engaged in divide-and-rule tactics by breaking up NDF alliances, and thus, fragmenting the KNU's alliances with other ethnic organizations. In an unprecedented move certain groups were allowed to retain their weapons as well as control territory. The KIO and NMSP benefited from this arrangement by being able to "hold on to its arms...until a new constitution has been agreed" (ICG 2003, 8; Delang 2000, 13). For the United Wa State Party and Army (UWSP and UWSA, respectively) autonomy was granted along with "material support and business opportunities for developing their areas" (ICG 2003, 8).

Meanwhile on May 27, 1989, hundreds of miles away in Rangoon, Saw Maung and the Tatmadaw announce the changing of the country's name to "Myanmar." Myanmar was "simply the historic ethnic Burman name for Burma" and essentially means Burman Country in the Burmese language (Smith 1999, 21).[46] Rangoon was renamed "Yangon."

On June 18, 1989, SLORC abandoned indigenous designations and colonial transliterations of territory and reassigned Burmese designations. The Karen State was changed to the Kayin State, the Karenni—cultural "cousins" of the Karen—had their Karenni State changed to the Kayah State (this reduced the territory and constituency of the Karen by about a third) and the Arakan State was renamed the Rakhine State. There were protests by ethnic nationalists as well as democracy activists. The name changes were viewed by ethnic nationalists as ethnic cleansing while Burmese democracy activists denounced the move as "an act of an illegal regime" (Delang 2000, 13).

Throughout 1989, a series of large defections by the CPB's ethnic minority Wa, Shan and Kokang troops would spell the end of the movement. The speed with which it occurred, however, "took its leadership by surprise" (Smith 1999, 363). The collapse of the CPB is eerily similar to the failure of the Second International during World War I: communist principles were

---

[46] SLORC utilizes astrology once again: May 27 was selected for the renaming of Burma to Myanmar because $2 + 7 = 9$, while the June 18 Burmanization of local names was significant in that $1 + 8 = 9$ (Fredholm 1993, 243). The employment of the number 9, aforementioned as Ne Win's lucky number, was indicative of how the rank and file of SLORC was still very much under Ne Win's influence.

abandoned in favor of nationalist ties. During March 1989 alone, ethnic Kokang and Wa troops of the People's Army seized the CPB's northern headquarters at Mong Ko, eventually allying themselves with leaders in the opium trade, including the figures such as Khun Sa.[47]

During the following months other ethnic units from the CPB People's Army, the Shans, Lahus, Akhas, and Kachins all defected from the CPB. The vestiges of the CPB's 15,000-strong PA began to break up into ethnic factions. The fragmented troops reorganized into five regional resistance armies, "four in Shan State and one in Kachin State" (Brunner et al. 1998). Within a month of the massive defections, the CPB was no more. By the end of 1989 "virtually all the CPB's permanent base areas…had collapsed" (Smith 1999, 375-377). Its remaining 300 leaders and their families were shamefully exiled to China. Delang describes this event as where the CPB "imploded" (Delang 2000).

The SLORC, concerned about the vast arsenal of leftover weapons and its heavily armed troops looking potentially to join with the NDF, began to placate remaining border insurgents. SLORC quickly began forming alliances with former CPB leaders that did not flee to China. Thus no longer worried about Rangoon, former CPB red guards such as U Sai Lin and U Kyi Myint from the eastern Shan State, turned former CPB ethnic factions "into the most heavily armed drug trafficking organization in Southeast Asia, outnumbering and outgunning even the hitherto most powerful opium warlord in Burma, Khun Sa" (Lintner 1994, 299). With the CPB no longer a nemesis, the Tatmadaw redirects their troops toward the central part of the country where demonstrations were frequently still occurring since 1988, as well as to the eastern hills, primarily toward the decreasing areas of Karen territory where many democracy activists had fled. Moreover, on August 10, 1990, the first of a series of weaponry shipments from China arrives in Rangoon. The dawn of the 1990s would see Burma emerge as China's main political and military ally in Southeast Asia.

1990 General Elections Results

The promised general multiparty elections were held on May 27, 1990.[48] Ninety-three political parties emerged to challenge the militarists. In anticipation of the coming multi-party elections the NDF and DAB members warn that election results would be tampered. The DAB drew up a

---

[47] Not all Shan armies were loyal to Khun Sa or were involved in drugs. The Shan State Army, South (SSA-South) is a true Shan nationalist force. It works with the Thai Army to combat opium trafficking and fought fierce campaigns against the military regime and other Shan "sell-outs." Fighting on several occasions has spilled over to Thailand, and in 2001, brought the two countries to the brink of war.

[48] Yet another example of astrological planning: May 27 was selected because 2 + 7 = 9; May 27 was also the *fourth* Sunday in the *fifth* month, once again, 4 + 5 = 9 (Fredholm 1993, 244).

"Provisional Government of Burma" to be headed by Mya, should the election turn out to be a fraud. It was modeled on the "tripartite Khmer coalition" set in place after the fall of the Khmer Rouge and which had United Nations recognition.

Bo Mya also engaged in preemptive diplomacy with Rangoon. In a letter written to Saw Maung on November 30, 1989, of which Smith has a copy, Mya expressed "the sincere goodwill and disposition of the KNU." Mya reminded Saw Maung that "thousands of young Burmans who had taken sanctuary in Kawthoolei since 1988 had been welcomed like their own 'kith and kin'" and that the KNU was thus not involved in a "racial war." Mya further notes, "The experiences of 40 years of civil war have proven beyond a doubt that the civil war, which is basically a political problem, cannot be solved by military means" (Smith 1999, 413). Saw Maung in his January 1990 address to army commanders discussed the details of this letter. However, there would be no resolution on the matter.

On May 27, 1990, in Burma's first multi-party elections since 1960, the SLORC awaited the results that they believed would legitimize their party's stay in power. Since the election field would not include any self-determination groups, their political organizations, or any "students now underground who had led the democracy movement from the beginning," it appeared as though the election results would be foregone conclusion (ibid., 22). Moreover, SLORC had taken a number of extraordinary measures prior to and during the election to further increase their chances of remaining in power.

- Martial law was applied before and during elections;
- Public meetings of more than five people were not allowed (Fink 2001, 67);
- Up until election day, hundreds of different party activists were still imprisoned;
- Aung San Suu Kyi, U Nu, and senior NLD and LDP leaders were under house arrest during the elections;
- International observers and journalists were banned from the country. At the last minute a small group of selected Western journalists was granted permission to enter the country;
- Restrictions on freedom of speech and assembly were enacted with old laws such as the 1950 Emergency Measures Act, the 1962 Printers and Publishers Registration Law, and the 1975 State Protection Law (which justified Aung San Suu Kyi and U Nu's house arrest);
- All party publications were censored, distribution of party literature possible only after approval by Home Ministry (Smith 1999; Fink 2001, 67);
- All 93 parties, representing 2,311 candidates were restricted to "one pre-

approved ten-minute statement on television and fifteen minutes on state radio";

- All existing party emblems were banned (religious symbols, astrological signs and pictures of animals, people and weapons were prohibited);[49]
- The SLORC propaganda machine and officials warned its citizens that "communist, rightist and foreign demons waiting in the wings to seize power if any other party should win" (Smith 1999, 412-414).

Indeed, SLORC's hubris even resulted in their rejection of the NDF's proactive attempts to offer ceasefire talks with Rangoon. In hopes of limiting the playing field so that the Tatmadaw would have all the necessary political advantages, how shocking it must have been when the election results clearly revealed that over 70 percent of 20.8 million registered voters in Burma desired democracy and change: Aung San Suu Kyi's NLD captures over 83 percent of the parliamentary vote (392 out of 474 parliamentary seats), resulting in a "crushing" defeat for the National Unity Party (NUP), the party of the militarists, which wins only 2 percent, or eleven seats. Moreover, NLD allies win 15 percent of the vote, and if one were to combine their numbers with the NLD, an overwhelming 98 percent of the parties have rejected militarism in one way or another (Fink 2001, 68; Lintner 1994, 378; Earth Rights International 1996).

SLORC's miscalculation backfired: it had anticipated winning the election and subsequently co-opting NLD members into the fold. The astounding NLD victory made this impossible. Adding insult to injury, thousands of soldiers and ex-BSPP members along with their families had voted for the NLD, as indicated by the NLD's wining of seats in predominantly military-districts of Rangoon. Neither did other pro-democracy old guards do well: U Nu's LDP won no seats while Aung Gyi's UNDP won only one seat (Fink 2001, Smith 1999, Lintner 1994). The United States, Australia, the United Kingdom, as well as many countries in Europe celebrated the outcome. Even the Chinese ambassador in Rangoon "personally congratulated the NLD on its victory and called for the release of Suu Kyi, saying his government wished to see 'national reconciliation in Burma'" (Smith 1999, 414). Amazingly, even the now shunned CPB announced their support for Aung San Suu Kyi and the NLD after their victorious 1990 elections.

Two months after the elections, Aung San Suu Kyi and her cadres in the NLD continued to demand a transfer of power to the new democratic government. Then Military Intelligence Service (MIS) chief, Khin Nyunt, begins to mastermind SLORC delaying tactics: after initially waiting six weeks to announce election results, SLORC further imposed a two-month

---

[49] According to Smith, "parties were forced to choose their insignia from a proscribed list of new items" which included an inspiring array of symbols such as "beach balls, combs, tennis rackets and umbrellas" (1999, 412).

moratorium for defeated candidates to lodge complaints. The regime then suggested a national convention would have to be created to draw up plans for a new constitution. Elected representatives would need time to write up the constitution which would require approval by military authorities. Finally, people would have to approve this via a referendum. The adoption of a new constitution was then promised, but no official date was assigned. There would be "no quick power transfer" due to the complicated process, says General Saw Maung (Lintner 1994, 379).

By the early 1990s three important forces competed for power: the SLORC and Tatmadaw, the NLD which by now claimed a mandate to rule Burma from its 1990 election results, and DAB. Meanwhile, Amnesty International releases reports estimating that 6,000 people have been arrested since 1988 and over 100 people have been sentenced to death by the regime's military tribunals. Even by September of 1990, Aung San Suu Kyi had yet to be released from house arrest. Arrests continue throughout the country. The military regime remained ensconced in Burma's immediate future and the KNU at the end of the 1980s was "struggling for its very survival" (Smith 1999, 440).

Bo Mya and the KNU in the 1990s: New Challenges

Observers such as Smith note that the role that Bo Mya played in the early 1990s was that of maintaining a sense of coherence among war-fatigued Karen in the impoverished regions of the eastern hills. Mya was also continuing the fight against the Tatmadaw, as well as engaging in transcommunal politics from the KNU headquarters at Manerplaw, or Victory Field.

Between January and May 1990 the NDF, mostly comprised of NMSP, KNU, and student-turned-soldiers of the ABSDF, launch counter-offensives against Tatmadaw lines, cutting it at various areas. Nevertheless, Tatmadaw forces experience victories in January 1990 by seizing the Karen base of Thay Baw Bo, which sheltered hundreds of Burmese dissident students, and Walay near the Thai border. In March 1990, NMSP and ABSDF troops attack the coastal town of Ye. Later in the year mostly 400 KNU commandos and ABSDF troops struck Papun, Yebyu, Bilin, Mokpalin and Kyaikto. At Kyaikto, only 65 miles northeast of Rangoon, the Tatmadaw's 9th Light Infantry Regiment headquarters was seized (Smith 1999, Fredholm 1993).

The KNU was even on the offensive even during the rainy-season, launching "hundreds of small and large-scale guerilla operations across Kawthoolei" (Smith 1999, 413). The Burma Air Force often intervened to provide cover for surrounded Tatmadaw troops, saving them from disaster. The Burma Air Force also begins bombing Manerplaw on April 10. From October 8-10, 1991, KNLA fighters clash with Tatmadaw in the town of

Bogale at the mouth of the Irrawaddy delta southwest of Rangoon, and far from the eastern hills. Tatmadaw forces use aircraft and boats in the battle.

Two important features need to be noted regarding the loss of KNU bases during the late 1980s and early 1990s. First was the complicity of the Thai military in making conditions advantageous for the Tatmadaw: General Chaovalit frequently allowed Tatmadaw troops to enter Thai territory to attack vulnerable KNU positions. This is how Klerday and Maw Po Kay were eventually lost in 1989. Similarly, Phalu and Three Pagodas Pass were lost in this way in 1990. The Karen base of Kawmoorah was also attacked in this manner but the KNLA was able contain Tatmadaw advances though the neighboring Thai town of Wangkha was completely destroyed. On January 24, 1990, the Karen base of Thay Baw Bo, which sheltered hundreds of Burmese democracy activists and students, was destroyed by the Tatmadaw. Over six thousand students, activists, and villagers fled to Thailand.

Second, the late 1980s also included clashes between erstwhile allies, the Mon and Karen. Thus, it is important to remember that the Mon and KNU clashes, specifically in the 1988 where territorial disputes erupted into warfare, "served as an important reminder that racial tensions in Burma are not simply an ethnic minority/Burman majority issue" (Smith 1999, 388). Moreover, with the demise of the CPB in 1989, the Tatmadaw was able to shift its focus back toward the ethnic armies. As aforementioned, it seizes the KNU/DAB/ABSDF headquarters at Klerday on January 19, 1989. By March of 1989 and after four years of fighting, the KNU base at Maw Po Kay is captured.

By having played his role in the NDF and DAB, as well as cooperating with the NLD, Mya reconfigures his strategic options with his "bulldog brand of nationalism" that exerted a "powerful pull" (Smith 1999, 388). In late 1990 at Manerplaw, Bo Mya allows over a dozen members of Parliament who escaped Rangoon after the pro-democracy crackdown to establish a government in exile, the National Coalition Government Union of Burma (NCGUB: 1990-present). NCGUB leaders have been accepted by Switzerland and Norway and both governments have given aid to the NCGUB government (Latimer, Hill, Bhumpakkaphan and Fehr 1992). The NCGUB consists of individuals legitimately elected to the People's Assembly but still not recognized by the military regime.

Members of the NCGUB pledged to work with the NDF and DAB to bring forth democracy to Burma even though there was often tension with its ethnic nationality hosts (Smith 1999, 434). Furthermore, on February 14, 1991, the KNU welcomes the NLD to set up an office at the KNU headquarters of Manerplaw as the NLD-Liberated Areas government (NLD-LA). The members of parliament that defected from the regime, along with other NLD activists, joined together to manage the NLD-LA office. According to Silverstein (1981), Manerplaw became the "border area capital."

For Smith, Manerplaw and Rangoon represented one of the "two centres of politics in Burma" (1999, 442).

On October 14, 1991, Aung San Suu Kyi is awarded the Nobel Peace Prize. However, because of her house arrest, Aung San Suu Kyi's eldest son Alexander accepts the Nobel Peace Prize in Oslo, Norway, on her behalf. In Rangoon, thousands of Rangoon University students celebrated by shouting anti-SLORC slogans. SLORC responded in the usual way by arresting 900 students. International recognition had once again centered on Aung San Suu Kyi, the protracted nature of Burma's warfare, the suffering of its ethnic minorities, as well as the refugee crises it generated. As a result, the SLORC rank and file began to suffer under the strain.

In a symbolic moment for democracy, SLORC chairman General Saw Maung—perhaps tormented by his legacy, cracks under pressure. By the end of 1991, Saw Maung's behavior was highly erratic, his public speeches "incoherent and rambling, covering subjects such as dying tomorrow and Jesus in Tibet" (Lintner 1994, 321). Once again, Lintner's vivid account of Saw Maung's journey toward a nervous breakdown is worth recounting.

> The deterioration of his health became obvious on 21 December 1991, when he was going to be the first to tee-off at a tournament at the military golf course in Rangoon. In front of the Burma Army's top brass and government officials, Saw Maung began screaming: "I am King Kyansittha!" Patting his holstered pistol, he warned onlookers to be "careful" or "I will personally kill you."

> His references to one of the kings of ancient Pagan empire was especially eccentric. Kyansittha, a powerful king whose name means "the remaining soldier" or "the one who was left behind," was the main character in a Moses-like story of a man who survived attempts on his life to become king. Saw Maung may have seen himself as the only SLORC member who also served with the pre-1988 regime (ibid., 321).

Despite talk that Saw Maung's demise might reinvigorate democracy politics, on December 28, 1991, General Khin Nyunt vehemently states that SLORC will "never accept" Aung San Suu Kyi or the NLD (Lintner 1994, 381). Khin Nyunt might have reconsidered his intransigence a month later when Saw Maung's performance was repeated, this time on television as he addressed SLORC officials. Apart from his repeated association with Kyansittha and Buddhistic themes,

> Saw Maung exclaimed in the middle of his speech: "Today our country is being ruled by martial law. Martial law means no law at

all...I always work with caution, perseverance and wisdom. Wisdom does not mean black magic" (Lintner 1994, 321).

Bo Mya did not have time to be amused with Saw Maung's detachment from reality. Mya was busy at the KNU capital of Manerplaw attending to the logistics of administering Kawthoolei and its free politics. Indeed by 1992, Manerplaw had become the democratic headquarters for all anti-government alliances and had gained international recognition as the site for democracy and freedom politics. In January 1992, the Tatmadaw launches a large Four Cuts offensive against the important KNU-NDF-DAB headquarters at Manerplaw as well as Kawmoorah, resulting in massive fighting with KNLA along the Thai border. Designated "Operation Dragon King," the Tatmadaw deployed between 10,000 to over 20,000 troops even though Lintner describes many as being ill-trained teenagers. Orders were for Manerplaw to be seized before March 27, Burma's Armed Forces' Day. Lintner notes:

> More than ten thousand government soldiers were mobilized for the campaign, and thousands of civilians were...forced to become porters. Almost the entire Bangkok press corps flocked to Manerplaw to watch the comparatively small rebel group resist the onslaught of the mighty Burma Army—with all its new Chinese equipment (Lintner 1994, 322).

The Tatmadaw seized the key forward position at Manerplaw, a series of craggy limestone crags known as Tipawicho, or "Sleeping Dog" Hill, on March 14, 1992, after three months of intense fighting. The Tatmadaw, however, failed to capture Manerplaw itself. Tatmadaw artillery that had been positioned atop Tipawicho but their 120mm Israeli Soltam mortars managed a range of only nine kilometers and thus was unable to reach Manerplaw, twelve kilometers away (Lintner 1994). There were at least 1,000 fatalities and at least 2,000 wounded in what Smith describes as "the greatest set-piece battle ever witnessed along the Burma-Thailand frontier" (Smith 1999, 425). Bo Mya and the KNU hold victory celebrations. The KNLA and ABSDF's defense of Manerplaw had been "the most stunning in many years" (Smith 1999, 444).

> The world media was full of stories of the heroic Karen rebels defending their base, interviews with female porters who had been raped, and pictures of burning villages (Lintner 1994, 322).

On April 23, 1992, the mentally dysfunctional General Saw Maung was forced to resign in favor of deputy General Than Shwe, who becomes SLORC's new strongman on April 24, and still remains in power at the time of this writing.

Than Shwe immediately begins to repair Burma's image amidst the international criticism directed against Saw Maung's brutal 1991 Four Cuts campaign against the Muslim Rohingyas of Arakan State.[50] In the campaign, the Tatmadaw also crossed into Bangladesh to attack a Bangladeshi army outpost. One border guard and three civilians are killed, but nearly 260,000 Muslims flee into Bangladesh, creating a humanitarian disaster. Than Shwe was undoubtedly nervous about the criticism directed at the regime from a furious Prince Khaled Sultan Abdul Aziz, the commander of Saudi forces in the 1991 Gulf War. After Aziz visited Dhaka and witnesses the humanitarian crisis that had befallen Rohingyas, he proposes a "Desert Storm" response to Burma, "just like what the UN did to liberate Kuwait" (Lintner 1994, 383).

The Tatmadaw also suspend operations against the KNLA and begin withdrawing troops from the frontlines at Manerplaw in the name of "national solidarity...although Sleeping Dog Hill and other forward positions which had been captured...were not abandoned" (Lintner 1994, 323). Rangoon didn't have to do any favors for the KNU however. At Manerplaw on July 31, 1992, to show the world that democracy and the Karen had prevailed, the important Manerplaw Agreement was signed by the NDF, DAB, NCGUB and NLD to further continue and promote a political platform for a federal Burma.

Resulting from the Manerplaw Agreement, another transcommunality designed to "streamline inter-party organisation" was born during August 1992: the umbrella organization known as the National Council of the Union of Burma (NCUB: 1992-present) was led by prominent leaders such as Bo Mya, Dr. Sein Win (Aung San Suu Kyi's cousin and former university mathematics lecturer), Brang Seng, and Nai Shwe Kyin. The NCUB was comprised of representatives from the NDF, NLD-Liberated Areas, and DAB, as well as pro-democracy members of parliament from the Members of Parliament Union (MPU) (Smith 1999, 444).

To prevent any further embarrassment to the regime, Than Shwe and SLORC implement reforms: Bangladesh and SLORC agree to the repatriation of Rohingya refugees despite cries of refoulement by international watchdog organizations.[51] SLORC also releases political prisoners. Than Shwe agrees to a National Convention and a new

---

[50] Rohingyas are the Muslims of the Arakan ethnic nationality group. The Buddhist Arakans are known as the Rakhines. Their territory straddles the Bangladesh border and Arakans make up about 4 percent of Burma's population. As mentioned in Chapter 1, The *Mujahid* Party, Burma's first Muslim resistance army, was formed in 1947, the same year as the KNU (Fredholm 1993, Lintner 1994).

[51] Human Rights Watch/Asia (HRW/A) defines refoulement as expelling or returning a refugee "in a manner whatsoever to the frontiers of territories where his or her life or freedom would be threatened on account of race, religion, nationality, membership of a particular social group or political opinion" (HRW/A, July 1997, 4). In the context of Burma's refugee crisis, a policy of refoulement, then, is when a government forcefully repatriates refugees back to where they initially attempted to escape from.

constitution for Burma. He even allows Aung San Suu Kyi's husband, Michael Aris and her two sons to visit in Rangoon. Universities were reopened and SLORC holds talks with the NLD. Journalists were invited back into Burma. On April 27, 1992, Than Shwe orders Maj. General Maung Hla, overall commander of the offensive against the Karen, to suspend operations along the Thai border. Manerplaw is temporarily spared.

Lintner claims that SLORC displayed goodwill gestures because it "could afford a few concessions" to various opposition groups. Lintner claims that this is primarily due to the mini-boom in free enterprise markets that were slowly emerging in Burma. In the early 1990s, SLORC had begun border trade with China in earnest. Thailand's concern that China could monopolize Burma's vast resources and emerging markets compelled the former to court the regime economically, engaging in lucrative logging enterprises with SLORC (See chapter 5).

However, another consideration must be Aziz's denunciation of the regime. Certainly SLORC did not want to incur the wrath of the United States and the European Community. Sensing that Thailand was already politically at the behest of the United States and fully aware that the US had nominally and indirectly backed the Karen via the KMT in the past, a two-pronged democracy "squeeze" from India and Thailand led by the West may have appeared highly plausible to the paranoid SLORC leadership.

Rangoon made three attempts to hold a national convention in 1993. The first attempt takes place on January 9 but is suspended after two days. On February 1, it is reconvened. Its third meeting in June was also not successful due to the Tatmadaw's demands that the army be guaranteed a role in shaping Burma's politics. It insists on having 25 percent of all parliamentary seats reserved for Tatmadaw members and that elected leaders must have military and political experience—which by definition discredits Aung San Suu Kyi's credentials. Burmese citizens married to "foreigners" are banned from holding office, once again, another condition which disqualifies Suu Kyi. By September of 1993, the third attempt at holding a national congress was adjourned because the Tatmadaw would not accept ethnic nationality parties' insistence on a federal system.

During 1993, the scope of Burma's civil war had attracted attention abroad. Over eight Nobel Peace Prize laureates, including the Dalai Lama and South Africa's Desmond Tutu, visit Thailand. Tutu and other laureates visit Karen refugee camps inside Thailand and call for Aung San Suu Kyi's release. Realizing the futility of negotiating with the regime Bo Mya travels internationally to pitch the Karen and democratic cause. Bo Mya would himself visit the United States during July of 1993 and hold talks with Department Officials. During October 1993, Mya visits London. His international trips would occur during a lull before renewed political and military developments would challenge KNU resolve again.

A. DKBA and the Fall of Manerplaw

A serious defection from the KNU, one that would have damaging consequences for the organization, occurs in December of 1994. U Thuzana, a Buddhist monk and strict vegetarian from Myaing Gyi Ngu monastery near Pa-an, along with over 1,000 Buddhist Karen decide to join SLORC as the Democratic Karen Buddhist Organization (DKBO) and the Democratic Karen Buddhist Army (DKBA). U Thuzana cited complaints by Buddhist Karen in the KNLA that they had suffered discrimination by the Christian KNU leadership. Their main grievance was that Buddhist Karen in the KNLA were rarely promoted and most were sent to the frontlines "without respite" (Rajah 2002, 535).

By the 1980s, many Buddhist Karen were frustrated with the disproportionate numbers of Buddhists who went and stayed at the frontlines for months, while the Christian KNU rank and file was "living a relatively comfortable existence by the river in Manerplaw" (Rogers 2004, 144). Indeed, for many years prior to the fall of Manerplaw, 80 percent of new KNLA recruits and two-thirds of the frontline soldiers were Buddhist. Exacerbating this inconsistency was that two-thirds of the senior officers at Manerplaw were Christian (Rogers 2004, 144). Min Zaw Oo, a Burman student that had fled to KNU areas after 1988, tells Rogers:

> There was no big animosity between Christians and Buddhists in the villages. The source of the problem was the distribution of wealth and power among the Karen. The remedy would have been to distribute resources wisely and proportionately. Through teak deals, many of the senior Karen Christian officers grew rich, while the front line troops remained poor (ibid., 144).

Colonel Nerdah Mya sums up the consequences of this division: "Once the SPDC see a crack in the opposition, they make it bigger" (ibid., 144).

During December 1994, U Thuzana ordered about 30 of his followers to block boat traffic at the confluence of the Moei and Salween rivers. Since the KNU utilized this part of the region to exact a tax on all goods crossing it, U Thuzana's actions were considered a direct challenge to KNU authority. Moreover, U Thuzana had arrested five Christian soldiers and demanded their conversion to Buddhism. The soldiers refused and were summarily executed after being tortured. U Thuzana then took eight boats to Manerplaw and demanded the disarmament of the KNLA; an intense firefight ensued (ibid., 148).

Sensing the implications of this defection the KNU sends a delegation of 16 officials to negotiate with U Thuzana on December 7, 1994. A Thai monk volunteered as an independent observer. Seven of the negotiators were then seized as hostages, only to be released. Although a tense agreement was reached, it was abandoned on December 28 when U Thuzana's men looted and stole from Thai and Karen boats navigating the regional rivers. By now U Thuzana and the DKBA had declared their resignation from the KNU on grounds of religious discrimination suffered by Buddhist Karen (Rogers 2004, 148-149). This was the last straw for the KNU. On January 3, 1995, the KNU declares war on the DKBA and DKBO.

For some time, the KNU had believed that U Thuzana had conspired with SLORC and that he was a SLORC spy. Indeed, just over a week before the coming second Manerplaw offensive the KNU claimed that SLORC was trying to incite a religious split in the organization (Lertcharoenchok 1995). In this regard, observers note that the Tatmadaw's second attempt to capture Manerplaw, unlike its first attempt in 1992, was based on infiltrating the Buddhist contingent of the KNLA and stirring up animosity against the Christians in the KNLA. What is known is that U Thuzana, Karen Buddhist mutineers, and fellow monks did meet for one hour on January 2, 1995 with the Tatmadaw Southern Command Chief, Maj. General Maung Hla and his 20-member entourage. The meeting was held at Myaing Gyi Ngu headquarters of the Karen defectors, located about 30 miles southwest of Manerplaw on the eastern banks of the Salween River.

According to the late Padoh Mahn Sha, a close adviser to Bo Mya, Maung Hla had promised to support the DKBA with food, money, weapons, development projects, and peace provided U Thuzana recruit more Buddhist Karen to leave the KNU.[52] In Lertcharoenchok's interview Mahn Sha noted that Tatmadaw General Maung Hla "told the mutineers [if they capture the KNU headquarters] they would be allowed to occupy Manerplaw. He also promised them the Karen State, peace and development projects in the area" (Lertcharoenchok 1995). Additionally, Maung Hla persuaded U Thuzana to recruit Buddhist Karen directly from the refugee camps, stir up rumors about anti-Buddhist discrimination, and if need be, kidnap prominent Buddhist Karen working for the KNU. Returning Buddhist Karen would then be given a one-year's supply of food. Now that old allies have become new enemies, the DKBA in alliance with the Tatmadaw was able to reinvigorate the latter's three year-old offensive against Manerplaw.

Although 1,000 soldiers may seem a small number compared to what the Tatmadaw could muster, it should be remembered that U Thuzana's Karen had previously fought side-by-side with the KNLA, and are as much experts at guerilla warfare as the their Christian brethren. Moreover, the DKBA provided the Tatmadaw with crucial intelligence regarding where the landmines were placed and was able to lead the Tatmadaw through the minefields that surrounded the capital (Rajah 2002, 531). Thuzana's DKBA,

---

[52] Padoh Mahn Sha was assassinated on February 14, 2008, at his home in Mae Sot, Thailand, by defectors working for the SPDC.

with the support of many Tatmadaw battalions, engaged the KNLA in battle. After three years of intermittent attempts at capturing the Kawthoolei's capital, Manerplaw falls on January 27, 1995.[53] Moreover six other bases to the north and south of the Karen capital are also captured by the Tatmadaw (Rogers 2004, 149).

In a lightning strike against KNU headquarters, the Tatmadaw generated over 10,000 refugees and pushed them across to Thailand. The KNLA force of 15,000 quickly dwindled to about "a third of its size, through defections and widespread resignation by disillusioned soldiers," and 4,000 KNLA troops reach the border as refugees (Rogers 2004, 149). Retreating KNLA guerillas blew up their own Law Wa Dee command post as well as Ba U Gyi's statue to keep them from being seized and denigrated. According to the Karen Human Rights Group (KHRG 1995):

> The day that Burmese troops arrived in Manerplaw, they immediately began a mortar barrage against Thai territory on the other side of the Moei River as a form of 'pursuit' of the Karen soldiers who had withdrawn to Thailand and disarmed themselves (ibid., 1995).

There was also shelling of Thai positions and "Thai soldiers from Task Force 35 had already been flown in to take up positions to secure their border" (ibid., 1995).

The capture of Manerplaw, the "last stronghold of democracy in Burma," was a severe setback for the Karen struggle and to a large extent, the democracy movement that fled to the area after 1988 (Rogers 2004, 144). For over twenty one years, Manerplaw was an important trading post and military base as well as being the main liberated area where a host of transcommunalities were formed. By the early 1990s, members of pro-democracy forces such as DAB, NDF, NLD-LA and NCGUB considered Manerplaw home. Whereas in 1992, the KNU/KNLA and their transcommunal allies successfully defended Manerplaw to sustain their revolution, in 1995, they had to destroy it so that their resistance would survive. It was a defining moment for the revolutionary potential of the KNU.

Four days later on January 31, the KNU releases a powerful and poignant statement regarding the fall of Manerplaw:

> The fall of Manerplaw, the KNU military headquarters, is not the end of the Karen Revolution. We will keep fighting until democracy is achieved in Burma and ethnic minority groups are free from

---

[53] The Tatmadaw still claims that the fall of Manerplaw was due to the DKBA split from the KNU. By this account the military engagement was an internal matter among rival factions within the KNU.

oppression. When we started the revolution over 40 years ago, we knew that there would be setbacks. Today we have lost the battle, but we will never lose the war. This is because as human beings, we all need freedom. Without freedom, there is no point in living. The Karen will continue to fight until we achieve freedom, no matter how many years that will take.

At this point, there are close to 10,000 refugees in three different areas on the Thai side of the border across from Manerplaw. There are also Karen refugees who are fleeing to Thailand near Mae Sot and Kanchanaburi. These refugees were able to bring only a few things with them, and within a week they will be short of food. The refugees urgently need food and medical supplies. Please send any contributions you can as soon as possible. Thank you.[14]

The KNU and KNLA guerillas would continue their fight but the capture of Manerplaw meant that the Karen struggle would have to transform its political and military strategies. By February 1995, the KNU instituted the Basic War Casualty Management Training Program as well as the two month-long Guerilla Rifleman Course for ABSDF trainees. By the end of August 1995, KNU members had participated in elections during the Eleventh KNU Congress that resulted in the election of General Tamalabaw as KNU Chief of Staff.

General Tamalabaw replaced Bo Mya after the latter failed to rally the KNU to hold on to Manerplaw. Concern was also raised about defections and the war fatigue among the soldiers. Delegates at the meetings, however, agree that they have not deterred the KNU from aiming for greater autonomy and the formation of a federal union. Nevertheless, the KNU accepts offers by the regime for ceasefire talks during this period, which are ultimately unsuccessful.

Manerplaw was not the only important KNU base and trading post seized. Other important trading posts and bases along the Thai border such as Kawmoorah, near the Thai border town of Mae Sot and roughly 240 miles northwest of Bangkok, and large adjoining areas in northern Kawthoolei were also captured.

The battle for Kawmoorah was fierce, transcommunally involving over 1,000 heavily armed KNLA and ABSDF troops and between 1,500 to 3,000 Tatmadaw troops, including an additional 300 DKBA soldiers (Rogers 2004, 150; Burma Net, February 8, 1995). The KNU had intercepted a Tatmadaw radio conversation between their artillery officers and commander expressing frustration as to why 40,000 artillery shells had not weakened the KNLA defenders at Kawmoorah (Rogers 2004, 151).

About 50 Tatmadaw troops tried to swim across the Moei to attack Kawmoorah from the rear but were repulsed by the KNLA and the Thai Army monitoring the fighting from Thailand. Nevertheless, over 150 rounds landed on the Thai side of the border during the assault and Thai forces, determined to keep the conflict off Thai soil, "fired warning smoke shells and later live rounds towards Burmese positions" (Birsel 1995). Some Tatmadaw troops were trapped at a horse-shoe-shaped loop in the Moei River which forms the border with Thailand. The KNLA then closed in, eliminating over 80 troops while it lost three KNLA soldiers.

Tatmadaw reinforcements were called in and instructed to seize Kawmoorah at all costs. Kawmoorah continued to be shelled without respite between January 30 and February 21, 1995. On February 21, the Karen and their allies relinquish Kawmoorah. Thai officials monitoring the fighting in Burma noted more than 800 mortar rounds and 1,500 rounds of gunfire daily, as well as 600 explosions at Kawmoorah in just a two-day period.

By the end of October 1996, the KNLA engaged in battle with 100 troops of SLORC's Battalion 257 near the border opposite Umphang district of Thailand's Tak province. Bo Mya notes at the end of 1996: "Along the border has been more or less quiet, but further inside there is always fighting…in the districts of Toungoo, Nyaunglebin, Thaton, Papun and Mergui/Tavoy" (Bangkok Post, December 8, 1996).

With the fall of Manerplaw and Kawmoorah, the KNU reestablishes its new headquarters in the Duplaya area of the 6th brigade. There, its rank and file would reconsider the merits of having relied on set-piece tactics and conventional warfare. They soon decentralize into smaller mobile guerilla units and return to the exclusive deployment of guerilla warfare. Furthermore there would be the dismantling of unnecessary military bases that could become sitting targets for Burmese security forces (Kasem 1997).

Although even more of the remaining Karen territory had to be conceded when adopting guerilla tactics, the relatively simpler logistics and mobile approach to fighting meant that the KNU could still carry on the fight. Even before the fall of Manerplaw, KNLA Maj. Walter had noted that guerilla war is a kind of war that the KNLA could wage "indefinitely" (Smith 1999, 413). Bo Mya still reinforces this position after the fall of Manerplaw. In an interview given to Ralph Bachoe of *Bangkok Post* on December 8, 1996, Bachoe asks Mya:

> *Bachoe.* Two years ago because of the dry season offensive the KNU lost Manerplaw and Kawmoorah, and you now have a new base. If there is one, how prepared is the KNU to defend the areas they still control?

Mya: We are well prepared to face a SLORC major offensive. We will employ guerrilla warfare tactics. And we can carry that on forever, and unless we surrender, there can be no defeat.

The DKBA continues to be an inimical threat to the KNLA but their effects are most deadly for unarmed Karen villagers. As we shall see in the Chapter 3, the DKBA would contribute to the refugee population in Thailand by attacking Karen refugee camps inside the country, claiming that the camps functioned as rear support bases. Thais along the border have died as a result. Up until mid-2003, fighting still occurred between the KNU and DKBA. By the late 1990s three more KNU units and a number of second-line leaders would surrender to Rangoon.

B. *Ceasefires*

The situation with the NDF transcommunality was also bleak as Rangoon's divide and rule tactics were able to lure away NDF members and non-NDF allies, some of whom were allies of the KNU. Between 1989 and 1991, the Shan State Progressive Party (SSPP), the Palaung State Liberation Party (PSLP), and the United Pa-O National Organization (UPNO) abandon the fight and sign ceasefires with Rangoon. By 1994, after holding a series of talks with Rangoon, the powerful Kachin Independence Organization (KIO) and its Kachin Independence Army (KIA) sign a ceasefire with the Tatmadaw. The Kayan New Land Party (KNLP) does the same within the year.

The NMSP, the last group to sign a ceasefire in 1995, appears to have relatively negative assessment of their ceasefire situation. Chan Du of the NMSP's Foreign Affairs Department noted that although there is no more fighting and movement of villagers are now freely permitted in certain Tatmadaw-controlled areas, over 8,000 acres of Mon land have been confiscated (Mon illegal migrations to Thailand has been one consequence of the land seizures) and there are more Tatmadaw troops in their state.

According to the KNU Joint General Secretary, David Tharckabaw, another damaging consequence of ethnic groups having signed ceasefires is their need to accept the Tatmadaw ban on political organizing. A decline in recruits along with the capacity to directly attend to the interests of their constituents is another consequence (Wechsler 2003). Since ethnic nationality groups sign ceasefires to embark on a purely political path to achieve their aims, a snub from Rangoon usually means that the groups' political agendas are not honored in good faith. As Chan Du noted eight years after the signing of the ceasefire:

We, the NMSP, constantly request the regime to start working on the political agenda, but up to now we have not received any practical response from the SPDC. We are disappointed to wait so long during the ceasefire period (Wechsler 2003).

All the aforementioned groups would subsequently be expelled from the NDF and DAB. The Wa and Kachin ceasefires deserve more mention.

In 1989, the United Wa State Army (UWSA) decided to throw in their lot with Rangoon. At one time, the UWSA had a self-determination army 15,000-strong fighting for the CPB that controlled the Wa hills in northern Shan State. Currently it experiences some autonomy and nominally accepts the military government, but has since been harnessed by the junta to engage in opium production.

The UWSA is one of the largest drug cartels in the world today. "The Wa have become a buffer for producing drugs in Burma and receive the blame from the rest of the world for it, instead of the Burmese regime itself," notes Pastor Lah Thaw. Indeed, most of the opium production in Burma is "under control of the armed groups who have had verbal ceasefire agreements with the Burmese government since 1989, as well as with different militias in the areas that enjoy partial or full autonomy" (Bangkok Post, February 1, 2004).

Attempts by local authorities to substitute opium with other cash crops have been met with little success, as it is hard to find markets for alternate crops. Furthermore, the price may not be enough for the average farmer to survive on. Opium production has since been supplemented with methamphetamines, particularly ecstasy, because "they are cheaper to produce and easier to smuggle than heroin" (Kaopatumtip and Wechsler 2004, 6). As a result, the Wa business sector is still highly dependent on drugs for their financial survival. According to the International Crisis Group (ICG), Myanmar and even Wa officials "admit that local army units and businessmen continue the trade in close cooperation with criminal networks in neighboring countries" (ICG 2003, 9).

Moreover, it is hard to assess how autonomy has manifested itself for the Wa. Its towns and areas resemble towns in China's Yunnan province. The Wa have their own administration and defense force, yet most schools teach in Chinese. Although the Wa region is described by ICG analysts as being "for most intents and purposes...an independent state," the ICG concedes that it has "much closer links with China than with the rest of Myanmar" (ICG 2003, 8). It is no understatement that the Wa economy is heavily dependent upon China: its local economy is Chinese, and most schools are Chinese, most immigrants to the region are Chinese, while "cigarette, beer, and whisky production are all accomplished with Chinese made machinery" (Bangkok Post, February 1, 2004). Its casinos draw 1.7 million Chinese visitors a year (Kaopatumtip and Wechsler 2004). Even Wa officials claim:

In fact, the town resembles China more than anything else…almost every shop has its name written in Chinese characters. The Chinese language and currency are widely used there (Bangkok Post, February 1, 2004).

Yet outside its few towns, there is "near 100 percent illiteracy and no social services whatsoever" (ICG 2003, 9). Currently the majority of the Wa remain impoverished and life is still very difficult for the overall population. Such are the complicated consequences of ceasefire and maldevelopment.

The Kachin Independence Organization (KIO) was for many years, one of the most formidable of the self-determination groups. During the early 1990s the Kachin Independence Army (KIA) numbered 6,000 to 7,000 regulars while others place the numbers at over 15,000 regulars. Its rank and file under Brang Seng, a former high-school principal, worked closely with Bo Mya and contributed to the emergence of the NDF. Although there was a long-standing rivalry between the two organizations and its two leaders, during the 1980s the KIO and KNU would significantly influence NDF's trajectory, resulting in the rejection of separatism for a federal union that would accommodate all of Burma's ethnic groups.

Prior to the signing of the ceasefire, Brang Seng and the KIO initially anticipated holding talks with SLORC alongside the KNU, KNPP and NMSP allies. The KNU, KIO, KNPP and NMSP were, after all, the four largest NDF and DAB groups. However, Mya was reluctant to support Seng's conditions for a conclusive ceasefire agreement. By October 1993, DAB and NDF members, weary of KIO's solo efforts and believing that the KIO had made a unilateral ceasefire with Rangoon, expelled the KIO. The KIO leaders continued to hold talks with SLORC, finally signing a ceasefire with Rangoon on February 24, 1994.

No one is certain about Brang Seng's legacy. Seng's life was cut short when he suffered a stroke a few months after the KIO ceasefire with Rangoon. His untimely death, while in his early 60s "left a vacuum that has been difficult for later leaders to fill" (ICG Asia Report 2003, 9). Seng was an intellectual with no military background—polar opposites from Bo Mya, who had been a "ruthless guerilla fighter" since World War II (Smith 1999, 390). However, during the 1980s, it was Seng who had garnered more international attention.

A regular visitor to China and, later, to Thailand and the West, he often appeared two or three steps ahead of his contemporaries… Indeed Brang Seng, a devout Baptist, was often mentioned as somebody who, in a more peaceful world, would have made an able and perceptive leader of the country (Smith 1999, 390).

ICG analysts shared the same sentiment, noting that Seng was a "major force in ethnic minority politics" and believed that he would have been a "worthy candidate for head of state under a different regime" (ICG 2003, 9).

The KIO today has formal administrative authority in the Kachin State, areas formerly under its control. It possesses parallel institutions but they are no longer in structural opposition to Rangoon. KIO social institutions include departments of health, education, agriculture, women's affairs, and development affairs. The Kachin State also has civilian hospitals and schools that teach Kachin language and culture. There is also development in the region. Infrastructural projects based on the construction of roads, bridges, hydroelectric power along with community-based programs have been implemented.

Unlike the Wa that has top-down feudalistic approach to its social organization, the Kachins has "stronger community networks than...any other ethnic minority group" (ICG Asia Report 2003, 9). In other words, the current goals of the KIO are said to be indistinguishable from the goals of local leaders and groups. The KIO rank and file, however, do not consider their ceasefire as political camouflage for any kind of surrender: "The government wants the KIO to surrender. We on the other hand, are protecting the Panglong Agreement. But we agree on the need for development. Instead of talking (politics), which will not bring agreement, we should practice development" (ibid., 10).

As of 2004, the drug problem has spilled over to many parts of the Kachin State. However, the Kachin Independence Army (KIA) has been effectively clearing their terrain of any opium production. During harvest season, many hundreds of KIA search for renegade fields and sometimes with the cooperation of the Tatmadaw they conduct joint anti-poppy operations (Bangkok Post, February 1, 2004). The KIO is proud to declare that there are no heroin refineries in their state. The US Drug Enforcement Administration, in its May 2002 Drug Intelligence Brief on the KIA agrees: "Trafficking of opium and heroin in the Kachin State decreased dramatically as a result of the KIA enforcing a ban on opium cultivation and drug trafficking" (ibid., 2004).

Yet like the Wa, the Kachins lament the lack of social progress following their ceasefire. Although the rank and file overall seem conciliatory, the ceasefire has caused the KIO to lose control over crucial income-generating enterprises such as lucrative jade mines in Hpakant and has "removed the justification for taxing the local population" (ICG 2003, 11). Moreover, it is believed that social progress cannot be achieved with the continuing confrontation between the Tatmadaw and the NLD.

ICG analysts describe the KIO's disdain of the confrontational approach between the SPDC and NLD since it overlooks the importance of working for national reconciliation and cooperation. In an interview of a KIO leader, the interviewee likened the confrontation between the SPDC and NLD as two elephants engaged in a fight yet the "grass gets trampled" (ICG 2003, 10). Like the vast majority of self-determination groups that have signed ceasefires with Rangoon, the KIO echoes the predominant sentiment of many ethnic nationalists in Burma, namely that they "doubt whether any of the Burman-dominated forces really have the welfare of ethnic minority communities at heart" (ibid., 10).

C. The Mae Tha Waw Hta Agreement: Hopes and Consequences

Despite the military and transcommunal setbacks for DAB, on June 30, 1996, Bo Mya is reelected as the organization's chairman. No longer able to host functions at Manerplaw, forty-six representatives from 18 democracy groups congregated at Pha Toei Village, opposite Umphang District of Thailand's Tak province. National League for Democracy leader Aung San Suu Kyi, released from her house arrest on July 10, 1995, was also present. Participants agree to renew their support for Aung San Suu Kyi, the NLD, and their political movement against SLORC.

By the mid-1990s, SLORC had made attempts to invite Bo Mya to talks by sending a delegation comprised of Lt. Khun Mya, Professor Tun Aung Gyi and Aye Saw Myint to visit the KNU leader. By then the KNU had formed a "go between" team to facilitate renewed diplomatic links. It engaged in seven meetings from 1995-1996 when SLORC was initially on the verge of granting full autonomy to areas under Karen control, provided the area was assessed by Rangoon first. During its last round of talks in November 1996, SLORC makes six demands:

1. The KNU should enter the "legal fold";
2. Engage in a ceasefire;
3. Agree to troop positions;
4. Begin development programs;
5. Go to the national convention as observers;
6. Lay down arms after the new constitution is approved.

The KNU also makes some demands to SLORC:

1. The KNU desires Rangoon to announce a ceasefire;
2. The Tatmadaw should then withdraw its forces from KNU-held areas;
3. Support to the DKBA must halt;
4. The Tatmadaw should also negotiate with the National League for Democracy during ceasefire talks with self-determination groups.

Sensing the futility of the inconclusive talks, Bo Mya sends a letter to President Bill Clinton asking the United States to cooperate with ASEAN and the European Union to push for freedom and human rights in Burma (Bangkok Post, November 28, 1996). ASEAN was in the process of preparing to admit Burma as a full member in July 1997. Mya takes the lull in the fighting to remind both ASEAN, the European Union and the United States that Burma should not be accepted into ASEAN membership because "SLORC is a government which has been ruthlessly suppressing the people" (Bangkok Post, December 8, 1996). Mya even writes ASEAN countries in hopes of persuading them to reject Burma under SLORC. Mya states that the "prestige of ASEAN" would be affected if it granted Burma admission.

Bo Mya is never given a direct response, prompting him to accuse ASEAN and the West as having "no sense of justice or fairness. All they want is to make profit" (Bangkok Post, December 8, 1996). With failed ceasefire talks occurring during the dry season, Bo Mya braces for the consequences: "Yes, SLORC will launch a major offensive if we reject their conditions totally" (Bangkok Post, December 8, 1996).

On December 31, 1996, Bo Mya and the KNU send SLORC a rejection letter. Two conditions the KNU could not meet centered around entering the "legal fold," which for Bo Mya would mean surrender and capitulation to a regime that they felt to be illegitimate. Moreover, laying down arms was out of the question, as that would mean violating Ba U Gyi's Four Principles.

Another main area of disagreement centers on the breadth of a ceasefire. The KNU desired to have a nationwide ceasefire that would affect all of its allies whereas the SLORC, keen on maintaining a divide and rule tactic, desired only a ceasefire with the KNU. SLORC also stipulated that regional development and disarmament should follow the ceasefire, a proposal unacceptable to the KNU and the NDF as both described the stipulation as "nothing but divide and conquer tactics" (Bangkok Post, February 19, 1997).

Interestingly, the *postponement* of development in the Karen State has been quite a consistent line with the KNU and its NDF allies. This is contrasted by the Wa and Kachin polities who continue to expect Rangoon to assist them in their regional development, only to subsequently be disappointed. But this is not the main reason why the KNU shuns "development" proposals from Rangoon. Even the NDF rank and file is aware that ceasefire agreements rarely result in a lasting peace "but only propagate ethnic cleansing programmes as they provide the SLORC with greater freedom to operate in the ethnic areas" (ibid., February 19, 1997). This was corroborated by my discussions with various commanders at the 202 battalion who often noted that development, via promises of roads and bridges, would only serve the Tatmadaw by providing infrastructure conducive for conducting more offensives against Kawthoolei.

In the case of Karen liberation ethnodevelopment, development means to have development on its own terms, not on terms imposed by the ethnocracy which in any case maldevelops Kawthoolei. The KNU, despite being one of the few remaining self-determination organizations to challenge Rangoon, would continue to resist. Yet because many ceasefires had already been signed by other groups the KNU was increasingly coming under more frequent Tatmadaw Four Cuts campaigns.

Not all political developments were threatening the KNU from Rangoon. Bo Mya was able to during September 1996 heal a dangerous split that had splintered the ABSDF organization at Manerplaw in 1991. Dr. Naing Aung led one group while Moe Thee Zun led the other faction. The separation soon turned bloody as local ABSDF in the Kachin State had undertaken a campaign to purge the organization of alleged SLORC spies. Two ABSDF leaders and 14 members were executed while reportedly 60 members were tortured. Mya sponsors a Reunification Congress for the ABSDF between the 6th and 16th of September at Teakaplaw Camp, opposite Tak province. Mya encourages the ABSDF to be pragmatic: "Instead of having two chairmen," he told them, "why not have one step down to become vice-chairman. After all aren't you all fighting for the same cause, with identical ideology and goals?" (Bangkok Post, October 6, 1996). He confronted ABSDF with tough questions, asking them, for example, "Is it for democracy or is it for your rights, is it a revolution for the entire country or is it only for the Burmans?" (ibid., October 6, 1996).

After the rapprochement of the ABSDF during January 1997, Bo Mya and the KNU sponsor a much-publicized Ethnic Nationalities Seminar in the 6th brigade area of Mae Tha Waw Hta, leading to the Mae Tha Waw Hta Agreement. The Agreement pledges to "dismantle the military dictatorship" and "join hands with the pro-democracy forces" of the country, specifically the NLD under Aung San Suu Kyi (Smith 1999, 431). The Ethnic Nationalities Seminar receives funding from overseas donors. By 1997, the KNU emerges from multiple NDF defections as one of the last few remaining self-determination organizations. Under Bo Mya's leadership, it also rises to the occasion to maintain the transcommunal potential latent in the Ethnic Nationalities Seminar and the Mae Tha Waw Hta Agreement.

The Ethnic Nationalities Seminar and its Mae Tha Waw Hta Agreement revealed that self-determination groups and democracy movements were far from being defeated. For SLORC, the implications of the agreement were highly destabilizing.

> SLORC strategists decided that the KNU was simply playing for time with two unspoken objectives: firstly, to win approval from the international community by allying its struggle with Aung San Suu Kyi, and, secondly, to win back ceasefire groups to the armed resistance side (Smith 1999, 449).

Not surprisingly, the regime's Khin Nyunt alleges that the KNU, NLD, ABSDF and NCGUB are organs of a massive US-sponsored conspiracy to overthrow the government. Khin Nyunt also accuses the NLD of being under the influence of many ex-communists who sympathized with the pro-democracy movement. This assessment may not be entirely untrue. Since the 1930s, tens of thousands of Burmese citizens who had once been involved with the CPB during its peak were now playing an "active role in very different walks of life…and it was from this group that many of the older leaders of the democracy movement emerged" (Smith 1999, 368).

Where Khin Nyunt's assessment is inaccurate is that the important distinction between those who still directly supported the CPB and those who "had long since moved on in new political directions" were never made (ibid., 368). The Mae Tha Waw Hta Agreement and unresolved issues with the CPB thus fuels the paranoia of the SLORC and prompts it to prepare for another large Four Cuts into the eastern hills during February 1997.

During the beginning of February 1997, the Tatmadaw supported by mules carrying supplies, bulldozers and civilians forced to work as porters, begin their assault on the KNU's Mergui-Tavoy 4th Brigade as well as the 6th Brigade from Duplaya (Smith 1999). With combined forces of over 3,000 guerillas, the KNLA was fighting over 100,000 Tatmadaw troops lined up against them at Kawthoolei's border with Thailand. More territory was lost by the KNU as the "two-pronged attack by the Burmese army along the Tenasserim and Paw Klo Rivers proceeded quickly with new villages being taken by the army on almost a daily basis" (HRW/A, July 1997, 11).

The Tatmadaw also shell the new KNU headquarters at Htee Ka Pler, jurisdiction of the 6th Brigade. It first launches several 82mm mortar attacks on two Karen refugee camps in Thailand, at Ban Klaa Thaw and Noh Ka Thaw, killing refugees and forcing the remaining 3,000 Karen and about 200 Thai villagers to flee deeper inland. Then it captures Ban Mai as well as a KNU outpost at Htee Soki. The KNLA were ordered to withdraw under the heavy onslaught, but only after departing troops burnt down their own headquarters to prevent them from falling into Tatmadaw hands (Bangkok Post, February 14, 2004). A unit of the 6th Brigade was defeated on February 17 when 300 KNLA troops from the KNU's 16th battalion, led by Colonel Tha Mu Hei[55], surrendered and "delivered much of the central 6th Brigade region to the SLORC" (Smith 1999, 449). Subsequently, the KNU headquarters at Htee Ka Pler base was captured by the Tatmadaw on February 17.

On February 17, there was also fighting opposite Ban Prak Thake between KNLA and Tatmadaw forces after the Burmese troops failed to persuade the KNLA to surrender. Over two thousand KNLA attempt to repulse the advancing Tatmadaw, but to no avail. The 4th brigade headquarters at Htee Kee was seized by the Tatmadaw on February 26 and over 700 Karen villagers in the region as well as over 9,000 refugees from other areas of

[55] Tha Mu Hei was then forced to kneel by SLORC's General Maung Aye to apologize for the rebellion while the latter stepped on the Karen flag.

fighting flee to Thailand (HRW/A 1997, Smith 1999, Bangkok Post, February 18, 1997). The KNU 11th battalion headquarters at Ler Ker were seized on March 18, 1997. Fleeing refugees swell up Thailand's refugee population to over 90,000. The offensives from Toungoo in the north to Mergui in the south were the Tatmadaw's most successful operations in decades.

> As another 20,000 Karen refugees fled into Thailand, Suu Kyi, wearing a Karen costume, made a video-taped statement of humanitarian support, and this…only appeared to confirm the SLORC's fears of a link up between the NLD and other anti-government troops (Smith 1999, 431).

Despite intensive fighting throughout February of 1997 that resulted in more Karen territorial losses, the transcommunal members who have been given shelter by the KNU try to maintain their poise and remain hopeful. U Tin Aung of the NLD-LA continues to support the Karen resistance. Aung denounces SLORC's ethnic cleansing offensives and accuses them of not desiring genuine peace. "Instead of sitting at the table to thrash out our political differences, they are bent on wiping out the democracy groups and the ethnic minorities by employing brute military force," says U Tin Aung (Bangkok Post, March 2, 1997). He further notes that the devastation suffered by the Karen and other ethnic minorities are due to "the lack of equality and the right to self-determination where the ethnic minorities are concerned" and within a state with an "absence of democracy" and a "federal union system of governance" (Bangkok Post, March 2, 1997). During the same period, the Tatmadaw invite the KNU for more ceasefire negotiations. However, two months later the KNU suspend talks with SLORC, claiming that SLORC "had acted in bad faith by making its position public" (HRW/A 1997, 8).

In spite of Tatmadaw victories, Smith notes, "in the 4th Brigade area of Tavoy-Mergui there was strong resistance, and virtually an entire government battalion was lost to mine warfare in the upper Tenasserim valley" (Smith 1999, 449). During the same year a splinter millennial Karen group known as "God's Army" emerged in the 4th Brigade area, previously under KNU administration. It was headed by two boy soldiers that dictated strategies from divine inspiration. With over 200 followers at one point, God's Army launched a number of successful (and unauthorized, attacks against the Tatmadaw). Dozens of Tatmadaw casualties were reported every month from 1997-1998 (Smith 1999, 449). Nevertheless, by the end of the 1997, all remaining KNU bases along Kawthoolei's border along with Thailand and virtually the entire Tenasserim River valley had fallen (HRW/A 1997, 11).

Burma's neighboring polities could have cared less about the strife generated by the Four Cuts campaigns: in July 1997, after being an observer country since 1994, and despite its continuation of mounting Four Cuts offensives against self-determination groups, Burma is granted admission to the Association of Southeast Asian Nations (ASEAN) at the annual ministerial meeting in Kuala Lumpur, Malaysia.

During November 1997, encouraged by its new international status and convinced that order, the beginning of market reforms, and stability were finally attainable, SLORC is replaced by the nineteen-man committee, the State Peace and Development Council (SPDC), with General Than Shwe still in charge. Although the SPDC moniker was meant to "project a softer image" many hardliners from SLORC ended up remaining in power.[56]

This has led to criticisms that the SPDC is no different than the SLORC that preceded it. There are minor variations however: the nineteen-man committee of the SPDC consists of regional commanders, unlike the SLORC which was comprised of 21 members and Burma's top three Tatmadaw generals: Army Commander-in-Chief General Than Shwe, Army Deputy Commander-in-Chief General Maung Aye, and then Director of Defense Services Intelligence Lieutenant General Khin Nyunt (Brunner et al. 1998).

Officially, the SPDC expressed confidence that its first objective of overall stability had been achieved and that economic development should now be the second objective (ICG 2003, 6). SPDC members who were viewed as potential threats were arrested. As a result of this coup, General Khin Nyunt and General Maung Aye used the SPDC to promote those who had been loyal to second-line leadership positions (Fink 2001, Smith 1999).

But the Tatmadaw had its own problems. By the end of 1996, Bo Mya had already hinted at the factionalism within SPDC. Mya's assessment is prescient and cautiously optimistic. When asked to confirm and describe the main factions within SLORC, Mya notes:

> Yes, we have got reports about it. There are two camps. One is Gen. Khin Nyunt's camp, which appears to be desirable about having a ceasefire. The other is led by Gen. Maung Aye which is more militant. They want to use military means to crush the opposition. On Khin Nyunt's side is basically the military intelligence and the secret police. There are altogether 50,000. They can be armed within a short time (Bangkok Post, December 8, 1996).

When asked whether this was considered "encouraging news" for the KNU, Mya is realistic:

> We can't say that is encouraging because whichever group that comes to power, they will use the same methods. They will still hold to racial chauvinism. So we will have to continue to fight (Bangkok Post, December 8, 1996).

---

[56] SLORC was also "widely perceived to have rather sinister connotations" (Fink 2001, 94).

The end of 1990s would expose the KNU to some more discouraging developments. During March 1998, the KNU Minister of Forestry, Padoh Aung San (cousin of U Thuzana), defected with a large amount of the organization's money (ICG Asia Report 2003). After arriving in Rangoon with 300 of his followers, "he made a strident denunciation of his former party and friends" (Smith 1999, 450). The KNU's official statement regarding his defection notes:

> In his press conference on 20/4/98, Padoh Aung San stated that some KNU leaders did not want peace, that some KNU personnel are staying in camps as refugees, that KNU is obstructing the refugees who wanted to return to Burma, that Refugee Camps were simply "Death Camps" which were all words without substance.

Also during this period, KNLA guerillas and armed villagers launch three unsuccessful attacks at the UNOCAL-Total pipeline (see Chapter 5). As a result of the attacks, five oil company workers are killed, prompting the US to warn the KNU to leave the pipeline alone. Moreover, by the end of the 1990s, the Tatmadaw increases its battalion size to 422 (in 1988 there were only 168 battalions). Tatmadaw troop strength had increased from around 200,000 troops in 1988, to 320,000 in 1995, to an estimated 500,000 troops by 2000 (Smith 1999, 426). With China supplying much of the regime's military hardware the SPDC would command enough troops and weaponry to have one heavily armed soldier guarding every 100 Burmese citizen (Fink 2001). Indeed much fierce fighting continues to rage on between 1998 and 2000, frequently underreported or even unreported in many areas of the Shan, Karen, and Kayah States where local ceasefires have failed.

Journalists and observers have frequently noted that the Karen resistance would be "finished" after a dramatic Four Cuts campaign. Over the years of working on this research, I often came across this sentiment over and over again. In 1995, John Hail, a United Press International reporter near Kawmoorah during shelling by the Tatmadaw, remarked that the fall of Kawmoorah would "bring the rebels' 47-year independence struggle to an end" (BurmaNet, February 8, 1995). Similarly, one of the Thai military officials interviewed by Hail noted, "The Burmese government has almost finished consolidating...if they take Kawmoorah the Karen will be finished" (ibid., February 8, 1995). Indeed, Falla—who explicitly noted that he was no apologist for the KNU—also noted this sentiment back in 1991, a few years before the fall of Manerplaw and Kawmoorah:

> Since 1984, the fighting has not let up, and no dry season passes without foreign journalists shaking their heads and pronouncing the Karen finished: "They cannot last another offensive." They do last,

year-by-year, losing some firefights and winning others, losing territory and regaining some of it later (Falla 1991, 29).

Bo Mya assesses the setbacks of the 1990s, primarily the defections, as due to "poor health, lack of true political conviction and deception by SLORC" (Bangkok Post, January 18, 1998). In hindsight he notes, "actually those really dedicated to the cause will never surrender. They are the veterans who have been fighting the Rangoon government for decades" (ibid., January 18, 1998).

Moreover, he reminds observers that other factors regarding the Tatmadaw should also be considered: "Although they [SLORC army] may be great in number I don't think they can carry on for long because of the low morale and lack of discipline among the ordinary soldiers" (ibid., January 18, 1998). Andrew Selth from the Strategic Studies Centre of the Australian National University, Canberra, agrees, noting "persistent reports of low morale in the army ranks" as well as "at the higher levels" (Selth 1995). Moreover, Tatmadaw casualties—despite being given better weaponry since the early 1990s—were high in the major campaigns. Nevertheless, Smith sums up the 1990s for the KNU: "Fifty years after its founding, the KNU was in deep crisis" (Smith 1999, 448). Most importantly, the destitution of numerous non-combatant Karen has not been reduced.

During January 2000, KNU Congress members elected Saw Ba Thin to replace Bo Mya as chairman of the KNU. After leading the organization for twenty five years, Mya—the hard-line Karen nationalist—stands aside as the more "modernist" Ba Thin takes the helm of the organization. Bo Mya retains the position of Minister of Defense and is elected Vice-President.

Ba Thin is described by Rogers as a "modernist who recognises that Karen independence is unrealistic and who frames the cause in terms of the wider struggle for democracy and equality in Burma." Ba Thin was born in 1927 in Henzada. Educated at the American Baptist Mission Karen High School, having served as head of the KNU's Educational Department during the 1970s and 1980s, and later becoming the KNU's General Secretary and Prime Minister, Ba Thin may be in a better position to harness the younger generation of Karen revolutionaries, intellectuals, and politicians that will emerge on the scene in the post-Mya KNU. Ba Thin tells Rogers:

> To be a free nation, to gain freedom, people need to be aware of the situation politically. At the moment illiteracy is very high and there are very few intellectuals among the Karen. We need to know about Burma, about Burman people, and about how to gain their sympathy and understanding (Rogers 2004, 153).

Whereas Ba Thin envisions the success of the KNU to be based on acquiring peace, justice and equal rights based on democracy, Mya's stance differs from Ba Thin in its emphasis on continuing the struggle, even after the arrival of democracy:

> Most people understand that our struggle is for the Karen nation. But some people think that if democracy comes to Burma, it will all be well for the Karen people. That is not the case. When democracy comes, we will still have to work for the Karen cause. There are different ideas, different ideologies. It is a question of whether this is a fight for democracy or a fight for Karen freedom. For me, this is an armed struggle for Karen freedom (Rogers 2004, 153).

Rogers' assessment of the KNU as it entered the twenty-first century is accurate: the KNU cannot afford another split in its organization. The KNU has, in over 55 years of its revolution, split along the lines of communism and religion. The implications surrounding the fragmentation have only served the interests of the military regime's divide and conquer policies.

Although the aforementioned views between Ba Thin and Bo Mya were politically healthy at the time and able to be debated within KNU circles, the continuation of the Karen resistance will have to be based on navigating between Ba Thin's vision of a Karen future and Bo Mya's legacy, but situated within the context where many war-weary Karen simply want peace. Moreover, the SPDC continues its machinations to divide the KNU since Bo Mya's passing on December 24, 2006. In February 2007, a faction of 300 guerillas defects from the KNU and establishes the KNU/KNLA Peace Council under Brig-General Htain Maung.

The Karen and other ethnic nationalities are not the only people suffering by the end of the twentieth century. Ordinary Burmans living under 46 years of military rule are also dealing with the disastrous effects of Ne Win's experiment with socialism. The main indicators of human development all show figures that are far below the regional and international average. Infant mortality rate was at 9.4 percent, under-5 mortality was at 14.7 percent, maternal mortality was at 14 percent, under-3 malnutrition registered at 32.4 percent, primary school completion was only at 27 percent (Brunner et al. 1998). The quality of education at the university level also suffered considerably: since the inception of the pro-democracy movement in 1988, universities have been closed twice between 1988 and 1991, the academic year shortened to five months or less between 1992 and 1996, with additional intermittent closures of universities by the end of 1996 (Irrawaddy 2003).

Much discussion hitherto has been centered on the development and maneuverings of the KNU political and military apparatus within a condensed history of the Karen struggle. I will now leave this format and continue our discussion by focusing on the consequences of internal colonization upon the KNLA and civilian Karen.

Chapter V
The Four Cuts as Maldevelopment

The Four Cuts upon the KNLA

> Colonel Nerdah Mya: This is not real fighting, it is shadow fighting. The real fighting is in the spiritual realms. The real enemy is here, in your heart. You have to overcome your mind before your enemy does. I tell the soldiers that they can win a battle but they can still lose the war if they don't know how to control their minds (Rogers 2004, 116).

> Robert Zan[57]: At last the enemy came… In the moonlight I could see them clearly. With my finger on the trigger of my Browning automatic rifle, I tried to concentrate on the firefight that was soon to come, but my mind was in conflict. On the other hand, I felt that the approaching enemy was responsible for my brother's death. They were the ones that burned our Karen villages and raped our Karen women. On the other hand, the enemy in front of me were young men who had not chosen to join the Burma Army but were forcibly conscripted. All of us had been born in the same country and we were all brothers. We did not know each other and we had no personal conflict with each other. I knew that soon they would be dying in front of me. I would be killing them. I felt both hatred and brotherly union spirit toward them (Rogers 2004, 115).

One cannot underestimate the devastating outcome of the Four Cuts as it pertains to the KNLA. The Karen have lost much territory in their own state since the Four Cuts campaigns have entered the eastern hills. Nevertheless, it should also be remembered that the Tatmadaw have not fully consolidated all areas within the Karen State. There are five main reasons for the KNU's staying power.

First, an important factor in sustaining the military aspect of the Karen struggle has been the KNU reemphasis on the merits of guerilla tactics. The days of defending bases and headquarters with hundreds of troops have since passed. As a result, the KNLA are able to wage guerilla warfare by fighting light, fast, and by avoiding large battles.

KNLA units, often traveling in mobile units of 20 to 30 soldiers, do not remain in any one area for long when the concentration of Tatmadaw troops

---

[57] Robert Zan is Mahn Ba Zan's son.

is high. As Desmond Ball, a professor at the Strategic Defence Studies Centre of the Australian National University, Canberra noted, the KNLA are experts at hit-and-run tactics and ambushes directed against Tatmadaw units or posts, "ignoring those where it's clear that they're not going to achieve victory…and only conducting operations when it's quite clear they will achieve the particular military aims" (Ball 2000). Furthermore:

> …over the last few years, although the overall strength of the various resistance armies has decreased, the military successes have in fact increased. And that applies to the…KNLA…where you have some quite substantial military successes, sometimes wiping out whole Tatmadaw battalions; in other cases directed more at hitting particular Tatmadaw and DKBA officers and really wreaking quite substantial punishment on the Tatmadaw (Ball 2000).

KNLA troops can also withdraw deep into the jungle, into familiar terrain conducive to guerilla warfare. An explosion maiming a Tatmadaw soldier signals an ambush-in-waiting. A KNLA commander describes the process:

> The mines are not designed to kill but to maim. Whenever the enemy troops step into a mine-field and a soldier is killed, the rest will leave him behind and continue to attack us. But if a soldier is crippled, they have to stop the advancement and carry the injured back for treatment. Then we can ambush them (Wechsler 2004, 6).

Second, the Four Cuts—though successfully employed in the Irrawaddy delta—is logistically more challenging to sustain in the thick, humid, and malarial jungles of the eastern hills. As Tatmadaw columns trek deeper into the forest they become vulnerable to KNLA ambushes, landmines, and thinning supply lines. Smith corroborates these views in his interview of Colonel Aye Myint, the former head of the Tatmadaw's North-East Command who fought against the CPB, KNU, KIO, and SSA.

> In these remote and sensitive border regions it is militarily impossible to tie down guerilla forces who have a back-door escape and supply line… In these mountainous borderlands the financial and logistical costs are too immense for the Tatmadaw to bear. Even for the smallest operation, for the campaign to succeed thousands of troops and porters need to be mobilized in advance and brought in to swamp the area (Smith 1999, 261).

In a January 18, 1998 *Bangkok Post* interview General Bo Mya confirms Colonel Myint's assessment by noting that Rangoon cannot afford the costs of providing frontline Tatmadaw with enough arms, ammunition, and food rations. "Because the logistics of supplying food to the troops is so poor...they have to plunder the villagers to survive," Bo Mya said.

Third, many Tatmadaw soldiers are conscripts and have gained a reputation for having poor discipline. Young male teens are customarily confronted by police or soldiers and literally told that they will now become soldiers or face imprisonment. Many are coerced off the streets, from bus stops, and on their way to or from school. They are then taken to military recruiting centers to be incarcerated and processed. It is no wonder many young Burmans soldiers have subsequently fled to KNLA or Karen areas to escape the Tatmadaw's brutal process of military indoctrination. Indeed, there are over 70,000 child soldiers in the Tatmadaw, roughly 20 percent of regime's army (Rogers 2004, 239). Falla shares a perspective from a KNLA soldier: "If the Burmese soldiers are given orders for a two-week operation, that means exactly fourteen days, and they know they will be punished if they return early. So they hide in the forest until it's time to go home" (Falla 1991, 219).

Bo Mya confirms this assessment as recently as 1998: "Although they...may be great in number I don't think they can carry on for long because of the low morale and lack of discipline among the ordinary soldiers" (Bangkok Post, January 18, 1998). Moreover, whatever state-induced courage that was instilled with Tatmadaw troops must have been counteracted when they were ordered to shoot their own people during the country's 1988 pro-democracy movement. The morale issue is due to a simple fact: economic hardships have not only befallen ethnic nationality regions, but since international sanctions have been tightened against the regime, coupled with the legacy borne from Ne Win's disastrous attempts at autarky through his Burmese Way to Socialism, destitution is also experienced among ordinary Burmans. Conscious of the destitution of ordinary Burmans under military rule, White Moon, a KNDO and expert boatman tells Falla:

> We don't hate the Burmese people...it is only their government and their army that oppress us. Some of the Burmese here are refugees too. They cannot stand the pressures that their own authorities put on them. You know, the KNU asks for a tax of just B.25 and one basket of rice from each household per year, but the Burmese government taxes their people almost to starvation. These poor people are our friends (Falla 1991, 346).

Bo Mya notes that as ordinary people, the soldiers also have their own families to support, "so they don't want to fight for the government anymore" (Bangkok Post, January 18, 1998). Tatmadaw child soldiers suffer the same destitution, with many of its child soldiers paid only 4,500 kyats a month, while a basket of rice costs 10,000 kyats[18]; one young Tatmadaw defector interviewed by Rogers "urges other child soldiers in the Tatmadaw to defect" (Rogers 2004, 240).

The KNLA accepts child soldiers, but the reasons for their enlistment are entirely different than child soldier conscripts of the Tatmadaw. Many Karen children voluntarily join the KNLA because they've witnessed the murder of their family members and friends, as well as seeing their villages razed to the ground. The KNLA discourages children from joining, "but if they chose to do so, they are accepted" (ibid., 241).

Fourth: KNLA guerillas are intimately familiar with the terrain that they make their home. Augmenting this knowledge is their improving utilization of better communications:

> They now understand the extent, for example, to which the Tatmadaw have been monitoring their communications and have been able to…more systematically monitor Tatmadaw and DKBA communications, so they're in a far better position in terms of knowing the details of particular Tatmadaw and DKBA movements so that they can therefore set up ambushes, or mine certain areas with landmines (Ball 2000).

The communication intelligence is also enhanced by villagers that provide the KNLA with intelligence regarding SPDC columns or DKBA units. In return, KNLA will warn villagers of advancing Tatmadaw. Yet the intimate knowledge the Karen have of the forest is not a new phenomenon. Even as early 1887, D. M. Smeaton noted:

> …the Karen is a dangerous fellow…from his perfect knowledge of woodcraft which enables him to live for months in the jungle without any supplies… He cooks his food in green bamboos, and will be off scouting for a month without giving his enemy a sign of his presence until he closes with him (Falla 1991, 358).

Finally, KNLA troops can frequently count on Karen villagers to provide for them food and shelter, that is, until the villages and villagers sympathetic to the Karen struggle are relocated or eliminated by the Tatmadaw. Rice is taken as a form of tax when "villages are stable enough to produce a reasonable crop" (Delang 2000, 75). A cash tax is expected from village elders who are in rich harvest areas. For example, in the Nyaunglebin District these demands are mainly levied against the relatively more fertile villages in the eastern part of the Sittaung River plains.

---

[18] The official exchange rate is 6 kyats to $1.00 US. Due to inflation, US$ 1.00 was worth 310 kyats in December 1997.

When KNLA units have to attend to logistics, they will also use porters, but their labor is not accompanied by physical abuse, and they only have to go for shorter periods. KNLA also utilize only able-bodied men as porters and those households without candidates fit for the task are exempted. The Tatmadaw have to force porters to carry their food, supplies, and military equipment to the site of an offensive. As a result, logistics are relatively less stressed for the KNLA when compared to the Tatmadaw.

Fleeing IDP villagers, regardless of ethnic background, can usually find safety when they stumble upon KNLA patrols—a well-known fact experienced by numerous pro-democracy activists fleeing the 1988 democracy crackdown.[59] Sick villagers can usually find shelter and medical treatment from KNLA units. Yet when KNLA and KNDO troops, along with other ethnic armies and communist groups, are cut off from these important links to the population they often have no choice but to abandon their areas and withdraw deeper into the thick jungle to conduct their operations.

As a result of the aforementioned factors, the Four Cuts campaigns against the KNLA are currently still unable to swing the tide of the military campaign completely in the Tatmadaw's favor. Even though some 1990s estimates show that the Tatmadaw outnumber the KNLA at least ten-to-one:

> Short of some bungle by the KNLA, it is therefore difficult for the 100,000 or so Burmese regulars to defeat them, even though they may temporarily overrun the territory. Nor do the Burmese seem to be able to prevent KNLA detachments from roaming about the coastal plains (Falla 1991, 29).

Nevertheless, the Tatmadaw do outnumber the KNLA: by 2000, the rapid expansion of the Tatmadaw has resulted in an estimated between 400,000 to 500,000 troops. Although numbers on exact KNLA troop strength is a confidential matter 1997 estimates place their numbers ranging from 5,000 to 11,000 (Smith 1999; Bangkok Post, February 19, 1997; Fredholm 1993; Falla 1991). Additionally, it is important to note that Rangoon has never directed its entire army in a Four Cuts campaign against the Karen resistance; it has to fight other self-determination groups as well. Yet when Four Cuts campaigns are successful,

> It is virtually impossible for guerilla forces to infiltrate back into their old stomping-grounds. Most of these counter-insurgency pressures have with time been relaxed, but the new military infrastructures have been kept intact and as a result vast areas of rural Burma, especially in the Pegu and Arakan Yomas and the mountainous

---

[59] The movie *Beyond Rangoon* (1995) captured such moments.

ethnic minority states, have not been repopulated since the rebels were forced out (Smith 1999, 261).

What are the resulting figures from the Four Cuts genocide? In spite of the staying power of the KNLA, the numbers of Karen lost to the Four Cuts, indirectly (as in Karen leaving for the interior or border) or directly (as civilian casualties) have steadily increased. Although exact and credible figures are unavailable, the military regime does provide some statistics, which we should use with caution. The Karen Women's Organization (KWO) cites government census figures for 1974 showing a decrease in the Karen population from 5 million to 3.2 million. On the contrary, Burma's total population had increased from 24 to 33 million. After the pro-democracy uprising of 1988, along with the increase in the size of the Tatmadaw resulting in more sustained Four Cuts offensives, 1990 figures by the KWO show that Burma's population had increased to 44 million while the Karen population had fallen to 2.9 million (KWO 2004, 15).

The Four Cuts upon Civilian Karen

War will always affect the fate of non-combatants most severely. By virtue of not being heavily armed soldiers, civilians are frequently most vulnerable to repeated, protracted, and systematic abuses by an invading army. Karen villagers and non-combatants, unlike the KNLA, often do not have a fighting chance. The pain and suffering experienced by the Karen thus needs to be documented.

Indeed, it is important to note that the Four Cuts campaigns—although ultimately aimed at capturing or destroying KNU/KNLA base areas—have always started first with the disruption, displacement, and murder of non-combatant Karen, followed by the destruction or relocation of Karen villages. Since the fall of Manerplaw and Kawmoorah, the intensity of villager and village dislocations has increased unabated. Yet in past periods when KNU-administered villages were free from strife or offensives there was certainly a functioning aspect to the KNU administration of Kawthoolei. Falla, who had stayed with the KNU and the Karen, vividly described the varying features of Karen villages.

> They are small villages for the most part, averaging some forty houses with five to a house, a population of about 200 is common... But you can hardly estimate the size of a Karen village without a guide, for you can't see more than two or three of the houses scattered among the trees. The effect can be exceptionally attractive, a forest variant of the garden-city principle, every house in its own areca-glade, its neighbors glimpsed between the slim ringed,

uncluttered trunks of palms—near enough to be reassuring, far enough to be unobtrusive.

Any village that figures in the Kawthoolei government scheme of things will have certain civic features: a football field, a school with its roof of thatch or tin depending on village resources, and the teacher's house nearby. There will be a shop in a locked side-room off someone's house, stocked with prawn crackers and vitamin pills, fishnets and flip flops. The grandest structure in a Christian village…will be the church, sometimes with the schoolroom tucked in underneath it. If the congregation is flourishing, this can be magnificent—painted timber with shutters, a portico and a bell tower (Falla 1991, 70-72).

For civilian Karen that have been subjected to the Four Cuts, their lives exist in a state of liminality. Whether as villagers in the remaining liberated areas of KNU control, as IDPs, as refugees, or as victims of war, what the Karen are still experiencing are Thai officials that are growing less sympathetic to their plight, KNLA defenses that are frequently outnumbered by the Tatmadaw, as well as the perennial marauding of their land, along with harassments and assaults by Tatmadaw forces. Moreover, in many areas of SPDC control many women are raped or gang-raped as part of the psychological warfare conducted to break the will of the Karen.

Since the 1970s, the military regime has believed that the single best way to counter self-determination groups "is to destroy the ability of the civilians to support them," or metaphorically speaking by "draining the ocean so the fish cannot swim" (Delang 2000, 15-16). As a policy, it has allowed Tatmadaw commanders and soldiers to engage in human rights violations of all articles under the United Nations' Universal Declaration of Human Rights, which applies to how governments should behave toward its citizens. The Four Cuts policy also violates international humanitarian laws "intended to protect non-combatants and the victims of such conflicts" (HRW/A 1995, 4).

It is conventionally acknowledged by watchdog organizations and pressure groups that the years from 1984 to 2000 contained the most recorded atrocities of Tatmadaw violations of human rights. Since the outflow of refugees to Thailand have saturated its refugee camps, the international community was forced to understand the historical context of the humanitarian crises directly from the Karen, other ethnic nationalities, and even Burmans that trekked through Karen territory to reach Thailand. I will rely on these secondary sources that contain important interviews with Four Cuts survivors. I also hope to utilize statistics and information provided by important conduits of the Karen struggle, the various international and local non-governmental organizations (NGOs) that have been able to document the depths of Tatmadaw brutality in its implementation of the Four Cuts.

Non-governmental organizations and pressure groups have done their share of reporting on the true climate of genocide and oppression the Karen face. The overall outcome of the Four Cuts, retold by countless refugees from all ethnic nationalities as well as by NGO activists that dare enter such areas is the same: there are gross violations of human rights via extra judicial killings, massacres, tortures, implementation of ethnic rape, and destruction of property. As a result, it is very important to view the Four Cuts as a development policy used by the military junta to maldevelop ethnic nationality regions; that is, the Four Cuts is an internal colonizing process by which an ethnocratic regime denies ethnic nationalities economic progress and political freedom.

The Four Cuts, when implemented, significantly disrupts six areas of Karen civilian life:

1. Villages and villagers are relocated;
2. Villagers are forced to become porters;
3. Karen women are frequently raped or gang-raped;
4. Villagers are forced to become IDPs;
5. Many villagers flee across the border as refugees;
6. The Karen regional economy is destroyed.

The above categories are not mutually exclusive human conditions. There is considerable overlap regarding the conditions of individuals in the aforementioned categories, especially regarding the condition of Karen women, as we shall see. To give readers a more visceral impression of the consequences of the Four Cuts, I have some cases for each of the categories, drawn from interviews conducted by activists from international and local NGOs that have treated Karen subjected to the Four Cuts. Villagers, be it women, men, elders, children, and even physically or mentally challenged individuals, are often forced into all the aforementioned states of destitution at one time or another. Villagers are "pacified" in this manner before actual military offensives begin.

Even when the KNU and SPDC were engaged in ceasefire talks during the first half of 2004, Four Cuts campaigns were still being directed toward villages. During my January stay at the KNU 7th Brigade base of Mu Aye Pu while the KNU and SPDC were holding ceasefire talks, Tatmadaw and KNSO troops set ablaze Noo Tha Hta church in the northern part of the Karen State.[60]

---

[60] The KNSO (Karenni National Solidarity Organization) is a faction working for the Tatmadaw.

Tatmadaw and KNSO troops had launched joint operations against Karen and Karenni villages along the Karen-Karenni border from January 11 to February 13, 2004. On June 25, 2004, the Tatmadaw's 135th light infantry battalion advanced upon the Karenni village of Paho, located at 4,500 feet elevation. Due to advance warning, the villagers were able to flee into the jungle with what they were able to carry.[61] These episodes are just reported cases. There have been other undocumented SPDC assaults on villages elsewhere.

A. Effects upon Villagers and Villages

In the past, the relocation of villages in conflict areas occurred at a localized level. From 1996 onward, the relocations took on an epic scale, involving relocations of hundreds of villages to army-controlled areas. Since 1996 over 1,500 villages with its 300,000 inhabitants in the Shan State were relocated. The Karenni, the "cousins" of the Karen, saw 200 of their villages relocated while other homes were put to the torch. In Kawthoolei, over 200 villages in Papun and Nyaunglebin districts were heavily shelled and burned. The fleeing villagers retreated deep into the forests as IDPs. In the Tenasserim Division between 1996 and 1997 over 100 Karen villages were torched.[62]

Statistics only capture a portion of relocations and its consequences. As the official KNU website notes: "economically, our fields and plots of land were nationalized and confiscated. We have to toil hard all year round and have to take all our products to the Burmese Government for sale at its controlled prices, leaving little for ourselves."

Relocation orders are dispatched when Tatmadaw units believe that resistance groups are active in patrol areas. Although many villagers may reside in villages that are not in contact with the KNLA, if the SPDC perceives that they are complicit in supporting the resistance they will be forced to move. The primary aim of relocating villages and villagers is based on establishing full control of populations so that labor and resources can be extracted. With strategic villages under Tatmadaw control, KNLA links to sympathetic villagers are severed.

Fredholm and Smith provide a helpful description on how a Four Cuts unfolds for Karen civilians: the first step in a Four Cuts campaign would be to surround the insurgent area "for a concentrated military effort." Villagers in the cordoned area, usually 40 to 50 square miles in size, are then given a

---

[61] Information provided to me by contact networking with the Free Burma Rangers.
[62] Due to problems of access, these figures are likely to under-represent the number and populations of relocation sites, and of affected villages in the selected areas. However, some relocation site residents may since have fled to Thailand, returned home, or adopted a life of hiding in the forest.

designated deadline—usually "between zero and a few weeks advance notice" depending on the orders to move to relocation sites or "strategic villages" (Burmese Border Consortium September 2002). According to Claudio Delang of the Karen Human Rights Group (KHRG), "many of the villages ordered to move do not even have any contact with opposition groups, but they fall within an area where the SPDC believes the opposition can operate" (Burmese Border Consortium September 2002).

After the deadline, Tatmadaw patrols are sent to destroy remaining villages and food supplies that may aid the KNLA. Village dwellings are almost always put to the torch but if heavy rains have recently drenched the area Tatmadaw troops would simply tear down the structures. Often landmines are planted in torched dwellings and rice fields to prevent any villagers from reestablishing their way of life. In 1999, at Kheh Der village in Ler Doh Township, a Tatmadaw battalion in the area planted 368 mines on pathways back to the village to prevent villagers in hiding from returning (Delang 2000, 149).

The goal of the Tatmadaw is to run the course of the counter-insurgency campaign by turning rebel-held areas, designated as "black" zones, into "brown" zones (also known as "free fire zones" because anyone seen within its confines will be shot on sight as an insurgent), and finally into "white" zones, a designation indicating that government troops have secured control over the area. Relocation orders are issued for villages in black and brown zones. Since the implementation of the Four Cuts relocation policies, the Tatmadaw has secured virtually all Karen villages near the border with Thailand, while "armed ethnic groups which have no cease-fire agreements with Rangoon no longer control any significant territory" (Burmese Border Consortium September 2002).

The Burmese Border Consortium identifies three general types of relocation centers. The larger relocation centers contain "residents...which have been forced to move from several outlying villages to one Tatmadaw-controlled location, often situated in the vicinity of infrastructure projects (e.g. car roads)" (Burmese Border Consortium September 2002). Villagers in large relocation centers may be able to retain "control over food stocks and access to farmland, although they are usually liable to various 'rice taxes', and subject to extensive forced labour." Due to the taxation drain on their income, it is difficult if not impossible for villagers to purchase basic necessities and commodities. As a result there are high rates of chronic malnutrition, hunger, and deaths. Some of the larger relocation centers "eventually dissolve, usually with the unofficial approval of local Tatmadaw and state officials." With the abandonment of these centers, some villagers return and attempt to rebuild their villages while others remain hiding in the forest.

The smaller relocation villages are those that have not been moved in their entirety, "although outlying houses and satellite hamlets are forced to re-settle on confiscated land in the village centre" (Burmese Border Consortium September 2002). Many of the smaller relocation centers are fenced in with armed guards patrolling its perimeter, and like residents of the larger relocation centers villagers are called upon to do forced labor. Some villagers are able to attend to farming activities. There are also non-state-controlled relocation sites managed by groups that have signed ceasefires with the regime. The pro-Tatmadaw DKBA and its political wing, the DKBO, have adopted this approach.

Soon after its formation in December 1994, the DKBO distributed leaflets ordering all Buddhist Karen to move to their headquarters at Myaing Gyi Nu, across the river from the Tatmadaw's command base at Kamamaung. The leaflets warned that those who failed to comply with the relocation would be considered pro-KNU and would thus face consequences. The Karen Human Rights Group provides an actual copy of such an order translated from the original, acquired from a refugee (Karen Human Rights Group 1995).

> Stamp: Hlaing Bwe Township, Myaing Gyi Ngu Old Town
> To: _____refugee camp
> Date: - -95
>
> Subject: All Buddhist people from the refugee camps are to leave and go back to Myaing Gyi Ngu
>
> We will take care and responsibility for the family needs of all Buddhists who return from the refugee camps. You will be accepted as the families of Myaing Gyi Ngu. Already many families from the refugee camps are joining us every day. We have learned from people who have returned that the KNU is harassing and frightening the Buddhist community in the refugee camps.
>
> To continue living in the refugee camps means to prolong the existence of the KNU and its harassment of the Buddhist community, and is a hindrance to a peaceful resolution. In order to dismantle the refugee camps, we have various plans. Therefore all nationalities must leave the refugee camps and return to Myaing Gyi Ngu. If you do not comply with this document, you will be considered as anti-Buddhists and KNU and we are going to uproot you. Families who return will be received at Myawaddy and will be sent to Myaing Gyi Ngu free of charge.
>
> Soe Thit Sa Ti (Kyaw Win)
> DKBA (Special Forces)

According to Human Rights Watch/Asia (HRW/A), more than 3,000 families from Hlaingbwe complied with the DKBO orders and relocated. The DKBO rewarded these families by granting them land, rice rations, and means of transportation. Moreover, families with members in the DKBA "receive two sacks of rice and 1,000 Kyats a month—considerably more than the regular army, whose foot soldiers are paid only 700 Kyats a month" (HRW/A 1995, 15).

Sometimes, "compassionate" Tatmadaw commanders do leave a parting message behind:

> I am so thankful for all your help, the food and everything else you gave when your battalion was in xxxx. I hope that all of you will understand and forgive us for what we said, ordered of and did to you. These were our duties and were done under orders. I do apologise for our previous deeds. Actually, we are all brothers and sisters. (SPDC Army captain's letter, dated December 1998, to villagers in Thaton district after he had been rotated out of the region) (Delang 2000, 203).

Since some villages in their original locations were not in ideal farming areas or located in deforested areas, many of those relocated complied because they believed they would be moved to areas with better land. However, since 1999 villagers were almost always forced to relocate at gunpoint. Although villagers are usually moved as entire village units, thus maintaining social and community structures, many are extrajudicially murdered, assaulted and raped, nullifying any potential benefit of communal coherence. Often villagers are transported some distance by trucks but many have to trek on foot.

Falla notes that the "Burmese Army knows very well that the KNLA is fed by the villagers," and therefore when the Tatmadaw seize a village, they relocate its population and confiscate all the rice to first feed their own soldiers. Leftovers are then redistributed to the relocated villagers (1991, 265). Confiscated foods are rationed daily, and no stockpiling of foods is allowed, lest they are smuggled out to the KNLA.

In a March 1997 Four Cuts campaign near Kyungchaung, Kawthoolei, the Tatmadaw, after conscripting a large number of porters from the village, "killed and ate pigs, chickens, cows and buffalos belonging to the villagers" (HRW/A 1997, 12). Villagers that remained or dared to return to their former villages or farms are arrested or shot on sight as insurgents. Since December 1999, villagers in the more than 100 villages of the Duplaya district of Kawthoolei were forced to "hand over their entire rice harvest to the Army and then move to Army-controlled sites or face being shot on sight" (Delang 2000, 16). A Karen villager recounts:

Recently, when a battle occurred at Saw Mu Theh involving DKBA, they [the Burmese] forced the villagers from 2 villages, Leh Wain Gyi and Kya Plaw, to move to a relocation site near the Ler Doh car road. They called it Pa Hee Ko village. The [SPDC] guerilla troops were working [on this] together with the DKBA. All the villagers had to move within 3 days starting on January 3rd [1999]. After they finished moving the villages were burned. They said that if the villagers couldn't move within 3 days they would find us and cause us pain. If we couldn't carry all of our things they would be happy because they could take them and sell them (Delang 2000, 87-89).

Life in relocated strategic villages is hard. Fredholm describes them as fenced-in concentration camps, situated at sites that allow the Army ease of control. Camps are usually patrolled by Tatmadaw troops ranging in number between 20 to 300 soldiers, and most are rotated out of the area every four to six months. Some rotations might yield a more lenient or compassionate Tatmadaw commander, while others may bring to the village a local tyrant. Curfew is customarily enforced by nightfall and depending on the intensity of conflict in the region, may be short-term or long-term:

From your village, children, men and all the villagers are absolutely not allowed out of the village on September 27/28/29, Thadin Kyut Hla Zan 7/8/9 [the corresponding Burmese calendar dates]. Don't go out at all to look after your cattle, buffaloes, farm affairs or to pick vegetables. Inform the villagers that they will be shot and arrested if the columns find out that they have left the village (ibid., 195).

In some accounts, to further ensure protection from potential attacks by rebel forces, the Tatmadaw would place its offices and barracks at the center of the strategic village, in effect utilizing the concentric ring of civilian villagers as a human shield. Most strategic villages are comprised of a dozen or more villages surrounded by fences further reinforced by armed guards/soldiers. In other cases, villages existing at the periphery of Tatmadaw-controlled areas are relocated to village centers. Some sites do have acceptable conditions.

Particularly in the longer-established settlements, there are functioning schools (to which however, not all residents can afford to send their children), some paid work is available, and—as in any community—people attempt to reestablish their lives. In such cases, residence is often no longer (or not entirely) a product of coercion, and it is debatable whether such 'new villages' should still be considered relocation sites. It is also worth noting that the state sometimes provides some rice to new arrivals in 'Relocation Centres' (although this has often been looted from their own or others' granaries), and that some support has also been distributed in relocation sites by church and other social welfare organisations working 'inside' Burma (Burmese Border Consortium September 2002).

The SPDC controls the strategic villages through Peace & Development Councils (PDC) with Tatmadaw battalions enforcing order. PDCs are usually comprised of villagers who comply with the Tatmadaw out of self-interest and fear. When Tatmadaw troops arrive in many villages, their commanders go directly to the PDC to issue orders for forced labor, cash, food, and materials. PDC members comply by attending to the aforementioned orders. Usually the chairperson divides the orders evenly between the households of the village by demanding a certain amount of money per house or having the households rotate the dispatching of laborers.

Some PDC members can profit from their position. The Karen Human Rights Group notes that in some strategic villages, people covet the position of becoming a village PDC member because they are able to impose a tax. In other districts, such as war-torn Thaton, few desire a position in the PDC because of the responsibility involved in meeting "the heavy demands for forced labour, food, materials and cash" (Delang 2000, 165). Elderly women often fulfill PDC positions because the villagers and the Tatmadaw perceive them to be less invested in supporting the KNU and KNLA.

The relocated villagers have to bring their own building supplies during their move. This sometimes requires villagers to dismantle their old homes and transport crucial materials to new sites. Once relocated, Fredholm describes the population as "virtually unable to leave their new village, and it is...impossible for them to regain contact with their relatives among the insurgents" (1993, 91). As a result, when villagers are aware of a coming relocation they flee deep into the forests as IDPs. Many are forced to take chances by growing some rice for family consumption in their new hideout areas. This is usually done deep in the forest in makeshift clearings.

Some Tatmadaw units do allow construction of makeshift infrastructure for relocated villagers. Delang notes: "In some villages it sanctions the construction of a primary or middle school, but usually it is the villagers who must pay the cost of the building...as well as the salary of the state-supplied teacher" (2000, 22). If the makeshift schools constructed by Karen villagers are not state-sanctioned Tatmadaw officials order them closed. Since 1999, the SPDC has adopted this policy in the Pa-an and Thaton districts of Kawthoolei. Karen villagers are understandingly upset at this approach toward education, since the "teaching of...Karen is strictly forbidden," with many children growing up "illiterate in their mother tongue" even though Karen nationalism has never outlawed the Burmese language (2000, 23).

In 2003, near the Paw Klo and Tenasserim rivers, two IDP sites opened schools totaling 50 students staffed by two teachers. According to the Free Burma Rangers (FBR), the small number of children attending school is due to their parents' fear that Tatmadaw attacks could happen at any time. As a result, although many Karen children desire to have a decent education, others shun the futility of schooling in times of war and do not attend. This is a perennial problem. One villager recounts:

> The situation is bad and we must move up and down, fleeing and sleeping outside whenever they [SPDC] come and tell us things [i.e. issue a new relocation order], so we can't send them to school. The situation is very unstable. There is a government school but we can't send them there. We learn Karen language at the pastor's house, mostly reading from the Bible. People dare not open a school to teach the villagers (Delang 2000, 90).

In the strategic villages, villagers are sometimes ordered to move to the village center, thus denying them proximity to their fields. One person in the family is forced to do work in one or two week shifts, while during the monsoon season able-bodied adults are forced to work in the fields while mothers and children fulfill tasks elsewhere. Enforced curfews that prevent travel between dawn and dusk "disrupts the entire crop cycle, because villagers are used to staying in field huts far from the village for much of the growing season to do all the intensive labor which is required" (ibid., 16). As a result, many villagers in the strategic villages are unable to produce their own food and are forced to flee, lest they end up starving or being used as forced labor. Moreover, the Tatmadaw continues to abuse villagers that have cooperated with the relocation.

It is also common for Karen intelligence to warn villagers of approaching Tatmadaw.[63] With KNDO assistance, villagers have the opportunity to flee into the forest and avoid capture. Many take their chances by returning to their abandoned villages to rebuild, a large segment of the population become IDPs, while still others end up as refugees inside Thailand. Usually a given Karen villager takes on all the aforementioned statuses at one time or another. Regardless of the outcome, the Karen lose the ability to sustain themselves. As a result, some Karen villagers decide to return to their abandoned or destroyed villages to rebuild and take their chances at a new life. They attempt to farm again so as to maintain some semblance of stability

---

[63] When SPDC commanders are aware of KNLA movement, they sometimes use the information to avoid the KNLA rather than engaging with them, "because most commanders would rather focus their energies on making money while in the field and…do not want to take personal risks by fighting the KNLA" (Delang 2000, 166). Skirmishes occur when SPDC and KNLA "stumble" upon each other, when the former is ambushed by the latter, or when the former launches military offensives against the latter.

rather than be reduced to living their lives by hiding in the forest as internally displaced peoples or as refugees in Thailand.

Some villagers are permitted by Tatmadaw officers to return, but with conditions:

> We were forced to relocate [to Yan Myo Aung] but later they allowed us to go back to live beside the Sittaung River and work for our fields. When we were working the fields, they demanded we give them 3,000 kyats per month and they also demanded we give them 1,000 kyats when any of them got married. Because of this, we went to live in Yan Myo Aung again. Now the orders are that we can't work our fields anymore, and anyone who does must pay a 100,000 kyat fine. There are 15 farm field huts in the area, and they will know if we go back to work because more huts will appear (Delang 2000, 92).

Many Karen villages in conflict-free areas are not far from Tatmadaw frontlines. As a result, Tatmadaw units frequently come to harass the villagers, further reinforcing the almost perennial presence of Tatmadaw abuse. Many village chiefs implore the KNLA to refrain from ambushing Tatmadaw units in their area. If the KNLA do attack, the swiftness by which they disappear into the forest means that reprisals are meted out upon the villagers. Indeed, after battles with the KNLA, the Tatmadaw soldiers usually descend upon the nearest village to exact revenge by punishing the villagers.

The effects of forced relocations of Karen villages and its accompanying abuses of Karen villagers mean that there is hardly enough social stability for the Karen to uphold and reproduce their way of life. Ordinary Karen can no longer sustain their economy because forced relocations prevent them from being near their fields. The thinning KNLA lines can only effect limited protection for the villagers. Allowed mobility only between dawn and dusk, unable to live in freedom, subjected to violations of their human rights, and forced to do hard labor, many relocated villagers are in essence, an enslaved people living in emotional turmoil, physical illness, and hardship. Moreover, the emotional strain and desperation experienced by Karen villagers as they simultaneously attend to the needs of the SPDC, DKBA and KNLA cannot be overemphasized. They must answer to at least two of the groups, perhaps all of them, within a scenario where informers on all sides are present.

B. Effects of Forced Labor upon Villagers

Burma is one of the "world's worst offenders with respect to the practice of forced labor" even though Burma formally ratified articles from the 29th International Labour Organization (ILO) Convention in 1955 under U Nu's "democratic" regime (Apple and Martin 2003, 28). During the ILO's 29th Convention, Article 1, point 1, stated "Each Member of the International Labour Organisation which ratifies this Convention undertakes to suppress the use of forced or compulsory labour in all its forms within the shortest possible period." Yet it was not until 1999 that the SPDC "outlawed" (but only nominally) forced labor throughout the country. Similarly, the SPDC continues to violate Article 2, point 1, of the Convention which states: "For the purposes of this Convention the term *forced or compulsory labour* shall mean all work or service which is exacted from any person under the menace of any penalty and for which the said person has not offered himself voluntarily" (ILO 1994).

At the time of the Human Rights Watch/Asia foray into Kawthoolei during 1995, SLORC has maintained that porters work voluntarily and that laborers do get paid for their work. Indeed, during the beginning of offensives against Manerplaw in November 1994, the Permanent Representative of Myanmar to the United Nations addressed the Secretary-General of the United Nations Assembly:

> Allegations of forced labour stem from a misunderstanding or ignorance of the Myanmar tradition... Voluntary contribution of labour is a tradition... People are free to contribute labour voluntarily and there is no coercion at all involved. Although such contribution of labour is voluntary in nature, the Government, in recognition of their contributions, had made substantial payments of remunerations [*sic*] for the community development of the local populace in the areas concerned (HRW/A 1995, 12).

According to Human Rights Watch/Asia that has been reporting on forced labor in Burma since 1990, none of the interviewees ever indicated that they were paid. Most laborers actually had to transport their own survival items such as food and tools. The SLORC justifies forced portering by referring to "British laws adopted by Burma when it was a British colony," which mandated that provisions be made for the treatment of laborers. However, the Tatmadaw also only nominally subscribes to this policy. Nevertheless, SLORC states:

> Members of the Tatmadaw who are on active duty and who are unable to perform certain tasks can hire civilian laborers to assist them. The laborers must be paid from the time they leave their respective homes until they return on completion of their duty. Apart from daily wages, they are entitled to receive rail and steamer traveling warrants or cash to cover the actual cost of transport to and from their homes and the operation area. The respective military unit

has the responsibility of providing accommodation, messing, and social welfare benefits of the hired labourers (HRW/A 1995, 13).

The SLORC further responded from its Office of the Quartermaster General, on March 30, 1993, that forced laborers receive a daily wage of 20 kyats. ILO representatives investigating SLORC claims regarding their continued subscription to British Laws concluded that they were "made redundant when Burma ratified the ILO Conventions" in 1955, thus obligating it to "suppress the use of forced labour in all its forms within the shortest possible period" (HRW/A, March 1995, 13). In 1994, the ILO published a report contesting the regime's claims and concluded: "The exaction of labour and services, in particular porter age service, under the Village Act and the Towns Act is contrary to the Forced Labour Convention, 1930 (No. 29), ratified by the government of Myanmar in 1955" (ILO 1994).

The fact remains that Tatmadaw officers overseeing relocated villages view villagers as potential laborers and a source of profit, utilizing them for profit-making activities such as brick-baking, rubber planting or digging fishponds (Delang 2000, 19). Other activities forced upon villagers include:

- Acting as messengers and sentries for Army camps;
- Building and maintaining Army camp fences, trenches, booby traps and barracks;
- Cutting and hauling firewood;
- Cooking for soldiers;
- Building and rebuilding military supply roads;
- Clearing scrub along roadsides to minimize the possibility of ambush;
- Standing sentry along military supply roads;
- Growing crops for the Army on confiscated land (Delang 2000, 21).

Conscripted porters are also drawn from Karen villages in non-conflict areas. Other forced porters farm crops for SPDC troops, a process documented in Thaton Township where villagers toil on roughly 100 acres of confiscated land (ibid., 2000). Road maintenance is also undertaken by forced laborers, as one villager recounted:

> They are building roads and bridges around Pa-an Township. They started at Myaing Galay and are coming step by step. At every river they build a bridge, so there are many bridges. They've hired villagers to do it for them, for building roads and bridges. Their aim is to send all their rations by truck. They hire people for 100 Kyat per day for bridge building, and 50 Kyat per day for road building. But as for sentries, they don't hire us, we have to hire ourselves. If you don't go as a sentry, you have to hire someone yourself (ibid., 189).

An ill villager unable to be forced into physical labor must pay between 100-1,000 kyats "per day of labour missed" (Delang 2000, 22).[64] Just to employ cash as a medium of exchange is problematic because many Karen subsistence farmers do not have the luxury of consistently operating in a cash-based economy. According to Delang, "all profit goes to the officers, who also confiscate most of the rations intended for their soldiers and approximately half of the soldiers' pay in the name of various 'fees' and 'contributions', then sell the rations on the market and tell the soldiers to get their food from the villages" (ibid., 21).

Forced portering is another form of forced labor. Since forced portering often occurs when Tatmadaw columns are on the verge of launching offensives, adrenaline and tensions against the villagers are often high. Within this emotionally charged context, there is much abuse against the porters. The Karen Human Rights Group (KHRG) reports that many of these porters are "say muh wah," teenage Karen girls from remote hill villages:

> Witnesses on the Thai bank of the Moei River saw 100 or more of these girls being held under guard in fenced enclosures along the Moei riverbank every evening. The fences were still visible in photos taken weeks later, each of their sharpened bamboo stakes with an empty milk-tin hanging on top so the girls couldn't get over the fence at night without making a lot of noise. None of them are known to have escaped (KHRG 1995).

In 1995, Human Rights Watch/Asia sent a team to survey human rights abuses inflicted upon the regional population of Manerplaw during its siege by the Tatmadaw. In their interview of 50 porter escapees, many of whom were "taken from their places of work, from cinemas, trains and even their own homes from October [1994] onward," all of them had indicated that they were subjected to physical abuse, inhumane treatment, and had "witnessed the deaths of fellow porters" (HRW/A 1995, 2). According to interviews conducted by the Human Rights Watch/Asia team in 1995, "porters were gathered at the foot of a mountain in groups of as many as 1,000 men" to sustain the offensive against Manerplaw. One escapee recounted:

> On the third day out, we were still going up a very steep path up the mountain and a man who was about forty tripped over, he was so exhausted. He fell off the path and over the side of the mountain. We could hear him crashing down and calling for help. The bag of

---

[64] Six kyats = $1.00 U.S at the "official" rate. The 2000 market rate, with 50 percent inflation, meant that $1.00 US = 300 + kyats (Delang 2000, 22, 30; Burmese Border Consortium 2004).

rice he had been carrying was close to the edge. A soldier went and picked that up, but they didn't even look to see if the man could be helped. Then, on the day I escaped, a man of about thirty five couldn't go on and took off his load to rest. A soldier hit him in the calves with the butt of a gun. He still didn't get up, so the soldier pushed him over the edge of the mountain, and I had to carry on up the hill and couldn't look back to see what happened to him (Delang 2000, 10).

Yet another account by a different escapee:

A battle started early in the morning. I had to carry the shells to the soldiers firing the big guns, right at the front. I was really frightened; it was so noisy with the guns going off, other bombs landing near us, smoke all around. It was terrifying. I was too scared to take the mortars to the guns, but a soldier poked me in the bottom with a bayonet to make me move. I saw seven porters like me get hit. There was no medical care for them, they were just left to die. Two soldiers near me were injured, and they were taken to the field hospital. The battle stopped by midday, but I knew I would die if I stayed, and the next day I ran away (ibid., 10).

Not all porters were ideal able-bodied men. Some were mentally unstable as well as possessing physical limitations. An escapee from Pa-an described the abuse of a twenty-five year old:

There was a boy who couldn't speak and couldn't hear very well. He wouldn't stop or move on when told to and they beat him all the time. His face and eyes were swollen. They beat him and kicked him all the way—he didn't know where he was going or what was going on. I had to pull him by the arm to make him sit down when we stopped anywhere. He was beaten so much, almost like they did it for fun. It was awful. After five days I didn't see him anymore. I don't know what happened to him (ibid., 11).

Another escapee tells of a fellow porter:

He had glasses and only one eye. He was moaning and kept saying he wanted to get off the truck. Two soldiers started hitting him with their fists, on and on, until their fists bled. They tied his hands behind his back and demanded that some of us hit him too, but all of us just kept our heads down and refused. He was not right in the head—it was terrible that they could beat up someone like that. He was covered with blood, his face was very swollen and he had cuts on his shoulders and arms too. Still they wouldn't let him go (HRW/A 1995, 11).

The escapees documented by the 1995 Human Rights Watch/Asia team eventually encountered Karen villagers or KNLA soldiers that directed them toward their base areas. The KNLA made them stay for their own safety. According to Human Rights Watch/Asia, interviews conducted with the escapees "with no Karen or others within earshot" revealed that although the porters were upset at the KNU/KNLA for not letting them return home, the Karen had treated them well.

> When I found the Karen camp, I was very tired and hungry, I had not eaten for three days. The Karen let us eat what they ate, chicken and rice, sometimes pork. They made me carry things for them too—one mortar shell. With the Burmese army I had carried six (Delang 2000, 11).

After the 1995 fall of Manerplaw, forced portering continued unabated. In other areas:

> They come and capture porters when their new friends [replacement troops] came. Every month they collect 7 porters from B'Naw Kleh Kee and Paw Baw Ko. We had to go for 3 days, then after 3 days those 7 people go home and another group has to go. They demanded the village head collect people for portering. If people cold not go they had to give money - 2,500 Kyats for three days. They didn't hire other people with the money, they just took it for themselves - Saw Po Doh (male, age: 36), B'Naw Kleh Kee village, T'Nay Hsah township. Interview #23, 8/99 (Delang 2000, 233).

Human Rights Watch/Asia documented the ordeal of a twenty-year-old Karen refugee during 1997:

> He was forced to porter for the Burmese army in Karenni State and spoke of how four older porters in his group were unable to keep up with the soldiers. They apologized to the soldiers for their lack of speed and pleaded for mercy. They were beaten up by the soldiers and each one pushed off the edge of a cliff (HRW/A 1997, 10).

Yet another account is provided from an interview with a thirty-eight-year old refugee:

> He also spoke of another occasion during the same operation when he and the other porters had to cross a fast flowing river, holding

onto a piece of rope as a guide secured on both sides of the riverbank. It was difficult for them to keep their balance due to the heavy loads they were carrying. The rope broke after he had crossed, but a number of the porters behind him were swept away down the river being dragged under the water by their loads. He believed that at least ten porters drowned (HRW/A 1997, 9).

The loads carried by porters are far from light. Accounts gathered by the KHRG indicate that porters are forced to carry at least 30 kilograms—over 60 pounds—of rations and/or ammunition (Delang 2000, 20). Other porters indicate heavier loads. During the siege of Manerplaw, Human Rights Watch/Asia reported that porters were carrying twenty five to thirty five *beiktha* (90 to 126 kilograms or roughly 180 to 275 pounds respectively). Undocumented numbers of porters were given some form of stimulant, most likely methamphetamines acquired from the Golden Triangle, to ward off fatigue:

> They gave me medicine, the kind that does not make you sweat but makes you happy to walk. In Kywe and Ta months (around April 1999) there was no shade in Lay Gaw, but because of the medicine we were not sweating. I don't know what kind of medicine it was, but when I arrived in Maw Pleh the people told me that you need a certain kind of medicine to counteract the medicine which I had taken. But they didn't give us that one, so I became very sick - Saw Mo Aung (male, age: 39), Pah Klu village, T'Nay Hsah township. Interview #13, 9/99 (Delang 2000, 235).

According to Delang, one of the most dangerous aspects about portering is the prevalence of landmines. Porters are thus never exclusively porters as such, since many have been forced to walk ahead of Tatmadaw columns as minesweepers, their body weights triggering the devices. There have also been reports that villagers, when not working as porters, are forced to walk ahead of Tatmadaw troops "dragging banana palms along the paths" to detonate any landmines along the way (Falla 1991, 109).

KHRG reports also cite SPDC columns using women and children for the task when no males are present. It is not surprising that Delang identifies one main compelling factor causing Karen villagers to flee is the fear of being forced by the SPDC to clear trails of landmines. Indeed, Delang cites data from the September 2000 *Landmine Monitor*, a publication by the International Campaign to Ban Landmines, which estimated that the number of landmine casualties in the Karen State "rose...to well over 1,000, more than the reported landmine casualties for all of Cambodia during the same period." Burma, according to Delang, has become "Asia's new landmine hotspot" (ibid., 19).

The places where we ran were full of landmines. We didn't know the direction to run, but we ran ahead and reached Pah Klu even though we'd never been there before. When we arrived at Pah Klu, the Sgaw women asked us, 'How could you dare to come back this way? Landmines are everywhere. We are surprised to see you arrive here safely.' Some people ran into Burmese soldiers, though, so the soldiers tortured them – Maung Hla (male, age: 30), Kru Bper village, Kawkareik township. Interview # 4, 4/99 (Delang 2000, 233).

C. The Rape of Karen women

Rape was formally constructed as torture during the 1998 trial of Hazim Delic, a Bosnian Muslim deputy camp commander at the Celebici prison camp. Delic was one of four accused for brutally and repeatedly raping two Bosnian Serb women held as prisoners at the camp in 1992. The trial was carried out by the International Criminal Tribunal for the former Yugoslavia (ICTY). The ICTY was established on May 25, 1993, to counter "the serious violations of international humanitarian law committed in the territory of the former Yugoslavia since 1991, and as a response to the threat to international peace and security posed by those serious violations" (ICTY 1996).

The charges brought against Delic for raping Ms. Grozdana Cecez and a witness "A" included two main counts: (1) a count of "Grave Breach," which is punishable under Article 2 (b) (torture) of the Statute of the Tribunal and (2) "A Violation of the Laws or Customs of War" punishable under Article 3 (a) (torture and cruel treatment) of the Statute of the Tribunal (ICTY 1996).

Rape is a systematic military strategy employed by the Tatmadaw as a means to demoralize, intimidate, control, shame and ethnically cleanse Karen communities in Burma (KWO 2004, Apple and Martin 2003). For over forty years the Tatmadaw has employed rape not only upon Karen women, but upon women from other ethnic nationalities as well, including fellow Burman women during the pro-democracy crackdown. International attention on this shameful legacy of the Tatmadaw only surfaced recently with the release in June 2002 of *License to Rape*, a publication made by the Shan Women's Action Network (SWAN) and the Shan Human Rights Foundation (SHRF).

With the release of *License to Rape*, the international community "expressed unprecedented but long overdue outrage" (Apple and Martin 2003, 13). Appalled, the US government called for an international investigation and even sent its own investigators to the Thai/Burmese border. Other reactions followed:

1. Members of the US Congress denounced the wanton acts committed by Burma's military regime;

2. Officials from other countries publicly condemn the regime;
3. The UN was forced to send a UN Special Rapporteur on Human Rights in Burma to address the issue with the SPDC;
4. Various government officials, NGOs, and UN personnel argued for an independent investigation.

In the report, 625 cases of rape directed against Shan women during Tatmadaw Four Cuts offensives into their state sparked an international proclamation of rape as a violation of human rights. The reported numbers, however, are still but a fraction of the actual number of rape cases.

The SWAN and SHRF methodology was replicated by other pressure groups assessing the issues of ethnic rape in rural villages across Burma. Similarly, groups like the KHRG, Refugees International, and the KWO employ a methodology based on harnessing "grassroots knowledge, participation, and decision making" to acquire stories, observations, testimonies and physical evidence from victims and/or witnesses (Apple and Martin 2003, 15). The KWO is correct to remind us that in times of crises, it is "the women who bear the greatest burden of these systematic attacks, as they are doubly oppressed both on the grounds of their ethnicity and their gender" (KWO 2004, 6). This can be contrasted with Karen men where although their human rights have certainly been violated, "sexual violence was generally not covered as an issue" (ibid., 13).

Ethnic rape violates the United Nations' Declaration on the Elimination of Violence against Women in which "violence against women" is defined as "any act of gender based violence that results in or is likely to result in physical, sexual or psychological harm or suffering to women, including threats of such acts, coercion or arbitrary deprivation of liberty, whether occurring in public or private life." Because the violation of a woman's rights is so consistently committed by the Tatmadaw, the importance of situating rape incidents within a human rights framework cannot be overemphasized since a large array of other international laws and multilateral treaties already exist to combat such practices.

To date, the SPDC has only ratified two important treaties, the Convention on the Elimination of All Forms of Discrimination Against Women (CEDAW) in July 1997 and the Convention on the Rights of the Child (CRC) in July 1991. However, the continued employment of rape against ethnic minority women "raises questions about Burma's commitment—even symbolic—to eliminating gross human rights abuses" (Apple and Martin 2003, 49). Refugee International identifies CEDAW articles 2, 14, and 16 nullified by the continued use of rape.

Article 2 mandates "state parties to condemn discrimination against women in all its forms" through a variety of constitutional, legislative, logistical, or other actions. Article 14: requires the State to ensure that rural women can "participate in all community activities" as well as "enjoy adequate living conditions," clearly impossible in the climate of institutionalized rape or gang rape.

Pertaining to the violation of articles 6 and 16 in the CRC, Article 6 recognizes that each child has an inherent right to life, requiring states and political parties to safeguard that life. Article 16 condemns attacks on a child's "honour and reputation" and allows children the "right to legal protection against such attacks" (Apple and Martin 203, 49). Even though the SPDC did not formally ratify the remaining international treaties regarding the treatment of women, the failure to "ratify these treaties does not entitle the regime to flout international community standards" (Apple and Martin 2003, 29). These international laws are designated as non-derogable, which means that even if a state does not ratify or agree with its terms, the state is obligated to enforce them.

Most significantly, the SPDC has not signed the Rome Statute of the International Criminal Court (ICC), which began operations on July 22, 2002. As an international court with authority to hear human rights violations based on genocide, war crimes, crimes against humanity, and crimes of aggression, it is not surprising that the military regime has opted out of an international contingent where 80 countries have ratified its principals while another 139 member countries will formally allow the Rome Statute to exercise its jurisdiction over them. The lack of the SPDC's membership with the Rome Statute means that not one SPDC perpetrator of rape has ever faced justice.

According to the Rome Statute of the International Criminal Court (ICC), rape is considered a "crime against humanity" as noted in Article 7 (1)(g)-1. Because the SPDC allows their officers and soldiers to engage in behavior that matches the ICC criteria listed below, the SPDC is committing crimes against humanity:

1. The perpetrator invaded the body of a person by conduct resulting in penetration, however slight, of any part of the body of the victim or of the perpetrator with a sexual organ, or of the anal or genital opening of the victim with any object or any other part of the body.
2. The invasion was committed by force, or by threat of force or coercion, such as that caused by fear of violence, duress, detention, psychological oppression or abuse of power, against such person or another person, or by taking advantage of a coercive environment, or the invasion was committed against a person incapable of giving genuine consent.
3. The conduct was committed as part of a widespread or systematic attack directed against a civilian population.
4. The perpetrator knew that the conduct was part of or intended the conduct to be part of a widespread or systematic attack directed against a civilian population (KWO 2004, 12).

There are also NGOs and local organizations such as the KWO that gather evidence regarding rape but admit that data are based on only reported cases. What is known, however, is that the various military regimes of Burma have indirectly reinforced their hegemony through rape as a means of "diluting" ethnicity for quite some time, but the international community was not exposed to the depth of the situation only until recently. According to the KWO this is due to four main reasons:

1. Many Karen villages have continued to be displaced by the Burmese military regime since 1975. During this period, hundreds of women have been raped and killed, particularly during the period 1975-1985 when the regime was actively implementing its Four Cuts Policy. As a result, the aggressive and continuous offensives by the military have made it impossible for Karen groups to keep records of all the incidences of human rights violations.
2. Many of the women who have been raped live in areas controlled by the SLORC/SPDC military. Their movements and activities are under close surveillance. Therefore they are unable to speak out for themselves. Many of the women fear repercussions by the military, against themselves or their families if they do speak out.
3. Women do not want to be reminded of their painful and unpleasant experiences of rape. It cannot be overemphasized the extent to which women want to avoid reliving their experience of rape each time they tell their story.
4. It is very unusual for women who have suffered from rape and other sexual violations to reveal what they have been through because according to the customs and traditions among ethnic groups in Burma being raped is a shameful experience. Women are afraid of being looked down on or being belittled by the men in their communities if they talk about their experience.

Only those who dare to escape the environment of their assault and are willing to share their experiences have their accounts documented. Between October 2002 and March 2004, 125 rape cases received documentation but this is just a small fraction of cases. The KWO notes: "Karen women tend not to speak about such incidents, their communities do not speak about them, and the Burmese military keeps silent about its actions at international gatherings" (KWO 2004, 10).

Although there is a paucity of statistics regarding rape, Refugees International notes that one fact is clear: "there are numerous women and girls inside Burma who undoubtedly experienced rape during flight, but who will never be able to tell their stories" (Refugees International 2003, 27). Despite the lack of data, the accounts compiled by the Karen Women's

Organization between 2002 and 2004 succeeded in revealing what Karen women must face when a Four Cuts campaign descends upon their village.[65]

Tatmadaw troops arriving at a village frequently rape women because the men are often in the fields tending to the crops. Tatmadaw officials accuse them of being married to rebel solders and there have been reports where women are held as hostages so that their husbands are compelled to return. In the absence of men, rape victims are often also subjected to other forms of physical hardship, such as forced portering and labor. In the presence of men, an abundance of reports often note that husbands are forced to watch their wives get raped. Moreover, many Tatmadaw officials and soldiers harass and attempt to court local women; it is not uncommon for them to force women at the new villages to become their new wives (Apple and Martin 2003, 49).

Tatmadaw troops are encouraged to marry ethnic women as a means of "diluting" their cultural identity. In the Karenni areas, Burman soldiers are given 6,000 kyats of rice if they marry a Christian Karenni woman. In Shan and Karen areas, military policy:

> ...stipulates an order by which Burmese soldiers are told to marry ethnic women... Soldiers that marry an ethnic girl would be rewarded, as these ethnic people "would only destroy Burma." They are not Burma nationals and therefore were to be oppressed until they all disappeared from Burma... The obvious intention being that if killing and guns can't get rid of them then breeding them out will. Not only would it physically dilute the ethnic races into oblivion but it would also succeed in eradicating the culture and identity of the ethnic groups (Rogers 2004, 161).

There are other important areas where rape is also employed. Rape is used during migration. Karen women and villagers leaving a scene of conflict due to forced relocations or when they are moving to a better site because their original villages have been destroyed will be exposed to Tatmadaw troops. Moreover, rape is usually inflicted as a punitive measure when women villagers cross the paths of Tatmadaw battalions during an escape.

> Thay Yu and her family were on their way to Thailand because they could no longer "endure the oppression of the Burmese Army."

---

[65] In the following pages, I will only include five cases out of the 35 profiled by the KWO in their April 2004 report *Shattering Silences: Karen Women speak out about the Burmese Military Regime's use of Rape as a Strategy of War in Karen State.* Those interested in more qualitative data regarding number of rape victims as well as their accounts should also certainly look into the report *License to Rape*, published in 2002 by the Shan Women's Action Network (SWAN) and the Shan Human Rights Foundation (SHRF), as well as those provided by NGOs such as *Refugees International.*

While in the jungle, they ran into a battalion of soldiers. Thay Yu hid in a nearby bush with her family when a group of Burmese soldiers caught another family of four traveling with her to seek refuge in Thailand. Thay Yu listened to the screams as the soldiers killed the infant with a swift blow to the back of the neck. The 6-year-old girl ran and hid behind a tree. Before they shot and killed him, the soldiers instructed the husband to stand and watch while they raped the wife and killed her by stabbing her with a bamboo stick through her vagina and abdomen. After the soldiers left, Thay Yu and her family buried the husband, wife and baby, and collected the six-year-old daughter, with whom they journeyed to Thailand (Apple and Martin 2003, 26).

Women who are incarcerated at cells or jails within military camps, often used as temporary transit points before they are relocated to strategic villages, are raped, often by the camp commanders and/or the soldiers guarding them. Rape also occurs when women are forced to do labor or work as porters. Usually when Tatmadaw units descend upon a village, they require the village headmen to provide a number of individuals to serve the army. Women and children are often used because many men have either fled or have joined the resistance. In addition, the problem of food scarcity in war zones means that many women have to tend to their crops when there is a shortage of able-bodied men. The journey between Tatmadaw-occupied villages and the fields is a dangerous one, as women have to usually walk past Tatmadaw soldiers or stations.

In spite of the January 2004 "Gentleman's Ceasefire" talks between the KNU and SPDC, the latter continues to perpetrate human rights violations against Karen women. In April 2004, months before the failure and suspension of ceasefire talks, the KWO reported on the continued rape and extra-judicial killing of Karen women by SPDC soldiers. The KWO describes the women that have come forth as "women of courage" because they have "shattered the silences behind which their rapists have hidden" (KWO 2004, 7). Some of the graphic accounts drawn from the KWO's 2004 publication *Shattering Silences* are presented in verbatim below.

Case 1: Naw Bway Paw's Story
Naw Bway Paw is a Karen Buddhist woman form a village in Kyain Township in the Duplaya district. On the 15th of May 1999 when she was eight months pregnant she was gang raped by eight soldiers. Shortly after the rapes her baby was born dead. She was a 23-year old woman with one child at the time:

> Story teller-One of Naw Bway Paw's fellow villagers. On 15 May in 1999 at 12 noon, 8 of the soldiers of SPDC troops LIB (210) led by Battalion Commander Maung Maung Ohn, came back from the

battle field fighting in the village of Kyong Doe, Koe Kyoung, and Noe Taw Pla. They came back with the wounded soldiers and when they arrived at the house of Naw Bway Paw, they went into her house and tied up her husband with ropes in three parts of his body, at his neck, his body and his leg. And 8 of the SPDC soldiers raped her. She was gang raped. At that time Naw Bway Paw was 8 months pregnant. All of the soldiers raped her and they captured her husband for 10 days as a porter to carry military ammunition.

After the SPDC soldiers left, Naw Bway Paw got serious pain because of her 8-month pregnancy and being gang raped. She could not move or even shout or cry. But two of her villagers came into her house and took her to the hospital nearby. When she arrived at the hospital, the nurse gave her treatment. Within a few days she gave birth to her baby. But her baby was dead. Her condition was so bad and she was suffering nearly a year after being raped. But there was no action taken for her case.

Case 2: Naw Cho Myint's Story

Naw Cho Myint is a Karen woman from a village in the Tavoy district. On the 6th of February 2003 she was raped and both she and her three year old daughter were murdered. She was a 23 year old married woman with a three year old daughter and was three months pregnant at this time:

On 6 February, 2003, Naw Cho Myint, returned to her deserted village, Ler Kwe Dot (Sinzwe) from the relocation area to tend her plantation. One of her villagers said that on February 6, a member of Pyithusit[66] named Maung Aye came to village when Naw Cho Myint was in her hut. When the other villagers returned to the relocation area Naw Cho Myint was not with them.

Then on the 14th of February 2003 her body was found outside the village of Htee Oo (Hpabyoke) near Kwe Dot village. She had been raped and then slashed to death by Maung Aye. He then threw her three year old daughter into Pi Stream and took kyat 40,000 and three gold necklaces from her. Naw Cho Myit was three months pregnant when she was raped and was slashed to death said her villager (KWO 2004, 62).

Case 3: Naw Htoo Htoo's Story

Naw Htoo Htoo is a Karen, Christian woman, who worked as a farmer in her village Wet La Daw in Kyauki Township in Nyaunglebin district. On the 12th of February 1994

---

[66] The Pyithusit is a Tatmadaw militia.

she was tortured and raped by Ba Kyi from the Burmese military. She was a 33 year old widow with three children at the time:

The SLORC troops from 60 Regiment often forced us to work for them. They made us sleep on the ground in the camp, but the mosquitoes usually kept us awake. We could only go to the latrine once in the early morning or once after work in the evening, and we had to urinate where we slept. Then after 3 days of this they said we couldn't go home, and we'd have to stay for a week. When we protested that we had no more food or clean clothes, a village elder was sent back to the village to get these things from our homes, but we weren't allowed to go.

Shortly after this system began, Paw Daw Moo camp closed for a few days while soldiers went to reinforce the troops at Yan Gyi Aung camp in some fighting with the Karen army. When they came back, they called a meeting and told all the villagers to cooperate with them and that they would give us some food if we worked with the army. But we still had to bring all our food with us every time; they only gave us some beans and a few other things.

One night, I remember it was February 12; Ba Kyi came back from a trip to headquarters and called a meeting. When we left the meeting we were split into small groups and kept under guard on the ground. But none of us could sleep because Ba Kyi went up the hill to the top of the camp and ordered the soldiers to fire their guns and mortars all over the place for no reason. There were all kinds of explosions and we were terrified, which must have been why he did it. Along with the other Christians there, I just prayed and tried to sleep.

Ba Kyi started calling villagers to his quarters one by one and questioning them, but we never got to see them afterwards to find out what happened. Eventually I was woken up and was the first of the 5 women there taken to see him. After I was left alone with him, he told me to tell him about Wet La Daw village, especially about the smugglers coming to buy cattle and buffaloes and any villagers who were helping the rebels. I didn't want to tell him anything, and he started yelling at me and threatening me with his knife. He demanded to know about Karen soldiers and Saw Lah Oo, their commander. I told him I'm too busy struggling to survive and feed my children to think about such things. He said he wanted to know what the villagers said about him. He told me he'd already tied up 2 villagers and killed them, and started firing continuous questions at me, especially about Saw Lah Oo. I didn't even have time to try to answer.

Then he pushed me into a small room behind a wall and tied one of my hands with wire so I couldn't move. He ordered me to sit quietly while he interviewed the others. Then he went and just pretended to call the next person in, but immediately came back to me and started asking more questions. I said, "Don't ask me, ask the men," and he accused me of working for the rebels.

Then he waved his knife at me again, grabbed my free hand and clutched at my breasts. I shouted, "Son, let me free!" But he told me since he was 24 and I was only 33, I must call him Brother, and started asking for sex. When I refused he said, "Then I'll send you up to the top of the camp—there many of my men will rape you and kill you, and we'll say the Karen rebels did it! If that frightens you, you'd better give in to me!" I told him, "Son, don't do this, you're single, if you need a woman you can marry someone much prettier than me. I'm a Christian widow, I have 3 children to support and I have to work here. I have too much trouble already."

He just kept threatening that he'd give me to his men who'd rape me to death, waving his knife and demanding sex. I kept fighting but he tied up my other hand, and then he pushed me down and raped me. I warned him I must tell the Church but he ordered me not to. When he was finished he asked me, "Are you satisfied?" All I could tell him was that my life was now nothing but darkness. He just said, "If you're so troubled and ashamed, go hang yourself."

He raped me 3 times that night. I was tied up so tightly that my elbows were dislocated while he raped me, and they still hurt even now. Then he told me that when I went the next day I would have to go and spy on 2 huts near the village that the Karen soldiers used and report back to him by letter, especially anything about Saw Lah Oo. I agreed just so he'd let me go. At 4 a.m. they woke up the other villagers and let me go with them but warned me not to tell them anything except that I'd been tied up under a tree overnight.

But back in the village, I felt I had to tell them and tell the Church. When I did this I learned that Ba Kyi had treated many women the same way before. But now that I'd told them I couldn't stay there safely any more, and I had to flee my home and bring my children here (KWO 2004, 39).

Case 4: Daw Win Hla's Story

Daw Win Hla is a Karen, Buddhist woman from a village in Kyaito Township in the Thaton district. On the 24th of January 1992 she was captured by the Burmese military and forced to work as a porter; she was raped every night by the soldiers during this time. She was a 42 year old married woman with six children at the time of the attack:

While I was cooking, a group of SLORC soldiers came to my house and forced me to go along with them to Byu Ha military camp. At the camp they made me join a group of over 100 porters, including 40 women aged from 15 to 50. The soldiers gave me 81 mm mortar bombs to carry, the same load as they gave many of the male porters. They made us carry our loads over high mountains all day, and then every night I was raped along with the other women. It was very hard for us to keep carrying our loads in these conditions. All we got to eat was a bit of rotten bad-smelling rice, and we didn't even get that regularly. For instance, one night in the forest when the birds were singing the soldiers said it was the enemy's signal, so cooking would be too dangerous. So we had to go hungry.

After 9 days I ran away with 3 other women, but the soldiers captured us in our hiding place. They were very angry, and they pointed their guns at us and shouted that if we ever tried to escape again they would kill us.

Along the way the SLORC soldiers were completely destroying the villages we came to. I saw them steal paddy from the villagers and burn down their houses and paddy barns. I also saw them steal an elephant from one villager, and they killed many village animals for food, but we never got any of it.

All of us only had the clothes on our backs, which quickly got torn and dirty, so it was very cold and uncomfortable. One day it rained and we all got soaking wet, which made it even worse that night. We were all very weak, and many men and women were ill with chills and fever, but the hurt and sick were still forced to carry their loads and keep up, even if they had to be dragged. There was one twenty year old Karen boy from Ma Kyi Hta village who got a bowel disorder. He was very weak and always vomiting but the soldiers still forced him to keep up.

When we were climbing Taung Ni, a very high mountain, he couldn't go on and begged and pleaded with the soldiers to be let go. But the soldiers said he had to come. They forced the rest of us to keep climbing and the Karen boy fell behind. We never saw him after that, so I don't know what they did with him. Another 45-year-old man showed me a large unhealed gash on the front of his left thigh, and wounds on both sides of his head. He said he'd run away during some fighting but the soldiers had caught him. They cut his leg and beat him on the head. When he told me this he was very weak, but they were still making him carry big heavy rockets.

When it was still dark one morning I heard Daw Khin Aye say she was going into the forest. I thought she was going to escape so I went with her. The four of us didn't know which way to go and walked all day in the forest. After dark, we followed a river until we heard someone shouting, "Daw bway! Daw bway!" [In Karen − "Sister! Sister!"]. When I first heard the voices I was very afraid, but when it turned out they were Karen soldiers and they were kind to us I was very happy (KWO 2004, 29).

Case 5: Naw Paw Eh's Story
Naw Paw Eh is a Karen, Buddhist woman from a village in Kyaito Township in the Thaton district. She was abducted by the Burmese military to work as a porter on the 24th January, 1992. She was gang raped every night. She was 17 years old at the time.

I was with Daw Khin Aye collecting firewood near our village when a group of soldiers came and ordered us to go with them. They took us to Byu Ha military camp, where we joined a group of at least 100 porters, including 40 women. We left the next morning for a long march over the mountains, and I had to carry four heavy 81mm mortar bombs, even though I am very small. They were so heavy I almost couldn't hold them on my back, but the soldiers made me carry them over high mountains.

We had no blankets and only the clothes we were arrested in, so it was very cold at night and easy to get sick. But I didn't have much time to think about the cold, because the soldiers always came for me at night. Because I am young and single, they all wanted to rape me and every night I got raped worse than most of the others. An officer who the soldiers all called "Ba Gyi" always came for me. He also raped a young Indian girl very often. All night long, the soldiers would gang rape all of us one after another. You could always hear women's screams at night, if they were strong enough to scream. Then in the morning they made me carry the bombs again.

This went on day after day, and I just couldn't bear it any longer. The other women said they pitied me but there was nothing they could do to help. They had their own loads to carry. I was so hungry and thirsty, tired and weak from carrying bombs and being raped that I was crying all the time. I never stopped crying and I was too weak to climb the mountains, and when the soldiers saw this they kept shouting at me and waving their guns and this just frightened me and made me cry even more.

Finally, very early one morning Daw Khin Aye called me to go with her. I didn't understand and I asked her where she was going, but she said to just follow her and not ask questions. We ran away but we didn't know where we were, so we traveled in the forest all day, and the next night we found some Karen soldiers who took care of us. They pitied me because I looked so weak and gave me a warm jacket, which I still have (KWO 2004, 32).

D. *Internally Displaced Peoples (IDPs)*

An IDP is defined by the UN as a person violently uprooted from home but who remains within the borders of the country. The United Nations' 1998 *Guiding Principles on Internal Displacement* defines IDPs as those that have been "obliged to flee or to leave their homes or places of habitual residence" (Burmese Border Consortium September 2002). Overall, between 600,000 and 1 million IDPs live in Burma today.

> For many of these people life is now a matter of running back and forth, spending much of their time living in the forest or their fields, where they must always be on the lookout for SPDC or DKBA columns, and sneaking back to stay at the villages for brief periods when they think it is safe. If they are found in the forest or living in their field hut, they face almost certain arrest, interrogation and torture as suspected KNLA supporters, and they may be shot on sight, taken as porters, or executed (Delang 2000, 199).

The Burmese Border Consortium 2002 field report gives more accurate figures, citing a total of 632,978 displaced persons living in hiding. The Border Consortium also identifies 2,536 of what they term "affected villages," or villages that have been "destroyed (usually burnt), relocated en masse or otherwise abandoned" for fear of marauding Tatmadaw activity (Burmese Border Consortium September 2002). The January 2004 Four Cuts offensives launched against Karen and Karenni in northern Kawthoolei generated over 5,000 displaced persons. Offensives in June 2004 caused an additional 3,000 villagers to halt work in the fields and flee their villages.

According to the Committee for Internally Displaced Karen People (CIDKP) and the Burmese Border Consortium, there are three types of

IDPs: (1) those displaced for political reasons, (2) those displaced for economic reasons, and (3) those that are displaced as a result of military operations (Burmese Border Consortium September 2002). The vast majority of Karen IDPs are all of the above statuses, sometimes sequentially, sometimes simultaneously. As a result, Karen IDPs are facing starvation, disease, and death, mainly from treatable illnesses such as malaria, pneumonia, dysentery, diarrhea, and measles.

The vulnerable segment consists of women (especially pregnant women), the elderly and children. Karen infant mortality rates due to these circumstances average about 20 percent (Brunner et al. 1998, 2). Many of the 100,000 to 200,000 Karen IDPs fleeing frontline battles between KNLA and the Tatmadaw, are a result of those who fled strategic villages to hide in "forests surrounding their farm fields," while some become "beggars in the towns" (Delang 2000, 17, 24). Relief teams such as the FBR risk their lives to enter these areas and provide IDPs with medical treatment, basic material supplies, and spiritual encouragement, as well as provide for the outside world compelling data and images.

Karen IDPs flee because they fear being forced into portering, raped, tortured, or killed. According to the Burmese Border Consortium the fact that many thousands choose to flee from relocation sites and take their chances as IDPs, "hiding, under conditions of minimal food and personal security, and subject to the full catalogue of Tatmadaw human rights abuses" is indicative of the deplorable conditions in the overwhelming number of strategic villages (Burmese Border Consortium September 2002). In 1987, Smith was able to witness a party of 220 Karen IDPs arrive at the Thai border:

> Government soldiers had killed 31 of their relatives, apparently at random, since the Four Cuts campaign was officially introduced amid much fanfare in the vicinity of their homes in the Shwegyin Hills in 1975. "Each year three, four, or five villagers have to die," said Pah La Hai, a 43 year-old farmer. "The Burmese shoot them without reason. They will kill all the villagers. No one must stay there anymore" (Smith 1999, 260).

However, even by hiding in the jungle, IDPs are not immune to further Tatmadaw reprisals. Tatmadaw patrols are frequently sent to seek out these temporary sanctuaries. Upon finding the IDPs, lives are lost, torture and rape implemented, makeshift dwellings are destroyed, while available foods are confiscated. As a result:

> Every IDP family has a place in the jungle prepared in case they need to run from the Burma Army. They keep extra rice and all non-essential possessions there. Animals sometimes find and destroy

their places in the jungle, so they have many different problems to deal with.[67]

Many IDP families try to situate themselves near rivers by sharing a hiding site. Those IDPs that are more conspicuous face grave consequences: even as far back as 1988, an Amnesty International report documented episodes of Karen "shot in the back as they worked the fields, of daughters seeing their fathers buried and burnt alive, and young men having the flesh stripped off their shins with bamboo rollers to make them talk" (Falla 1991, 361).

E. Refugees

As a result of the quickly changing nature of warfare in the region, refugee movements manifest in one of three ways. Refugees may be arriving, existing refugees may be moving to different camps, while others choose to return back to Kawthoolei. The first large wave of arriving refugees occurred in 1984 when over 10,000 Burmese refugees fled to Tak province, Thailand. By 2003, there were over 130,000 predominantly Karen refugees at camps inside Thailand. Although the Karen resistance started in 1949, most Karen displaced by war prior to 1984 resolved to remain inside Burma. Most of the refugees in the 1980s were migratory because they returned to Kawthoolei, crossing the porous border, when fighting had diminished. However since the 1990s, Karen refugees in Thailand have tended to remain at the camps due to the intensification of fighting between the KNU and the Tatmadaw.

The years following the 1988 pro-democracy crackdown increased the population of Kawthoolei as Burman and pro-democracy activists fled to the eastern hills for safety. The Tatmadaw hunted the Rangoon protesters and those granting them safe haven. The formation of the 20 insurgent-strong DAB transcommunality in 1988 compels the Tatmadaw to respond. Fearing that self-determination groups like the KNU were providing military assistance to them, or at the very least providing a new source of potential anti-SLORC recruits, the Tatmadaw re-intensifies its Four Cuts campaigns in the eastern hills, generating another exodus of Karen refugees. Once again, waves of refugees either fled to the border or became IDPs within Kawthoolei's liberated areas.

After the capture of Manerplaw, several thousand KNU families similarly made their trek to Thailand. By of February 1995 many were already in refugee camps. During 1997, when over one hundred representatives from various self-determination groups, including groups which have already signed ceasefires, participated in the Ethnic Nationalities Seminar in KNU territory, Rangoon took notice.

---

[67] Information provided by contact networking with Free Burma Rangers.

Since the event concluded with the ethnic nationalities' endorsement of Aung San Suu Kyi and the NLD, Rangoon launches yet more Four Cuts campaigns, resulting in a wave of 20,000 refugees fleeing to Thailand. By the end of 1997, over 115,000 refugees of all ethnic minorities, but mostly Karen, were in camps along the border. Since 1997, over 8,500 refugees were forced back to Kawthoolei by the Thai Army's Ninth Division (HRW/A 1997, 2). In addition, over three thousand refugees that escaped localized battles were prevented from entering Thailand.

KHRG figures from 2000 estimates that approximately 110,000 Karen and Karenni refugees are still registered at various camps in Thailand. Refugees International has described the continuing exodus of people from Burma as Southeast Asia's largest migration movement. Moreover, an additional 150,000 refugees are estimated to have fled deep into Thailand's major cities and constitute its large illegal migrant population (Burmese Border Consortium September 2002). Since the KNU and KNLA no longer control any significant territory, areas previously under Karen control are now subject to Tatmadaw laws, policies, and abuses. Subsequently, new ethnic refugees continue to make their trek toward Thailand. According to the Burmese Border Consortium's 2002 report:

> With the ethnic resistance "defeated" and their territory "lost" it might have been expected that the refugee flow would stop, or at least decrease. But it has not. Refugees have continued to enter Thailand until the present day. The total border camp population, including the three Mon resettlement sites on the Burma side, now totals around 143,000 and the rate of arrival has been remarkably constant since UNHCR [United Nations High Commission for Refugees] registered the refugees in 1999, averaging just under 900 per month for the last three years.

It is also difficult for any organization to ensure that basic necessities are consistently supplied to camp inhabitants. The main reason is that the vast majority of camps are located within ten kilometers of Kawthoolei, and some are even located on the banks of the Moei and Salween rivers, banks that once constituted the liberated areas under KNU control. Yet since many of these banks have fallen into Tatmadaw control the refugee camps are vulnerable. Since the Tatmadaw "have never shown respect for international borders," many camps are raided by groups working for the Tatmadaw such as the DKBA.

Exacerbating the situation is Rangoon's tendency to blame border incursions upon the DKBA/DKBO "which the SLORC claims it does not control in any way" (KHRG 1995). In the past, the Thai Army did not have to worry about its borders as significantly because the KNU had control over the areas. But ever since the fall of Manerplaw, simultaneously combined with the Thai Army's vacillating stance on their policy with the KNU, SLORC and the DKBA have frequently exploited the ambivalence of Thai forces to raid across the border.

International NGOs and charity organizations play a pivotal role in aiding refugees. The Karen Relief Committee, a predominantly Christian organization that has close links to the KNU, manages all Karen refugee camps. Many charitable organizations descend on groups of camps at one time or another. Charity personnel from different parts of the world have often stayed at these camps to attend to medical, educational, and religious matters. Visiting groups are hosted by organizations such as Asian Tribal Ministries, a Christian-based organization that assesses the human condition regarding the victims of Tatmadaw policies and offensives.

According to Human Rights Watch/Asia, since Karen refugee camps were established throughout the border regions between Kawthoolei and Thailand, "non combatant members of the KNU have routinely lived in the camps, where they often worked as camp administrators" (HRW/A 1995, 17). Karen refugee camps have also installed local Karen governments within the camp boundaries. Fellow refugees elect leaders of camps, and the elected officials manage the smooth functioning of institutions within the camp, primarily the health and education departments. The Karen leadership also utilizes a lottery system for determining allocation of available plots of land for farming in the surrounding areas. The Thai Army ostensibly protects the camps but this protection is intermittent, as we shall see.

The KNU does not desire that refugees be returned to Burma during times of war or a precarious peace. Bo Mya was aware of their fate: "We don't want the Karen to be repatriated because they would become minesweepers and forced to work in fields or construction sites. They won't have the opportunity to return to their choice of occupation but will have to do whatever the SLORC tells them" (Bangkok Post, January 18, 1998). According to Mya, intelligence sources from the ABSDF identified large shelters built in preparation for the returning refugees so that they could be screened, photographed, and fingerprinted. The DKBO would then distinguish those associated with the KNU and those sympathetic to the DKBO movement. The returnees would then be divided into three groups: to work as porters, to build roads or to be sent to detention centers.

Another surprising fact is that Thailand is not formally obligated to help any refugees. It honors "customary international law" to grant asylum to persons fleeing from persecution. This, however, is not the same as direct refugee assistance. Indeed, the Karen and other ethnic refugees at Thailand's refugee camps have no official status. Thailand is not even a signatory to the 1951 United Nations Convention Relating to the Status of Refugees nor its 1967 protocol. Nevertheless, Thailand tolerates the camps, allowing a network of charities to provide basic necessities such as food, blankets, and mosquito nets. It has also allowed groups such as the Médecins Sans

Frontières (MSF), more popularly known as Doctors Without Borders, to provide basic medical needs to Karen refugees, as well as accommodating research on malaria. The UNHCR leaves the process of admitting Burma's refugees to the Thai authorities; indeed, the UNHCR is not in the position to determine whether escapees from Burma are eligible for refugee status.

Moreover, Thai public opinion would grow less sympathetic toward Burma's refugees. In 1999, Burmese students laid siege to the Burmese Embassy in Bangkok. In 2000, a breakaway Karen group called God's Army[68] made attempts to take hostages at a Thai provincial hospital in Ratchaburi. These developments, coupled with Thailand's desire to court the military regime, have meant that Thailand is eager to rid their border of Burma's refugees and refugee camps. To make matters worse, the SPDC is reluctant to grant the UNHCR permission to monitor the departure of refugees. Moreover, within the last ten years Thailand has resorted to repatriation and refoulement policies, sending many Karen refugees back to an uncertain fate (HRW/A 1997, 2).

In August 1986, after visiting refugee camps where 18,000 Karen and Karenni have taken refuge, Roger Winter, Director of the United States Committee for Refugees had this to say:

> Karen refugees have been received rather well in Thailand, in part because there is substantial ethnic Karen population of Thai nationality there. However, the Royal Thai Government does not formally recognise the Karen from Burma as refugees...Nothing of a developmental nature that might encourage the refugees to stay in Thailand or draw others, or that would antagonise the authorities in Rangoon is permitted (Falla 1991, 194).

Thailand's anxiety about international organizations disrupting their ties with the SPDC has meant that access to the camps is strictly prohibited: outside governmental organizations are not granted access and neither is the International Red Cross.

Although one may suppose that refugee camps offer Karen a safe haven, the fact is they are only relatively safer than areas within Kawthoolei. Refugee camps are concentrated in two areas between Kawthoolei and Thailand. The northern camps are close to the Thai town of Mae Sot in Tak province while the southern camps are located in Ratchaburi province. Each region falls under the jurisdiction of a different division of the Thai Army. Since almost all of the refugee camps in Thailand are just a few kilometers from the

---

[68] The KNU has vehemently denied that it sponsored any activities by the God's Army which, after all, was a KNU breakaway faction. The Thai government claims that the hostage takers fought back when the Thai Army stormed the hospital—this despite hostage eyewitness accounts that tell a different story: the vast majority of the God's Army surrendered inside the hospital and were summarily executed by the Thai Army.

Kawthoolei border, Tatmadaw incursions via the DKBA are not infrequent events. The many moves, consolidations, and dismantling of camps are thus due to the threat from across the border. Yet these activities must be balanced with Thailand's wish to make certain that camps are close enough to the border should repatriation need to occur en masse.

At the beginning of 1995, DKBO leaflets were distributed to refugee camps near Mae Sam Lep just inside Thailand, where over 9,020 Buddhist and Christian Karen have fled since the fall of Manerplaw. It urged Buddhist Karen to return back to Burma. DKBO leaflets found at refugee camps argue that the refugee situation inside Thailand only "prolongs the KNU," further warning that "those who still remain in the refugee camps will be considered anti-Buddhist KNU and will be destroyed" (HRW/A 1995, 16). Aid workers from NGOs in the area estimated that 200-300 families took these threats seriously and returned back into DKBO-controlled areas.

The beginning of February 1995 would see the DKBA/SLORC launch a series of raids into refugee camps and nearby Thai villages. The raids were meant to demoralize and destabilize what Rangoon and the DKBA perceived to be a pro-KNU population. Within the year, over sixty refugee shelters would be razed resulting in 10 refugee deaths while five Thai civilians and six Thai policemen were also killed (HRW/A 1998, 40). During the same month 400 sacks of rice, provided by international aid agencies and reserved for refugee camps further north, were stolen by twenty DKBA/SLORC soldiers at Ka Htee Hta.

By the end of February, DKBA troops had already made repeated raids into various camps and had stationed themselves opposite some camp sites. By this time four refugee camps were already relocated deeper inland to counter DKBA forays. DKBA soldiers patrolled the camps in plain clothes and trucks coming to and from camps were stopped and searched by them. On February 23, a truck transporting four families to Huay Haeng was ambushed by the DKBA. As the refugees tried to run away two women were killed, as was the Thai driver, while a six-year old boy was shot in the chest and severely injured. Trucks behind the scene hurriedly turned back and although "medics heard the shooting…they did not know what happened until they reached Mae Sariang by a different route" (HRW/A 1995, 17).

By March 1995, SLORC radio documented 9,495 returnees (KHRG 1995).[69] Unlike resistance units in the past which surrendered to Rangoon amid positive fanfare, the refugees that willingly capitulated to Tatmadaw control are still derided:

---

[69] The Karen Human Rights Group notes that in reality, the "total is more like 1,500-2,000, primarily from two of the largest camps, Baw Noh [Mae Tha Waw] and Sho Kloh" (March 29, 1995).

Articles in the state-run media have described all refugees as KNU supporters, maligning them and the international agencies that give them support. "The refugee policy of the Western bloc is nothing but a policy of enslaving other nations under a neo-colonialist policy by breeding thugs...In fact they [refugees/KNU] are all scoundrels and swindlers, rogues and rascals, crooks and scam artists. They keep swindling contributions made by the international community to look after refugee funds" (HRW/A 1995, 16).

During April 1995, more refugee camps are sacked by the DKBA/SLORC. Mae Ra Ma Luang camp with 4,583 refugees, Kamaw Lay Khlo camp with 4,000 refugees, Mae Tha Wah camp with 6,400 refugees, Shoklo camp[70] and Kler Ko camp with 3,726 refugees are all attacked and "whole sections of these camps were razed, [while] Kler Ko and Kamaw Lay Khlo were entirely destroyed" (HRW/A 1998, 40). This time Thailand was compelled to respond. Its helicopter gunships conducted reconnaissance at the border for two days, but "there were no moves to permanently improve security" (HRW/A 1998, 40).

By the middle of 1995, smaller camps were dismantled and its inhabitants incorporated into Mae La camp, swelling its population from 3,000 in 1995 to a staggering 30,000 refugees by 1998. As of January 2003, Mae La is constituted by an astounding 42,032 refugees, making it by far the largest primarily Karen refugee camp in Thailand (Burmese Border Consortium September 2002).

On January 28, 1997, Don Pa Piang camp, located about 15 miles north of Mae Sot, was sacked by over 100 DKBA/SLORC troops that had crossed the Moei River from the west, only one mile away from the camp.

> The attackers surrounded the camp, which is much smaller than Huay Kaloke, at about 9:45 p.m. Then the refugees heard a single shot fired, and the soldiers stormed the camp in two groups. One group of about 30 DKBA headed for the clinic and the houses of the medics, demanded admittance to the clinic and searched it for the microscope.[71] Witnesses say they appeared to be on drugs. Even though a medic offered them medicine, they said it was the microscope, not medicine, that they wanted. They finally found it, then set the clinic on fire and commenced burning the surrounding houses. A larger group headed for the market section of the camp and began looting. Upon realising what was happening, a Thai merchant who was spending the night in the camp ran to his truck...and tried to drive out of the camp. The soldiers blocked the

---

[70] The DKBA was also looking for an unidentified KNU officer at Sho Kloh camp.
[71] Microscopes, as will be discussed in Chapter 6, are coveted because they detect malaria.

truck and ordered him to stop, but he attempted to drive past them and they opened fire on him, shooting him dead.

The troops fired into the air and set much of the camp on fire. As in Huay Kaloke, the houses are bamboo huts with leaf roofs tightly packed together, so the fire spread on its own and about 95 percent of the camp was completely destroyed—only a couple of rows of houses were left behind the market section. As Huay Bone was burning, some refugees in the camp saw the glow in the sky coming from the burning of Huay Kaloke, 10 km. to the south, but they did not realise what it was (KHRG 1997).

The KHRG then interviewed "Naw G'Mwee Paw," a 49 year-old Christian medic at Don Pa Piang camp:

I was under my house, I looked at the clinic and I saw the fire start to burn. Then my house and the camp office [next door] started to burn. They were about 30 soldiers there, and at other places maybe a lot more, but I just saw the ones who were near my house and the clinic. They were dressed in uniforms and all of them had guns, but I don't know which kind. One of the guns was very short and a lot of them had long ones. I could not see very well at nighttime. We could not shine our torchlights, and they were shining their torchlights on us. Only some of them were DKBA. SLORC soldiers were also amongst them. As far as I know, the soldiers who came and talked to me were DKBA, but outside the clinic many of the soldiers were staying silently and they didn't speak. One woman told me that when they were outside the camp she heard them speaking Burmese to each other, but inside the camp they didn't speak at all...

First, they surrounded the camp, then after the gunshot, some of them ran to the clinic and my house but another group went to the market. They shot one Thai [a merchant who sold things in the camp]. I didn't see that. Early the next morning I came back to the market and I saw a lot of blood on the ground, and the people told me, "Oh! Min Yen's husband was shot last night!" When he heard that the DKBA were close to us, he jumped into his car and tried to drive out of the camp. Then he saw one DKBA soldier in front of him who ordered him to stop the car, but he tried to drive through and they shot him dead. He was hit in his leg and his bladder, inside the car. I don't know his name. He was Thai. His wife is also Thai. They do business here. They have a shop in the market. He was staying alone in the camp that night [without his wife]...

At that time, we didn't know that they were also burning down Huay Kaloke camp. We could see the light of the fire in the sky but we didn't know where it was from. It was nearly at the same time that they set our camp on fire. There was no Thai security in our camp and nobody was staying at the checkpoint. Usually they stayed in the day time, sometimes at night too. But if they hear that the news is not so good [i.e. that there may be an attack], they go away. It happened at night time, so there was no security for us. But the next morning, a lot of Thai soldiers came, checked the situation and asked many questions (KHRG 1997).

The second attack launched on the same night was directed to Huay Kaloke camp sheltering roughly 10,000 refugees and located six kilometers inside Thailand. Huay Kaloke sheltered refugees that were sympathetic and loyal to Karen National Union and Bo Mya. Its fires were seen by fellow Karen refugees in the other aforementioned camps, but it survived.

During 1998, attacks against refugee camps were again renewed. On March 11, 150-200 DKBA and Tatmadaw troops again attack Huay Kaloke camp. They had launched their attacks from the recently captured KNU stronghold at Kawmoorah. Five lives were lost and twenty-five were wounded in the assault. Two of the fatalities were women, shot on sight, one of them pregnant and unable to flee the flames that engulfed her shelter. In this foray, over 85 percent of the 1,613 shelters at Huay Kaloke camp were burnt to the ground and nearly 9,000 refugees were left without any shelter (HRW/A 1998, 41).

Not surprisingly, one of the few structures left standing was a Buddhist monastery on the campgrounds. One survivor said that "the whole camp was blazing and we jumped into a trench. We heard the soldiers saying 'We told you to go back to Myanmar!'" (Bangkok Post, March 11, 1998). Refugees that did not flee to Mae Sot after the attack hid in adjacent rice fields. Four days later, attacks were launched against the bloated Mae La camp, but it held on. On March 23 at roughly 1:30 A.M., Mawker camp, with over 8,500 refugees was shelled with 60 mm mortars as well as RPG7s, and M79 grenade launchers. Over 2,000 shelters were attacked and fifty completely razed.

One of my Karen colleagues, a 21 year-old name Roni was there during the late night assault at Huay Kaloke. Only 15 at the time, Roni described the eerie quiet that evening since everyone at the camp had already been forewarned of an impending attack. According to Roni, the Thai soldiers that had guarded Huay Kaloke "disappeared" by the evening hours, a typical response by the Thai Army that was observed in the first Huay Kaloke attack as well as at Don Pa Piang in 1997. After midnight, fires started to surround the camp as mortar assaults, grenades, and automatic gunfire commenced. Soldiers in black with blackened faces then descended upon the camp. Roni had to seek shelter by hiding underneath some of the bamboo barracks that served as dwellings in virtually all refugee camps in Thailand, while the DKBA and Tatmadaw units looted and razed the camp for about two hours with impunity. He then made his escape by fleeing toward Mae Sot.

Roni's account is telling because during the aftermath of the second Huay Kaloke raid, international condemnations were not only directed toward Rangoon but also toward the Thai government for not protecting the refugees. Both the United States and the Karen Relief Committee also slammed Thailand's Third Army for not responding "despite having at least two hours' warning that an attack was imminent" (Bangkok Post, March 13, 1998). The UNHCR representative based out of Bangkok, Amelia Bonifacio, condemned the attack as an "act of violence against innocent civilians in refugee camps" (Bangkok Post, March 11, 1998). Tatmadaw officials denied any SPDC troops were involved and blamed the fighting on the internal divisions within the KNU.

While the UNHCR immediately sent a team to assess the aftermath, the United States followed with its own condemnation of the attack, with the US State Department spokesman James Rubin immediately calling on Burma to halt its "campaign of terror and violence" (Bangkok Post, March 13, 1998). The NCUB condemned the raid as a "serious violation of the sovereignty of Thailand and a direct insult to the Thai government and the Thai people" (ibid., March 13, 1998). Indeed, one anonymous medical worker noted "several separate groups of refugees said Thais had guided the marauders into the camp" (Bangkok Post, March 11, 1998). Thai authorities denied accusations that they failed to prevent the attack against the unarmed refugees. Thai officials responded by citing that Thai security forces did guard the camp and "engaged the raiders in a small arms battle" (Bangkok Post, March 13, 1998). In any case, there was no resistance when DKBA and Tatmadaw forces descended upon Huay Kaloke.

The refugee camps in Thailand are currently saturated. Frustrated with a consistent flow of refugees, Thai authorities are addressing this situation by decreasing the number of camps built by consolidating smaller camps into larger ones as well as by enforcing some form of forced repatriation of refugees already at the camps. Indeed, after the Rangoon Embassy episode of October 1999, Thai authorities had pressured the UNHCR to "speed up the repatriation of refugees" (Delang 2000).

The protracted nature of raids, extra-judicial killings and kidnappings of prominent Karen from the camps is making visible a real possibility in the minds of many analysts that there is a "Fifth Cut," that is, "in addition to the Four Cuts program to cut off the opposition from civilian support" the military regime "now seems to be doing everything it can to cut off the escape route of refugees to Thailand" (KHRG 1995). The Karen Human Rights Group and other analysts have made an incisive observation: "Over the past year or two, SLORC seems to have realized that the flight of refugees is a weak point in its complete control over the country" (KHRG 1995). Moreover:

> In recorded conversations last year, some senior SLORC Intelligence officers discussed how in the Irrawaddy Delta they have no problem with forced labour projects because the people can't escape, but in areas closer to the borders such as Arakan State and the Ye-Tavoy railway, people flee to neighbouring countries, causing problems for the projects and international bad publicity for SLORC (KHRG 1995).

The Tatmadaw has continued to pressure neighboring countries, primarily Bangladesh to the west in regard to the Rohingya exodus and Thailand in regard to the Karen exodus, to return the refugees. What this means is that the SPDC is actively persuading the two governments to engage in a policy of refoulement, and Thailand in particular has, on many occasions, indirectly deferred to their demands.

F. The Destruction of the Karen Regional Political Economy

During times of peace, most eastern hill Karen families utilize the *taungya*, or swidden agriculture (also known as shifting cultivation) to farm the areas of the eastern hills. Their most important cultivation is upland rice. Kunstadter (1976) and Hinton (1976) have detailed the Karen approach toward swidden agriculture, as has Latimer et al. (1992), who noted that only already disturbed or secondary forest is used for agriculture and "rarely is primary forest cleared for that purpose" (1992, 7).

Cash crops such as honey, betel, chili, sesame, and fruits such as fresh bananas, tamarinds, durian, kapok, coconut palms, pumpkins, lime, jackfruits, and papaya, as well as vegetables and maize, are cultivated. Bamboo is harvested to sell to Thai construction firms that utilize the strong plant for scaffolding, with some being made into toothpicks and chopsticks for the Taiwanese market. The raising of livestock occurs throughout the year, but meats are acquired from hunting monkeys, deer, wild boar, squirrels, and jungle fowl.

Those that do not move to new villages have established home gardens that possess a "maturity and diversity of species" (ibid., 7). Furthermore "some of these gardens are truly impressive with various palms dominating the system" (ibid., 7):

> In the villages along the Tenasserim River most households maintain integrated home gardens surrounding the house or fruit tree gardens in the village. Older gardens are dominated by trees [that produce]

coconut, betel nut, mango, jackfruit and a palm used for roofing. Younger gardens are characterized by species such as banana, lime, bamboo, castor bean, chili and yams. Other practices include...boundary plantings and [building] fences around homes and villages (Latimer et al. 1992, 8).

Close to major rivers such as the Salween and Moei fish is an important source of protein for the Karen. Reports in 1992 indicate that there is an abundance of fish in the rivers, and most riverine families are engaged in "some sort of fishery activity" (Latimer et al. 1992, 7). Traditionally, families utilize methods such as gill netting, trot lines, and cast or throw nets to acquire their catch, but with war disrupting lives for decades, a sense of urgency has prompted many families to use poison, electricity, and dynamite to secure their catch.

Karen crops thrive in the frequently heavy rains during the monsoon months. Karen families tend to rotate every year to local hill fields on a 5 to 15 year cycle, cutting and clearing the foliage that have grown since the field was last harvested. Under non-crisis circumstances a rotation occurs when used land requires regeneration. The fallow period, or where land is tilled but no seeds are planted, allows the land to naturally restore its soil fertility as well as control the increase in the amount of weeds and pests that accompany swidden practices.

Nevertheless, during colonial times British observers shunned swidden farming, regarding it as "iniquitous, primitive and destructive; the farmers appeared to wreck the forest willfully, grab one harvest, and then move on" (Falla 1991, 189). Indeed, it was this concern that prompted the British to introduce to many hill Karen the raising of cattle for trade. Yet Falla notes that current "experts have in the last two decades realised that they were wrong" (ibid., 189). It is only in the initial few years of the fallow period, however, that weeds and grasses grow in the old abandoned plots. Ultimately, as the fallow period progresses, soil recovery and the regeneration of trees establish themselves at the end of this cycle and the plot of land is ready to be cultivated once again. The Karen, far from laying waste to the land, have practiced *taungya* in this manner for "at least a hundred years with no obvious detrimental effects" (ibid., 189).

The key factor affecting the utility of a working swidden method is population: the land can only provide so much for Karen farmers. If we observe the general swidden practices of Karen in Thailand, the generally accepted figure is that 5 to 6 hectares of land are required per head of population (Rerkasem 1996). If the population were to boom, farmers would thus be forced to return to the same field only after a six to eight year cycle (Rerkasem 1996). A typical Karen family in the Mergui-Tavoy area cultivates approximately 2 hectares annually (with variation), with total rice acreage at approximately 1,200 hectares annually. If families utilize a fallow period of 5-

6 years, then each family will have roughly 6,500 hectares under fallow (Latimer et al. 1992, 7).

Yet the Karen in Kawthoolei have been at war for decades and there is less land available for Karen to farm due to its seizure by the Tatmadaw. Should this pattern continue, there will be "leaching and erosion of the soil; the fertility falls. Crops decline and human malnutrition follows. Eventually the soil is ruined" (Falla 1991, 189). In other words, the lasting war and territorial losses experienced by the Karen have made swidden agriculture with long cultivation and fallow periods precarious at worst and inefficient at best.

In an ideal year, Karen farmers usually follow a schedule not unlike their Karen cousins in Thailand (although the latter group possesses more options due to sociopolitical stability): between March and October, there is the clearing and burning of land for upland rice, sweet corn, and maize. Between July and November farming activities include the gathering of bamboo for use and exchange value. Cabbage, carrots, a double crop of potatoes, and beans are usually grown between the months of October and January (Rerkasem 1996). By December and January, the beginning of the dry season in the region, rice harvests are completed while preparation for new fields need not occur until April (Latimer et al. 1992, 17).

Karen supplement their income with other profit-generating activities that provide for a "dry season income" (ibid., 1992). The most popular activities revolve around groups of Karen, sometimes "composed of men and women, and sometimes children," trekking one or two weeks through the forest in search of bee hives, collecting honey as Karen climb over one hundred feet on bamboo scaffolds to acquire it (ibid., 16). Falla (1991) notes that the honey is excellent, and with its "citron" scent, one liter of honey sells for 40 baht (approximately $1.00 at the time).

The Karen and the KNU do well in their trade with cattle, for it is "politically less sensitive than timber" (Falla 1991, 355). Thais in the region often buy the cattle tended by the Karen. In the late 1980s and early 1990s, cattle purchased at the Burmese coast for 2,000 kyats can be resold to Thai border merchants for 3,000 kyats. Before it reaches the Thai merchants, the KNU would have already exacted a toll tax on them. Falla notes that in the district he resided, the KNU had "two herds of some fifty animals" (ibid., 355).

Yet the unstable circumstances of war affect not only people, but also livestock: "Fattened at the coast and unused to the mountains and forests, the cows might sicken and die on the way" (ibid., 352). Moreover, although the raising of livestock may alleviate deforestation, the effects of this undertaking are only temporary. A vicious cycle has already begun. The growing demand for cattle in the region will only compel the clearing of land for cattle to graze. Indeed, Falla's observation that Kawthoolei's forests are becoming less of a resource and less of a refuge is not an exaggeration (Falla 1991, 359).

The size of farming families in the remote hill areas can be as low as 8 to 10 families, while families who live close to one hundred homes tend to populate the larger towns. The Karen in the more fertile flat areas live in villages with several hundred households. For the Karen, rice is a significantly important staple and is usually eaten at all meals with accompanying dishes of assorted vegetables, whatever meats can be spared, and salted fish. Even IDPs use swidden farming to survive if it is safe to do so. The IDPs who do have enough rice share with others who are less fortunate. Some IDPs create a small income from hunting and the selling of chili and/or honey.

Families not engaged in shifting swidden agriculture tend to areca groves, "so extensive that there are insufficient laborers to harvest it all. Poor Burman migrant workers satisfy the demand, and are readily hired by the Karen. By harvest time, the migrant workers and their families have already established settlements along with their livestock and shops" (Falla 1991, 344). The local economy is usually situated more or less within the parameters of regional village clusters with "loans and payments often being made in rice" (Delang 2000, 15).

Surplus cash crops are sold in surrounding villages or the nearest market town. Forest exotics such as baby elks, dried bear's gall bladder, monitor lizards, anteaters, songbirds, and eaglewood are also exchanged. All these aforementioned commodities have passed through Karen territory for as long as the Karen have resided in the hills. The Karen also raise needed cash by selling Burmese valuables to Thai merchants.

The Thais represent the merchant class that manages the smaller retail shops within the quasi-free market present in Kawthoolei's remaining liberated border towns. "The wholesalers supplying the shops are all Thais" and their business acumen usually means they get to the producers first (Falla 1991, 351). The relationship is quite symbiotic in that "Rangoon sophisticates" have quite a demand for luxury goods available in Thailand. Televisions, radios, and cheap nylons go into Burma; rubber and timber flow out. All these pass through KNU areas, its officials levying a tax. However, the protracted nature of the war means that the KNU control only the borders and passes in areas without Tatmadaw presence, and these jurisdictions function with low levels of local enterprise.

The small income generated from this enterprise allows villagers to purchase goods that enhance their basic needs. However, Delang notes, "this...system is very delicate because there is little or no safety net in hard times; if one family has troubles the village can pitch in to help them, but if an entire year's crop fails the village goes hungry for the following year" (Delang 2000, 15). Moreover, within the context of the Four Cuts:

There is also no built-in capacity to deal with the scenario of several Army battalions moving into the area, restricting the movements of villagers and demanding food, labour, and building materials. However, under the rule of the...SPDC this is what the farming villages are being forced to deal with (Delang 2000, 15).

Regardless whether there is a surplus in the annual harvests, villages under SPDC-controlled areas must give a proportion of their yields to the Tatmadaw. The rate in 2000 was roughly 30 percent of the entire crop, but when farmers factor in "seed stocks, payments in rice for previous loans, use of other villagers' buffaloes to plough, etc.," then the quota exceeds 50 percent. The Tatmadaw usually pays much less than the asking market price for the rice. Tatmadaw officers also compound matters by personally adding on more deductions so that it is not unusual for farmers to receive no more than 10-20 percent of the market price for rice. When a state of war and a state of destitution already exists, the aforementioned quota quite literally destroys the Karen swidden farmers' way of life of. The quotas increase yearly and no provisions or corrections are made for extraneous factors such as natural disasters caused by floods, heavy rains, or droughts.

> When we work in our field and get 50 baskets of paddy, we have to give them 25 baskets. Then there are only 25 baskets left for us, but we still must give taxes and fees so each year we never have enough rice left. Each year I had to borrow from others. There are many taxes, like taxes for pigs and taxes for goats. If they come to the village you can't keep your livestock. They come to take one pig, and if the villagers cannot give them one pig, then they fine the village head and torture him. We are just villagers so we must give to the village head whenever he collects money from us. When we don't have money to give we must sell things from the house - Saw Eh Htoo (male, age: 37), xxxx village, Bilin township. Interview #1, 7/99 (Delang 2000, 191).

As a result, many Karen farmers are forced to buy rice from the market—rice that they could have easily grown collectively given stability. Even in areas of severe destitution, Karen farmers still have to face "regular demands for rice meant to feed the local Tatmadaw camps, and armed patrols often enter villages to loot rice, livestock and valuables" (ibid., 22). This devastation of the Karen civilian economy is thus achieved primarily through the destabilization and destruction of swidden agricultural practices as well as subsistence farming. The mechanisms that ensure this outcome can be attributed to: (1) the implementation of forced labor—thus taking away important labor from the fields, (2) cash extortion, and (3), unreasonable crop quotas that are demanded from villagers regardless of the political climate or demands made by the natural environment.

Petty taxes are also implemented upon Karen:

> They also demand donations when their officials come to the village. They call it 'sah kywe' [eating tax]. They come and eat food in our village, and after they go back we have to pay for them. We have to pay 50 or 60 Kyat each. Now in our village the DKBA are showing videos of their battles, and when you go see it you have to pay 50 or 60 Kyat each night. Even if you don't go to see it, you still have to pay. That's why the women are very angry; but nobody dares to complain to them and everyone is keeping quiet - Naw Mu Mu Wah (female, age: 29), xxxx village, Pa-an township. Interview #7, 7/99 (Delang 2000, 191).

The exorbitant "fees" charged by the Tatmadaw compel many families to send their small children to do forced labour so that the adults can remain in the fields. Under the guise of "porter fees", "servants' fees", "development fees", "pagoda fees" and so forth, the Karen face constant demands to pay these superfluous taxes. According to Delang, a family usually pays local Tatmadaw on average 100 to 3,000 kyats in monthly taxes. Although the money is meant for paying laborers involved in construction projects in the immediate area "in reality it is pocketed by the officers and forced laborers are not paid" (Delang 2000, 22).

In our examination regarding the effects of the Four Cuts upon the KNLA and the Karen civilian population, I attempted to detail the processes of internal maldevelopment affecting the Karen way of life. We now shift our focus to a more detailed discussion of the various KNU institutions that represent the organs of their self-determination struggle. Although some of these institutions are severely battered and no longer function at full capacity, I attempt to delineate how some of the remaining KNU institutions continue to press forward within the context of internal colonization.

Chapter VI
Liberation Ethnodevelopment and Key KNU Institutions

In this chapter, I continue my task of equating the Karen self-determination struggle with liberation ethnodevelopment. Liberation ethnodevelopment functions as a sociopolitical and sociocultural system to sustain the survival of the Karen by inculcating and reproducing Karen agency nationalism. The institutions, infrastructure, political economy, and material culture will now be observed as it empowers the remaining Karen to continue their fight for freedom. The link between ethnicity, development, and freedom is poignantly addressed throughout the Preamble of the 2003 Proposed Draft of the Constitution of Kawthoolei:

> We the Karen people, in the spirit of fraternity, unity and liberty and for the sake of peace, stability, security and social progress, join together with the other nationalities of the land to be part of the Federal Union of _____. We will always remember how relentlessly we had to struggle, for our freedom, equality and self-determination, and be ready to defend our basic human rights to freely develop ourselves socially, culturally and economically within the framework of the Federation.
>
> During the days of feudalism, we, the Karen people had been systematically and severely oppressed, exploited and prevented from advancement in all the fields of human activities. When the system of oppression and subjection was removed, we made rapid advances through industriousness and self-reliance, in a matter of 60 years, to become a civilized community, capable for sustainable development.
>
> However, after independence from the British, the political immaturity, intolerance and above all ultra-nationalism of those in power had led the country to civil war and the Dark Age of oppression, subjugation and exploitation, for more than half a century. In this Dark Age, all suffered immeasurably and the country suffered a disastrous setback.
>
> Accordingly, we, the Karen people in the State of Kawthoolei as well as in other States will join together with all peace-loving nationalities to prevent the return of the Dark Age and always work for harmony, stability and prosperity of the Federation.

In the above four paragraphs, the ideals and hopes of Childs, Sen and Stavenhagen become inextricably fused, albeit situated within a protracted and bloody conflict. The dystopian context of the Karen human condition thus behooves us to further understand the potential of liberation ethnodevelopment as underpinned by key KNU institutions. In this section, I discuss the institutions that have been pivotal to the Karen struggle: the (1) Karen National Union that governs the State of Kawthoolei, the (2) Karen National Liberation Army, along with the KNU's, (3) Forestry Department, (4) Health and Welfare Department, and (5) Education Department.

The Karen National Union

The KNU is the political organization that aims to serve the aspirations of the Karen people engaged in their fight for freedom. The KNU was in many ways similar to its predecessor, the Karen National Association of 1881 (KNA). The KNU and KNA were both created and initially led by Christian Karen but remained open to all Karen, regardless of their faith (Lintner 1994, 27). Indeed, freedom of religion is an important aspect of the Karen identity as constructed by the KNU but also at the level of experiences. Smith observed that "there were Buddhist temples...even a number of Muslim mosques...in many villages in KNU territory" (Smith 1999, 393).

The majority of details regarding the structure of the KNU stem from the collaborative work between KNU Joint General Secretary 2 David Tharckabaw and *Dictator Watch* headed by Roland Watson. Published as a November 2003 article, *The Karen People of Burma and the Karen National Union*, it presents a brief history of the Karen people as well as the layout and goals of the KNU. Most of the presented information in this section will be drawn from this excellent publication.

The positions within the KNU are as follows:

- President
- Vice-President and Defense Minister
- General Secretary
- Joint General Secretary 1, Organizing Department
- Joint General Secretary 2, Information Department
- KNLA Chief of Staff and General Officer Commanding
- Vice Chief of Staff, Forestry and Mining Departments
- Foreign Affairs Department Head
- Relief and Rehabilitation Department Head
- Transport and Communications Department Head
- Alliance Affairs Department Head

Kawthoolei's jurisdictions are divided into seven districts established during the late 1960s: Thaton, Toungoo, Nyaunglebin, Mergui-Tavoy, Duplaya, Pa-an, and Papun. Districts are comprised of several townships. A district governor, a committee of administration officials, and military officers administer each district (Latimer et al. 1992). Smith notes, "this full district committee was then the supreme administrative body for each district and liaised closely with the governor and the regional KNLA command, which also maintained a presence in the villages through the local KNDO" (Smith 1999, 392).

A nine-member committee as well as a township leader, the latter of which is elected for a two-year term, manages the townships. The township committee is comprised of persons from women's groups, a secretary of the committee, and village representatives. A voting system elects the village representatives that constitute the Township Standing Committee of Secretaries (Latimer et al. 1992, 3). The Township Standing Committee nominates a Township Chairman, and a township representative is sent to the District Committee, which then send the delegates to the Supreme National Congress (Falla 1991, 42). The main departments at the township level are the Information, Health, Education, Agriculture, and Forestry departments. Other KNU departments are created "depending on the requirements of the specific township" (Tharckabaw and Watson 2003).

Townships are further divided into tracts "roughly equivalent to British Regions, Counties and Parishes" (Latimer et al. 1992; Falla 1991, 42). Roughly ten to twenty villages comprise a tract. Within each village tract, village committees with members drawn from the health, agricultural and education boards would elect the tract committee, which includes a chairperson, vice-chairperson, and secretary. The KNU, at its very foundation, is a village-based electoral organization. Within each village a committee and a village head is elected, the latter for only a one-year term because of the demands required to administer a village within a context of war. Moreover, most villages also have a youth organization and a women's committee which are "well-integrated with the local administration system" and "perform important social functions" (Latimer et al. 1992, 6).

KNU congresses are held every four years, where each district nominates six representatives to congress. The congresses lasts three weeks. All representatives of the KNU are able to attend congresses, nominate candidates, and vote in elections. Elections for President and Vice President occur during this period. There are approximately over 1,000 KNU officials and over 60,000 KNU members (KNLA are automatically considered members of the organization) democratically managing the social and military apparatus of Kawthoolei.

By the end of the Ninth KNU Congress in 1974 administrative wings were also established. There is a "party organization" wing administered by the KNU president, who is also responsible for propaganda and external affairs. There are also "justice" and "military" administrative wings. It also publishes the *Policy of Rules and Regulations of the Karen National Union* for governing and administering Kawthoolei. There was a brief hiatus of KNU congresses after 1974 because the Four Cuts entered the remaining liberated areas in Kawthoolei's eastern hills. KNU Congresses have since resumed after the fall of Manerplaw.

With warfare now inside Kawthoolei, it would be difficult to hold meetings in the 500-mile stretch of mountainous terrain. Even before the fall of Manerplaw, when radio contact with frontline KNLA was maintained, officers operating at distant brigade districts "rarely came back to Bo Mya's general headquarters...near the junction of the Moei and Salween Rivers" (Smith 1999, 390). During the KNU's hiatus from holding congresses, Bo Mya selected a central standing committee and a cabinet of ministers to administer their respective departments from Manerplaw. Even non-combatant Karen officials found their work only advisory, since "the distances and lack of easy communication preclude any direct involvement. In 1991, the only departments controlled directly from the general headquarters are the mining and...the forestry departments" (Fredholm 1993, 118). Mining enterprises have been substantially curtailed due to the virtual collapse of the tin market in the late 1980s.

On a daily basis the KNU governs Kawthoolei through its Executive Committee, with personnel drawn from the Health, Education, Agriculture, Finance, Mining, and Forestry Departments (Smith 1999, 295). The committee is comprised of eleven members, although in 2003 the KNU notes that only nine positions were filled. The Executive Committee meets weekly and reports to the General Secretary, a position equivalent to Prime Minister. The KNLA also reports weekly through the Defense Department. The KNU also organizes a Central Committee, a parliamentary body that meets once a year. The thirty full members and fifteen candidate/probationary members discuss relevant issues to the struggle and if needed vote on them.

The KNU also administers fifteen departments that branches to the district level (the Foreign Affairs Department does not have branches at the district level). The KNU report states that "most departments are quite small, one or a few individuals, and an assistant or two, reflecting budget constraints" (Tharckabaw and Watson 2003). The fifteen KNU departments are: (1) Agriculture, (2) Alliance Affairs, (3) Defense, (4) Education, (5) Finance and Revenue, (6) Foreign Affairs, (7) Forestry, (8) Health, (9) Information, (10) Interior, (11) Justice, (12) Mining, (13) Organizing, (14) Relief and Rehabilitation, and (15) Transport and Communications. The departments are centralized in that their progress is reported to the KNU's general headquarters. In practice most departments, especially in finance-related matters, have tremendous freedom and are self-sufficient (Smith 1999, 287).

Smith provides a 1999 summary on the impact of KNU institutions and its organizational capability in the various districts of Kawthoolei:

> It was here, in the 'liberated' mini-state of Kawthoolei, a country unmarked on any map, that the flame of the Karen rebellion was kept alive. And here, into the 1990s, travelers could see an alternative vision of Karen society, very different from that under the military-dominated governments in the Delta, where all public expressions of Karen language and culture have been disappearing. From the Mawdung Pass to the Toungoo hills, an impressive network was established of KNU government departments, hospitals and clinics and hundreds of village schools, serving the seven main KNU administrative districts...Given the lack of resources, standards remained surprisingly high. Indeed, most of the teachers were university graduates, including the children of KNU veterans...The main medium of education was Sgaw, but in the ethnic Pwo villages, which lie mostly in the valleys to the west, Pwo was also used. Burmese, too, was taught but categorised (and only half in jest) alongside English and Thai as a 'foreign language' (Smith 1999, 391).

Since the beginning of the Karen struggle, the KNU organization has remained a self-supporting entity. Throughout the decades the KNU funded their revolution through taxes levied in a variety of ways. The most important mechanism for collecting taxes was through customs gates at key KNU bases, such as Manerplaw and Kawmoorah prior to their capture by the Tatmadaw. Prior to the fall of Manerplaw, the KNU imposed a flat 5 percent tax on the majority of goods being traded in their territory. Revenue was also acquired from a variety of sources through taxes on local households and functioning industries such as timber mills and rubber plantations.

In spite of the establishment of trading posts situated near the border with Thailand, income and revenue generated from the aforementioned methods did not generate much profit. As a result, KNU and KNLA units had to generate their own income as well as acquire their own weapons. As mentioned earlier in the text, the differences between different KNU regions in terms of wealth and purchasing power meant that certain brigades were stronger and better equipped than others. Smith notes that during the 1950s the KNU's entire Eastern Division was only able to contribute about 200,000 and 300,000 kyats annually towards the Kawthoolei Revolutionary Council's four million kyats annual budget. The rest was acquired from the Karen in the delta, where "there were numerous fish farms and forestry plantations" (Smith 1999, 283).

During the 1960s, a main factor contributed to a dramatic increase in the coffers of the KNU. Ironically it was Ne Win's establishment of the Burmese Way to Socialism after his 1962 coup and its subsequent nationalization of all sectors of the Burmese economy that resulted in opportunities for the KNU. Within this context, there were massive shortages of commodities that affected the basic needs of the Burmese population.

> Distribution now became so badly organized that few consumer goods which were now produced in the country reached outlying areas months after they had left the factories. Umbrellas appeared when the hot season set in and blankets when the rains began—if anything at all was available (Lintner 1994, 179).

There were also other important macro-level crises that advantaged the economy of the KNU:

> Once self sufficient in petroleum, fuel was now scarce with oil production having barely reached half of pre-war levels; during the 1961 monsoon the government was knocked back even further by disastrous floods which left 200,000 homeless and wiped out an estimated 300,000 acres of paddy (Smith 1999, 187).

> During late 1966 and early 1967 rice shortages, famine and growing numbers of anti-government demonstrations were reported in towns and villages across Burma. Official rice allocations were proving woefully short (ibid., 225).

Ironically, the main means for acquiring needed commodities were through Thailand's bustling economy. The informal economy emerged because the items that the general Burmese population needed had to be transported through Kawthoolei. During this period, teak, cattle, and luxury consumer goods were prime commodities traded by the KNU. Natural resources were relatively more available at this time because the KNU had substantially more territory under control. A series of customs gate and trading posts were established to facilitate the transfer of the goods, with the KNU imposing a tax on the value of all goods going into Burma. Regardless of which brigade area the goods passed through, local KNU commanders were able to benefit from the levies imposed, thus increasing the region's income. As a result, Thai and Karen traders had a healthy economic rapport. Thai traders were often seen on the Moei and Salween rivers selling their goods. During the 1960s,

> With swift access to Moulmein and the Delta, the KNU rather than any other rebel force became the main beneficiary; and with the Tatmadaw tied down by the war with the CPB in central and north-east Burma, the KNU's Eastern Division suffered relatively few disruptions (ibid., 283).

The first customs gate was opened at Phalu in the 6th Brigade Area, just south of Rangoon-controlled Myawaddy—the latter town located directly west of the Thai town of Mae Sot. The very important KNU base and trading post of Kawmoorah, in the 7th Brigade area, was opened a few years later north of Mae Sot. Trade was booming, the KNU profiting, and more trading posts were opened. Between Mawdung Pass in the south and the trading post of Sawta bordering the Kayah State in the north, there were 400 miles of lucrative trade activity. The important Three Pagodas Pass was also a crucial trading post, jointly administered with another liberation ethnodevelopment ally of the KNU, the NMSP. Three Pagoda Pass would grow and become a "frontier settlement of 5,000 Karen, Mon, and Indian inhabitants with a cinema hall, temples, churches, and even a mosque" (Smith 1999, 283). One can only speculate how the Tatmadaw must have felt at Myawaddy during the 1960s, as the town was one of the few BSPP-controlled areas on the Thai/Burmese border.

Yet another indirect boost to the KNU's coffers came not from Thailand, but of all places Australia:

> In the early days, it took three days for a mule convoy carrying contraband to reach the main highway at Tak, eighty kilometers distant in the central Thai plain. But in the late 1960s, the Australian government financed the construction of a new…road that wound its way from Tak over the hills up to Mae Sot on the Moei River, which formed the border. It was all part of the so-called 'Asian Highway Programme'—a pipedream which would connect Istanbul with Saigon. But hermetically sealed Burma allowed no roads to be built through its territory; the fine Australian-financed road ended on the banks of the Moei. For the border traders, however, it was a boon (Lintner 1994, 180).

Karen chroniclers give much credit to Bo Mya for the increasing size of KNU coffers. Smith notes that the large KNU income during this period improved the fighting capacity of the Karen. Indeed, the 6th and 7th brigades, once relatively weak and poorly armed of the KNU divisions, "rapidly expanded during the 1960s (fuelled by 'Vietnam-surplus' weapons bought on the Thai and Laotian black markets) to become the KNU's strongest" (Smith 1999, 283-284).

Although exact figures for the informal economy of the period are always hard to come by, observers such as Lintner and Smith argue that Karen liberation ethnodevelopment via the KNU have also contributed to the economic growth of Thai border towns such as Mae Sot. Indeed, even Thailand as a whole "owes much of its rapid economic growth and development to the thriving cross-border trade with Burma" (Lintner 1994, 180). Moreover, Rangoon had to "turn a blind eye to these smuggling activities along the border, since no goods at all would have resulted in political and social unrest" (Lintner 1984, 180).

The tax levied on the goods by the KNU and other self-determination groups generated numbers that cannot be accurately calculated. The World Bank, however, estimates that in 1988, the "annual value of this two-way traffic was at a remarkable $3 billion, or some 40 percent of Burma's total Gross National Product" (Smith 1999, 25). It is important, however, to note that a portion of this amount came from the CPB's involvement in the opium trade, and that the KNU, which despised the trade due to the moral standards instilled by the highly religious Bo Mya, still managed to generate significant amounts of income through non-narcotics trade.

Liberation ethnodevelopment processes were not limited to the KNU or the Shans, and neither were all liberation ethnodevelopments created equal. Major differences exist between, for example, Shan and Karen self-determination political economies. This distinction is important because readers need to be aware that certain factions of self-determination groups like the Shan and the Wa, since their ceasefires with the Tatmadaw in 1989, have engaged in opium trafficking as a means of financing their regional administration. Other ethnic nationalities were able to harness and exploit coveted resources from their own territory. The KIO traded jade from their state while Muslim Rohingyas and Rakhine nationalists profited from medicine and rice.

For Burma's people the disastrous consequences of Ne Win's demonetization policies resulted in shortages of essential commodities such as medicine, gas, textiles, and even bicycles. These, in turn, were purchased with raw commodities such as rice, teak, cattle, opium, and jade that were exported to pay for the imports from Thailand. The lack of many commodities inside Ne Win's Burma meant that the flow of goods going through Karen territory also included radios, watches, high-quality sarongs, and other manufactured goods that were hard to come by in Burma. Other consumer goods that generated income included machinery, spare parts for vehicles, and medicine, as well as minerals, jade, and precious stones, many of which were acquired through joint business deals with local Thai merchants and military authorities who often shared common business interests.

> After a few years, at Wangkha [Kawmoorah] alone, the sum of 100,000 Thai Baht was being collected by the Karen rebels per day in taxes—at the rate of 5-10 percent of incoming and outgoing merchandise. In other words, between one million and two million Baht was in circulation every day at Wangkha alone (Lintner 1994, 180).

Smith notes that by the 1970s, the border trade had a dramatic effect on several towns in neighboring Thailand. Mae Sot had by now become a bustling new market town. Indeed, even in Mae Sot today, one can see first hand the importance of Karen and Burmese as means of communication, heard everywhere throughout Mae Sot's downtown markets and bazaars. During the 1970s, Bo Mya's main base at Kawmoorah "was sometimes producing as much as one lakh[72] kyat in a single day's trading when up to 1,000 cattle would splash across the Moei River into Thailand at the end of the long journey across the Dawna Range from central Burma" (Smith 1999, 283).

By the end of the 1970s, the KNU and KNLA utilized their tax revenues to purchase supplies and other high quality weaponry. From the profits the KNU was able to eventually establish the fifteen significantly important aforementioned departments that reinforce their autonomy and self-determination political economy. Because the lucrative trade provided the KNU and KNLA commanders with an expanding source of income, the once ragtag Karen guerillas "started to look almost like a regular army with smart uniforms, steel helmets and officers' insignia" (Lintner 1994, 181). Karen citizens in non-combat areas begin to experience some normalcy with daily life.

It is no overstatement that the informal economy saved Burma's peoples from absolute destitution. During this period, the vast majority of the goods that were available in Burma were often, as aforementioned, from Thailand, smuggled through mostly KNU and Shan territories that stretched along 500 miles of border. During this period, China had yet to court the military regime and had little to offer in terms of providing necessities for Burma's populations. The irony that Smith points out is worth reflecting on: "the major beneficiaries from this…trade were the very insurgent movements the BSPP government was fighting" (Smith 1999, 25).

By the late 1980s, the Four Cuts campaigns in the eastern hills were intense enough that it affected KNU liberation ethnodevelopment. KNU Finance Minister Pu Ler Wah cited 1983 figures for KNU earnings as worth over 500 million kyats (£50 m at the official exchange rate). By the late 1980s, the Four Cuts reduced the KNU income by as much as 50 percent to 60 percent (Fredholm 1993, Smith 1999). Nevertheless, the KNU "partly recovered by opening up other trade routes" (Fredholm 1993, 113).

Further exacerbating matters, in 1989 China abandons its neutral stance. With the disintegration of the CPB that same year, Beijing was no longer interested in walking the fine line between its ideological support for the CPB and its political support for Rangoon. Beijing sells the Tatmadaw fighters and gunboats worth over 1 billion dollars. With newer weaponry and the demise of the CPB as a viable military force, the Tatmadaw's advance in the eastern hills increases in intensity. KNU bases engaged in the border trade were repeatedly sacked during the early 1990s, leading to the first assault against

---

[72] One lakh equals one hundred thousand.

Manerplaw in 1992, its fall in 1995, and the capture of the KNU's lucrative trading post at Kawmoorah in 1997.

By 2003, David Tharckabaw of the KNU concedes:

> Unfortunately, and in summary, given our available resources the KNLA is unable to successfully mount a comprehensive Karen defense. We have inadequate personnel, supplies and arms. One reason for this is that territory losses over the years have reduced our ability to raise taxes (on legitimate trade) and hence finance defense requirements. Also, the present Thai government is opposed to a vigorous Karen defense against the SPDC, other than Karen efforts against narcotics, which the Thais generally support (Tharckabaw and Watson 2003).

The Karen National Liberation Army

The current jurisdictions of KNLA brigades are presented below. When combined with other Karen defense forces such as the KNDO, the Karen police, and village guards, the KNU cites over 10,000 fighting troops (exact numbers are not disclosed by the KNU due to the sensitivity of their struggle). I refer to the Brigade jurisdictions by their Karen names, with the more familiar Burman names in parentheses:

1st Brigade, Doo Tha Htoo (Thaton)
2nd Brigade, Taw-Oo (Toungoo)
3rd Brigade, Kler Lwee Htoo (Nyaunglebin)
4th Brigade, Blee-Taweh (Mergui-Tavoy)
5th Brigade, Papu (Papun)
6th Brigade, Duplaya (Kawkareik)
7th Brigade, Pa-an (also Pa-an)

A brigade's jurisdiction covers one district. Since the KNU slowly decentralized during the post-Manerplaw era, most brigades have become quite autonomous institutions. This was simultaneously a drawback and an advantage because although KNLA units frequently had to fight without assistance from other brigades, the Tatmadaw have been unable to pin down and "destroy a central command structure" (Fredholm 1993, 119). Individual brigades are expected to be self-supporting. Forty percent of the income generated by KNLA brigades is sent to headquarters. In turn, the leadership redistributes foods, arms, supplies, and ammunition back to the brigades.

Each brigade is comprised of up to five battalions with each battalion ranging from 300-500 troops. Four companies constitute each battalion, with each company consisting of three platoons. Each platoon is divided into three twelve-man sections. There are also four special battalions created especially for guarding designated headquarters. The KNU notes that the KNLA has intelligence, quartermaster, communications, medical, training and recruiting departments (Tharckabaw and Watson 2003). The standard practice is for most battalions to be rotated. As a result some companies will be held in reserve while others are stationed at the frontlines (Fredholm 1993, 119).

> Although in organization following the Maoist guerilla system, the KNLA is still mainly run along British lines. The ranks and names of formations are also British. This is natural, as most if not all of the leadership are veterans from World War II (Fredholm 1993, 119).

Karen families in KNU territory usually nominate one son to join the KNLA. Military service is at least for seven years, and marriage is not encouraged during this period. Smith notes that since the mid-1990s, marriage is not encouraged before 35 for Karen men and women in the service (Smith 1999, 394). KNLA soldiers are not paid monetarily, but receive "a token sum for cheroots as well as a substantial rice ration" (Fredholm 1993, 119).

The main goals of the KNLA are based on countering Tatmadaw offensives and protecting the Karen "since without such a defense force the Karen likely would be exterminated" (Tharckabaw and Watson 2003). Other than protecting villages and providing for the security of villagers, the KNLA also has important non-military roles such as providing security for humanitarian relief missions. International audiences sometimes forget that other than being expert guerillas, the images, reports, and data acquired regarding Tatmadaw abuses, offensives, and issues regarding Karen basic needs, are only able to reach the wider world due to KNLA protection of representatives from the international community.

Charity organizations will often send a handful of representatives to a refugee camp or a base to assess the humanitarian issues at hand, and these groups must be protected until the completion of their survey. Moreover, international aid workers are often welcomed to KNU areas so that they can report on the conditions of the Karen, of the KNU/KNLA, and of Tatmadaw activities in the area. KNLA soldiers also provide protection for mobile medical teams that travel to IDP sites. Since medics and their staff have to trek through areas patrolled by the Tatmadaw, KNLA soldiers fulfill demanding roles as bodyguards, guides, as well as intelligence officers by warning medics and their staff about Tatmadaw troops. In my case, and despite the precariousness of then ceasefire talks between the KNU and SPDC, I felt that my visit and stay at Mu Aye Pu was only made possible by the safety of KNLA bodyguards that accompanied the KNU rank and file I held dialog with.

Another important role for the KNLA is their interdiction in all issues related to narcotics and narcotics trafficking. The KNLA and the KNU also discern themselves clearly from the other self-determination groups that are engaged in opium trafficking. The KNU and KNLA vehemently do not want to be lumped as part of an underground Golden Triangle political system that finances their struggle through drug production. The KNU have always made it a point to denounce Khun Sa's Shan army and the Wa armies for currently working with Rangoon to produce and distribute drugs. The KNLA also enforces KNU policies regarding drug eradication:

1. Kawthoolei, the Karen State, has always had a drug-free policy. It has successfully achieved this to date.
2. We must now adapt to the increased threat presented by the drug production in Burma.
3. The KNLA has established special operations units to confront this threat.
4. The problems include the manufacture, distribution, and sale of amphetamines, opium, heroin, and other narcotics in and through Karen territory.
5. Anyone involved in these activities will be apprehended with all necessary force.
6. We would like to work with other groups to develop a coordinated approach to this problem, and request any and all assistance from interested parties worldwide (Tharckabaw and Watson 2003).

As a result, the KNLA aggressively captures and destroys drug production facilities and their "trans-shipment" into Thailand. In other instances, the facilities are handed to Thai authorities. They also notify Thai authorities to incoming shipments that aid Thai officials in making arrests.

Smith describes the KNLA as functioning like a parallel institution within Kawthoolei. At the district level KNLA bases are the hubs of KNU authority. It also distributes up-to-the-minute status reports of the fighting. In the villages the KNLA collaborates with the KNDO village militia, comprised of villagers and retired soldiers. The KNLA full district committee, the largest administrative organ under the regional KNLA command, manages schools, courts, and prisons while "for more serious offenses, including banditry, spying, and opium trafficking, the general headquarters send out a judge" (Fredholm 1993, 119).

> In secure rear base areas, a string of permanent KNLA strongholds were built in strategic military positions, usually close to the forest trade roads leading towards the Thai border (Smith 1999, 392-393).

Prior to the capture of significantly important trading posts and bases such as Manerplaw and Kawmoorah, the KNLA were able to acquire light weaponry from the informal economy. The conclusion of the Vietnam War in 1975 meant a significant surplus in arms flooded the region. From revenues earned at the customs gates, the KNLA were able to secure access to Vietnamese, Laotian, or Thai surpluses of US arms. According to Phongpaichit, Piriyarangsan and Treerat (1998), regardless of the origin of the weaponry it is through Thailand that weapons are acquired (132). Smith and Phongpaichit et al. note that KNLA arms are also a reflection of nearby wars:

> Into the late 1970s most of the KNLA's arms were described as 'Vietnam surplus' (sometimes 'Laotian' or 'Thai'); today most are Chinese made 'Khmer surplus'. The result has been that, though lacking in field-guns and larger conventional weapons, KNLA units have frequently been as well, if not better, armed and equipped than their Tatmadaw counterparts. Certainly, in radios and battlefield communications the KNLA for many years stood some way in advance (Smith 1999, 300).

The KNLA is also a member of a military transcommunality known as the Five Party Military Alliance (FPMA), a front comprised of other self-determination groups still engaged in overthrowing the military. Other FPMA members include the Karenni National Progressive Party (KNPP), the Arakan Liberation Party (ALP), the Chin National Front (CNF), and the Shan State Army-South (SSA-S). As a military transcommunality, FPMA coordinates their defense and intelligence sharing.

The Forestry Department

> From Ceausescu's Romania to Saddam Hussein's Iraq, modern experience has repeatedly shown that governments which are amongst the worst abusers of human rights are also, very often, the worst abusers of the environment (Smith 1994, Chapter 4).

The primary task of the Forestry Department is about "nurturing the Revolution's natural resources" in one of the world's most diverse biodiversity ecosystems (Falla 1991, 41). The KNU Forestry Department emerged from attending to the surplus of logs available at the time the British departed Burma in 1948, abandoning its log and timber depots in the forest. When the KNU controlled substantially more land prior to the Tatmadaw's advance toward the east, forest resources, mining enterprises, and agricultural production generated much revenue for the organization.

As the Tatmadaw advanced through the delta forested areas under KNU jurisdiction were eventually captured. The lucrative Mawchi mines were also captured by 1953, an important source of revenue for the Karen at the time. Moreover by the 1970s, as the war edged the Karen toward the hills at the Thai/Burmese border, there were declining entitlements for many Karen to earn a decent livelihood from the forest. The environmental degradation caused by decades of war as well as heavy logging would severely test the relationship between the aims of the Forestry Department and the ecosystem that sustains the Karen.

The Forestry Department is divided into three branches: (1) administration, (2) timber revenue and tax, and (3) survey, wildlife, and forest conservation (Latimer et al. 1992, 4). Its jurisdiction is divided into seven districts that administer reserved forests within each district, "notably where teak was abundant" (Bryant 1997, 4). The KNU assigns each of Kawthoolei's districts forest guards and rangers to work in the field. It also has "conservators" at the district level, at the headquarters level, as well being directed by a department minister. Indeed, the protection of Kawthoolei's forests is so vital that a Forestry of Ministry had already been established by 1950. It has contributed substantially to Kawthoolei's state finances and thus, serves as an important source of income for the KNU. By 1994, one year before the fall of Manerplaw, the Forestry Department had become a key organ in the KNU administration with 463 forest officials representing all of Kawthoolei's forest districts and additional staff at Manerplaw (ibid., 1997).

Bryant argues that the Forestry Department ensures that Kawthoolei's rainforests serve three main functions. First, the forest serves as a place of refuge. KNLA guerillas require the thick foliage for their military maneuvers while IDPs and refugees in transit desire the same coverage. Second, the forest provides a livelihood for all Karen, and in this regard the importance of the forest for sustaining a Karen way of life is "as great to the KNU as it has traditionally been to individual Karen farmers" (ibid., 4). Karen utilize the forest for fuel, building homes, constructing dugout canoes, and for "farm and household utensils" (Latimer 1992, 9). Karen are also able to exploit the roots and edible leaves for medicinal purposes as well as its game for food.

Third, the forests foster a sense of nation. The human saga of the Karen struggle is intimately tied to their natural surroundings. For the vast majority of all Karen, even the geographically distant delta Karen, the once large forests are symbolically relevant for their identity and "resonate with meaning…symbolized most vividly in the many Karen myths and prophecies that are set in the forests…a reminder of the historical origins of the Karen people" (Bryant 1997, 7).

A Karen, P'Doh Thaw Thai, had remarked to a survey team that assessed Kawthoolei's forest during the 1990s, "the forest is the home of the Karen, if you remove the Karen from the forest you remove the Karen from the people" (Latimer et al. 1992, 20). The ethnogenesis of the Karen is told through their "ancestral culture-hero" Toh Meh Pah, and his family's trek through the forest in search of richer soils (Falla 1991, 11). For missionaries as well as Christian Karen from the delta, "the notion of the Karen as a lost tribe of Israel wandering the forests…serves as a powerful symbolic reinforcement of the link between the forests and Karen identity" (Bryant 1997, 7).

A. Kaser Doo Wildlife Sanctuary

One of the Department of Forestry's most impressive achievements was the 1982 establishment of eleven wildlife sanctuaries in KNU-controlled areas. KNU district forestry officers advanced this view during the first annual National Forestry Meeting in 1982. The proposal for Kaser Doo (Big Mountain) Wildlife Sanctuary (WS) was forwarded to Manerplaw by the Mergui-Tavoy government and was accepted by the KNU Department of Forestry. By 1990, five members of the district committee finalized the WS boundaries by factoring the effects of intensive logging in the region. As a result, the Kaser Doo WS—a habitat that the World Wildlife Federation considers to be one of the world's 136 most threatened terrestrial ecosystems—covered 460 square kilometers (42,000 hectares) of forest, and was located 20 kilometers from Thailand's largest national park at Kaeng Khrachan (Brunner et al. 1998, 9; Latimer et al. 1992).

The panorama of Kaser Doo WS is dominated by Kaser Doo Mountain, rising 2,000 meters (over 6,500 feet) above the surrounding area. Other than the rich flora that vary with changes in elevation, Thailand's Regional Community Forestry Training Center (RECOFTC) and the KNU report that Kaser Doo WS also nurtures a variety of habitats nestled within its ridges and valleys that contain mineral springs, meadows, and "truly virgin forests untouched by human hands" (Latimer et al. 1992, 4). Indeed, "Burma's most biologically diverse and intact habitats are found in the areas inhabited by the ethnic minorities" (Brunner et al. 1998, 9).

Kaser Doo WS also contains the Tenepaw River, a large tributary of the Tenasserim River, along with two smaller tributaries the Kaytha Klo and Kase Klo streams. Several endangered and vulnerable animals also reside in the region such as the Java and the Sumatran rhinoceros, "the tiger, tapir, clouded leopard…as well as the headwaters of three large tributaries of the Tenasserim" (Brunner et al. 1998, 9).[73] As early as 1970, the KNU Department of Forestry had already devised a list of endangered species to protect them from illegal hunting and poaching.

---

[73] Brunner et al. cite findings from the World Wildlife Fund and Wildlife Conservation Society: "40 percent of Southeast Asia's highest priority tiger habitat areas lie in Burma, all of them in the border regions" (1998, 7).

A significant publication regarding Kaser Doo's management as well as how the KNU approach the managements of its forests was released in 1992 by Wyatt Latimer, Glen Hill, Naris Bhumpakkaphan, and Clemens Fehr through RECOFTC. The *Report and Proposals for Kaser Doo Wildlife Sanctuary* assesses how Kaser Doo could be extended to connect to Kaeng Krachan, Thailand's largest national park, which would result in a major transboundary and transnational reserve.

Much of my discussion will be drawn from this excellent publication which addresses Kaser Doo Wildlife Sanctuary as a product of Karen nation construction and subsequently analyzes how the forestry personnel structure and manage its resources within park boundaries. Most importantly, Kaser Doo exemplifies how institutions are structurally opposed since SLORC's Ministry of Forestry was concurrently consolidating territories that would superimpose its larger Myinmoletkat Nature Reserve over Kaser Doo Wildlife Sanctuary.

The Forestry Department even welcomed international assistance in managing the park's "unique combination of riparian forests, extensive mineral springs and high-altitude montane forest...one of the greatest natural areas left in Indochina" (Brunner et al. 1998, 9). The KNU had by the early 1990s, already invited RECOFTC, from Thailand's Kasetsart University, a contingent of international personnel with backgrounds in forestry, agriculture, community conservation, ecology and flora and fauna management, and photography to assess the management of the Kaser Doo Wildlife Sanctuary (Latimer et al. 1992, 1) as well as examine the "integration of villager rights to use forest resources and their ability to manage the same resources" (ibid., 5). During this period the RECOFTC team met with the KNU District Forestry Officer, the Governor, and other administration and military officers to assess the logistics of managing a WS, as well as trekking for six days through the WS and spending three days visiting various villages in the region.

Another notable feature of the Kaser Doo Wildlife Sanctuary was how local populations willingly participated in environmental education and village meetings, supplemented with patrols of the WS. The RECOFTC team expressed satisfaction in being able to work with local Karen "who have developed a traditional harmonious relationship with the forest" as well as with the local KNU government that was "eager to establish a condition where community development is enhanced and conservation preserves cultural values" (Latimer et al. 1992, 4).

In spite of the coordinated efforts to establish and maintain Kaser Doo WS, local and district administration have been hard-pressed in providing personnel to actively manage the sanctuary. Although it would be war that would ultimately destroy Kaser Doo WS, during the period of RECOFTC's survey of the WS this was not a problem. The main problems were forest fires, illegal hunting, and poaching. Villagers not familiar with WS boundaries may mistakenly farm and exploit natural resources from within the sanctuary. The Department of Forestry held meetings with the local population to notify them of the establishment of the WS, as well as walking the WS boundaries with many of the village leaders. One advantage for conserving Kaser Doo WS was that it did not have any significant population of farmers clearing large tracts of land for farming. As a result, Latimer et al. noted "this showed that the administration is able to enforce, at certain levels, the integrity of the WS" (1992, 18).

The decision by Rangoon to gazette their vision of a natural reserve, the Myinmoletkat Nature Reserve, ultimately meant that new and larger boundaries would be superimposed over Kaser Doo WS. By 1996, villages to the west of Kaser Doo were already relocated close to Tatmadaw areas on Mergui-Tavoy Road. After failed ceasefire talks in 1996 was followed by a series of Four Cuts offensives in the area, Kaser Doo WS falls under Tatmadaw control and is subsumed within the larger boundaries of the Myinmoletkat Nature Reserve project. In January 1997, the KNU declared:

> The KNU does not recognize the superimposition of biosphere reserves or wildlife sanctuaries by the SLORC...or foreign companies whose intentions are questionable, dishonest, and only face-saving, and whose actions are devious and oppressive toward the Karen people and the proper aims and methods of ecosystem management (Brunner et al. 1998, 9).

KNU complaints of interferences from foreign companies point us to the multitude of different actors that have been complicit in the annexation of Kaser Doo WS. For example, during the period when Myinmoletkat was being established, it would be UNOCAL that proposes to SLORC the merits of officially establishing Myinmoletkat as a nature reserve to encompass key territories where gas pipelines could be built. Myinmoletkat also covers a planned highway project that would link Thailand with a deep-sea port. Since both the proposed road and pipeline projects would cut through Karen and Mon villages, forced relocations occurred along the project areas.

A more detailed exploration of how oil transnational corporations have shaped much of these developments will be presented in Chapter 7. Suffice to say that to observers like Brunner et al., Rangoon's maneuverings were fraught with contradictions; that is, the Tatmadaw's attempts to project to the international community its environmental-friendly image via Myinmoletkat was countered by a "policy of unrelenting aggression against the Karen, the very people with the most to gain from, and the most to contribute to, forest conservation" (Brunner et al. 1998, 9).

B. The Significance of Teak

The Forestry Department also places tremendous importance on teak. Southeast Asia's rainforests is one of the world's largest rainforest ecosystems after the Amazon, with numerous virgin teak forests. Within this system, Burma and Laos are the most "richly endowed countries in the region" with more forest cover per capita than first tier countries (previously prosperous forestry countries) such as Thailand, Indonesia, and the Philippines. In Kawthoolei, teak logging and production as well as the maintenance of elephants for teak production represent an economic sphere where the Karen have traditionally dominated.

Teak, known as the "king of woods," is one of the hardest types of wood found in the world. Teak grows endogenously in the remote ecological systems of Burma, Kawthoolei, Thailand, Laos, and India (although they are also cultivated elsewhere in Sri Lanka, Indonesia, and in certain parts of Africa and the Americas). The World Resources Institute states that "the physical and mechanical properties of teak are superior to other well-known temperate timber species, including ash, beech, oak, pine, and walnut" (Brunner et al. 1998, 5). Moreover, because teak is saturated with natural oils that stay in the wood even when it is dead, matured teak is resistant to boring insects, fungi, and decay. This natural response is not surprising when one considers the steamy atmosphere of tropical rainforests where pathogens thrive. As a result, teak is incredibly strong and resistant to the eroding effects of water:

> It is extensively used for shipbuilding, furniture, carving, and numerous other purposes. The properties of teak that make it so valuable are lightness with strength, stability, ease of working without cracking and splitting, resistance to termites, resistance to fungi, resistance to weather, and non-corrosive properties (Kaosa-ard 1989).

The incredible strength and resiliency of this closely-grained wood has meant that ancient civilizations of Southeast Asia have for millennia recognized teak for its immense infrastructural and cultural potential. Teak products have even "contributed considerably to the wealth and regional importance of Siamese rulers" (Buergin 2000).

When the Tatmadaw capture Karen territory abundant with teak its production and distribution is redirected to Thai and international markets. Since over two-thirds of Thailand's teak forests are depleted, the Thai government has had to look to the forests of Burma. As a result, Burma—despite being one of the world's most impoverished nations and desperate for economic capital as they slowly abandon their autarkic economy in favor of freer markets—welcomed the new links with Thai merchants.

The most efficient way to accomplish this is to fill the vacuum left by Thailand's decreased timber exports by inundating it with Burma's mature and relatively unspoiled teak forests. Currently, Burma possesses an impressive 70 percent of the world's teak forests, and accounts for about 80 percent of the teak on the global market. It is in this regard that we can understand the soft line that Thailand has taken with the SPDC. Many Thai military officials have personally profited from the teak trade. Yet much of this teak is not drawn from the lowland areas, but from the hills of Kawthoolei and Burma's northeast regions. Teak production in areas still under KNU control represents an untapped resource for generating income for the regime as well as a means to deny the KNU/KNLA and Karen civilians the very forests they depend on for sustenance.

Historically Karen were known throughout the region as being expert teak loggers and excellent elephant drivers (in a non-mechanized setting, elephants are the only animals able to haul teak logs). Such a characteristic makes elephants invaluable for the local Karen who, under non-crisis circumstances, rely on them for the generation of use and exchange values. Even when teak extraction occurs inside northwest Thailand, Karen Thais usually constitute the workforce, with many running the industry. The owners of elephants used for logging teak and managers of the workforce are usually Karen (Keyes 1979, 15). The Karen excel in acquiring this main resource, and were "from the outset, heavily involved as logger and elephant drivers" (Falla 1991, 353). This reputation goes back over a century. Neither were the intimate links that the Karen have established with the teak forests overlooked by the Burmans. In 1837, the British Captain Low remarked that "few countries yield such a variety of useful woods as the three Tenasserim provinces... The Burmans once forced the Karen to fell a certain quantity yearly, without receiving any wages" (ibid., 353).

During the 1960s, the Thai-Karen had a near monopoly on logging elephants. By contracting their services to timber companies much profit was generated for the local economy as well as the KNU. In the 1950s and 1960s, the Karen possessed about 3,000 elephants that worked the forests, all managed by the KNU's Forestry Department. Fifteen hundred of the 3,000 elephants were owned by the KNLA, which in 1991 still employed them for cavalry and long-range patrols requiring reconnaissance and transport (Falla 1991, 130). Horses and mules do not possess the ability to carry heavy weight of arms, and neither can they penetrate the thick foliage of the rainforests of Kawthoolei. During the same period, however, Karen with capital begin to exploit the forests by trucks and tractors, changing the landscape within a generation. Bulldozers now bring the "road to the logs" (Falla 1991, 354).

The hyper-deforestation of Kawthoolei's teak forests is due mainly to investor anxieties. Business people know better than to trust the unstable political and military climate of Kawthoolei. Investors "want the fastest possible returns" which could only be achieved by "rapid stripping of the forest" (Falla 1991, 354). No longer do they chose the more romantic route of awaiting elephants, rains, and rivers to be conducive to business—and none display the "slightest interest in replanting trees after they've gone" (ibid., 354). Left behind after swathes of forests are cleared are telltale signs of the direct relationship between environmental destruction and genocide. Here, the Thais appear to be repeating history, one where their own deforestation lessons a few kilometers away seems to have been forgotten. As a result, certain districts have seen a shift in the demographics of forest extraction. Falla noted that in one of the districts where he resided all aspects of teak logging, "from felling, hauling, sawmills, middle and senior management, and all the capital behind it" were in Thai hands (ibid., 354).

The 1998 defection of Padoh Aung San, head of the KNU's Forestry Department and member of the KNU Central Committee, must have been preceded with SPDC promises of lucrative profits. While head of KNU's Forestry Department, Padoh Aung San was responsible for managing and redirecting the profits generated from the logging business toward the coffers of the KNU. According to an official KNU statement released after his defection:

> He misappropriated the income for buying land, buildings and cars for his own personal benefit. From our information we have come to know that he made secret contacts with the DKBA and participated in the illegal logging scandal in cooperation with some greedy businessmen. He made secret purchase of fire-arms and formed his own pocket-army to achieve power by dubious means. The KNU had been investigating the activities of Padoh Aung San for some time. Aware of this, he enticed people who had close connections with him into going back to Burma with him. This was his way of escape from being exposed. As one responsible for the Forestry Department, he took the opportunity of being trusted by the central committee and manipulated the income from the logging business.[74]

A better understanding of the difficulties faced by the KNU forestry practices will need to encapsulate the geopolitical factors that have influenced the dynamics of the KNU struggle. In Chapter 7, I revisit the deforestation topic through the examination of Thai logging activities in Kawthoolei.

---

[74] http://www.karen.org/knu/updates.htm#aung

Health and Welfare Department

The KNU's Health and Welfare Department operate at the district level through mobile and refugee camp clinics (Tharckabaw and Watson 2003). The clinics are staffed by nurses, medics, and doctors, often in dwellings made from endogenous materials. A small clinic usually houses up to "two medics, up to six bedridden patients, and a cooking area."[75] A typical clinic within a district serves all of its inhabitants, which includes soldiers and villagers. All clinics have an operating area, an area for recovering patients, as well as bamboo platforms for additional patients.[76] The infrastructure, however, is less effective now as compared to the period prior to the fall of Manerplaw. Then, the KNU's Health Department staff, local NGOs, and international NGOs collaborated to train Karen health workers. The trained health workers were often able to manage their own districts with aid from NGOs based in Thailand.

> Even large hospitals like at Htee Hta in Mergui-Tavoy district could be supported and used to build capacity for local staff. However, the focal point of most of this work was, naturally, in stable KNU-held areas since security and transport of supplies had to be carefully managed (Burma Ethnic Research Group (BERG) 1998).

During 1990, for example, the KNU's 4th Brigade and Special Township Region (STR)[77] consisted of three hospitals attending to between 2,600-3,150 people or 576 families. There are also additional clinics that serve the daily health needs of the people. Metameeta Hospital, in the village by the same name, was staffed by 20 community nurses as well as 33 volunteers (Latimer et al. 1992). Latimer et al. comment that the three medical nurses at Metameeta are "well-trained and are able to perform basic diagnosis and treatments to conduct tests" (ibid., 5). A rotational system means that one nurse makes house calls throughout the village, one is teaching volunteer nurses, while the others work at the hospital. In the case of STR, an NGO also provided the services of an English lab technician who advised at the local hospital, while medicines and testing equipment were provided by other NGOs.

During periods between fighting, the most common illness in Karen areas is malaria, which affects all age groups. Diarrhea is a serious problem for young children, often requiring hospitalization.

---

[75] dictatorwatch.org: http://www.dictatorwatch.org/karenclinic.html
[76] Ibid.
[77] The actual township name is withheld by authors due to the sensitivity of their research.

The center is able to test for various diseases such as tuberculosis. Malaria, hepatitis, stool and hemoglobin tests are also administered. Basic stitching for surface wounds is not a problem and will be done in the center. The center has people trained as midwives and almost 3 mothers/month come to the center for delivery. The manager of the center estimates that this would be approximately 50 percent of the births that occur in the villages (Latimer et al. 1992, 6).

Unlike the KNLA and the Education Department, the Health and Welfare Department does not have a regular budget. Sixty percent of Kawthoolei's total budget is directed toward the KNLA, which in turn, provides necessities such as medical care in liberated area villages (Fredholm 1993, 118). Falla notes that ultimately "the hospital was taken over by the Army, its nurses put into uniform...the takeover was inevitable because, in modern Revolutions, health is too important; the soldiers cannot bear to leave it to the civilians" (Falla 1991, 99). Moreover, since the KNU controls less territory today, much of the Health Department initiatives have also focused on IDPs dispersed throughout areas once under KNU control but now controlled and patrolled by the Tatmadaw.

The KNU Health and Welfare Department also has another task. Not only are the ill attended to within Kawthoolei's remaining liberated areas, but the KNU has a mandate to attend to refugees as well as IDPs. Since Thailand has grown significantly less sympathetic to all refugees fleeing Burma, some Karen IDPs do not attempt to trek to the Thai border. Should they get caught by Thai officials they may forcibly be sent back across the border. Instead, mobile units accomplish this task by trekking into IDP areas, with trips lasting six to eight weeks. The allocation of medicines is made possible by funds from NGOs based in Thailand, channeled through border clinics and the KNU. During 1997 alone, 22 separate trips were made, averaging 800 patients treated per trip (BERG 1998).

> The KNU health department reported that at least one trip has reached every district; though of course no one area can receive continuous care, care being provided only when a team passes through the location (ibid., 1998).

Regardless of whether the KNU Health and Welfare Department is conducting medical care with IDPs, soldiers, and/or villagers in areas under KNU control or near the Thai border, logistics frame their medical exigencies. Since dictatorwatch.org and the KNU have embarked on programs to establish clinics near the Thai border, but within reach of IDP sites, the dual jurisdictions—often with great distances between them—mean that requests for medical supplies from local and international NGOs tend to revolve around certain general items. I have since taken the liberty of cautiously extrapolating that the following materials are required by any KNU-administered clinic, in varying degrees (note that these items are presumed to be more available in non-combat areas—in combat zones there may be a dearth of the items).

As of February 2003, the material and nutritional requirements for patients and staff include rice (approximately one-half kilo per person per day), salt, chili peppers, fish paste, sugar, spices, tea and coffee, tins of sardines, fresh vegetables, fruit, and meat. Various vitamins such as multivitamins, iron tablets, vitamin B complex, folic acid, vitamin C, and re-hydration salts are also dispensed. Medics also have their own equipment such as uniforms, boots and socks, T-shirts and under shorts, belts, hammocks, sleeping bags, mosquito nets, backpacks, water bottle, and knives/machetes that can cut through the thick foliage. Porters who are hired to carry the load for the medic teams may also need the same equipment. The medical team's mobile instruments include scalpels and blades, forceps, artery clamps of various sizes, large and small scissors, stethoscopes, blood pressure gauges, thermometers, notebooks, pens, torches, and disposable cameras used for documentation.

Kitchen and other supplies are also needed to maintain one's dietary needs. They include cooking pots, steel plates, spoons and forks, small and large knives, cups, water containers, 40kg waterproof containers for the equipment and medicine, blankets and mosquito nets, plastic floor mats, radios for communication with the backpack teams, hammers and nails, saws, and heavy-duty plastic sheeting for roofing.

Medicines, especially those that combat malaria are in high demand. Most desired medications include quinine sulfate, quinine I.V., chloroquine, paracetamol, co-proximal, analgesic, and pain ointments (for malaria joint pain). Dictatorwatch.org and the KNU have also noted that sometimes:

> The clinic will not have a microscope, so the specific type of malaria protozoa will not be diagnosed. Because of this all malaria cases will be treated with quinine sulfate. This may lead to quinine resistance in the future, but due to operational necessities there is no alternative.

Microscopes are in high demand by all parties involved. Even DKBA raiders into refugee camps are often instructed to acquire microscopes from the refugee clinics. Other medicines dispensed include Imodium, laxatives, de-worming pills, hydrocortisone cream, eye drops, conjunctivitis cream, and eardrops. The maintenance of patients' hygiene is accomplished through soaps, toothpastes, toothbrushes, shampoos, and combs. The following antibiotics are also utilized: Ampicillin, Amoxicillin, Amoxicillin powder (oral form for children), Penicillin and Penicillin V tablets, Tetracycline, Metronidazole, and Doxycycline.

Since many villagers and soldiers have serious wounds from injuries acquired through fighting, forced portering, and rape, materials for treating such wounds are also required. The most common are alcohol, hydrogen peroxide, povidine solution, iodine, gauze, cotton wool, cotton swabs, sutures, cyclocane (local anesthetic), syringes, disposable needles, plastic forceps (disposable), dressings and bandages, scalpel and blades, micropore tape, plasters, surgical gloves, and kidney dishes.

The 2003 costs to run such a clinic for six months with the aforementioned supplies and materials can be broken down as follows.

Medicine: 60,000 baht
Communication equipment/radios: 14,000 baht
Clinic setup: 10,000 baht
Six months operation: 50,000 baht
Other expenses (truck hire, travel): 10,000 baht
Total expenditure: 144,000 baht

To sustain a clinic for six months, with the 2003 exchange rate of approximately 40 baht to $1.00 US means that $3,600 is required for half-a-year's treatment of a designated Karen population.

The Free Burma Rangers (FBR), a medical movement constituted by relief workers, whose mission is to "bring help, hope and love to the oppressed people of Burma," also attends to health conditions of the IDPs. It also aims to "strengthen civil society, inspire and develop leadership that serves the people and act as a voice for the oppressed" (FBR 2004). Established in 1997 at the height of the Karen humanitarian crises, the FBR was founded with KNU support. Its founders, Tha-U-Wah-A-Pah and Htoo Htoo Lay of the KNU, also coordinate activities with members of the Ethnic Nationalities Seminar and the NDF.

Customarily, an FBR team consists of a "soldier, a medic, an assistant medic, a pastor and videographer, a photographer, and reporter and a nurse" (Rogers 2004, 189). FBR teams typically launch missions to IDP sites that last up to three weeks. During FBR missions, the sick and wounded are treated and whatever medications that are available are dispensed. The team "pull teeth, deliver babies, sew up wounds, treat diseases, and perform basic surgical operations" (ibid., 195). Other skills of the entourage are also harnessed. Photographs capturing the conditions of IDPs are taken, interviews are conducted, faith and hope are instilled, and whatever additional resources that could be used to satisfy the IDPs basic needs are distributed. The assessments from their missions are then publicly reported through their own website as well as to other NGOs.

During June 2002, the FBR was first to provide photographs taken by a Karen relief team of a massacre at Htee Law Bleh, in the Duplaya district where the Tatmadaw's Infantry Battalion 78 executed twelve Karen. But there were more episodes. At the end of April 2002, the Tatmadaw had already burned six villages to the ground, torched fifteen churches, killed fifteen villagers—including children no more than three years old, generated over 5,000 IDPs, and tortured three pastors, Happy Htoo, See Pa Thru, and Pareh, for five days outside their churches (Rogers 2004, 205).

There have also been casualties on the FBR side. Five battalions of the Tatmadaw chased a relief mission conducted by the FBR in 2002 after the Duplaya massacre. The FBR team was in the process of leading 96 IDPs to Thailand when the pursuing Tatmadaw began shelling the group, killing two of its team members, wounding one, and capturing another. The IDPs and remaining FBR members made it to the Thai border.

The FBR institution has an impressive record worthy of much praise. Since 1997, the FBR have successfully implemented over 40 missions into warring zones of not only the Karen, but of other ethnic nationality regions. The IDPs of the Karenni, Shan, and Arakan states have all benefited from their visits. Since the founding of the FBR, the organization has trained over 30 teams, and since 1998, has averaged "at least five missions a year, each one month long" (ibid., 194).

> Some of their trips involve hundreds of miles of walking—one trip to Karen State was only about 70 miles deep as the crow flies, but involved 350 miles of walking. They often walk 20 miles or more in a day, stay overnight in a village or in the jungle, carry out a clinic the next day, and walk through the night to get to the next location. On each mission, an average of 2,000 patients are treated and at least 4,000 receive help of some sort (ibid., 194).

While KNLA are holding the SPDC troops at bay, the FBR engage in their own struggle to overcome despair and illness of Karen unable to defend themselves. The risks that FBR relief teams face are equal to, if not greater than KNLA troops. Should the Tatmadaw spot an FBR team this would almost certainly mean torture or death for its members. After all, FBR teams trek to the most "needy and remote" places in Kawthoolei, which often means that they are going near or into the areas of fighting. The safety of the FBR teams is usually ensured by the increased number of soldiers that travel with the crew, supplemented by good informants and intelligence.

Education Department

Traditionally, the Karen culture and the KNU strongly emphasize the merits of having a good education. It is an emphasis all Karen are proud to share with chroniclers. Schools in Kawthoolei also serve the important function of grooming young Karen to internalize Karen nation construction.

Falla comments on the efficacy of schools as part of the revolutionary struggle: "In the name of education, links could be made with churches and charities abroad, in Asia, Europe and the United States, attracting supplies and money, interest and visitors" (Falla 1991, 298). According to Fredholm's data in 1993, there were "hundreds of schools and five high schools, of which three have been forced to move to refugee camps in Thailand by the recent fighting" (Fredholm 1993, 118). The Karen Teachers Working Group (KTWG), a local Karen NGO with the aim of assisting Karen educational aims within Kawthoolei, notes that despite the unstable social and political environment, Karen educators at the villages, when given the opportunity, are able to "set up well organized schools for their children" (KTWG 2004).

The KNU's Education Department draws its lineage from American missionary work in the Karen areas during the mid-nineteenth century. Missionaries had trained pastors and teachers while the British government provided grants which resulted in a "system of hundreds of Christian village schools in Karen areas" (Naw 1989). Indeed, the current educational system administered by the Education Department "is based on a curriculum established by the mission schools that appeared in Burma in the post-World War II era" (ibid., 1989).

By 2004, there were 564 documented schools in Kawthoolei employing 1,302 teachers with 31,071 students. The school year traditionally begins during the first week of June and concludes in March. However, due to the volatile situation caused by fighting, many schools end the academic year a month early in February. This pattern has occurred numerous times as the month of February lies within Southeast Asia's dry season, and for the Tatmadaw and Rangoon hawks, the continuation of the year's offensives against ethnic nationality armies takes place during this period.

Ne Win's 1962 coup ended all hopes of having a Karen educational foundation in the delta. After seizing power, Ne Win nationalized schools and universities, and Burmese was exclusively used in the Rangoon approach to education. Indeed, many Karen in the Delta today are Burmanized and do not know how to speak the main Karen dialects of Sgaw and Pwo. The Karen language based on its two main dialects owes its continued reproduction to the KNU Education Department which has attempted to administer a system through decades of challenges and systemic crises.

Today SPDC-controlled schools do not teach in Karen and if a Karen village is predominantly Christian, Buddhist monasteries are constructed in the occupied areas, as was undertaken in the predominantly Christian towns of Myitta and Pway Poe Klah of the Kamoetheway area (KTWG 2004). The deculturalization of Christian Karen is especially damaging since "the Karen...look on Christianity and education as inseparable factors in their civilization. A school must always have a church, and a church can never be without a school" (Falla 1991, 48).

In spite of this, Rebecca Naw notes in her 1989 article *Karen Education: Children on the Front Line,* the KNU's educational goals was not a Christian conversion project. Although many Karen teachers were hired from Christian Karen communities, it was the villagers that supported the school financially since the Karen of animist and Buddhist faiths made up the majority of faiths in the villages. Karen children's illiteracy was eradicated not through a theocratic program, but one based on acquiring knowledge of "math, history (world, Karen, and Burmese), general science, and geography...hygiene and civics at the elementary levels, and all students at all levels...learn domestic science, which consists of physical training, gardening, cooking, and needlework" (Naw 1989). Most importantly, Karen children are taught the core principles of their heritage based on understanding the virtues of "brotherhood, sincerity, honesty, simplicity, and humility" (ibid., 1989).

Naw's account of the KNU established educational system was written at a time when the war had yet to saturate the Mergui-Tavoy district in earnest. As a result, the Mergui-Tavoy district prided itself on having 36 schools: 3 high schools, 2 middle schools, and 31 elementary schools totaling 2,026 students. By 2004, the Kawthoolei Education Fund (KEF) reports that the Mergui-Tavoy district has only 2 schools, with two teachers, and a total of 50 students (KEF 2004). In Duplaya, district schools closer to the delta areas have already succumbed to Burmanization policies and only teach in Burmese. The Karen in the hills of Duplaya are still able to manage their own education since they "retain relative autonomy and set up community-based schools where Karen is the language of instruction" (KEF 2004).

When Latimer et al. visited the STR in the early 1990s they noted that in most villages there were at least 16 elementary schools, 1 middle school, and two high schools, all following the British style of education with standards 1-10 (1992, 4-5). Not all villages will have elementary schools but those that do will include village school committees staffed by the students' parents. Middle and high schools are relatively expensive.

During better times, the Education Department oversaw Karen villages and their construction of schools. In turn, the villages provided their schoolteachers with some small funds and food. At the time of Falla's stay with the Karen in 1991, "revolutionary teachers" received no financial earnings, "only a rice and salt stipend" (Falla 1991, 352). Latimer et al. corroborates this by noting teachers are only paid "1 tin of rice a month" along with "salt, clothes, and other basic necessities" (1992, 4). Due to displacement and lives lost from war, several teachers are "past the retirement age while others have never attended a real teachers college" (ibid., 1992, 4). Since teachers, teaching supplies, and materials are always in demand, the famed "backpack" teachers that trek for days to visit villages carry "packs of books, inks, chalks" weighing over twenty kilos "slung from their foreheads" (Falla 1991, 310). Falla noted in 1991 that "it was the only way the schools in the Western Valley could be supplied" (ibid., 310). Some teachers are sent to township headquarters "to keep abreast of the subject material" (Latimer 1992, 5).

> In theory, every child had access to a village school and the reality almost matched that. Those not attending were poor forests animists who lived well away from the villages... Most villages could provide only primary education... At every stage the children were drilled and tested. Those who failed their exams stayed down a year. The children took their exams quite as seriously as their teachers... Many of the key words, especially in the sciences, were of course in English (Falla 1991, 309).

In the case of high school teachers, annual summer training courses are sponsored and conducted at KNU headquarters. Teachers able to make it to KNU headquarters receive more training by Karen educators in all aspects of teaching as well as being able to teach in a state of conflict. However, a continuing problem is that Tatmadaw troop concentrations in many districts of Kawthoolei have made it hard for teachers to travel, communicate, and network safely with other teachers located in different districts.

In more destitute areas closer to conflict there are also many teachers with "little or no formal training themselves nor do they have educational texts to rely on for support" (KEF 2004). Women outnumber men because men usually are off fighting or engaged in farming and caring for the family. Military personnel are thus assigned to teach should a teacher-shortage result from the fighting.

A shortage of teachers is not the only obstacle affecting Karen students, with teacher recruitment "reported to be the most difficult aspect faced by township officers every year" (Latimer et al. 1992, 4). School materials and supplies are lacking. School blackboards are poorly constructed and for chalk, "diluted carbon powder from used dry cell batteries" is used (Naw 1989). Moreover, many of the texts that have Karen script are books over twenty years old. Even in the Mergui-Tavoy district where Rebecca Naw taught in the late 1980s, at a time when the KNU was relatively better off:

> A Karen student has only four pencils, two ballpoint pens, and six composition books for the academic year. Because there is no printing press in the area, textbooks are hard to get; we have to copy the old school texts in Thailand to use in our schools, and the expenses are very high (ibid., 1989).

Like many students worldwide, Karen students begin their education at the elementary level, between ages of 5 to 8 years old. They usually complete high school between ages of 16 and 20 years old. Karen, English, and Burmese are taught at schools in ideal conditions, but usually there is a shortage of materials to facilitate English lessons. Moreover, the main Karen dialects of Pwo and Sgaw are taught "according to the needs of the local inhabitants" (Naw 1989). According to Naw, "lessons can be taught in any language that will facilitate learning" (ibid., 1989). Yet sadly, what many students learn first and foremost is how to take flight from war. Naw provides a powerful insight and assessment on the psychological trauma that is internalized within many Karen students:

> Most of the schools are in villages that can be reached by Burmese soldiers during the dry season; as a consequence, nearly every Karen child who comes from a village has bitter and fearful experiences. These children became war victims without knowing why their properties were looted, their villages razed, their parents killed, and their sisters and mothers raped by Burmese soldiers. The only thing they came to know through their experiences is they had to flee for their lives from the Burmese soldiers when fighting broke out in their villages (Naw 1989).

It is hardly surprising that some of Kawthoolei's high schools, "to instill more discipline and to understand that military training is an art," have basic military training programs for their students conducted during summer (Naw 1989).

Today, schools in Kawthoolei's liberated areas will be administered by the KNU Education Department, but should the Tatmadaw capture KNU villages, the schools it spares from the torch then fall under the jurisdiction of the Tatmadaw. More frequently, Tatmadaw reprisals against Karen schools take the form of the physical destruction of the schools, harassment and/or the killing of teachers and their families. The destruction of livestock and fields by passing SPDC means that there will be little food to feed anyone, more or less teachers. Many schools have been systematically eliminated along with Karen villages. According to the KEF:

> The SPDC views the mountainous areas as KNU controlled and thus treats local communities as the enemy. The SPDC burns homes and shoot people on sight in this area. Karen run schools are seen as signifying KNU influence in the community notwithstanding the fact that communities manage and support their schools themselves... Schools have been targeted as "signs" of KNU presence...and are burned. School materials are destroyed and stolen. Teachers are becoming seen as KNU supporters and thus more in danger of SPDC brutality (KEF 2004).

As Karen experiences with a protracted war have made managing the affairs of state expensive, an alternative source of funding for sustaining the educational apparatus of the Kawthoolei comes from an array of charitable individuals, NGOs, and the Karen diaspora. Through groups such as the KEF, finances have been redistributed to administer another unique program managed by the KTWG, that of maintaining or establishing an educational system at refugee camps and in remote areas where IDPs have congregated.

The KNU Education Department provides safety and grants autonomy to many of the KTWG programs. Both organizations know that the survival of the Karen identity will rest on maintaining a Karen educational system. The difficulties of managing and funding the educational apparatus are alleviated somewhat by the initiatives of the KTWG. With 32 active members in 2004 (31 Karen and 1 Canadian), the KTWG has devised a program to help facilitate a decent education in war-torn Kawthoolei through the mobile teacher training team (MTTT).

The MTTT visits Kawthoolei's schools three times a year. During their visits funds from the Kawthoolei Education Fund are allocated to the selected schools. Supplies and much needed materials are then purchased. Subsidies for teachers, basic needs, and supplies for school infrastructure are also covered by the fund. Along with the monitoring of fund distribution, the MTTT also facilitates correspondence between the school and donors. Individual primary schools average about 5,000 baht in donations, middle schools average about 10,000 baht in donations, and high schools receive an average of 15,000 baht. Moreover, since January 2004, the KTWG has already distributed 9,000 books throughout Kawthoolei's schools.

Without NGO assistance such as that provided by the KTWG, Burmanization will run its full course. Already a number of schools have been reduced due to SPDC incursions and raids into villages. Although IDPs make a concerted attempt to teach in the forest, most of the IDP schools lack supplies and their personnel are forced to migrate from place to place, while many remain difficult to access due to their remote locations. When the military government does assign teachers to the districts of Kawthoolei, these teachers get paid while the hiring of Karen teachers must be paid out of the pockets of the Karen.

Over fifty-five years, the Educational Department has had to whether the continuing onslaught of the Four Cuts. One consequence is that most young Karen males have had to leave school by fourteen to serve as helping hands on the fields. With war interrupting crop cycles, the desperate need for harvests requires an intensive labor force, meaning that able-bodied youths are needed on the farm. Enough parents have already utilized their children to work on the farm that the KNU imposes a fine against any family which does not send their children to school. Naw also points us to another scenario that still applies to many young Karen today:

> There are very few paths open for good students after they finish high school; no college or university is available for Karen students

at present. The only thing teachers can do to help them is to send them to vocational training sponsored by KNU headquarters, which offers medical, technical, electrical and radiomechanic, and English teaching training (Naw 1989).

My survey of key KNU institutions reveal the essence of ethnic self-determination dynamics subjected to a totalitarian, ethnocratic and genocidal military junta; that is, Karen institutions have to be established in structural opposition to Rangoon so as to maintain group survival. With these established Karen institutions, Karen notions of economic, social, political and cultural development can then be engaged on their own terms, and not on terms dictated by an exploitative Tatmadaw.

In the next chapter, I make visible the geopolitical and economic forces that are confronting the state of Kawthoolei and the Karen Revolution. The interplay between geopolitics, economic interests, and foreign policy positions will be used to debunk the myth that attending to the Karen "insurgency" along with "insurgencies" by Burma's other ethnic nationality self-determination groups, are issues that belong in the "internal affairs" of the country. As the Tatmadaw elites further this myth, SPDC generals further their capacity for oppression by internationally linking up with governments that sell arms and engage in corporate dealings with the Tatmadaw.

Chapter VII
Myth of the "Internal Affair": Geo and Petropolitical Complicity

In this chapter I hope to make visible the links the Tatmadaw has to various state governments as well as to oil transnational corporations (TNCs). This task can conceivably be an entire project in itself, so I have decided to focus on only a selected group of actors complicit with Burma: Thailand, China, and oil TNCs. Other countries and TNCs complicit with the SPDC regime will also be identified but only briefly. Interested readers who desire a more expanded view on regional interferences should explore the wide variety of publications on the international community's complicity in sustaining the military regimes in Burma.

At the historic ceasefire talks in Rangoon during January 2004, Bo Mya and a KNU delegation met with the Tatmadaw's Khin Nyunt and SPDC commanders. Khin Nyunt, during the middle of the discussion, reiterated the need to keep foreigners out of the internal affairs of Burma. "We must be aware that outside interference can cause difficulties...especially with the interference of...western countries," noted Khin Nyunt. Mya then replied, "You said you don't depend on foreign countries...but I've seen that you also depend on China for their economics and military support."[78] Nyunt promptly quieted his voice. The pause had an effect and Bo Mya readied himself for Khin Nyunt's response. Nyunt then disclosed that Burma needs China's support due to "American sanctions."

Bo Mya did not note otherwise but China isn't Burma's only ally. Indeed, insofar as forging diplomatic links with the regime, the Thai polity's growing relationship with Rangoon is inversely related to the Thai government's sympathy toward the Karen, even though a substantial part of the Thai population is still sympathetic to the Karen cause (HRW/A 1997). Beijing has its own interest in manipulating Rangoon so as to acquire access to the Bay of Bengal as well as enticing the overall Burmese population to be consumers of China's exports. Competing with these interest are those by transnational corporations (TNCs) who want to establish gas pipelines and hydroelectric dams through the Karen and Mon states.

Since the early 1990s, nearly all of the SPDC's diplomatic links and its subsequent income stem from the sale of natural resources. Due to the poor industrial infrastructure of Burma, much of Burma's exports and sales revolve around timber, rubies, oil and fishing concessions (Smith 1994).

---

[78] Observation derived from the *KNU and SPDC Peace Mission: January 2004* DVD. DVD provided by Pastor Lah Thaw and is on file.

Rangoon has allowed these pull factors to prompt rapacious international governments and TNCs to have a vested interest in the country. Yet as Khin Maung Kyi, former professor of Economics at the Rangoon Institute noted:

> The Myanmar leaders still seem to place much store on the supposedly rich natural resources of the country...it should be realized that countries gain competitive advantage not through the richness of natural resources, but through development of technology and the skills of their work force (Smith 1994, Chapter 3).

Rather than highlight the geopolitical inputs as mutually exclusive activities, I have decided to present their trajectories within a chronological format. This method will reveal how geopolitical links "fan out" from the regime at different geopolitical sites during the last fifteen years.

I hope to reinforce the notion that the relationships formed between the Tatmadaw, state governments, and economic institutions only lend credence to what international observers have known all along, that although the Tatmadaw expects the international community to stay out of its internal affairs it aggressively fosters international links with not only sympathetic governments, but corporate and economic entities that allow the continuation of military rule with impunity. From the perspective of the Karen, the links mean that the Tatmadaw will have the finances to bolster their fighting capacity, as well as exploit and "develop" Karen territory it captures.

Thailand

The Karen and Thais have coexisted relatively harmoniously throughout the centuries, and the Karen population was "generally well-received" (Falla 1991, 187). There has also been a sizeable Karen population that assimilated into Thai culture in Thailand's west and northwest. The relationship between the two cultures was symbiotic. The Siamese populace in the Chao Phraya River Valley respected the forest and scouting expertise of the Karen. Even Thailand's historically revered and modernist king, Chulalongkorn (ruled 1886-1910) was fond of the Karen. Falla points us to some romanticized poems Chulalongkorn wrote about the Karen after visiting their hills:

> Girls, girls; these Karen are lovely
> Hair-bunned with pins comely, so fair,
> Decked with pins richly, at great cost,
> Their faces talced, they're so, so demure (1991, 37).

And about the Karen way of life:

So tranquil they plant their rice.
Birds in paradise, the dense woods.
Glad bodies entice; minds at ease,
They scorn worldly progress (Falla 1991, 188).

Falla notes that although the Karen were "not given full citizenship until they came under the patronage of the reforming King Chulalongkorn in the late nineteenth century, they were not persecuted" (1991, 187). In 1904, French observer Lunet de Lajonquiere noted of the Karen:

> As regards those populations that are dependent on the Kingdom of Siam, there is a hierarchy with the Siamese at the top of the social ladder and the Kariengs [Karen] at the bottom. They all live quite content with their lot, moving in their proper spheres with some degree of independence (ibid., 187).

Falla's accounts from his stay with the Karen and his travels through Kawthoolei provide for us fascinating insights into the symbiotic relationships that characterizes Karen-Thai relations:

> Thais didn't enjoy the work of tin mining—it offended the soil deities—but Karen would do it. Before Western medicine came to Thailand, Karen-prepared cures based on forest products were sought after even by those potion-connoisseurs, the Thai Chinese. Karen cloth was appreciated (partly because of the inordinate time it took to make). Above all, the Karen supplied most of the forest exotics that Siam both desired and exported.

Trade between Siam and Europe took on a different character with the opening of the Suez Canal. Falla noted that bulk commodities and manufactures became the preferred units for conducting trade. With the onset of a world network of trade links being forged with Europe, the awareness of Karen culture went into decline. After Ne Win's seizure of power in 1962, followed by decades of military oppression against the Karen, Thailand began to employ Kawthoolei as a buffer zone.

Although the scope of my analyses does not cover the tumultuous history of Siamese-Burmese relations, it is well known that the kingdoms of Burma and Thailand have engaged in many bloody wars throughout the centuries, culminating in the second and successful attack on the Siamese capital of Ayudhya. In 1767, renewed Burmese expansionism under King Hsinbyushin (ruled 1763-1786) meant that soon the capital of the Siamese empire would have to face troops consisting of Burmese, Shan, along with regional troops from the recently defeated Lan Na Kingdom (based out of what is today

Chiang Mai province, Thailand) and Luang Prabang (kingdom from what is today Laos). Over a period of many months, Siamese attempts at countering the tens of thousands of Burmese troops were fierce, but ultimately unsuccessful. On April 7, the bloody siege succeeded and Ayudhya was razed to the ground, many of its citizens brutally massacred:

> The Burmese wrought awful desolation. They raped, pillaged, and plundered, and led tens of thousands of captives to Burma. They put the torch to everything flammable and even hacked at images of the Buddha for the gold with which they were coated. The Siamese King Suriyamarin...fled the city in a small boat and starved to death ten days later (Wyatt 1982, 137).

The many thousands of Thais brought to the Burmese Court at Ava (near present-day Mandalay) were forced into slavery; many became incorporated into the court as courtesans, court staff, and musicians. Those that were not hauled into captivity experienced a slower demise, as indicated by a local high-ranking Siamese monk of the period:

> The populace was afflicted with a variety of ills by the enemy. Some wandered about, starving, searching for food. They were bereft of their families, their children and wives, and stripped of their possessions and tool... They had no rice, no fish, no clothing. They were thin, their bodies wasting away. They found only the leaves of trees and grass to eat... In desperation many turned to dacoity... They gathered in bands and plundered for rice and paddy and salt. Some found food, and others could not. They grew thinner, and their flesh and blood wasted away. Afflicted with a thousand ills, some died and some lived on (Wyatt 1982, 136-137).

Although modern assessments of Thai-Burmese foreign policy cannot discount the Thai's historical links to this episode in Thai history, one must be careful not to exaggerate how this has determined the current state of affairs between the two countries. That said, the sacking of Ayudhya does provide much insight into how 20th century Burman aggression against its ethnic nationalities has perennially multiplied the anxieties of Thai citizens and the Thai government. Even today, Burmans or Burmese-language speakers in Thailand, as told by many pro-democracy Burmese and Karen students who found shelter there after 1988, are susceptible to discrimination.

How much this indignation is dispersed across Thailand's foreign policy spectrum is hard to say. Two Thai trajectories in dealing with the military regime and the Karen have emerged. One is sympathetic to the Karen struggle and shares the Karen aspirations to see Burma's military dictatorship overthrown (circa 1960s to the 1980s), the other is to placate and exploit the

SPDC regime through economic interests, relegating Karen interests aside (1980s to the present). The simultaneous interaction of these two trajectories is indicative of Thailand's return to a buffer zone policy where Karen indirectly safeguarded the sovereignty of Thailand.

Thailand has always exploited the Kawthoolei as a buffer state whenever it suited the Thai government's interests. Indeed, buffer zone politics continues to "influence the thinking of Thai policy-makers down to the present day" (Phongpaichit et al. 1998, 130). As a result, the Karen struggle was at times enhanced and in other times disadvantaged by Thailand's stance. Currently, Thailand's desire to exploit Burma's natural resources based on teak and natural gas has allowed both the military regime and Thailand to forge links. Yet, as Phongpaichit et al. noted, it makes certain the regime cannot fully consolidate the country and thus become a direct threat to Thailand. In their interview with a Thai police general:

> The Thai government recognized the dictatorial regime in Burma but did not want it to have unity and peace. Thus the Thai government supported minority groups and provided them with arms. However the Thai government did not trust the minorities either. Thailand did not want the minorities to win for fear that the conflicts among themselves would have a negative impact on Thailand. In other words, the Thai government did not want any party to win the war. SLORC could be the government but there should not be complete peace in Burma. In this way Thailand would achieve security and freedom from the Burmese threat (Phongpaichit et al. 1998, 129).

This evidence of a buffer zone policy has been vehemently denied by Thai government officials, but its use in the 1980s was exploited by Thailand's Chaovalit "while gaining a reputation as an astute, thinking-man's general" (Bangkok Post, June 16, 2002). The buffer zone policy "slip" emerged again in 2002 when Thailand's Prime Minister Thaksin Shinawatra reiterated, "Before we didn't stress this but it will be made clear now we must give up the buffer state policy" (ibid., June 16, 2002). This statement incited uproar within the Thai government because it implied that a buffer zone policy was still being used. The uproar compelled Chaovalit to clarify, "We have shifted from the buffer state policy to intelligence operations outside Thai boundaries, or defence diplomacy as it is called by this government" (Bangkok Post, June 11, 2002).

Thai fears of an independent Burma and its implication for Thailand's adoption of a buffer zone policy date to 1953, when the Tatmadaw was struggling to repulse remnants of the Chinese Nationalist Kuomintang who set up base in Burma.[79] The Tatmadaw's Air Force was called in, and in its attempts to stop advancing KMT troops, bombs were accidentally dropped on a Thai village, killing two villagers and injuring five others. This infuriated then Thai Prime Minister and Field Marshall Plaek Pibulsongkram. He threatened to "shoot down any aircraft that violated the country's airspace" (Lintner 1994, 118). During the same period, Pibulsongkram "invited leaders of the Mon and Karen rebel armies to Bangkok, where for the first time secret negotiations were held between ethnic minority groups...and senior Thai officials" (ibid., 118).

For many decades, the Thai government quietly accepted ethnic nationalists along its border with Burma.

> In particular, local Thai-Karen, Mon or Shan relations have always been extremely cordial. Indeed, many Thai officers have always greeted the arrival of any Burman soldiers on their borders with apprehension...the sacking of the Siamese capital at Ayut'ia [Ayudhya] by the Burman king Hsinbyushin, has never been forgotten or forgiven (Smith 1999, 397).

The Thais needed the Karen and other ethnic nationalities to help patrol the porous 2,100 kilometer border between Thailand and Burma. Patrolling the border with large numbers of Thai troops risked instigating a response from Rangoon. Moreover, it was costly endeavor for a country that at the time was nowhere near the economic capacity that it is at today. The meetings that Pibulsongkram had with the Karen and Mons resolved this problem. Although Thailand never formalized any agreement with the Karen, "the rebels were allowed to set up camps along the frontier, their families were permitted to stay in Thailand and they could buy arms and ammunition" (Lintner 1994, 119). Even as recently as 2005, many KNU meetings were still held in Thailand and the late Bo Mya's health was attended to at Bangkok hospitals.

In 1958, the KNU struggle received a significant bolster, albeit an indirect one. Thailand's field Marshall Sarit Thanarat and his cadre of followers launched a coup in 1957 that disposed of Pibulsongkram. Lintner notes that during this period, Sarit was admitted to Walter Reed Military Hospital in Washington and was paid a visit by US Secretary of State John Foster Dulles and President Dwight Eisenhower. The outcome of this meeting was an agreement that Thailand had to resist the growing communist threat surrounding the region. Sarit had reached an agreement with the United States where Thailand pledged to be a "bulwark that the US needed to halt Communist advance in East Asia" (ibid., 156).

---

[79] Some of Chiang Kai Shek's Kuomintang troops fled into Burma after Mao succeeded in winning the Chinese Civil War in 1949.

Thailand was developing during the 1960s; its GDP during this period averaged 8 percent and its indoctrination against Communism by a mighty capitalist power such as the United States also forged strong bonds between the two countries. Thailand's link with the United States would indirectly lay the groundwork for Bo Mya—a staunch anti-Communist—and his ascension to power over a decade later. Moreover, by 1975, the nationalist KNU under Bo Mya, having tempered Mahn Ba Zan's leftist orientation, also successfully prevented the CPT and CPB from coordinating their efforts.

Phongpaichit et al. (1998) note that these machinations were born from the historical enmity between Thailand and Burma. It thus served the interests of the Thai government to fan the flames of conflict because Bangkok continued to view the Burmese military dictatorship as a threat to its national security. As a result, the implicit support given to the Karen struggle occurred as Thailand allowed and continues to allow arms to be sold to the KNU.

Arms emanate from different sites. During the 1970s, weapons were Vietnamese, Laotian, or Thai surplus US arms (Fredholm 1993). Weapons have also been acquired from Cambodia's "Khmer surplus," a product of Chinese support when it assisted the Khmer Rouge in countering Vietnam's 1979 invasion and occupation of the country. Even by 1995 the Khmer Rouge, though having lost Phnom Penh, still numbered around 30,000 irregular troops along the border with Thailand, with roughly 10,000 permanent soldiers. Thailand thus became the middleman between Burmese ethnic nationality groups and the Khmer Rouge by securing arms for its allies. Phongpaichit et al.'s interview with an ex-officer of Thailand's National Security Council confirmed that "all the armed forces of these minority groups rely on the weapons purchased from the Thailand market" (Phongpaichit et al. 1998, 132).

By 1988, during the beginnings of the pro-democracy movement in Burma, Rangoon was already fighting twenty-seven self-determination groups throughout the country. With a combined insurgent troop count of over 60,000 soldiers, the demand to supply various groups was overwhelmingly lucrative for those in the Thai Army with access to weapons. Even though many of the self-determination groups had signed ceasefires with SLORC by 1994, over 30,000 troops, many from the KNLA, were still fighting. Phongpaichit et al. note that at the time, the largest non-ceasefire groups numbered about 18,000 for the Shan, 5,000 for the Karen, and 2,000 for the Burmese armed pro-democracy students, with the Shan and Karen having "the most purchasing power" (ibid., 132). As a result of this complex network even Chaovalit concedes that seizures of contraband were frequent events.

Phongpaichit et al. note that arms sales to the ethnic self-determination groups are accomplished through middlemen from different strata of Thai society. Some are Thai military officers or police, while others are arms trade specialists that are legally licensed to trade arms. In reality, these are not mutually exclusive operations. There is much overlap when one considers the fluid movement of the middlemen who acquire arms. The role of licensed arms trade specialists, for example, is quite unique. Sometimes they are prominent personalities that are middlemen to other unknown middlemen, further blurring a trail to the source of the arms. When the traders import the arms, they may underreport the actual quantity that is shown on the paperwork and then sell the surplus in the informal market. Some arms-related businesses also supply the Thai army and police. As of 1998 there were thirteen corporate suppliers of arms to the military (Phongpaichit et al. 1998, 139-141).

Since the 1990s the position of Thai foreign policy regarding the Karen is slowly being transformed by it warming relations with the SPDC. The Thai government's treatment of Karen refugees, through instances of refoulement, for example, is indicative that its relationship with the Karen is currently waning. Although denied by the KNU, observers have argued that Bangkok is pressuring the KNU and the SPDC to come to some sort of agreement, with pressures upon the KNU to concede more.

The buffer zone policy is still there, but as relations between the SPDC and the Thai government thaw, this policy is being reconstructed in a way that will likely disadvantage the Karen. As we shall see, a section of the Thai government views the Karen struggle as a thorn toward Thai and Burmese business relations. Pastor Lah Thaw sums up the exploitative nature of the buffer zone policy insofar as the Karen are concerned: "like a material that is no longer useful" to the Thais, they "threw the ethnic minorities away."[80]

The beginning of warming of relations between Thailand and Burma occurred with initiatives by Thailand's then Army Chief of Staff General Chaovalit Yongchaiyudh. An often-overlooked fact is that Chaovalit was the first foreign leader to recognize the SLORC regime in 1989 in spite of protests from Thais within the country. Two general reasons prompted Chaovalit down this path: Thailand coveted the teak forests of Burma while China was wooing the military regime and coveting the same resource among others. The country had to minimize this influence by acquiring a share of the Burmese market. The conventional interpretation of Chaovalit's move is that he had sold out to business interests. Indeed, Pastor Lah Thaw notes that many "Thai politicians are self-confessed close friends with the Burmese regime and are acting as a shield for them."[81]

Logging

In the mountains of Thailand during the 1980s, timber production was occurring at a feverish pace. The regional ecosystem was slowly being

---

[80] Interview with Pastor Lah Thaw, February 2004.
[81] Ibid.

destroyed. The felling of numerous tracts of rainforest had caused land denudation and soil erosion. Fahn notes that since the 1960s, Thailand's forests have already been halved; with unofficial estimates suggesting that only 20 percent of the country is still forested (Fahn 2003, 112). During November 1988, while the population of Burma was living in the aftermath of the first pro-democracy uprising, the results of environmental destruction within Thailand resulted in one of the worst floods in a century, compounded by landslides that killed over 400 people. Within two months, Bangkok enforced a complete logging ban, effective January 1, 1989, followed by the cancellation of 300 logging concessions. Brunner, Talbot and Elkin's (1998) wonderfully in-depth and detailed research into logging at the Thai/Burma border reveal that due to the ban domestic timber production fell from 4.5 million cubic meters in 1988 to 2.7 million cubic meters in 1992.

Indeed, a visual assessment of the border ecology points to a substantial dwindling of Thailand's teak forests. Through my travels to Thailand's Kanchanaburi province, east of the 4th brigade area in the Mergui and Tavoy districts of Burma's Tenasserim Division, the teak forests that were present in 2004 were very much the product of *reforestation* by the Thai government. The road passed by many miles of carefully manicured forests, with teak trees evenly spaced apart from one another, most of them the same height, in what are clearly orchestrated attempts to replant timber in the region. The teak trees were young, not very tall (about 30 feet), with trunk circumferences of about 30-40 inches, and evenly spaced out across the numerous hills that dot this part of the Thai border. It was visually obvious that a systematic plan was designed to replant the trees in evenly spaced intervals, ranging from three to six meters.

The lost logging concessions compelled Thai companies to seek abundant sources of teak elsewhere. In their attempts to pacify Rangoon as a competitive seller as well as boost KNU coffers, the KNU precariously allowed Thai timber companies to log large tracts of Kawthoolei's forests. Timber companies also began crossing into the forests of neighboring countries; by the late 1980s "timber imports increased sevenfold" (Brunner et al. 1998, 14). The most obvious site was Kawthoolei's forests. From a purely business perspective it made sense.

By the mid-1980s, Thailand had only 167,425 square kilometers of forest, compared to Burma's 448,238 square kilometers. Moreover, if we examine Brunner et al.'s data longitudinally, we see that although in 1973 Thailand possessed over 225,567 square kilometers of forest cover, it was still less than half of what Burma had at the time, 487,050 square kilometers of forest cover. By 1985 Burma had over two and a half times more forest cover than Thailand.

The political move by the KNU at the time ensured Thailand's insatiable appetite for teak would not cause the country to view the Tatmadaw as its sole supplier. Yet by 1997, Brunner et al. note that border forests "have been largely depleted, undermining a key element in the Karen resource base" (Brunner et al. 1998, 18). As more land is captured by the Tatmadaw, access to teak is becoming more constricted. Although teak forests are still relatively abundant in the rainforests of Kawthoolei as well as in the northeastern Burma, deforestation rates have increased significantly over the years on Karen land now under Tatmadaw control.

With the advent of logging inside Burma's borders, Thailand reported an increase in timber imports from 43 percent in 1988 to 67 percent in 1992. Burma's share at the time also increased, from 26 percent to 41 percent during the same period. Brunner et al. note that as a result of Thailand's deforestation:

- The total volume of timber available for processing in Thailand more than doubles when the illegal harvest in Thailand and the illegal inflows from the surrounding countries are added to the official production figures.
- Burma is the single largest supplier of illegal timber into Thailand, supplying 1.6 million to 1.7 million cubic meters in 1992, or 70 percent of total illegal imports.
- There are also reports of large-scale illegal exports of timber from Burma to China (which in 1996 imported more than 80 percent of the logs it consumed), but no statistics are available (1998, 15).

Another reason why has Thailand embarked on this path toward diplomatic relations with the Tatmadaw—even though Thailand is a "democracy" is Thailand's concern that Rangoon would fall under the orbit of China and India. This concern almost completely explains Thailand's geopolitical maneuverings that have since the 1990s, severely affected its relationship with its erstwhile Karen allies. The Tatmadaw knows this, and with China and India courting the SPDC, the Tatmadaw is adeptly playing off the countries against one another. The neighboring governments of SPDC Burma, along with their insatiable appetite for Burma's teak, other kinds of timber and natural resources, have meant that the SPDC has easily harnessed their political clout to disadvantage the Karen and other ethnic nationalities.

The regime realizes that Thailand, China and India covet the untapped natural resources of Burma, and in the case of Thailand, teak is a highly desired commodity, both for symbolic and local uses as well as for export. The figures for the teak trade are, however, impossible to come by because virtually the entire area is off-limits to scientific scrutiny (Smith 1994). But what we do know is not only are China, India and Thailand the regime's biggest customers, they also "report the greatest difference between their imports and Burma's declared exports" (Brunner et al. 1998, 15). With this in mind, in 1998, Thailand was still Burma's number one customer when juxtaposed to the China and India. However it must be known that the most official figures only capture declared exports to Thailand.

There are gross discrepancies in the figures, however, and one should consider them as indicative of shady trade practices between those involved in business relationships with the regime. Brunner et al. note that Thailand reported imports that quadrupled Burma's declared exports in 1994, as well as double Burma's exports in 1995. A more fascinating discrepancy is via India, which reported 1995 import figures to be 30 times higher than Burma's declared exports. The regime provided no figures for 1995 in regard to Chinese demand, but China declared imports of over 500,000 cubic meters.

> There can be some legitimate reasons for mismatched export-import figures, but when these discrepancies persist for several years in the same direction, they point to a systematic attempt by Rangoon to conceal timber exports and the illegal income it generates, a pattern that has been well-documented elsewhere in the region (Brunner et al. 1998, 16).

For example, Rainforest Action Network (RAN) has estimated an annual felling rate between 800,000 to one million hectares, making Burma's deforestation rate "one of the five highest in the world" during the mid-1990s (Smith 1994). In 2001, the United Nations Food and Agriculture Organization (FAO) designated the Southeast Asia region as experiencing the highest rates of deforestation in the world, surpassing even the much publicized deforestation rates of Amazonian Brazil (Fahn 2003,112). Indeed, R. B. Singh of the FAO noted that Southeast Asia "is losing forests five times faster than the global net annual forest loss of 0.2 percent experienced between 1990 and 2000" (Fahn 2003, 337).

In December of 1988, as Thailand was exhausting its own supplies of timber, and weeks from declaring a complete logging ban in the country, Rangoon's Ministry of Forestry granted logging concessions to foreign logging companies. According to Brunner et al. (1998) Thailand received 36 contracts, or over 85 percent of the 42 applications for five-year logging concessions inside Burma while Smith notes that Thailand received 34 out of 40 contracts. This shouldn't be too surprising as many leaders of Thai logging firms "enjoyed close links to senior Thai military officials," especially General Chaovalit Yongchaiyudh, a "soldier turned politician who seems to have had more political lives than a Siamese cat" (Bryant 1997, 6; Fahn 2003, 133).

Most of the contracts were given to Thai "military interests" rather than forestry-based companies. These interests are in turn tied to Thai logging companies who are linked to influential and powerful Thai politicians. For instance, the companies *Mae Sot Panakit, Muang Pana, Vinives and Sila International Trading* are all owned by M.P., Suchart Tancharoen. *Boonsawat and Friends* is owned by Boonsawat Duang-jaiekarat, a former Social Action Party

M.P. from Chiang Rai. *Union Par* belongs to Seri Tanchukiat and Precha Nawawong, sons-in-law of an important army officer. *Sirin Technology* belongs to Boonchu Trithong, a member of the Thai parliament and an arms trader with "connections to many high ranking military officers" (Phongpaichit et al. 1998, 142).

These interests were further solidified when General Chaovalit and his 150-strong delegation visited Rangoon in April of 1988 (Ne Win had visited Thailand a year earlier). In Rangoon arrangements were agreed upon regarding the need for more diplomatic exchanges. The increased trade between China and Burma, much of which had previously gone through Thailand and CPB-held territory in Burma's northeast "was one of the main reasons for the Thai government's swift recognition of the Saw Maung regime after the 1988 coup" (Smith 1999, 361). With the CPB and CPT no longer a serious threat, Thailand's military circle seized the initiative in hopes of preventing a monopolization of the Burmese market by China. Thus, Thailand, under the immense power wielded by then Thai Army Chief of Staff General Chaovalit, quickly granted international recognition to the Union of Myanmar. Not even the beginning of Burma's pro-democracy uprising and its subsequent suppression during August of the same year would alter Thailand's stance on trade with the regime.

> The lucrative fishing and timber deals struck with the Saw Maung regime…by General Chaovalit, immediately following the military take-over in Rangoon, were interpreted by many observers as simply an opportunistic attempt to compensate for the ecological devastation of Thailand's own environment and to win back the economic initiative from China (ibid., 361).

Moreover, the timber agreements between the SPDC and Bangkok "had a clear counter-insurgency motive" (Smith 1994). Many of the logging concessions granted to Thai loggers were in territories controlled by the ethnic nationalities. Logging roads were required to transport heavy machinery to the lumber sites that would harvest the over 18,000 square kilometers of rainforest. As a result, when the Tatmadaw launched their offensives against the ethnic nationalities, "Thai companies began bulldozing logging roads along which troops and supplies could also be rapidly transported" (Smith 1994). Brunner et al. note:

> In addition to generating revenue, logging along the Thai border coincided with Rangoon's desire to control rebel-held territory. The most strategic consideration was the construction of logging roads. The regime had been unable to bear against the ethnic armies because there were few roads in these areas. Once the logging roads were bulldozed, however, the Burmese army was able to advance

rapidly. There is a close correlation between the granting of a concession and the initiation of military offensives against the ethnic minorities (Brunner et al. 1998, 17).

In December 1989, Britain's Channel Four captured footage of Tatmadaw troops pillaging the Karen village of Sitkaya which already experienced mortar barrages from the night before. Seven villagers were killed and twenty were forced into portering while over 200 villagers escaped by swimming across the Moei River into Thailand. However, "within a week...Thai loggers had moved in to Sitkaya to begin cutting and transporting timber" (Smith 1994).

Rangoon relished at the possibilities. Other than the annual $112 million income generated from logging, the Tatmadaw was in essence, allowing the Thais to streamline the initially difficult logistics posed by the thick foliage (Brunner et al. 1998, Smith 1994). On paper, this was a win-win situation for the regime insofar as suppressing ethnic self-determination groups are concerned. Logging concessions were assigned to areas that straddled the Thai-Burmese border at a time when pro-democracy students were fleeing to Karen territory. At the time it was well known that the KNU provided shelter and even contributed to the training of its pro-democracy army, the ABSDF. Logging thus occurred during a period when there was continuous fighting between the Tatmadaw and the KNU, NMSP, KNPP and other ethnic self-determination groups along the border (Smith 1999).

For generations, the Karen, Mon, and Karenni have harnessed and exploited the availability of timber in the region, and for many years, in direct control of its production. However, these groups have utilized "low impact harvesting methods that protected the forest" (Brunner et al. 1998, 17). The forest was "managed" in this manner and the Karen were able to harness its forests for "timber, fuel wood, fruit, nuts, medicinal products, and game" (Bryant 1997, 2). The Karen have historically planted teak alongside their swidden crops and "as the cultivators moved to a new area after a couple of years, the process was repeated, and teak plantations were created" (Brunner et al. 1998, 5; Bryant 1997). Bryant (1997) notes that on average the Karen villagers practiced forest clearing to provide fertilizer for the crops on a ten-year cycle. Moreover, the KNU organization, other self-determination groups, as well as Rangoon, harvested teak utilizing a more refined system of teak cultivation known as the Brandis Selection System.

The Brandis Selection System was named after German botanist Dietrich Brandis, who was employed by the Government of India and stationed in Burma during the 1850s. The Brandis Selection System exacted conditions for harvesting teak. A 30-year felling cycle is prescribed, sizes of trees that can be cut are prescribed, and the method of preparing teak for cutting and production are laid out (Brunner et al. 1998). When the Brandis Selection System is properly implemented, the system "has proved successful at maintaining a high yield of top-quality timber with minimum environmental impacts in the mixed deciduous forests of central and northern Burma" (Brunner et al. 1998, 6). Given the efficacy of the Brandis Selection System by all groups involved, how then does the military regime secure an advantage in the process of exploiting teak?

It does so through the regime's two forestry institutions, the Ministry of Forestry and the autonomous institution known as the Myanma Timber Enterprise (MTE). The MTE has direct powers to make "on-the-spot decisions" regarding "harvesting, marketing, and trade of forest products on a commission basis" (Brunner et al. 1998, 6). From the perspective of the Karen, the MTE was competing directly with the KNU Forestry Department. The two governmental institutions with their arsenal of elephants, of which teak harvest in areas with no roads would be impossible, render teak wood the most coveted hardwood in Asia. As a means of maldeveloping Kawthoolei (and cutting into the market of a rival), the MTE, in collusion with the Tatmadaw's Ministry of Forestry, has stood by as logging concessions were purposely granted to Thailand in predominantly Karen, Shan and Kachin areas, areas which supported armies fighting Rangoon. Moreover, felling cycles have been shortened for the region, with younger trees being harvested and regeneration severely affected.

Imagine the surprise to Chaovalit and the Thai government when, in 1993, the Tatmadaw cancelled Thailand's logging concessions: in the midst of politics between the relatively giant neighbors of Thailand and Burma, the KNU had their say in the matter. Even though Thai logging firms are intimately linked to the military elite of Thailand and even though the KNU was not able to halt the advance of Thai logging companies on their soil, it was still able to tax the Thai loggers (Phongpaichit et al. 1998, Brunner et al. 1998). The Thai Army was not going to stop the KNLA from enforcing their tax: if Tatmadaw couldn't do it with its military machine, Bangkok was not going to try. In return, the KNU dare not alienate its quasi-ally and allowed the logging to occur. Bangkok may have made deals with Rangoon, but this was also very much the Karen State of Kawthoolei, and goods that passed through Kawthoolei passed through the KNU.

Whether Thailand paid the taxes willingly should also be questioned—if it complied readily with KNU tax requirements, the Thais are then indirectly reinforcing the Karen resistance, a pattern that must have resonated with Chaovalit and his insinuation to a buffer zone policy in use at the time. Yet Falla's interview of a Karen presents another view, primarily that "not all Thais support the Karen, you see. Thai businessmen don't want fighting on the border, they want it quiet and wide open so that they can take all the trees without trouble" (Falla 1991, 315). In any case, it was soon apparent to Rangoon that it had made the mistake of granting logging concessions in the Manerplaw and Three Pagoda Pass areas. Here, the KNU profited heavily from the tax it levied on Thai timber companies. The profits acquired by the

KNU further reinforced the welfare of Karen in the region. Since the Tatmadaw was unable to "cut the KNU out of this activity" the logging concessions to Thailand were cancelled in 1993 (Brunner et al. 1998, 17).

> The Burma logging trade has become a desperate business in which few parties emerge with their reputations intact. Though on a lesser scale, many of the country's armed opposition groups have also become increasingly active in logging deals since 1988 as one of their major sources of revenue to buy arms and ammunition. The most serious...overfelling have reportedly taken place in areas where insurgent armies have signed cease-fires with the SLORC (Smith 1994).

The price of keeping Thailand from throwing its lot with Rangoon was high however. Between 1989 and 1993, the KNU Forestry Department, not to be outdone by the MTE and Rangoon in the "teak war," permitted Thai logging firms to over-cut "as part of a desperate attempt to maintain forest-based revenues in the face of SLORC's efforts to cut the KNU's income" (Bryant 1997, 6). Thai loggers received waivers that required Thai logging firms to follow the strict guidelines for sustainable forestry. Thai loggers also frequently extracted more timber than their contracts allowed and even went so far as logging in areas not designated for such purposes. Indeed, Bryant notes "logging outside designated areas was ubiquitous as loggers took advantage of the political turmoil along the border to extract extra timber free of charge" (ibid., 6). As a result the Thai teak industry rapidly deforested large areas of Kawthoolei along the border.

Nevertheless, the KNU profited from their trade in teak. Since the KNU never publishes revenue data, estimates of prices range between $60 per cubic meter of teak (Brunner et al. 1998) while others cite a range of $40 to $80 per cubic meter of teak (Bryant 1997). With a significantly small population in the hills, much of the wealth was allocated to improving the quality of KNLA weaponry, attending to the welfare of Karen living in a war zone, as well as improving the Karen quality of life in the remaining liberated areas of Kawthoolei.

Within this context, Thailand was also in a win-win situation. It reestablishes its influence in the region at a time when Beijing's interests were quickly transforming Burma into a quasi-satellite state of China. This is an important point to remember because Thailand's desire to establish economic influences over Burma resulted in yet another geopolitical maneuver: Thailand and the Association of Southeast Asian Nations (ASEAN) granted membership to Burma in 1997 as a means of situating its opening economy within the orbit of Southeast Asian interests, a decision which has garnered international condemnations against the trade bloc. Indeed, ASEAN, like many of the oil TNCs we shall soon examine, attempted to escape scrutiny by arguing that human rights issues and trade issues are separate dynamics.

As Thailand once utilized its buffer zone policy with the Karen in dealing with Rangoon, it now needed to utilize Rangoon as a buffer against China. In this hop-scotching of diplomatic ties, the Karen have become expendable. This explains why Chaovalit jumped at the opportunity to engage in business dealings with the Tatmadaw; his dream of envisioning trade where ultimately hydroelectric dams would be established along the Moei and Salween rivers, in the heart of the Karen State would soon, or so he believed, come true (Smith 1999).[82]

China

During October 1989, at the time Bangkok's elite were celebrating a renewed source of profits through Chaovalit's business acumen, Rangoon sent a delegation, the "most high-powered Tatmadaw delegation ever," to visit China and hold talks with then Chinese Prime Minister Li Peng. Their partnership would further be strengthened after Ne Win killed thousands of students during Burma's 1988 pro-democracy crackdown, followed a year later by Deng Xiaoping's eerily similar reaction to Tiananmen pro-democracy protesters. As a result of the dramatic events that befell Burma in 1988 and China in 1989, there was "no doubt both governments felt that in their crushing of student-led 'democracy' uprisings they had something in common" (Smith 1999, 360). Moreover, with the CPB no longer in power, China switched sides and courted Rangoon.

Then Chief-of-Staff Lt. General Than Shwe and General Khin Nyunt, head of the Military Intelligence Service, had received assurances that both countries would continue to foster growth and political relations. With the CPB having disintegrated into ethnic factions in 1989 and with worries that punitive measures against Burma would push it to seek Soviet support (which could conceivably place Kremlin interests near China's southern province of Yunnan), China strengthens its ties with the Tatmadaw.

The warming of Sino-Burmese relations began during this period, when Deng Xiaoping and Ne Win were cementing their diplomatic ties. The eventual cooperation between the two leaders, and consequently, the two countries, may ironically be due to the CPB. As CPB leaders conducted their campaign against Rangoon during the first three decades after Burma's independence, they followed a strictly Maoist line. Many CPB members had traveled to China to consult with Chinese Communist Party officials. Moreover, during Mao's Cultural Revolution, CPB cadres were following suit by denouncing the "rightists" in their own country—but not before they vehemently denounced Deng.

---

[82] Interview with Pastor Lah Thaw, February 2004.

After Mao's death and the unsuccessful grab for power by the pro-Maoists Gang of Four, the CPB was politically cast adrift by Beijing. By the time Ne Win visited Beijing in May of 1985, Deng Xiaoping greeted him as an "old friend" while Ne Win announced "there were no special problems between the two countries" (Smith 1999, 360).

Rangoon was not necessarily encouraging Chinese trade in the informal economy to be as intense as it would turn out to be. During the 1985-1986 period Rangoon only controlled 60 kilometers out of the northern border that stretched for over 2,100 kilometers. The rest was Kachin, Shan, and CPB territory, and their own liberation ethnodevelopments were beyond Rangoon's administration at the time.

During 1986, Chinese goods began to flood Burmese markets. Ethnic nationalities in the northern Burma acted as middlemen who supplied much of the bankrupt Burma with "cigarettes, crockery and rice cookers" as well as manipulating prices to "undercut the price of locally made goods" (ibid., 361). In spite of being named the "Burmese" way to Socialism, by the late 1980s Chinese commodities outsold Burmese-made products. With such asymmetrical but lucrative trade, Tatmadaw elites willingly sacrificed Burma's long-term interests for short-term survival.

The Frontier Trade Division of the Yunnan Province Export Corporation also traded with Burma. Over 2,000 items, ranging from "rice, jade...manufactured consumer goods such as bicycles, medicine and household items" were traded with the regime (ibid., 361). China also established an effective economic intelligence gathering system with Beijing agents assigned to Lashio, Rangoon, and Mandalay, to study the market needs of the region. The Yunnan governor cited 1987 trade at one billion dollars. Within the next two years trade increased by 500 million annually (ibid., 1999).

Although China wanted Burma as a trade ally, it also desired to establish a friendly Burma where it militarily did not threaten Beijing's interests. Beijing's main priority has always been the security of its vast borders, especially in Yunnan Province, "scene of a bloody border war with Vietnam in the late 1970s... [and]...always...regarded as a particularly dangerous flashpoint on the soft underbelly of the country" (ibid., 360). Not surprisingly to ensure stability, weapons sales were formalized with Rangoon, amounting to billions of dollars since the 1990s. No other economic transaction would have such a profound consequence upon Karen lives and the Karen struggle than this endeavor.

By August 1990, the first shipments of Chinese arms arrive in Rangoon. Soon Chinese F-7 jets, Hainan-class naval patrol boats, 100 light medium tanks and the Chinese version of the Soviet PT76, APC vehicles, single barrel anti-aircraft guns of 37mm and 57mm variety, radio equipment, radar equipment for jets, "and enough light arms and ammunition to equip seventy-four new battalions" arrived (Lintner 1994, 314). Chinese military advisers also arrived, the first foreign military personnel to do so in Burma since the 1950s. One could argue that Burma was, in essence, transforming into a Chinese satellite state. Other than guns, over 200 heavy-duty trucks were also delivered, along with "unspecified air force weapons," multiple rocket launchers, and artillery. In March 2004, new negotiations with Beijing included the purchase of older weapons no longer valued by the People's Liberation Army. Future weapons purchase will likely include combat helicopters, minesweepers, anti-ship missiles, and naval mines, and ship hulls (Ashton 2004).

Weapons sold at "friendship prices" further facilitated Chinese arms sales to Burma. By 1997, Tatmadaw generals Than Shwe and Maung Aye along with China's Li Peng formalize the Sino-Burmese Pact. Part of the pact included provisions for the training of 300 Burmese air force and navy officers in aviation skills and naval duties, as well as development loans to the regime—overall an agreement to strengthen military cooperation between the two countries. By June of 1998, the sale of NAMC/PAC Karakorum-8 (K-8) training aircrafts worth $20 million was commenced (Selth 2000).

Exact figures of Tatmadaw arms purchases are unknown as a sizeable part of its purchases are financed by heroin sales estimated to be worth $1 billion to $2 billion during the mid-1990s. In 2004, estimates place military contracts at 3.5 billion dollars (Ashton 2004, Ball 2004). China also began to assist Burma in the development of its infrastructure, especially roads. By the end of the 1990s, China and Thailand would be the most important trading partners of the SPDC regime.

Smith's (1999) speculation that China was developing naval and intelligence listening facilities at various locations around the Andaman coastline would be corroborated by Desmond Ball of the Strategic Defence Studies Centre of the Australian National University, Canberra, an important center for acquiring a comprehensive analysis of the Tatmadaw. In an interview granted to the Irrawaddy newspaper, Ball corroborates the "continuous" Chinese-SPDC presence at the Great Coco Island as well as the presence of Chinese technicians at six to seven smaller listening stations on the Andaman coast. Ball further notes that of all of China's listening stations, the ones in Burma are most critical because they allow monitoring of two dynamics: (1) the "telemetry signals which are generated during Indian ballistic missile tests" that land in the Andaman Sea and (2) all naval and commercial maritime movements (Irrawaddy On-Line Edition 2004).

Additional Players

The evolution of the Tatmadaw was also very much shaped by its historical acceptance of weaponry from a host of other countries, a revelation of the grossly contradictory diplomacies that have historically characterized how the international community deals with Burma. The following players in the discussion below are also important actors that reinforce the staying power of the regime.

During the beginning of the Karen Revolution in 1949, Rangoon had approximately 2,000 well-equipped troops. By the time Doi Tung was seized from the KMT in 1955, General Ne Win commanded over 40,000 soldiers, equipped at the time by India and Britain, as well as receiving substantial aid from Australia. By the mid-1950s, Burma's navy was receiving cannons from Sweden (Lintner 1994, Selth 2000).

After Josef Tito's visit to Burma in January of 1955, Yugoslavia began to supply a battery of the Burma Artillery with 76 mm Yugoslav cannons, as well as pledging to supply "an entire Burmese brigade with weapons" (Lintner 1994, 127). Relations between Burma and Japan also thawed. North Korea, for example, has been engaged with the Tatmadaw since the 1990s. Sales to the Tatmadaw included small arms ammunition as well as sixteen 130mm artillery pieces sold to the SPDC in 1998. By 2003, North Korean technicians were sent to Rangoon to install surface-to-surface missiles on ships. Discussions have been in place for the purchase of naval submarines and even SCUD short-range ballistic missiles. Speculations for the future revolve around Pyongyang's potential construction of Burma's first nuclear reactor and its first nuclear weapon (Ashton 2004).

India has also provided the military regime with an assortment of weapons, ammunition, and equipment. In 2003, New Delhi sold the SPDC eighty 75mm howitzers (also known as "mountain guns"). Advanced communications equipment has also been sold to the military regime. India's Defense Minister has demonstrated further willingness to sell the SPDC naval vessels. A performance staged by India's Air Force in Burma during 2004 might indicate that the SPDC is interested in buying aircraft from India (Ashton 2004).

The Ukraine is also involved. As part of the cash-strapped ex-Soviet system, Kiev signs a contract in 2002 with the SPDC to provide the regime with 36D6 radar systems. By mid-2003, fifty T-72 tanks were sold. A $500 million contract was signed in May 2003 to provide the SPDC with components to service 1,000 BTR-3U light armored personnel carriers. During the next decade, the vehicles will be supplied with parts and assembled in a purpose-built facility in Burma. In February of 2004, secret delivery of air defense weapons arrives in Rangoon (Ashton 2004).

Serbia is also complicit with Rangoon. In December 2003, Serbia sells the SPDC "Nora" self-propelled howitzers marketed by Jugoimport-SDPR. In March 2004, thirty Serbian technicians arrive in Burma to repair the 12 Soko G-4 jets of the Burma Air Force, purchased from the Republic of Yugoslavia in the 1990s. According to Ashton (2004), the jets are often grounded—many for several years—due largely to the unavailability of spare parts. During the same period, Slovakia ships machines that manufacture artillery or rocket-propelled grenades through the Unipex Company of Slovakia (Ashton 2004).

The SPDC has made a few dramatic purchases from Russia, including the sophisticated MiG-29B-12 jet fighters, of which it purchased eight in 2002, perhaps to replace the unreliable F-7 jets purchased from Beijing. Two dual-seat MiG-29UB training jets have also been purchased. By July 2002, Rangoon and signs a contract with the Russian Ministry of Atomic Energy (MINATOM) to construct a nuclear reactor. A new communications system has also been purchased (ibid., 2004).

During the late 1950s, the Federal Republic of Germany via Fritz Werner Industries (FWI), an armaments engineering firm, was an important contributor to Burma's arms technology as well as to its defense industries (Lintner 1994, Smith 1999, Selth 2000). The enterprise was such a success that Fritz Werner's Gewehr 3 (G3) rifle became the "standard infantry weapon" (Selth 2000, 9). By the 1970s, FWI was manufacturing mortars and grenades in its other facilities. FWI paid for Ne Win's recreational and health trips abroad. By 1985, there were accusations that FWI was assisting Rangoon in the manufacture of chemical weapons. Accusations emerged from academics, the international news media, the Stockholm International Peace Research Institute (SIPRI), Christian Science Monitor, as well as by the US Director of Naval Intelligence, Rear Admiral William Studeman and his successor Rear Admiral Thomas Brooks. Although Chancellor Helmut Kohl cancelled all official aid to Burma after the 1988 protests, indirect assistance is still occurring between FWI and Rangoon despite the former government's protest.

By the mid 1990s, reports from the Kachin Independence Army and the KNU claim that there were "tear-gas like rockets" used in the attacks on Manerplaw and Kawmoorah, fired through heavy artillery. Villagers and soldiers reported chest pains, difficult breathing, nausea, stinging eyes, "mysterious ailments" and "ugly sleeping wounds." No independent sources could verify the accusations by the indigenous peoples and the international community (Selth 2000).

Singapore also maintains close link with Rangoon. By the mid-1980s, Singapore consumed 15 percent of Burma's exports in timber, fish, and agricultural goods. In spite of the crackdown on pro-democracy activists, Singapore continues to maintain "highly pragmatic and self-interested ties" with the Tatmadaw. It supplies the country with mortars, ammunition, and raw materials for rifle construction, and Carl Gustave recoilless guns manufactured by Chartered Industries of Singapore (CIS). By 1989, Singapore ships second-hand caches of 40mm rocket propelled grenades (RPGs) and 57mm anti-tank guns of "Eastern-bloc origin." M16s and 5.56mm ammunition, 7.62mm assault rifles and ammunition, possibly landmines, and communications equipment have all been sent to Rangoon. In 1997, Singapore even defends the Tatmadaw at the United Nations "when it attempted to weaken a General Assembly resolution which criticized Rangoon for its harsh treatment of human rights activists" (Selth 2000, 30). Singapore, member of ASEAN, continues to court the regime to prevent the Tatmadaw from falling into the orbit of Beijing, the same approach adopted by Thailand and other ASEAN members.

Israel's links with Rangoon go back to Burma's Independence since as a "former British mandate...[Israel] shared a certain identity with Burma" (ibid., 45). Burmese local militias have been modeled after the defense units that protected collective settlements in Israel. Most transactions are clandestine in nature, but to date many weapons have been sold to the regime. During the 1950s, Israel supplied Burma with 30 second-hand British Spitfires and trained Burma's post-independence air force pilots. Over 50,000 rifles were also sold during this period. By the 1980s 40mm RPGs and 57mm anti-tank guns of Eastern-bloc origin were sold. Currently, Israel has engaged in activities based on upgrading the notoriously unreliable Chinese-made F-7 jets sold to Burma (a derivative of the venerable MiG-21 "Fishbed"). Sixteen Soltam 15mm howitzers were sold to the Tatmadaw via Singapore. Naval weaponry such as 76mm OTO Melara compact guns has also been sold to outfit the Burmese Navy (Lintner 1994, Selth 2000).

Pakistan also maintains a close link with Rangoon because of their shared concerns over India and China. During the late 1980s, Pakistan capitalized on Rajiv Gandhi's support of Aung San Suu Kyi and the NLD by warming its relationship with the military regime. Islamabad sold SLORC over 150 machine guns and 5,000 120mm mortar bombs. KNLA troops have uncovered unexploded ordinance with markings of the Pakistan Ordinance Factories (POF). The KNU has also claimed that Pakistan was training Tatmadaw pilots. Indeed, since 1988 over 40 Tatmadaw officials were sent to Pakistan for training while between 1990 and 1994, 34 Tatmadaw officers (16 from the army, 11 from the navy, and 7 from the air force) even attended Pakistani military schools (Selth 2000, 65).

Other weapons provided by Islamabad also include 106mm M40 A1 recoilless rifles, of which the Tatmadaw fastened to its jeeps, mortars, rocket launchers, assault rifles, and ammunition valued at about US $20 million, and likely "siphoned" from shipments meant to supply Afghanistan's mujahadeen fighting the Soviets. Ammunition was also sold to the Tatmadaw, specifically for the .38-caliber revolver, 7.62mm machine gun, as well as 77mm rifle-launched grenades, 76mm, 82mm, and 106mm recoilless rifle rounds, 120 mm mortar bombs, 37mm anti-aircraft gun ammunition, 105 mm artillery shells and ammunition for the Tatmadaw long-range 155mm guns (ibid., 63).

Petropolitics

Oil transnational corporations (TNCs) and their interests began moving into Burma following the wake of the 1988 pro-democracy crackdown. Earth Rights International (ERI) and the Southeast Asian Information Network (SAIN) provide detailed information on this area of the Karen struggle from their 1996 publication *Total Denial: A Report on the Yadana Pipeline Project in Burma*. I have drawn much of my data from this excellent report.

After SLORC dismissed the 1990s election results amid mounting arrests and executions, ironically it would be oil companies from *democratic* nations that decided to invest with Rangoon. Plans were created to build a natural gas pipeline through the Tenasserim Division into Thailand (KNLA 4th Brigade and NMSP territory). Although Thailand is relatively rich in natural resources, it is relatively poor in fuel resources. Gas deposits do exist in the Gulf of Siam but much of it is contaminated by mercury. Thailand's neighbors fare much better with their gas fields, especially Burma, Malaysia, Indonesia, Brunei, and even Vietnam (Fahn 2003).

By 1989, at least ten oil TNCs were lured by Rangoon's pitch of allowing businesses to operate without environmental regulations as well as assurances that Rangoon would employ Tatmadaw units to protect their workforce. Constituting what Smith describes as the first wave, Petro Canada, Royal Dutch Shell, Amoco (USA), Broken Hill (Australia), Premier (UK), Yukong (South Korea), and Idemitsu (Japan) had purchased exploration licenses. By the early 1990s, most of these TNCs withdrew their operations due to "poor discoveries, high operating costs and, though never publicly admitted, in at least two cases concern over the poor human rights condition in Burma" (Smith 1994, Chapter 6).

However, during the same period, two major offshore gas fields were discovered in the Andaman Sea. During late 1989, California-based UNOCAL pays SLORC $5-8 million dollars US to secure rights to explore the large gas fields. SLORC's Minister of Energy, U Khin Maung Thein announced the presence of over "six trillion cubic feet of natural gas...more than three times original estimates" (Smith 1994, Chapter 6). In the midst of the announcement, various new and old oil TNCs vied for access to the fields. Eventually it would be Total (France) and UNOCAL (USA) that would secure the rights to tap into the Yadana gas fields, located 200 miles offshore from the Mon State and the Tenasserim Division. Texaco (USA), Premier (UK), and Nippon Oil (Japan) would harness the Yetagun fields further south.

By 1992, SLORC's deal with Yadana consortium member, France's Total, was so lucrative that the regime soon imported over $390 million in weaponry purchased primarily from China, "an all time record for military spending" for the regime (ERI/SAIN 1996, 5-6). In 1993, UNOCAL secures a deal with Total (France) to joint-administer drill the Yadana fields, and along with SLORC, back a pipeline project to bring natural gas to Thailand by 1998. By 1995, the Petroleum Authority of Thailand (PTT) signs a thirty-year contract with SLORC's Myanma Oil and Gas Enterprise (MOGE) to facilitate this project. Soon after, Texaco and ARCO secure drilling rights in the Gulf of Martaban (ERI/SAIN 1996).

The planned arrangement was for the PTT to purchase natural gas drawn from gas fields located off Burma's coast. Approximately 220 miles of the pipeline is submerged under forty-five meters of sea, while the remaining thirty miles is terrestrial and would cut through the northern Tenasserim Division, predominantly Karen and Mon areas, finally reaching Thailand. At Three Pagoda Pass located in Thailand's northern Kanchanaburi Province, the gas will feed a giant power plant in the region. PTT is aiming to tap into over 250 million cubic feet of natural gas per day. According to Fahn (2003), the construction of the Yadana pipeline is one of the most contentious environmental issues in the developing world.

The importance of rich gas fields in the Gulf of Martaban and its transport to Burma's biggest customer, Thailand, meant that Karen and Mon areas within the Tenasserim Division had to be neutralized. SLORC would then be projected to earn $400 million annually from its sales, the "regime's single largest source of foreign currency" (ERI/SAIN 1996, 1-2; HRW/A 1997; Smith 1994). To the extent that the pipeline would be crossing KNU territory, the activities of these members, also known as the Yadana Consortium, would leave a legacy of death, displacement, lies, and denials.

Pro-democracy forces in Burma denounce the partnerships between SLORC's MOGE and the oil TNCs. The oil TNCs have no allies among the pro-democracy groups or ethnic nationalities who do not have formal ceasefires with Rangoon. The protests were vocal enough that the World Bank and International Monetary Fund continue to refrain from loaning to Burma. A KNU communiqué from the period states:

> The KNU and the KNU's Mergui-Tavoy District wish to state clearly that they are not opposed to the pipeline per se but oppose any business venture that strengthens the illegal SLORC's hold on power and hence fuels the civil war. With the establishment of conditions for peaceful resolution of the country's problems the KNU will welcome and cooperate fully with any business activity that serves to improve the living conditions of the Karen people and that does not abuse internationally accepted standards of human rights nor have detrimental effects on the environment (ERI/SAIN 1996, 4).

The National Coalition Government of the Union of Burma (NCGUB) states:

It is the responsibility of the National Coalition Government of the Union of Burma to remind these companies that they are dealing with an illegal regime that represents no one but a small group of military personnel in Burma. The military regime has no mandate from the people to exploit or sell off the country's natural resources. Hence, any agreement undertaken with an illegal regime will not be honored by the Burmese people...

We hereafter would like to reiterate our call for the international communities and transnational foreign companies to wait and hold their investments in Burma until the democratic government is formed and allowed to give protection, rights, and benefits to all Burmese people.

Nai Shwe Kyin of the New Mon State Party (NMSP) informs UNOCAL:

Dear Mr. Denis Codon,

This letter is to inform you that the New Mon State Party and related organizations have decided to take legal action against UNOCAL...due to the environmental damage [caused by] the State Law and Order Restoration Council's security activities [against] Mon, Karen, and Tavoyan areas. [83]

Aung San Suu Kyi's response to ERI/SAIN:

Q: Currently, the government is promoting foreign investment, and many companies, including UNOCAL, have investments here. What's your message to those companies?

A: We always said—very, very clearly—that Burma is not ripe for investment.

DAB and NDF have also issued strong warnings against pipeline construction, similarly discouraging investment from the international community until the restoration of democracy (Smith 1994).

Two main pull factors lure Yadana consortium partners and foreign investors. The first is the lack of environmental regulation. As of 1996, there was still a "legal vacuum" in Burma and Burma was technically without a

---

[83] Plaintiffs from the Tenasserim region have successfully sued California-based UNOCAL in the Superior Court of California. The fact that the Superior Court of California is trying UNOCAL is an unprecedented event since this is the first case in US history where a corporate entity settled on human rights abuses committed abroad (see page 300).

constitution. Its laws are based on "whatever the ruling junta of generals or local military decree," which meant that the oil TNCs would not be held accountable for environmental degradation from the project (ERI/SAIN 1996, 3). Oil TNCs and their practices are unmonitored.

Moreover, oil TNCs have yet to make public environmental impact assessments (EIAs), a precarious stance "given the consortium's lamentable environmental record" (ibid., 3). Existing and future environmental problems are not brought forth in social discourse. As a result, consortium partners "exert absolute decision-making control" regarding environmental practices in the areas under their jurisdiction (ibid., 54). Being notorious polluters that international oil companies are the *carte blanche* given to the Yadana consortium must have been a dream come true for its members.

The second factor consists of two interrelated political dynamics. Because SLORC fails to address human rights and indigenous issues, the TNCs need not either. The resulting process of establishing pipelines thus excludes local participation at the grassroots level by people who have the most invested in protecting their natural environment. Yet without a public process or an independent judiciary, Karen and Mons do not have "legal protection against, nor any legal remedies for, abuses perpetrated by the repressive SLORC regime" (ERI/SAIN 1996, 3). This situation is further exacerbated since farmers and villagers do not have access to a free flow of information to better their daily situation. Inevitably, local leaders are unable to formulate any effective policies due to a lack of data. Aung San Suu Kyi protested against these ethical violations:

> If businessmen do not care about the numbers of political prisoners in our country they should at least be concerned that the lack of an effective legal framework means there is no guarantee of fair business practice or, in cases of injustice, reparation (ibid., 46).

The Yadana consortium was also tight-lipped with its shareholders. UNOCAL has rejected calls by its US shareholders to acquire comprehensive information on their enterprises in Burma. UNOCAL's own lack of corporate responsibility is particularly distressing: ERI/SAIN cites a 1995 Citizens for a Better Environment (CBE)[84] report which argues that UNOCAL "may be one of the worse actors in the oil industry" (ibid., 59). Not only has UNOCAL threatened California's Bay Area with toxic dumping as reported by the *San Francisco Chronicle* in 1994, when a

> ...clear, diesel fluid covered the California Coast with a film of at least 8.5 million gallons of petroleum thinner, it was also responsible

---

[84] The CBE is now known as Midwest Center for Environmental Science and Public Policy (MCESPP).

for a massive oil leak from a pipeline at their Guadalupe field in California...estimated to be the largest in the state's history and the fourth largest ever in the United States (ERI/SAIN 1996, 59).

However, other oil TNCs were also complicit since many have tried to convince the US Securities and Exchange Commission to "remove resolutions on human rights and environmental issues aimed at their projects in Burma" (ERI/SAIN 1996, 56). Information and access to the Yadana operations were strictly enforced and only the SLORC and companies involved were allowed to project areas. The restrictions make EIAs impossible. As a result, few people locally or internationally outside of the companies were aware of the environmental practices and policies of the oil TNCs. ERI/SAIN's analyses also made visible the ulterior motives of the Yadana consortium: "SLORC may actually consider such environmental harms as watershed destruction and deforestation as strategic tools by which to further disempower opponents of the regime" (ERI/SAIN 1996, 57).

A. Consequences

One of the most important lessons one can draw from oil TNC practices in Burma is the link between genocide/deculturation and environmental degradation. Should anything go wrong, indigenous peoples "have had to bear the costs of clean up, environmental pollution, ethnic and cultural destruction, and some have lost their lives in pipeline explosions or had their resources destroyed for future generations" (ibid., 59). The Yadana consortium's use of technology and large-scale development projects further divert much needed resources from local groups, ultimately destroying what Fahn (2004) describes as "traditional forms of civil society." In the case of the Karen and Mons of the Tenasserim, these trials are exacerbated since they go hand in hand with the systemic crises caused by war.

Watchdog/pressure groups such as Amnesty International, Anti-Slavery International, SAIN and environmental groups such as ERI and Rainforest Action Network have already documented much of the abuses against Karen and Mons, as well as the link between human rights and environmental rights abuses. The construction of the pipeline by UNOCAL had required SLORC to utilize their infamous Four Cuts strategy, further reinforcing the notion that large ethnocratic development projects are about power and centralization. Villages have been relocated as recounted by an ERI interview of a 66 year-old Karen villager who fled to Thailand:

> Just before we came here, SLORC burned so many houses in Mi Chaung Luang. Pan Polo's house and Kyaw Shin's. I saw the ashes of Tharamu Ye Yta and Saw Htee Day's houses. They burned the

houses because no villagers were living there. They said the KNLA was there. These houses were bigger than others, and on the edge of the village. Then SLORC dismantled some houses. They took planks and wood... In the new village, you know, we have nothing. We have no farm, no crops, no house. In the new place we were not allowed to plant or grow. We lived in our old village since we were born. Our old village was perfect for us if there are no soldiers (ERI/SAIN 1996, 42-43).

In typical Tatmadaw fashion villagers are harassed and many extra-judicially murdered, raped, and forced into portering and construction of pipeline projects. A forced laborer who escaped recounted:

The main work was cutting the trees and the bamboo, making the ground level, carrying the metal pipes from the coast to places they ordered, building up the barracks made from bamboo and wooden buildings. They told us the wooden buildings were for the guest house. I do not know what the reason was for the metal pipe. They were about 20 feet long and 10-12 inches wide. There were about 500 pipes as far as I saw. We also needed to build three mini-airfields. First we had to make the ground level and put the bamboo mats painted with white colour and a red cross on it. There were about 200 inmates in uniforms and in chains working on the island. Their place was separate from us. We saw them every morning and when they were coming back in the evening. I do not know what kind of work they had to do on the island. They looked malnourished and worse than us. They were not allowed to speak with us (ERI/SAIN 1996, 33).

A railroad infrastructure is also required to maintain the pipeline. The 1993 construction of the north-to-south Ye to Tavoy railway line resulted in the forced mobilization of 30,000 villagers to work on the railway. In October of 1993, up to 2,000 forced laborers toiled everyday on the railroad. The process predictably did not include assessments by any local grass roots organizations. Land was confiscated "without compensation along the entire 100 mile route" (Smith 1994, Chapter 6).

In the very area where the Death Railway was completed by allied prisoners of the Japanese in the Second World War, a party of 20 Mon villagers who fled to Thailand in April 1994 described to Article 19 how they and their relatives had been compelled to work 10 hours a day, provide their own food and medicine, and sleep in the open in a series of eight forest camps to the south of Ye town. The oldest of the escapees was 67 years old, and husbands had sometimes been separated from wives and forced to work at different forest camps (Smith 1994, Chapter 6).

In 1995, UNOCAL's Vice Chairman John Imle, head of the ill-fated Burma pipeline project, continued to maintain, "we will build our own roads, with our own labor, with no impressed labor and with no labor that is not paid... There is no way that any government can impose on us the use of slave labor. We will not do it" (ERI/SAIN 1996, 36). The UN Special Rapporteur for Burma, Yozo Yokota, dismissed these claims when in February 1995 he pointed to the number of Karen and Mons killed by the Tatmadaw during these "development" operations:

> Forced labor, forced relocation, arbitrary killings, beatings, rapes and confiscation of property by the SLORC are most commonly occurring in the border areas where the Army is engaged in military operations or regional development projects...with virtual impunity (ibid., 21).

By May 1996, the Tatmadaw's Light Infantry Battalion 408 conscripted over 600 porters to attend to the pipeline in the Nat Ein Daung area where it crosses into Thailand (ibid., 37).

During this same period UNOCAL proposes to SLORC the enlargement of Myinmoletkat Nature Reserve boundaries to encompass sections of the pipeline that will (1) ship gas to Thailand as well as to (2) areas that cover a planned highway project linking Thailand with a deep-sea port in Tavoy. Not surprisingly, the Myinmoletkat boundaries encapsulate Kaser Doo Wildlife Sanctuary. Since both the proposed road and pipeline project will cut through Karen and Mon villages as well as Kaser Doo WS, the Tatmadaw force relocations along the project areas as well as engage in incursions to drive out KNU and NMSP fighters. In the name of protecting the delicate ecosystem, Myinmoletkat thus becomes an off-limits "nature preserve," that is, off-limits except to the oil TNCs and SLORC officials.

B. Justifications Used by the Oil TNCs

In response to international criticism against Thailand and the oil TNCs' relations with the military regime, the excuses used by various oil TNCs and Thai officials is that human rights and business endeavors are not related issues. They also claim incorrectly that development schemes provide jobs and stimulate economic growth in the region. This is the stance taken by the major oil companies that have had their turn in exploiting the rich gas fields in the Gulf of Martaban, believing that their contracts "encourages the military elite to open Burma's doors to the world community" (ERI/SAIN 1996, 8). Even Akapol Sorasuchart, a Thai government spokesman noted:

> This matter has got nothing to do with Burmese politics... Purchasing natural gas doesn't mean Thailand supports the Burmese junta. The two issues are not related. Thailand has never closed the door on its neighbors. Thailand doesn't agree with the way the Rangoon government administers Burma but it can still be one of Burma's best neighbors (ibid., 8).

Oil TNC representatives are fully aware that they are propping up a military regime, as noted in an interview with an oil company analyst:

> There are a lot of folks in the industry who would rather deal with an authoritarian regime than with the chaos often associated with an emerging democracy... Human rights remain off the table until such issues begin to jeopardize the likely conclusion or the bringing to fruition of projects. When those issues begin to have intermediate to long-term economic implications, then they become relevant, but exclusive of that, they're not (ibid., 12).

Even at the time of this writing, Total dedicates a portion of its website to explain its position on Myanmar.

UNOCAL's previous ties with the Taliban regime, made popular in the Michael Moore's 2004 documentary *Fahrenheit 911* reveals the insidiousness of this kind of corporate worldview. Indeed, UNOCAL supported the Taliban regime in the mid-1990s in hopes of securing pipeline agreements that would cut a north to south path in the western region of Afghanistan. UNOCAL's complicity with the Taliban was matched by Pakistan's preference and aid for the Pashtun-dominated Taliban theocracy. With a pipeline that crossed from Herat southward through the Chagai Hills of northern Pakistan, the pipeline would have eventually reached the sea, benefiting the Taliban, Pakistan, and UNOCAL interests.

The main consequence of this corporate belief is that the interests of oil TNCs can only be sustained if the regime stays in power. Of course this is never acknowledged formally. Oil TNCs maintain that they are welcomed in the country by all of Burma's peoples including the ethnic nationalities. In reality, the Yadana consortium views the ethnic nationality presence in their project areas as a nuisance. They also readily comply with a SLORC-imposed "gag clause" in its contracts with the oil TNCs, prohibiting them from communicating with groups "not aligned with SLORC" (ERI/SAIN 1996, 7). In clause 25.2 of SLORC's contract with South Korea's Yukong:

> The Contract shall be terminated in its entirety by MOGE if it is proved that the CONTRACTOR is involved in any manner whatsoever with political activities detrimental to the Government of the Union of Myanmar. On such termination the unexpended portion of the minimum expenditure in Section 5 and all equipment purchased by the CONTRACTOR and brought into Myanmar under Section 6.1 shall pass to MOGE (ERI/SAIN 1996).

Furthermore, UNOCAL also claims that its presence allows insight into the situation within Burma. UNOCAL claims that "human rights groups do not have direct access to on-scene information in Myanmar. We do" (ibid., 21). Furthermore, UNOCAL has "categorically" denied that there are even human rights abuses in the area. Then UNOCAL president John Imle noted "We will not allow those [human rights] violations to take place to our benefit, meaning our project" (ibid., 21). However, Imle noted that when the military is involved in "transgressions" the fault lies with the agitation caused by ethnic nationality self-determination groups. Total also responded by noting that it is:

> ...pledged to ensuring that the construction and operation of the Yadana pipeline is approached and managed in a manner which is consistent with the local communities' expectations, traditions and requirements...and in line with the policy of established international guidelines (ibid., 21).

During December 1994, U Win Mra, Permanent Representative of the Delegation of the Union of Myanmar, addressed the 49th session of the United Nations General Assembly and continued the denial:

> I would like to state that there is no element of coercion or force involved concerning the use of civilian laborers. In fact, the development projects are for the benefit of the local populace... The daily wages for the laborers are found to be commensurate to those prevailing in the areas concerned... A point worthy of mention is that donating labor is a tradition deeply rooted in Myanmar's culture... It is widely accepted in my country that voluntary work for the good of the community is not tantamount to forced labor or a violation of human rights (ibid., 32).

In January 1995, Imle further justified UNOCAL's position regarding forced labor to human rights activists:

> Let's be reasonable about this...what I'm saying is that if you threaten the pipeline, there's going to be more military. If forced

labor goes hand-in-glove with the military, yes, there will be more forced labor (ERI/SAIN 1996, 32).

But he backtracked after realizing the incriminating implications of his words, stating "the troops assigned to provide security on our pipeline are not using forced labor" (ibid., 32). Total spokesman Herve Chagneaux "was not able to share the confidence of Total's investment partner" (ibid., 32):

> I could not guarantee that the military is not using forced labor…all we can really guarantee is what we ourselves are doing, the contract we make, the people we employ. What is being done nearby we do not know (ibid., 32).

The oil TNCs of the Yadana consortium have done more to sustain a military regime than the vocal denunciations by the international community to destabilize it. ERI/SAIN commented on the quiet retreat of UNOCAL when Aung San Suu Kyi was freed from her first house arrest after six years, on July 10, 1995:

> While the Burmese people rejoiced, and the international community expressed new hope for democracy in Burma, UNOCAL remained silent. Two days after Aung San Suu Kyi's release, UNOCAL refused to comment on how the release would affect the company's investments. The people of Burma and their supporters expected something more from a company purportedly committed to the development of their country (ibid., 1996).

Although members of the Yadana consortium continue to maintain that there is no link between railroad construction and gas production, human rights pressure groups point out that the construction of its railway line is linked to increased militarization in the area, citing the new military camps that have emerged along the railway route. According to the KNU, most of the documented forced relocations began during 1991 and 1992 when SLORC forced Karen villagers to move to non-Karen areas and away from the pipeline construction route.

In late 1991, the Tatmadaw captured the KNU Mergui-Tavoy District Township offices at Nat Ein Daung, generating a large outflow of refugees toward the Thai border. Shin Ta Pi village was forcibly relocated in 1992 since the pipeline has to pass through the village. By the time Total signs a production sharing contract with MOGE, fifty-nine households have already been relocated to Nam Gaeh, five miles away. A villager recounts:

> Over 1,000 soldiers from 408, 409, and 410 came to move the village. SLORC told the village head, "Your village has to move in one

month starting from today. After one month, your village will be a free-fire zone." Then no villager dared to stay, so they all moved (ERI/SAIN 1996, 41).

By 1995, this vulnerability to exploitation resulted in the forced relocation of eleven Karen villages in Laydoozoo to clear the way for pipeline construction (ERI/SAIN 1996, Kardlarp 1995). The Electricity Generating Authority of Thailand (EGAT), which purchases gas from PTT confirms the relocation in the April 17, 1995, edition of the *Bangkok Post*. EGAT justifies the relocation in business terms:

> The Myanmar government aims to complete its part of the gas pipeline system by 1996. The pipeline will pass through Karen villages in Laydoozoo District, Mergui-Tavoy province and in Mon villages, Ye-Tawai province. Myanmar has recently cleared the way by relocating a total of 11 Karen villages that would otherwise obstruct the passage of the gas resource development project...

> If there are any deviations from the plan, we must ask ourselves what would happen to the investment in this 60 kilometer pipeline worth hundreds of thousands of million baht[85], not to mention the investments required for the power plant in Ratchaburi, which because it is being specially designed to use different types of fuels so as to reduce the supply risks associated with relying solely on natural gas, will cost an additional 70,000 million baht (ERI/SAIN 1996, 42-43).

Not surprisingly, SLORC subsequently increased military activities in the region aimed at stifling all armed opposition. When in 1990 there were only five Tatmadaw battalions in the region, by 1991, SLORC's Light Infantry Battalion (LIB) 273—responsible for the security of consortium personnel—and LIBs 408, 409, and 410 arrived to permanently safeguard the pipeline by building their military camps along the 39-mile long route. LIB 273 is stationed between two Total base camps. LIBs 401, 406, and 407 further reinforce Tatmadaw presence in the region (ibid., 1996).

Although ERI/SAIN note that Tatmadaw battalions are not usually at the full strength of 800 troops, the aforementioned battalions are at full strength, with at least 3,000 Tatmadaw troops protecting the pipeline route. Moreover, with at least ten other battalions patrolling the region, pipeline security exceeds over 10,000 Tatmadaw troops, not including Tatmadaw intelligence officers, police, or special forces (ERI/SAIN 1996, 13). A villager from Ohn Bin Gwin, near a Total base camp, remarked:

---

[85] In 2004, US $1.00 was worth approximately 37 Thai baht.

Before 1991, we saw Burmese soldiers very seldom, only Karen soldiers. But after 1991, LIB 408, 409, and 410 led by Major Han Htin started to base their outpost in our areas... I never saw any foreigners when I was in my village. In 1988, we seldom saw soldiers so that soldiers did not cause us problems as they did in 1992. In 1992, we saw soldiers almost everyday (ERI/SAIN 1996, 13-14).

Military incursions are soon launched against the KNU and NMSP. Between July and August 1994, two attacks are launched against Mon refugee villages in the Halockhani area near the Thai/Burmese border, while 6,000 refugees flee toward Thailand. SLORC and the Mon National Liberation Army (MNLA), the military wing of the NMSP, engage in battle with SLORC, causing over 500 Mon refugees to flee to Thailand.

By the end of 1994, the Tatmadaw launch Operation Spirit King (*Natmin*), based on two objectives: (1) "the destruction of rebel forces in the pipeline area" and (2) "the securing of the pipeline against attack" (ERI/SAIN 1996, 66). A bogus "pipeline" tax is imposed on villagers remaining in areas near the pipeline. Since the regime has not passed this as actual legislation, it is only nominally a tax; Tatmadaw soldiers call it a "donation" while the ERI/SAIN and villagers refer to it as extortion. The tax varies with the commanders of the areas. Fees begin at 500 kyats and can go as high as 2000 kyats.

Attacks have since been launched at the Yadana project, one resulting from the civil war while the other two were aimed specifically at the pipeline. In February 1995, arguing that the natural gas from the Andaman Sea belongs to all peoples of Burma, Karen and Mon guerillas renew their threat to destroy the pipeline (ibid., 1996). In response, on March 7 1995, KNLA soldiers attack two SLORC battalions in the area. KNLA units ambush a military convoy carrying SLORC and gas pipeline survey teams with 62mm single-use rocket launchers and 79mm mortars, followed by M16 and AK47 fire. It had departed from one of Total's base camps, Ohn Bin Gwin, and was traveling on a "newly renovated road" that encroached upon KNU territory (ibid., 15). Five people were killed and eleven were injured in the ambush.

On December 2, 1995, armed villagers launched an unsuccessful 107mm rocket attack at Total's Kanbauk village. In response, SLORC promises Total that "you will never hear gunfire again" (ibid., 15). On February 2, 1996, armed villagers repeat their attempts by launching three 107mm rockets from Kyauk Than Ma Ni Pagoda Hill. ERI's interviews gathered from local sources state:

One of the rockets landed at Total's heliport but did not explode; another rocket landed and exploded at the building that houses Total's employees; the third rocket landed and exploded at Lan Bar

River near Mi Chaung Ei Village. Initial reports counted six employees wounded and no deaths (ERI/SAIN 1996, 16).

A frustrated SLORC Brigadier General Zaw Htun threatens a scorched-earth policy for Ein Da Ya Za village for the February 2 attack. Zaw Htun would also be humiliated in an argument with a Total employee,

> ...who, according to eyewitnesses, slapped the SLORC commander twice across the face and punched him once... Following this altercation, the Total employee returned to Paris (ibid., 16).

In response to the February 2 attacks, the Tatmadaw LIB 273 and 403 entered Shin Byn village near Kyauk Than Ma Ni Pagoda Hill. Major Ko from the LIB 403 ordered his troops to seize Saw Kyi Lwin, the head of the village:

> He was accused of collaborating with the KNLA, interrogated and tortured. He was later executed by SLORC soldiers. Following Saw Kyi Lwin's death, SLORC troops made their way to Ein Da Ya Za village and arrested twelve villagers. They were taken to Mi Chaung Laung village, where four of them were marched into the forest at Pyin Gyi and executed... The remaining two villagers were arrested and jailed (ibid., 16).

KNLA attacks are unable to entirely repel the Tatmadaw and by 1996 fourteen battalions are stationed in the Mergui-Tavoy District of the Tenasserim.

During this period, the lack of access to dialog with the TNCs meant that effective action against the policies of the consortium was impossible. As a result, the potential activism that local grassroots Karen actors have against private sector tyranny remains stunted, and once again impoverished Karen remain vulnerable to future environmental disasters along with the perennial suffering caused by war. KNU and KNLA attempts at alleviating the situation are further disadvantaged by the oil TNCs' use of Tatmadaw troops to further their business interests.

By the late 1990s, however, villagers in the vicinity of the Yadana project were able to sue UNOCAL under the organization and activism of Earth Rights International, who put the case together with fifteen of the plaintiffs, many of whom have fled the area into Thailand to avoid certain death. An eight year court case ensued, with UNOCAL settling out of court in April 2005. It was, according to *The Nation* journalist Daphne Eviatar, a "big win for human rights" (The Nation, May 9, 2005). Not all lawsuits end in favor of the plaintiffs; during my writing, cases are still pending against Royal Dutch/Shell, Chevron-Texaco, and Exxon-Mobil. With this in mind, the role of oil TNCs and their relationship to authoritarian regimes like the Tatmadaw, and their culpability in ethnic cleansing and genocide accompanying petropolitical activities, must be viewed not only as a maldevelopment problem but a moral one as well.

Chapter VIII
2004 Ceasefire Concerns for the KNU

On January 16, 2004, a 21-member KNU delegation arrives in Rangoon, invited by the SPDC for historic ceasefire talks. General Bo Mya, now Vice-Chairman of the KNU, leaves Bangkok with his entourage and begins personal dialog with the SPDC rank and file. The ceasefire talks had actually begun during December of 2003, but the initial KNU contingent did not yet include Bo Mya. Indeed, the last time Bo Mya had set foot in Rangoon was in 1947, when the British were in the process of granting Burma its independence.

The January 16, 2004 issue of *Bangkok Post* would report that the KNU and SPDC have "stopped fighting for the first time in years," the reality is that less than six months after talks began the SPDC had already instigated over 240 engagements against the KNLA. The reason the Tatmadaw does not fully honor the informal ceasefire with the KNU has much to do with the internal power struggle between the SPDC's Than Shwe and Khin Nyunt, a struggle that would ultimately purge the latter and leave only Tatmadaw hawks behind.

Although Khin Nyunt wielded immense power over intelligence as well as through his role as Prime Minister, he did not have the full backing of the Tatmadaw, who were loyal to hardliners like Than Shwe and the SPDC's No. 2 man, Maung Aye. One may surmise that Than Shwe was behind the scenes urging the Tatmadaw to continue intermittent strikes against the KNU. This strategy would serve to discredit Khin Nyunt and his reform-minded policies which were aimed at improving relations with Burma's ethnic nationalities as well as with Aung San Suu Kyi.

Moreover, the much touted National Convention convened in May 2004 was a sham. The crucial players in Burma's democracy and ethnopolitical movements were not invited. The Karen delegation that actually attended the conference was handpicked; they were never recognized by the KNU nor the NLD, NDF, or DAB. The main stickler that forced the self-determination groups and democracy activists to abstain was the Tatmadaw insistence that the new constitution guarantee a governing role for the military, so that it could continue to participate in the political dynamics of the country. This was unacceptable to the NLD, NDF, DAB, and KNU.

A few days after the convention began, the May 22 *Bangkok Post* reported on some conference conditions that are worth our amusement. Delegates were advised to "put on suitable clothes, avoid having a bath at an unreasonable time and [not] eat junk food." Another crucial condition laid by the organizers of the national convention was that criticism of the forum would result in up to 20 years of jail time. On a more chauvinistic level all attending representatives must bow to the Union of Myanmar flag as they enter the convention hall, located at a heavily guarded conference center in the small town of Nyaung Hna Pin.

Burma's only newspaper, the state-run *New Light of Myanmar*, proudly reported that "TV, karaoke, newspapers, movies, a stage show, gymnasium and golf course are being provided for health and recreation of the delegates... A hospital complete with specialists, modern medicine and medical equipment is being opened in the camp while restaurants, a beauty parlour, barber shop, optical shop and grocery shop are being opened for the delegates." Yet the May 22 issue of the *Economist* reported, "Local television has shown them nervously swiping at golf balls and singing quavering karaoke under the watchful eyes of the top brass" (Economist 2004, 29).

The rejection of the national convention by the NDF, DAB, and NLD is a sign that ethnic transcommunalities and pro-democracy transcommunalities are still working in unison—a tough course to maintain with Burma's heavily factional politics. Political dissidents and activists from DAB and the NLD have unanimously noted:

> Gen. Khin Nyunt, along with the country's head of state, Gen Than Shwe, are manipulating collaborators, submissive political groups and others into drafting a constitution which will allow the military to enjoy immunity from severe human rights violations (Erlich 2004, 29).

The generals, however, hail the convention as a successful first phase for its "road map to democracy." Richard Ehrlich's May 22 *Bangkok Post* designation is less charitable: a road map to mockery. Nevertheless, the geopolitical implications of a sham convention spill over to the international community. Burmese dissidents hold a noisy demonstration outside the Myanmar embassy on May 18. Even Cambodia's Sam Rainsy Party (SRP) reiterated its "unwavering support" for Suu Kyi, declaring "The SRP condemns the sham May 17th constitutional convention orchestrated by the hardline military regime, and demands the immediate release of Suu Kyi and other prisoners of conscience" (The Nation, May 18, 2004). Thailand's former prime minister, Thaksin Shinawatra similarly noted:

> I don't feel comfortable because we expect all the parties concerned must be included... I will urge the minister of foreign affairs to ask Myanmar what they have in mind because a meeting without the participation of the opposition is affecting the international image of Myanmar (ibid., May 18, 2004).

Not a bad statement from Thaksin, considering he is a longstanding apologist for the regime (Economist 2004, Erlich 2004).

On October 18, 2004, the SPDC purged and arrested Khin Nyunt. The SPDC also purged other moderates and consolidated their power with hardliners. A KNU delegation that had traveled to Rangoon for a fourth round of talks was told by the SPDC to leave. Talks between Rangoon and the KNU were suspended. Without a moderate like Khin Nyunt to represent a growing nexus between ethnic nationalities and democracy activists, the future of a lasting ceasefire between the KNU and the SPDC appears unlikely. Indeed, all ethnic nationalities in Burma, even those that have signed ceasefires, were understandably nervous about the negative implications from Khin Nyunt's purge.

Within a week of Khin Nyunt's ouster, India, the world's largest democracy, welcomes the arrival of General Than Shwe and a high-level cabinet delegation from Burma's energy and communications industries. Than Shwe soon meets with India's new Prime Minister, Manmohan Singh, for what India said would be wide-ranging talks on bilateral, regional and global issues. In the name of India's "Look East" approach, the high-level visit by Than Shwe from one of the world's most brutal dictatorships breaks the 24-year hiatus between Rangoon and New Delhi.

The resumption of Indo-Burmese diplomacy can better be appreciated if we, once again, situate warming New Delhi/Rangoon ties as a result of Indo-Sino competition for influence of the region. Moreover, because groups such as the National Socialist Council of Nagaland and the United Liberation Front of Assam are operating out of Bhutan, Bangladesh and Burma, Singh and Than Shwe's dialog attended to cross border strategies to contain the problem. The world's largest democracy had become the world's largest hypocrisy.

Since the failure of the Gentleman's Ceasefire of 2004, the KNU continues to maintain their commitment on certain key issues that affect the well-being of non-combatant Karen. The following observations and interviews were drawn from my visit and stay with the KNU during the early months of 2004, when the ceasefire talks had not yet failed. Since the period was full of cautious optimism, journalists from around the world had flocked to Mu Aye Pu camp on Karen National Day January 31, 2004, home of the KNLA 202 battalion where I resided.

I had the privilege of seeing key members of the organization interact with the press and have decided to include some KNU views of the ceasefire situation. Throughout the duration of National Day, and well into the evening, I was fortunate to be able to listen in on very important interviews given by Bo Mya and Colonel San Htay, as well as conduct an important interview with former KNU congress member, Pastor Lah Taw. Although interviews with other Karen and KNU members would follow, I have decided to include only the interviews conducted on National Day, January

31, 2004, since other journalists were also present to ask important questions, many of which have been included in this work.

National Day, January 31, 2004

On January 31 2004, KNU's National Day, I awoke to find my freelance photographer friend Trent readying his camera for the day's activities. He had not slept well since the camp was active all evening as villagers and soldiers prepared for celebrations. Trent and I shared a room inside Bo Mya's home. Although I had already been at the Mu Aye Pu camp for two weeks, Trent had only arrived the night before and noted that the biting night chill prevented him from having an honest night's sleep. "It was one of those nights where though your eyes were closed, you could still hear everything going on around you," remarked Trent.

By 5:30 AM when I stepped out of our room, I see Bo Mya quietly being dressed in military uniform by his assistants. Colonel San Htay was also ready, and we managed to take a quick photograph together before the day's festivities began in earnest. Bo Mya then slowly descended his home, and with a cane assisting his walk, approached the center of the quad to greet a dozen other Karen rank and file that had also arrived for the celebrations. By now, a brass band had started playing music on the stage while KNU generals from Bo Mya and San Htay's generations were led to their assigned seating.

Stepping out into the misty morning, I see KNLA troops already in formation while camp caretakers, vendors, veterans, and bodyguards of the Mya entourage, along with international observers, all stood close to the stage to watch the ceremony. Prominent KNU leaders took turns speaking into the microphone, leading to Bo Mya's speech to the Karen gathered at celebration. During Bo Mya's speech I was able to finally speak to Pastor Lah Thaw in earnest. Having met him for only a few hours prior, we spent our morning discussing the spirit of the Karen struggle in the festive and crowded quad of Mu Aye Pu. I was immediately impressed by Pastor Lah Thaw's spirit and energy. He was forthright and analytical about the Karen cause.

Pastor Lah Thaw and I segued into a deep discussion about Karen self-determination. I asked him whether the Karen people still dreamt about the formation of an independent Karen state, along the lines of what Karen nationalist, Dr. San C. Po, had pitched in the mid-1920s. He thought this a worthwhile question and answered, "In the hearts of every Karen they want their own state but that goal is not realistic." We then talked about the more measured KNU strategy for self-determination and greater autonomy. Pastor Lah Thaw then continued to explain that because the Karen have been fighting such a long war, certain people have emerged with their own "self-agenda" in the struggle. Pastor Lah Taw noted that SPDC officials have intoxicated some of these Karen, asking them to abandon the struggle in return for having roads and highways built in their areas, only to later have the SPDC use the infrastructural development to launch offensives.

Pastor Lah Thaw also noted that the international community focuses too much on pitching democracy without fully understanding the ethnopolitics of Burma. I paraphrased his statement: "So you're saying, Pastor Lah Thaw, that democratic politics misses the bullseye of what is happening in Burma, the real issues being the ethnic politics that has plagued the country since British decolonization?" Pastor Lah Thaw concurred. I then proceeded to explain to him my perspective on the Karen struggle, and how its dynamics could be situated within the context of ethnodevelopment that framed the self-determination trajectory of the Karen.

A. Bo Mya Talks with International Journalists

After the ceremonies, Bo Mya sat patiently as throngs of people lined up to have photographs taken with him. I was part of this contingent and was extremely fortunate, as I was the last person to have my photograph taken before he was led away to another part of Mu Aye Pu. As the crowd slowly thinned and the soldiers relaxed and greeted friends from other visiting battalions, Karen *Don* dancers and drummers who had rehearsed diligently the day before began to stand in formation for their performance. The drums began, and in the cool morning air, their dancing commenced. A great sense of excitement filled Mu Aye Pu.

Colonel San Htay, Pastor Lah Thaw, and the late KNU General Secretary Padoh Mahn Sha, had by now situated Bo Mya toward one corner of Mu Aye Pu's quad, near its southern entrance. They were surrounded by a swarm of international reporters from Ireland, Australia, the United Kingdom, and Thailand, Karen bodyguards, and KNLA troops. I too placed myself in the swarm to position my tape recorder close to the speakers. Bo Mya had to answer a variety of questions from different journalists, to which Pastor Lah Thaw and San Htay translated into Thai and English, respectively, for the international contingent of reporters:

Thai journalist: *What are the details of the ceasefire, and how will this affect the Karen refugees inside Thailand?*

> Bo Mya: First, I would like to remind all of you that talks are in the early stages and thus the ceasefire details are not clear just yet. As a result, the decision to repatriate the refugees inside Thailand have not been decided. Neither can the refugees be brought back into Burma at this current time, for we do not know what will happen to them nor do we know where to situate them. Moreover, there are

also internally displaced Karen that require assistance. In this regard we need NGOs to assist us with the provisioning of food for internally displaced Karen peoples and Karen refugees. Another important issue that must be addressed other than the ceasefire is the release of Karen political prisoners still being held.

Thai journalist: *How many Karen political prisoners are still being held in Rangoon, and what is the SPDC stance on this issue?*

Bo Mya: The SPDC has nominally agreed to this request, but they claim that they do not know how many are held in Rangoon. They have requested from us a list of names. In reality, there will be an exchange of prisoners because the KNU also have some Burmese soldiers under captivity. However, we do not have that many prisoners because we set many of them free after making clear the demands of our struggle.

Irish journalist: *Are any of Saw Ba U Gyi's principles on the bargaining table?*

Bo Mya: Ba U Gyi's Four Principles will not be compromised even though the issues surrounding the four principles have been brought to the table for negotiations.

Irish journalist: *So there will not be any surrender?*

Bo Mya: The Karen will still never surrender and will never give up their arms. These principles are still upheld. The other two principles, where the Karen State must be recognized as its own entity, and where the Karen will decide their own political destiny will still be upheld.

Irish journalist: *And is there a united front, where the KNU and KNLA are as one?*

Bo Mya: The KNU and KNLA are still a united front.

Irish journalist: *And where does this leave the DKBA?*

Bo Mya: As for the DKBA, we've already let them know that if they want to back they are always welcome to come back with us. If they make a choice to stay with the Burmese, then it's up to them, we won't push them.

Irish journalist: *What are the conditions for coming back?*

> Bo Mya: For us, we don't account for what they've done in the past. They can come back freely and there's no condemnation for the DKBA.

Irish journalist: *So there will be an amnesty?*

> Bo Mya: There will be an amnesty. However, if the DKBA come back to join us, they will be placed under KNLA command, same as before.

Irish journalist: *How confident are the Karen people that this is not just a PR stunt by the SPDC to appease the international community? And how much more international pressure is needed against the SPDC?*

> Bo Mya: Current negotiations between the KNU and the SPDC should not stop the international community from continuing to pressure the SPDC. The international community should go on pressuring until the KNU achieve our victory, freedom, and self-determination. Indeed, the international community will have to put more pressure on the SPDC so that the SPDC dialog with the KNU will be more effective.

> The international community should know better and know what they should do. While the dialog is continuing between the SPDC and the KNU, they should carry on the way they do and the way they're doing it right now. They also have to look at the SPDC and how they have changed as well as how they have not changed. If they have changed for the better, then the international pressure should naturally decrease, but if they have not changed for the better, then the international community should continue the same. Changes must be based on how sincere the SPDC actions are and not just based on words that encourage change. They need to improve their activities in a politically beneficial way. It all depends on the regime and how they improve their politics and minimize their military actions.

Bo Mya then retired to his home, had a change of clothes, discussed the early morning developments with close aides, and traveled to another area of the camp to greet the *Don* dancers that had performed that morning.

B. Colonel Nerdah Mya Grants Interview to Australian Journalist

Not long after the initial crowd of journalists disbanded Colonel Nerdah Mya granted an Australian journalist a brief one-on-one interview, close to the dancers who congregated around Bo Mya. I was fortunate to be able to listen in on the dialog.

Australian journalist: *Are the KNU negotiations with the junta damaging to the NLD, since they're not included in the discussions?*

> Nerdah: No, Aung San Suu Kyi is campaigning for democracy while KNU is fighting for ethnic issues. The two roads are different, and it is important not to confuse the two.

Australian journalist: *Why are you now going to negotiations when she's locked up?*

> Nerdah: We must remember that Aung San Suu Kyi has been locked up for 10 years already and the people need change. We have to find new tactics for change. The military regime is also looking for change, and not only are the KNU dealing with them, but the international community is also dealing with them so as to effect the needed changes.

Australian journalist: *Are you 'selling out' Aung San Suu Kyi by having the KNU negotiate with the SPDC?*

> Nerdah: You have to remember that Aung San Suu Kyi is not our leader. We have our own leader. She is fighting for democracy, while we are fighting for ethnic issues based on Ba U Gyi's four principles that state: (1) surrender is out of the question, (2) recognition of the Karen State must be completed, (3) we shall retain our arms, and (4) we shall determine our own political destiny.

After listening and tape recording the aforementioned series of important interviews, I decided that I would follow the international contingent that same day back to Mae Sot. I did not anticipate hearing General Bo Mya, Colonel Nerdah, and Pastor Lah Thaw—in one given day—speak volumes on Karen politics. I initially planned on systematically approaching them individually over many weeks, asking questions. The arrival of the large KNU and international contingent, as well as journalists that asked pertinent questions of them, provided for me the "thick" and intense data that I had hoped to acquire, all in one long day. In any case, I was scheduled to return to Mu Aye Pu, and found comfort in that.

I then stepped into the living room and had a brief conversation with a contingent of English pastors that were traveling around the Thai/Burma border assessing the refugee situation. I found out that they too would be leaving later that afternoon, so I asked them to notify me when they were ready to depart. After notifying Trent, Tha Doh, and Colonel San Htay's assistant, Roni, about my change of plans I promptly returned to my room to quickly pack.

Walking across the quad toward the northern dock area I see throngs of villagers and vendors also descending the steep banks to the Moei below, with the noise of the boat engines echoing up the ravine. Many people were leaving. National Day celebrations were over. Tha Doh was accompanying me by now and we were laughing and exchanging kind parting words. By now I looked up to him like an older brother. Moreover, he in his very unique way, taught me about the individual Karen in life, struggle, and perseverance. I told Tha Doh that I would develop the photos and have Colonel San Htay give it to him within a month's time. We smoked a *muertoo* together—a Burmese cheroot cigar—and gave each other a hug.

Getting on the boat in the midst of a crowd was no easy task. With my 45 pound hiking backpack altering my center of gravity, I was clumsy climbing into the boat which was already close to the waterline. Seeing the smiles and gestures of my British friends, I climbed aboard. I did share my concern, however, on how close we were to the waterline, which by now was only a shocking 4 inches, possibly even less, above the Moei River. There was already water at the bottom of the craft, covering its beam. It was very noisy and departing activity around the entire area added to a sense of false urgency, and perhaps to an unnecessary sense of haste.

Sho Jun, a KNLA veteran, was next to climb on board. Most of us assisted him by gripping his arm and hips. Sho Jun stepped on a landmine a few years back and now wears a prosthetic from the left hip down, and was hardly able to stabilize himself to board a boat that was swaying in the wake other departing boats. Sho Jun had only placed one leg on board when the driver gestured from the rear that we needn't take more. At that moment, a child which appeared to be no more than five or six years old, and who certainly meant well, attempted to assist in the launching of the vessel. He then pushed, with all his might, the craft away from the dock in hopes of making clearance for the boat operator to steer the vessel away from the river bank. Sitting on the ledge of the starboard side, with my heavy hiking gear on my upper back containing my notes, tape recordings, digital camera, and photos, the boat violently tilted to the point of almost capsizing. The spectators at the dock caterwauled aloud as the banana-shaped craft scooped in massive amounts of water. Sho Jun and I were able to grab the rocky edge of the dock to keep the boat from turning over, while the passengers immediately threw their bodies over the port side to level the boat. Nevertheless, the bottom quarter of my backpack, as well as my buttocks, got submerged in the Moei. Fortunately only my boots, mosquito repellants, and thermos were in the lower area of my backpack; my journal, tape recorder, and cassette tapes were in the top compartments, spared immersion in the water.

Within a few minutes of leaving Kawthoolei, we were in Thailand. By now the afternoon sun was falling low but still remained above the mountain ridges. I had to stare into the sun to catch a glimpse of people still descending the cliffs of Mu Aye Pu. On the edge I see Tha Doh waving to me and I waved back.

After crossing the bank and reaching Thailand we loaded our gear aboard Pastor Lah Thaw's awaiting minivan and made our slow crawl on the dirt path back toward the highway. We were all going back to Mae Sot. Since our minivan was packed to capacity, the drive back toward Mae Sot was slow. On board were the members of the Asian Tribal Ministries. Their guests, British preachers by the name of Benny, Michael and Weatherly, were on board. Karen youths working for the ATM such as Roni, Dawn, Angelica, Hope, and her husband were also aboard the packed minivan.

During the ride, as if all of us needed to immediately make sense of the amount of stimuli at Mu Aye Pu, conversations literally exploded upon topics of self-determination, ideas of the state, and the political implications of current ceasefire talks. Weatherly, in his late twenties, was most engaged in sorting out the role of ethnicity in development and inquired a great deal about the topic. Pastor Lah Thaw was at the front of the van listening intently to the dialog emanating from the rear which by now had included viewpoints by Roni and Dawn. We all talked with great excitement, but Angelica fell fast asleep.

C. Interviewing Pastor Lah Thaw

After reaching Mae Sot, my own insecurities and sense of vulnerability vanished in the parking lot of our hotel. I was now in Thailand, just barely. Most of us were exhausted and checked into our respective rooms. Upon taking a great shower, I went downstairs to meet with Pastor Lah Thaw and his contingent. We would all be going into downtown Mae Sot so that Pastor Lah Thaw could get his haircut. Arriving at the shop bodyguards "Johnny" and "Captain Tony" kept watch outside while Pastor Lah Thaw gestured that I go into the shop with him. I would be conducting my interview while he got a good shave and hair cut. With my tape recorder readied, I began my inquiry:

Today is a very exciting day for the Karen. I was wondering: if there's one thing you'd like for me to bring back to the United States regarding the Karen Revolution at this current stage, what would it be?

Pastor Lah Thaw: I want the United States to support and highlight the KNU struggle and its political dialog with the regime the same way that they support the NLD. Because you know, as everyone else knows, the Karen are not rebels—I mean, if somebody comes and takes your house, and kills your family, rapes your sister, destroys your village, and commits these atrocities, you can't call those who resist rebels. We are calling the wrong group rebels. Thus, it's time for the United States to be mature in how they are dealing with the current information.

You had mentioned something today that stuck in my mind regarding how the international community seems to have missed the point in their assessment of democracy and ethnicity. Do you see democracy and ethnicity as separate issues in Burma, or do you see them linked in some way?

Pastor Lah Thaw: You have to understand that the problems of Burma today did not start with democracy and neither will it end with democracy. It started with the internal conflicts based on the unfair treatment of the ethnic nationalities through the violations of conditions as promised under the Panglong Agreement for a Federal Union. This unfair treatment did not start under the regime in the first place, it came under U Nu's "democracy." U Nu knew of the agreement to uphold for ethnic nationalities such as the Karen, Chin, Kachin, Shan, all the Mon, Arakan, and others, but he didn't want to recognize it and give the states its independence as promised under the Panglong Agreement. This is why the conflict lasted so long. Moreover, instead of peacefully negotiating on the table, which takes time and patience, the regime resorts to brutality and genocide.

Many are asking about and watching the KNU's next move. What do you think is the most important next move for the KNU?

Pastor Lah Thaw: I spoke with an official of the Thai government last night, specifically the Tak governor. I told him that through the recent negotiations and developments, the KNU at the moment carry on a big responsibility for the whole future of Burma. The negotiations are not just about the KNU or the Karen, but about the right of all the ethnic nationalities, as well as Burmans who are also suffering under the regime. So the KNU is carrying a very heavy burden now.

In the past the UN came and tried to persuade the regime—it didn't succeed, the United States, EU, and even ASEAN has not had any success. So now all of the burden is on the shoulders of the KNU.

At the national level, the only group that has access to the regime and can talk at an equal level is the KNU; not even the NLD can because the NLD is just a political word without any troops. This military regime does not recognize words, they only recognize guns. But one advantage the KNU has is that they have the forces, they have the guns. So that is the reason why the regime sees us as very important.

So what I'm trying to say at the moment is that access to the regime is currently most effective through the KNU. So what we need is the international community's support instead of the international community misunderstanding us, condemning us, or even just being neutral. They shouldn't act that way. They should urgently say, "we support the KNU role at this moment over the regime." They should also explain this and work together with the educated Thais.

How does the SPDC's relationship with China fit into the current situation?

Pastor Lah Thaw: During the ceasefire negotiations in January, Khin Nyunt was saying to General Bo Mya, "We cannot trust outside interferences on our internal affairs." General Bo Mya then responded, "Well, I agree with you," to which Khin Nyunt enthusiastically said "yes." But then Bo Mya responded to Khin Nyunt again by saying, "but why do you then buy weapons from China and use it on the Karen, to destroy us, to commit human rights abuses against us and against other ethnic minorities?" Khin Nyunt sat there and laughed nervously—he did not know how to answer.

Do you think the split that has occurred in the past with the DKBA is one of the most damaging episodes to have occurred with the KNU?

Pastor Lah Thaw: I think the media should not focus too much on the DKBA. Most of the DKBA commanders and leaders are defectors from the KNU. One, most of them are doing criminal work, you know, like torturing their own people. Also, they are being used by the regime to maintain a split in the Karen. But even right now, the KNU have many Buddhist groups. So right now, I encourage the international news media to not focus on the DKBA. Number one: they're a small group. Number two: they're killing and causing all these problems for their own people to please the regime. Number three: they're involved in drugs and drug trafficking.

And so why the media is so concerned about the DKBA—for what? That's why Bo Mya wrote a letter to them and asked them to come and we will forgive whatever they've done to their own people— they're not representing their own people, they're representing the regime for their own survival. The regime is using the DKBA to fight the KNU. But now the regime knows there's no way to defeat the KNU. That's why they're willing to talk to the KNU directly. Thus, the media shouldn't misunderstand the role of the DKBA— they're not important. If they continue to focus on the DKBA, then they're not responsible journalists. The DKBA is a criminal organization—killing their own people, even causing a lot of problems in Thailand, killing Thais, placing stray land mines. A lot of the drugs that make it to Thailand and the international community also come from the DKBA. The KNU are saying: "We'll forget what you're doing. Okay come back, now is the time. Do you want to stay with the Karen, your own people, or do you want to stay with the regime and continue causing problems to your own people?"

Who do you think is the greatest ally of the Karen, if you could single out one? It could be a country or an organization, or even a coalition.

Pastor Lah Thaw: The KNU's biggest supporters are western countries: the EU and America are looking out for and feeding our refugees. They have tremendous sympathy for our people. ASEAN and its leaders are not even concerned about us and do not even see what the harm of their "neutrality" is doing to their own ASEAN people. But the westerners, how come they can feel terrible about what the ASEAN people suffer, you know? ASEAN leaders are showing no concern for what the regime is doing to their own ASEAN people. They're only interested in business and the natural resources the Karen areas have. That's very shameful. As an ASEAN person, I find it very sad, very shameful. There's a lot of poor and corrupt people in ASEAN, and under them ASEAN people suffer. ASEAN is supporting the regime and it's very sad. They may say, "We have our own different way of dealing with the problem," which is not true! If you want to deal with the problem then stop engaging in trade with the regime. Only this will show ASEAN sincerity in providing assistance.

Do you think the junta will insist that the KNU disarm? Or do you think the junta will know better than to ask such a question?

Pastor Lah Thaw: The regime has been fighting the KNU for more than fifty years. They may be able to persuade other ethnic nationalities to disarm and they have, but for the KNU it's implied only because they know that arms are the Karen's security. And they know no matter what, the KNU will never surrender. The regime knows this.

I want to tell you something: in the Karen military force, the soldiers do not have a salary, they do not have good food, and they do not have an ordinary soldier's life. And no one supported the Karen for so many years. Yet Karen fighters, faced with the regime's 500,000 strong army, powerful with all its arms, have never feared them. Why? Because the Karen fight with their heart, they fight with the love for their country and for their people. This is their power. This power cannot be defeated with ordinary weapons. So the Karen know that as long as they keep that love for their people in their heart, they will win the fight, they'll be on the winning side. Remember that the Burmese people also suffer under the crush of this regime. Many of the Burmese people, Burmese students, Burmese soldiers—they're tired. Also, for the Burmese soldiers, their heart is different, their zeal is different.

What did your conversation with the Tak governor entail, since Thailand has a role to play in encouraging the ceasefire?

Pastor Lah Thaw: He asked if the situation at the border can improve? I said "Yes, but to be able to improve or not we all must work together." I told him it's not fair to put all the heavy burden on the Karen's shoulder, you know what I mean? Don't throw the entire burden on the Karen. The Thais also have a responsibility. I had to remind him of two important points:

One: don't let third parties come in and put a knife behind the Karen while the Karen are talking with the regime. These "self-agenda" groups and their people will ruin the whole thing.

Two: While we are talking, don't talk about road-building because that will be encouraging one side against the other. The whole world is looking, the international community is also looking at the Thai approach. We've got to be very careful because Prime Minister Thaksin said he will support bringing peace to both sides. But we must ask, "How?" If you're talking about building roads, highways, or whatever, when international community hears this it won't be good for Thailand because it sounds like Thailand wants to do business instead of politics. This is an important point to remember. Also, Thailand will be showing the world that they're promoting their own economic self interests. If this is the case, the Thais must know that if everything fails, it will fail not because of the Karen, or not because of any other people, but because of the Thais.

If the Thais want to help bring peace, then it has to be based on truth and sincerity. Otherwise if it fails, then the whole world will blame Thailand. But if the Thai government is sincere then they can do things that the UN cannot do, things that America cannot do, things that ASEAN cannot do, and things that the Europeans cannot persuade the regime to do. But if Thailand can sincerely support and encourage the Karen as well as the regime, then Thailand will make history. Thailand is at a crucial historical moment too.

What do you think of Thaksin's position?

Pastor Lah Thaw: Prime Minister Thaksin is sincere and is doing a very good job. But within the Thai government, there are people behind him in third parties interfering, trying to manipulate him for their own self-interests. That's what I see, and I find it regrettable, and I feel very worried about this. So I want the prime minister to be aware of this, these "self-agenda" people, these corrupted people. In other words, there are other groups within his government that are going to ruin and destroy our whole policy. And what I want America to do is keep pressure on the regime, and publicly recognize the cause of the Karen with the same status accorded to the NLD. Indeed, at this time in history it is very important to recognize the KNU with the same energy, if not more, than the NLD, you know.

Interview of Bo Mya by Mizzima News: February 20, 2004

On February 20, 2004, Bo Mya granted New Delhi-based *Mizzima News* a forthright and succinct summary of ceasefire talks and issues:

Mizzima: *At present the KNU is talking with the SPDC, building confidence and has entered into a gentleman's agreement for ceasefire. Can we say that all these are the victorious results resulting from 50 years of the Karen nationals' revolution?*

Bo Mya: We have been in revolt for many years now. Since it has been for a very long time now, it is necessary for us Karen to unite. Only through unity can we achieve our goals. If we are not united, we will not achieve as we expect. That's how I see it. Moreover, I believe that our revolution has the right cause. We do not fight out of hatred toward the Burmans. We are fighting for the rights of the Karen people.

During the British colonial times, we were allowed to learn Karen literature up to the tenth standard in schools... But when Burma obtained independence everything changed. The Burmans did not allow us the right to learn Karen literature anymore. They stopped all ethnic nationalities from learning their own literature. That's how they suppressed us educationally.

They had also suppressed us even in religion. As far as I know, during the AFPFL time, many religious institutions were nationalized. That's why the Karen have suffered a lot. Moreover, they [the Burmese] also made Buddhism the national religion. This may seem unimportant without careful thought, but it is not as benign a decision as it seems. After Buddhism became the national religion, we can see Karen and other ethnic nationalities having to convert to Buddhism if they want to become national leaders. They have to shave their heads and take up the robe [become a monk] for at least a week. If they do not shave their heads, they cannot become leaders. If we look at the case of Mann Win Maung (a Karen national), he had to shave his head to become the President of the country and had to take up the robe for a week. Otherwise he would not have the right to become president.

That's how the Burmans suppressed us. It is because of Burman suppressions and discriminations that our country is in turmoil. They do not give the due rights to other nationalities. They believed that independence was only for the Burmans and seized the country all alone. And they rule the country by Burmanising and suppressing all ethnic nationalities. That's why there is no ethnic group that does not revolt in Burma. The reason why all nationalities are revolting is because nobody is happy and because nobody is getting their rights. Burmans should also understand this.

It is high time that the Burmans realise it and change their ways. And if they do not change, this conflict will never have an ending. I believe it is impossible to go on using the power of weapons. I have known many Burman politicians: Communist Party of Burma (CPB),

Ye Baw Phyu, and Ye Baw Ni, U Nu—all of them stand on the same policy of Burmanisation. During U Nu's time we created combined forces... But U Nu refused us. He said that if he grants self-determination for us, he would be harshly accused, so he told us to take our demands to the people's government. This is the same with the Communist Party of Burma (CPB). We had joint forces with them also. But when the Karen leaders demanded self-determination, they [the Burmans] refused. They told us that they couldn't give such demands.

So as for me I see that all Burman political leaders are holding the same policy of Burmanisation. Therefore, we the National Democratic Front (NDF) members used to say that Burmans are not allowed in our organization. Even if they request us to join we would not allow them. But all nationalities do not understand that decision. And they do not understand the value of the NDF. They take it lightly. I see that only we [Karen] understand the value of the NDF.

Mizzima: *Do you expect the present talks and discussions will bring the Karen nationals much expected self-determination?*

Bo Mya: The talks are not over yet. Whatever form the talks take, we have to continue until the end. We have to continue until we achieve what we want. It is important that the Burmans understand that and I believe if they understand that they will give the Karen what we ask for.

And if they do not give us our demands, then they will not be able to solve the problem. And we will not settle until we achieve our demands.

We have also supported groups that are against the government of Burma, for example, students. Many students, at least 5,000 of them, fled to Te Baw Boe (former stronghold of KNU in Burma's border with Thailand). They said they would fight the military regime. We thought that it would be good to have Burmans in the revolution fighting against the military regime, a common enemy. So we helped them in every way. We Karen had to feed 5,000 of them for at least one and a half months. We gave them weapons and they formed the student's armed forces. And when they formed, I told them, "all of you fled our country because of the government's ill behavior, so be united and stand together, do not get divided and scattered here and there." But my words lasted only for a few moments. They started fighting among themselves and I had to solve their problems. I told them "don't behave like that, you need to be united to be successful. Now that we have given you weapons, they are not to be used against each other but to fight the enemy" but it did not help. I told them "forgive one another and put away the wrongs and be united again, I will buy you a cow for you to eat together." So I bought them a cow [laughs], but it didn't help much.

And later, they decided that it was not necessary to hold arms. They said "if we are an armed force we cannot get aid from others." So, they dispersed and only a few are left scattered here and there. But the majority left. We thought they should return our weapons. But they never returned the weapons, and we don't know where these weapons went. Later they formed organizations and sought financial aid from others through projects, and that's how they lived. How can the revolution end [if we follow their example]? Therefore, we cannot follow their ways, and if we do it would be a crazy act.

After that experience came the national coalition government (NCGUB). Before the coalition government came, we the KNU had done all the seals. We wanted to form a government with all nationalities. We had done all the seals and also selected the people. When they arrived, they made requests to participate. We agreed and allowed them and gave them seals and everything.

Previously we thought we would be included, but we were not. As we are rebels and they the "government," they said, "both the government and the rebels cannot work together" so they rejected our group altogether. However, the coalition government that we had formed still exists today.

Mizzima: *When the KNU met General Khin Nyunt in Rangoon, he said to leave those that came before in history, and that those people are deceased now. "Now, Pha Hti [uncle] and I should work together," General Khin Nyunt told you. What is your opinion of his view?*

Bo Mya: When he said that I replied it cannot be like that. We cannot leave everything in history: we have to learn from them. We cannot put them aside. We cannot forget them. We have to study Burma's problems and learn from them. Only when we are able to learn from past experience will we be able to solve our problems. Otherwise we will never find a solution. He was saying that all these are the past and they have become history, but I told him we have to learn from them.

Mizzima: *In the on-going process, how do you think self-determination for the Karen people will be achieved?*

Bo Mya: I will continue with our demands [for self-determination]. We should have self-determination and the Karen State should be recognised. We should have the right to do what we want to do. And as for us, we will not leave the Union. We will stay together as part of the Union. And if they do not accept this offer from us, then we have no choice but to leave the Union. Isn't that good? We will take self-determination but we will not separate from the Union. We will stay together in a Federal Union.

Mizzima: *How about Karen in other States? What do you think for them?*

Bo Mya: They will have to be given rights of whatever state they reside. For example, in Myit Wa Kyun Paw, there are a lot of Karen, so I think the administration heads should be from the Karen communities in the area.

Mizzima: *At present Daw Aung Suu Kyi and U Tin Oo are under house arrest. What will be their role?*

Bo Mya: To have peace inside Burma, they cannot be kept like this. They should also be freed and should also be allowed to do what they want to do.

Mizzima: *What do you think of the 1990 election?*

Bo Mya: During the election in 1990, reporters and journalists used to ask this question. They asked General Saw Maung whether he would hand over power to the successful party. General Saw Maung said he would. He said that the military would go back to the barracks. But after the election, when reporters and journalists asked him again, he did not have power any more. The regime people said that this General Saw Maung is crazy. So they put him aside and he can do nothing...

Mizzima: *What will be the role of the DKBA and how will you handle the DKBA?*

Bo Mya: The DKBA is formed by the SPDC. Frankly speaking, the Burmese government cannot fight against us, even when it comes to military skills. So when they cannot fight against us with military skills, they use every possible means. They fought us with the help of other countries. They used all kinds of weapons and fought us in Te

Baw Boe. They even used their air force to fight against us. They would bomb us with four fighter planes from 10 in the morning to 5 in the evening. But they could not defeat us. When they realised they could not fight us with the military they used religion instead, that is, from within our community. That's the story of the treacherous monk.[86] He doesn't know any politics and he also doesn't know what religion truly means. So when the SPDC lured him, he became an easy prey. He started fighting against us in various ways. Moreover, he used our enemy to fight against us. So, we have to retreat. That's it. These people are not trying to improve religion but are rather spoiling it. Therefore, if the government does the right thing then improper acts like this should not be used. But since they are using futile people like this, we are facing the consequences.

Mizzima: *Will you ask for the abolition of the DKBA to SPDC?*

Bo Mya: We have not demanded that yet. We will do it later. Be slow and take your time.

Mizzima: *What is the future for the 5 organization's military alliance (which includes the KNU and four other armed groups)?*

Bo Mya: I am not very sure about the 5 organizations' military alliance. The KNU President formed it and he must have his own reasons. I am not sure about it. He didn't tell me anything about it.

Mizzima: *If you sign a ceasefire agreement, will it still be possible to work together with the National Council of the Union of Burma (NCUB)?*

Bo Mya: That is politics. We consider NCUB as an alliance. The NCUB is an umbrella alliance as well. It is described as that in its formation.

Mizzima: *What is the future role of the KNU in that umbrella?*

Bo Mya: The KNU does not have much of a role. The KNU is supportive only to get funds. Frankly speaking, the Burmans do not use us much. When they go to foreign countries they don't speak much about us even though we are supposed to be included. In the NCUB they only speak of the NLD. When I used to listen to them (chuckles) they speak only of Saw Suu's issues[87], no one else's.

---

[86] Bo Mya is referring to U Thuzana of the DKBA.
[87] Another way of referring to Aung San Suu Kyi.

Mizzima: *During the past 50 years of revolution, how much help has the KNU and the Karen Nationals received from international communities and from among the rest of the people within Burma?*

Bo Mya: The KNU has asked the international communities for help. But the international communities consider that they cannot help us, as KNU is an armed group. So, I stopped asking for help. We stood on our own as much as we could and as much as our capacities allowed us to. But if we look back over the past 50 years when we did not receive any help from the outside, we could still stand and fight. If we compare this with the SPDC, they receive aid from outside the country for education, business and even weapons: but they fail in their fight against us. That is because we always can find what we need. We are always together with God, and that's why they could not fight against us. Moreover we do not have a single debt to repay, while the SPDC has a lot of debt. They have thousands of millions in debt. We, the Karen national revolution, do not have any debt (chuckles), don't you believe it?

Mizzima: *What do you think of neighboring countries like India and China, who are cooperating with the SPDC? What would you like to say about them?*

Bo Mya: What they say is that they will not interfere in another country's affairs. But economic collaborations are signs of interfering, they are stepping in another country's territory. Even constructing roads are acts of interfering. But they do not see that as interfering. As for us, we leave it up to God.

Mizzima: *There are reports that the Thai government is brokering the peace talks between the SPDC and the KNU. What is your opinion on that? Do you think there will be more on this matter?*

Bo Mya: The Thai government initially wanted to do it. But since the Burma junta did not allow them to, they could not do it.

Mizzima: *Will there be anything regarding Karen refugees in the upcoming talks with the SPDC?*

Bo Mya: The Karen refugee issue is the next step. Right now we are talking about issues within the country. We haven't discussed anything about exiled refugees. It will take a little more time.

Mizzima: *What about the Karen internally displaced peoples (IDPs)?*

> Bo Mya: We will discuss with the SPDC for the safe return of the IDPs. We will continue the discussion. But we haven't discussed the matter of IDPs yet.

Mizzima: *What is the KNU stand on the proposed National Convention by the SPDC?*

> Bo Mya: It's all about how far the SPDC's National Convention will help us. If it is going to help us then we can think about it. If it doesn't then there is no question of thinking about it.

Additional Ceasefire Issues

When the most recent rounds of ceasefire talks were reinvigorated in December 2003, observers were immensely hopeful about the possibilities. Colonel San Htay was more guarded, however, and had told me that the KNU is "hoping for the best, but preparing for the worst." Nevertheless, the fact that Bo Mya accepted an invitation by Khin Nyunt to visit Rangoon in January 2004 is quite significant. At the time, hopes were high since it was the SPDC that invited Bo Mya and the KNU delegation, not the opposite. Khin Nyunt also organized a large birthday party for Bo Mya that was attended by, unbelievably, the high-ranking officers of the Tatmadaw and KNU.

Up until the suspension of talks in October of 2004, the most consistent obstacle to effective negotiations centered on the KNU insistence to remain armed and not enter the "legal fold." Nevertheless, up until as recently as May 2003, the SPDC has always felt that it had the upper hand in its political negotiations with the KNU. The regime has always presented stringent conditions in its dialog with the KNU. Although the regime's hubris ignored the international sanctions imposed upon the country, Burma, already an impoverished nation, continued its economic and cultural decay. Internal colonization still continued in the following years, further undermining its credibility and legitimacy as a nation-state. Since 1988, twenty years later, the SPDC regime still has a death grip on its own people and against the ethnic nationalities. That said, their ability to run amok with their Four Cuts has been curtailed due to international scrutiny and outcry. It is within this war-fatigued context that the SPDC via Khin Nyunt has made more overtures for a ceasefire with the KNU.

The KNU is still maintaining its organizational and ideological poise. The KNU leadership at the time was only cautiously optimistic. There are two main reasons for this caution. The first reason is the KNU familiarity with the Tatmadaw penchant for using a cessation in warfare to resupply their troops for renewed offensives when the talks "fail." For decades, this notorious tactic of trickery was repeated during previous ceasefire talks with virtually all of Burma's ethnic self-determination groups. Second, the KNU, with its advantages of over five decades of hindsight, is fully aware that many self-determination groups that have signed ceasefires with the regime have succumbed to broken promises regarding the development of their areas. When development did occur, the resources acquired from ethnic regions benefited only the ethnocracy.

Most notably, the main consequence of past ceasefires has resulted in ethnic nationality areas rendered vulnerable to Rangoon influence and exploitation. Moreover, the regime has not established appropriate discussions or links with the local leadership, often bypassing them in their desires to secure business deals that can tap the rich natural resources of the mountains and hills—home to the vast majority of ethnic nationalities. According to the ICG report in May 2003, many people remain disappointed with the lack of more substantial political and economic progress. Ethnic nationality grievances are rarely attended to, and "no progress has been made towards a political solution" (ICG 2003, 13). The report further notes the continuation of repression:

> The government discourages them from making political statements or engaging in any overtly political activities. Most...leaders of the ceasefire groups appear to trust Aung San Suu Kyi's promise...for increased ethnic autonomy and equality, but they...emphasize that, as a Burman leader, she does not represent their groups. They are...anxious to get directly involved in the talks (ibid., 13).

The Kachins have made such a complaint, claiming that the regime is exploiting the natural resources of its areas yet "few profits are spent for badly needed development of the state" (ibid., 20). The regime has also sold off resources such as gold, teak, as well as important mineral resources such as various gems "without consultation with, or compensation for, local communities, who thus both lose the income and suffer the social and environmental consequences of extraction industries" (ibid., 21). A Kachin development worker told ICG:

> The government has never done any development programs in Kachin State—we do it ourselves. We have plenty of natural resources. They come here and dig it up and sell it to other countries to get dollars. But they never use it to develop our state, the gold, teak and jade (ibid., 20-21).

Suffice to say, historically these two main outcomes of past ceasefires have tempered the enthusiasm among KNU and international observers. Indeed, the historical trajectory of negotiating a ceasefire with the regime has often resulted in not only internal maldevelopment, but at best when there is some development as in the Wa and Kokang, it is certainly an anti-Senian one, where development is not freedom.

Colonel Nerdah noted that "after the junta made peace overtures last November, we realized that we should do something, and whether we get it or not, we should be able to tell what the Karen people want, what the Karen people should get: self-determination" (Peck 2004). Colonel Nerdah further emphasizes that current negotiations can be distinguished from those made since 1989 between SLORC/SPDC and 17 self-determination groups: "Our ceasefire is different. We don't want to enter the legal fold, we don't want to surrender, we don't want to stay under their constitution. We want to have a ceasefire and continue our political dialog and see what they can give and cannot give" (Peck 2004).

The inclusion of the term "legal fold" in Nerdah's response has an important historical significance as well as a negative connotation for the KNU. For the KNU rank and file, entering the "legal fold" is tantamount to surrender. The term was first employed in a 1993 speech in yet another SPDC-sponsored ceasefire talk with the KNU, where Khin Nyunt had urged ethnic self-determination groups to relinquish their struggles. During this period there was only a handful of self-determination groups still resisting Rangoon. SLORC had grown confident in the sudden implosion of the CPB and the subsequent defection of its many factions to Rangoon. Khin Nyunt thus continued to encourage other self-determination groups to do the same:

> We invite armed organizations in the jungle to return quickly to the legal fold after considering the good of the government... We extend our invitation with genuine goodwill. We do not have any malicious thoughts... This is official. Please respond as soon as possible (Smith 1999, 449).

Three years later in November of 1996, a SLORC delegation under Col Kyaw Win reiterated the conditions to the KNU in six demands: (1) The KNU should enter the "legal fold," (2) implement a ceasefire, (3) agree to troop positions, (4) begin development programs in Karen areas, (5) attend the National Convention as observers, and (6) upon the creation of a new constitution, lay down arms. Bo Mya and KNU advisers found two phrases problematic: agreeing to enter the "legal fold," they worried, might be a self-incriminating posture of admitting to the illegality of the Karen struggle; "laying down arms" was out of the question because it would force the KNU to violate Ba U Gyi's Four Principles of the Karen Revolution, which according to Smith, represent the cornerstone of KNU ideology.

Eight years later, Colonel Nerdah's responses to a *Bangkok Post* interview are just as telling, especially in his phrases "we don't want to surrender" and "we don't want to stay under their constitution." The former and latter statements still remain true to Ba U Gyi's principles, with the proclamation of "we don't want to stay under their constitution" echoing sentiments similar to Ba U Gyi's "we shall decide our own political destiny." The one optimistic development is that the SPDC regime "seems to have abandoned its long time insistence that the Karen soldiers relinquish their arms" (Peck 2004).

The KNU also insisted that there be a nationwide cessation of fighting where the Tatmadaw would withdraw from ethnic nationality areas, especially from roads near major Karen towns, and return to their bases. Concomitant with this act, the KNU also demanded that an international monitoring system comprised of a multilateral or UN peacekeeping force be established. By late summer of 2004, the KNU also submitted a request to have all future ceasefire talks held in neutral countries such as East Timor, with an international mediator. All these aforementioned demands by the KNU have been rejected by the SPDC (Watson 2004).

Observers have their different opinions on the Tatmadaw and KNU's last attempt at a ceasefire. Burma scholar Josef Silverstein argues that the Karen were dealing from a position of weakness. He remarked that "the Karen people are hurting badly and that the military has not let up in its military assaults...to destroy the KNU... I think this lies behind Bo Mya's present manoeuvres" (cited in Peck 2004). Silverstein's observations display a clear diagnosis of the KNU's military situation when pitted against overwhelming Tatmadaw forces, but it also overlooks the political advantages the KNU currently possesses. Conversely, although the KNU/KNLA were not in a position of military advantage, neither were the SPDC dealing from a position of political advantage: Harn Yawnghwe, a prominent exiled Shan activist notes that the Karen were "shrewdly cutting the best deal possible while international pressure is on the junta." He further notes:

> The KNU is the backbone of the movement—democratic and ethnic...they have fought the longest, suffered the most and have the most at stake. They know what they're doing. To think any less is to insult the Karen (Peck 2004).

International sanctions and pressure had slowly but surely tugged at the reformists within the regime. Under the watch of Khin Nyunt, the military dictatorship, with its monopoly on social apparatuses of violence, has opted to accommodate his diplomatic route instead of deploying its military as it often does. For many, the SPDC accommodation of Khin Nyunt's moves hinted that the SPDC may finally be yielding to international pressures. However, the international community would be disappointed when in October 2004, Than Shwe ousted Khin Nyunt in a coup that completely altered the diplomatic scenario. Hardliners have always engaged in dramatic maneuvers to maintain a political trajectory that preserves the Union, be it Ne

Win's coup in 1962, or the large scale Four Cuts offensives launched after the Ethnic Nationalities Seminar in 1997. In spite of international pressures and condemnations the SPDC decided to regress back toward totalitarianism.

Chapter IX
Conclusion

As I conclude my examination of the Karen epic I harbor the same insecurities and questions as Varese (2002) when he immersed himself in the culture of the Ashaninka people of Peru: would the many hundreds of pages of historical data mining and research, some interviews, and normative development paradigms capture the experiences of the Karen Revolution as Varese was able to capture with the Ashaninka? Only readers can answer this. I begin this final section by exploring the major factors that will continue to influence Karen liberation ethnodevelopment. I then cautiously assess and extrapolate from the Karen struggle for self-determination its implications for development doctrine. A discussion of how ethnodevelopment can enhance the understanding of a materialist ethnicity will also be undertaken. Finally, the future of Karen liberation ethnodevelopment and its implications for understanding nationalism will be explored.

In the discussions to follow I use the term "future" with two intentions in mind. First, I employ it as an invitation for scholars to *cautiously* extrapolate from my observations the role ethnicity plays in the development of the human condition. Second, I also employ the term to indicate my own scholarly desires to, in the near future, revisit some of the theoretical cues and additional considerations generated in this work.

The Future of Karen Liberation Ethnodevelopment

At the beginning of my work, I posed two questions. The first asked how the KNU and Karen sustain their self-determination struggle in a context of systemic crisis spanning over five decades. The second question asked what additional local and global factors will continue to shape the future of Karen liberation ethnodevelopment.

In the body of my work, specifically chapters 4 to 8, I responded by arguing that Karen liberation ethnodevelopment, an agency nationalism that harnesses its institutions and regional political economy to resist ethnic cleansing, along with its transcommunal links, sustained and continues to sustain their struggle. The struggle continues because Karen liberation ethnodevelopment contains institutions that are in structural opposition to an exploitative ethnocracy. The institutions serve three instrumental functions: to reinforce the social, political, and economic administration of Kawthoolei, to reproduce the Karen sense heritage, history, and nationhood, and to protect the natural environment that all Karen depend on for their sustenance. In this regard, the Karen have infused their struggle for self-determination with strong instrumentalist and primordial articulations. Moreover, the urgency of systemic crisis has, for many Karen, mated their individual rational choices with the imperatives of a collective movement.

The trajectory of Karen liberation ethnodevelopment is also pivotal in making visible how ethnocratic Burma is a "weak state" because its "Union" has always been "internally contested to the point of violence" (Buzan 1983, 67). Indeed, the "Union" articulated by the pro-Burman hawks to forward Burma's nation-state project has never materialized. However, the KNU has yet to formally birth Kawthoolei in the likes of how East Timor gained its independence from Indonesia. Neither has the KNU been able to fully provide for the Karen all the basic needs required of a functioning state due to the advantages that are now skewed toward the Tatmadaw:

- Hardliners in the Tatmadaw purged the more "reasonable" SPDC general Khin Nyunt in October 2004;
- Regional powers China, India, and Thailand continue to acknowledge Tatmadaw rule with economic and/or military support;
- Aung San Suu Kyi remains under house arrest while the international community's general indignation yields no political results;
- In March 2006, the Tatmadaw promulgated its new and geographically advantageous capital at Naypidaw, directly adjacent to Kawthoolei;
- The pivotal and legendary KNU figure, General Bo Mya, dies on December 24, 2006;
- The much respected and able KNU General Secretary, Padoh Mahn Sha, was assassinated on February 14, 2008;
- There exists a population of war-fatigued Karen refugees and IDPs that want a cessation to war at all costs.

The Tatmadaw is currently—if one were to measure a polity by weaponry and regional support—stronger and more ensconced in the political terrain of Burma than it has ever been. Being relatively sealed off from the international community allows the Tatmadaw polity to snub world condemnation of its rule. Although the SPDC still must address internal contradictions among their own ilk, specifically in the guise of having to attend to competing Burman ideologies espoused by Burman hawks and Aung San Suu Kyi's NLD, the latter of which has the overwhelming support of the population, the regime stays in power because greedy corporate entities from, ironically, many democratically-oriented states, continue to do business with the regime.

Nonetheless, because the SPDC is unable to simultaneously attend to the numerous political demands forwarded by the ethnic nationalities as well as failing to provide for its own Burman population, Burma is experiencing what Habermas designated as a *legitimation crisis* (Habermas 1973). The dramatic September 2007 uprising by Burmese monks in major Burmese cities, supported by the people as well as ethnic nationality groups, was a vivid indicator of this crisis.

Given these complex factors, the future of the Karen struggle is entering a period of uncertainty. A new generation of younger KNU leaders will soon be poised to attend to these circumstances as they navigate the political changes in a post-Bo Mya period, a situation the SPDC will certainly exploit to their advantage. The manner by which the Karen leadership manages its synchronicity with the will of the Karen people, without compromising the ideals of the struggle, will be the basis for how its self-determination unfolds. Although the Karen Revolution is far from finished, its capacity to administer its social institutions and construct a nation will additionally be tested as the SPDC continues to be courted by regional powers.

In spite of the complex obstacles faced by the KNU, the organization still exhibits the following diacritica that continue to thwart the construction and consolidation of a "Union" of Burma:

1. The KNU and the Karen elite continue to administer their own state, with their own social institutions and with their own approach of generating income from a regional political economy, albeit an impoverished one. Should warfare cease the Karen will be able to harness a trajectory that further establishes institutions of civil society and of a prototypical state.
2. The KNU has walked the diplomatic tightrope with Thailand throughout its struggle, dealing with the latter's vacillating political stance which has become progressively less sympathetic over the years. The role Thailand plays in the future of the Karen struggle cannot be underestimated or ignored.
3. The KNU is able to articulate their struggle on a geopolitical landscape, such as requesting ASEAN to sloganeer democracy for Burma and urging demotic Karen to make visible their cause diasporically.
4. Much of the Karen diaspora around the world have formed offices in exile, have maintained their cultural autonomy and identity, and have made visible their cause through international channels.
5. The Karen struggle still possesses the KNLA that can frequently keep the Tatmadaw at bay.
6. The plight of the Karen has garnered the sympathies of the international community which the KNU has harnessed into their articulation for nation. This status grants the Karen a relatively high degree of legitimation that the Tatmadaw has never possessed. The Karen can thus claim the moral high ground.

The staying power of the KNU and the Karen struggle for self-determination requires the consideration of additional factors.

A. The Transcommunal KNU

Additional considerations regarding the KNU's staying power center on the organization's involvement with various transcommunalities. The ultimate effectiveness of the transcommunalities, which by 2003, included "over one hundred alliances, associations, armies, committees, fronts, leagues, parties and unions" stretched along the 3,610 miles that border Bangladesh, India, China, and Thailand remains to be seen (Wechsler 2003). The transcommunalities explored in this text have been used as referents insofar as they supplemented the interests of the KNU. However, there are many other transcommunal groups such as Marxist-Leninist groups, ultra-nationalist transcommunalities, as well as religious transcommunalities. Wechsler notes that "the ordinary Burmese is relatively tolerant of all religions, so is the resistance movement. Buddhists, Christians, Hindus, Muslims and others stand side-by-side" (2003). Moreover, the KNU and the KNLA have also supported smaller transcommunalities such as the ABSDF. Interestingly, few people in the smaller towns throughout Burma are aware of these dissident transcommunalities "and they were very much surprised when told of the number of these groups" (Wechsler 2003).

One outcome of this is the potential lack of unity in the ethnodemocratic project. The numerous groups may play into the hands of the SPDC's divide and rule tactic. Simply stated, there are too many "united fronts" at this moment, prompting Wechsler to note "had there been a contest for the biggest number of opposition organizations in one nation, Burma would be the winner by a large margin" (2003). Many of the transcommunalities are also hard to track because they often quickly form, disband, split apart, or completely change ideologies, further complicating the efficacy of their activism. Although all aspire to remove the military dictatorship and replace it with a democratic one, the ideological similarities end there.

Wechsler provides some diversified opinions on the role of transcommunalities from those engaged in the struggle against the Tatmadaw. For example, U Thein Oo, Judicial Minister, NCGUB, noted:

> At this moment there are too many opposition groups. This is not good. We need unity, we must have a strong united front and we must have a common goal and then we can win.

Prince Maha Sang of the Wa National Organization (WNO):

> If there are so many organizations without unity, there will be problems. The more organizations there are, the less effective we are

going to be. Therefore, all organizations should unite and help each other.

David Tharckabaw, the KNU's Joint General Secretary 2, noted:

> Having many organizations weakens the movement, since it is very difficult or takes a long time to lay down policies and programmes acceptable to all. The movement often has to hold large meetings which are costly and difficult to arrange.

Colonel Nerdah Mya, however, sees a benefit in a decentralized struggle that is militarily advantageous:

> Several groups committed to an armed struggle, including us, continue to battle the Burmese army with guerilla warfare, a tactic that enables us to take heavy casualties on the enemy in surprise attacks.

As does U Kyaw Hla of the Muslim Liberations Organisation of Burma (MLOB):

> The Burmese people have been under the dictatorial regime for a long time. They all want democracy and freedom. And whenever they get the opportunity, they will form a group. This is good for us. We can't form [large] organizations because of SPDC repression, and that's why we can only have small groups. This will change after the regime falls. Then we should all join and have the same platform.

The larger transcommunalities can still work their politics effectively given the conditions of repression. For example, the DAB, NDF, and NCUB have "greatly improved cooperation with regular meetings, the costs of projects shared, political and military activities organized, and assistance given to people in Burma" (Wechsler 2003). There is another benefit to the transcommunal dimension of struggle in Burma. Since the 1988 pro-democracy crackdown, many pro-democracy members of these transcommunalities are widely dispersed throughout Australia, Canada, Europe, Japan, and the United States. For example, the NCGUB, formed in the former Karen capital of Manerplaw in 1990 and constituted by members of parliament rejecting military rule, is currently an exiled government based out of Rockville, Maryland, United States of America. There is thus a transnational contingent of diasporic activists that continue to lobby their host governments to promote democracy and change in Burma.

B. Transnational Self-determination

The third factor is how the Karen struggle is enhanced by its international links with transnational supporters in democratically-oriented governments, international and local NGOs, and the Karen diaspora. KNU preemptive diplomacy has a long international tradition dating back to the early days of their struggle. Their efforts at linking up to global communities have been successful in garnering international attention to their cause. Today a myriad of other border-based Karen social organizations serve as links for channeling resources to Karen in areas such as educational development. Assistance is also given to Karen women victimized by war (especially rape survivors), survivors of forced labor and land mine injuries, and Karen civilians that have to respond to issues related to basic needs.

Many Karen elites hope to pattern their liberation struggle along the lines of East Timor. They desire the United Nations to enact similar policies with Burma where a referendum vote is established and due processes enforced to honor the vote (which will certainly result in at the very least, a federalized Burma). Thereafter, United Nations personnel and peacekeepers would work with the local polity to ensure a smooth transition to federalism and self-determination.

The KNU's hopes are not premature. The KNU, like many other ethnies engaged in conflict for a greater autonomy, constitute a bloc of polities that have historically attracted "outside patrons" (Khosla 1999, 1143). Khosla has observed that ethnonationalists like the Karen constitute a group that is most likely to be recipients of external support (1999, 1153). According to Heraclides, ethnic minorities with external allies have a better of chance of achieving their goals (1990). Between 1990 and 1998, 975 such interventions occurred all over the South. Yet this assistance is not yet entirely decisive for the KNU because it has received mostly moral, charitable, and economic support, especially for Karen refugees and IDPs, and no large distribution of arms or direct military intervention are forthcoming (Saideman 2002).

The efficacy of international support in augmenting the political goals of an ethnie is still not entirely conclusive. According to Khosla, even lower level support may create or deepen regional insecurities because it increases the "scope and duration of intra-state conflicts, along with threatening to spread the dispute across state boundaries" (1999, 1151). Khosla further notes that between 1990 and 1998 most support for the Third World stemmed from regional powers such as India and China, both of which currently accept the legitimacy of Burma's military regime. In an examination of 224 interventions by regional powers, 119 interventions (60 percent) constituted military aid. However, in the case of 235 interventions by major powers in the Third World (defined by Khosla as the United States, Russia, France, and the United Kingdom), 139 interventions (59 percent) were achieved through diplomacy (Khosla 1999, 1151). It is in this regard that I believe that Western-assisted diplomacy can politically steer Karen liberation ethnodevelopment toward resolving its conflict and achieving its aims.

Regional interventions have thus far mostly benefited only the SPDC. This is currently happening as China—a totalitarian regional superpower, India—the world's largest democracy, Thailand—the vacillating ally of the Karen, and ASEAN, continue to court the military regime. As aforementioned in previous chapters, China's regional assistance has been primarily military and directed to the pro-Burman military ethnocracy. Bo Mya had explicitly confronted Khin Nyunt on this matter prior to the latter's purge from power. Consequently, much of Burma's ethnic nationalities lamented when Than Shwe and India's Singh fostered diplomatic ties a week after Khin Nyunt's purge. In this regard, the KNU was prescient for having continued to maintain their diplomatic ties with Western powers.[88]

What the Karen need are more peace-oriented political interventions on their behalf. Here, NGOs, charity organizations, human rights groups, and pressure groups have already paved the way for the Karen. The Karen can also benefit from a more unified, direct, and aggressive political role from Western democratic powers. Regional powers such as China, Thailand, India, and ASEAN have already failed the Karen. The rapaciousness of their polities has directly maintained the staying power of the Tatmadaw. From the perspective of many Karen regional powers are the problem not the solution.

C. Self-determination on the Information Highway

The fourth factor is how the Karen nation is constructed and internationalized through cyberspace. That is, the Karen struggle for nation in the late 20th and current 21st century has expanded from an indigenous/irredentist movement toward a geopolitical one, as can be seen in how the Karen diaspora construct the Karen nation on the information highway. Indeed, Yagcioglu notes that in our information age, authoritarian governments will ultimately fail in its capacity to regulate and control the content and amount of information available to activists abroad. Because groups like the Karen are not able to find consistent refuge in their local and regional governments, the hopes, memories, and problems of nation construction are sublimated in cyberspace.

In addition, there is, in any movement, a contingent of young intellectuals and activists that will be able to harness this information and effectively place it in a public discourse for international consumption and activism. Yagcioglu insightfully observes:

---

[88] For example, General Bo Mya had represented the KNU and DAB when he visited the United States in July 1993 to meet with State Department officials; in October 1993, Bo Mya visited London.

Today, the leaders and intellectuals of ethnocultural minorities (and not only them) are aware of and are closely following the developments in other parts of the world. They know about the struggles other minorities, they know about global trends favoring democracy, and they also know that they can internationalize their problems and their agenda much more easily than before. It is therefore almost impossible for any government to oppress a minority or suppress its demands, without creating international reaction.

At the three-day *Impact of Globalization, Regionalism and Nationalism on Minority Peoples in Southeast Asia* international conference, held in the northern Thai city of Chiang Mai in November 2004, scholars and activists came to the conclusion that information provided by the cyber-Karen ends up not only in the international arena but back at the refugee camps. As such, Karen refugees along the Burma-Thai border, despite their lack of access to modern technology, are able to have a "window to the outside world" (Yeni 2004). The information flow is gleaned from intermediary border-based Karen social organizations such as the Karen Teachers Working Group, the Karen Women's Organization, the Karen Office for Relief and Development and the Karen Environment and Social Action Network. K'nyaw Paw of the Karen Women's Organization said that she "believed international participants in the conference were aware of what was happening in Burma and sympathized with the 'suffering of the Karen people'" (Yeni 2004). At the conference attended by over 300 representatives from Thailand, Laos, China, Malaysia, and the Philippines, Lee Sang Kook of the National University of Singapore's Department of Sociology observed the Karen as a "scattered but connected people" (ibid.).

D. A Role for the United Nations?

Will the United Nations be able to assist the Karen? One must not forget that it is not unknown for the UN to historically recognize non-state actors as legitimate representatives of peoples during periods when they have not yet achieved statehood; the African National Congress (ANC) under Nelson Mandela, South-West Africa People's Organization (SWAPO) under Sam Nujoma, and even the Palestinian Liberation Organization (PLO) are but some examples (Southalan 2000). On December 1, 2004, the United Nations announced that it will embark on reforms that are unprecedented in its organizational history, "a moment no less decisive than 1945 itself, when the UN was founded" (Economist, November 20, 2004, 25). Topping the list is for the UN to be more "forceful against genocide and ethnic cleansing by confronting tyrannical regimes" (BBC news report, December 1, 2004). Moreover, the UN declared in a strongly worded language that they will "consider preventive early action" (BBC news report, December 1 2004).

One of the leaders of this new UN movement is led by Gareth Evans of the International Crisis Group. This stance points to the real possibility that more preventive and early action will be taken against genocidal and state-sponsored terror regimes. The UN's embarrassing failures with Bosnia, Rwanda, and Somalia are finally forcing the organization to come to the realization that genocide is symptomatic of failed states. Burma is no exception. However, one should remain skeptical of UN sloganeering and its course of actions: the ethnic strife experienced in Sudan's Darfur and the UN's slow response was disappointing; the inability of the UN to compel the Tatmadaw to negotiate with Aung San Suu Kyi in the wake of the September 27, 2007, Buddhist monks' uprising is another example of their current inefficacy. One must also remember that alas, the United Nations is but a "club" of member states with their own regional self-interests.

What remains to be seen, however, is how the application of sanctions will be applied by a reformed UN. A divided and contentious issue at best, international governments and bodies such as the UN will have to reassess the track record of sanctions. Sanctions hitherto, and this should be remembered, hurt the poor and destitute significantly more than it does the governing elite. Thousands of miles to the west we have seen sanctions fail against Saddam's Iraq, Castro's Cuba, Ahmadinejad's Iran, and Kim Il Jong's regime in North Korea. The efficacy and prudence of sanctions in bringing down the SPDC should thus be evaluated from the streets of Rangoon and from the soil and farmlands of rural villages throughout Kawthoolei.

As discussed in Chapter 1, within the last two decades the global community has been showing greater interest in the plight and suffering of oppressed ethnic minority peoples. For decades, however, it lacked the courage and resolve to intervene. Perhaps the coming years will see the UN emerge to question the premise of the nation-state if its construction yields an anomalous society where human rights abuses are protracted in nature. Although they can celebrate their ethnodevelopment efforts in East Timor, at this point the UN cannot claim too much success on preventing ethnocratic oppression worldwide.

That the UNDP already considers an alternative development approach should be considered a move in the right direction. The autonomous United Nations agency, the UNRISD, also emphasizes a non-economistic perspective on development and notes that it is "deeply concerned with the many negative aspects of globalization and the concentration of economic and political power in the hands of international economic institutions—the WTO, IMF, World Bank and also TNCs—and a few governments" (UNRISD 2005).

Perhaps with the successes of the East Timor example, the UNDP and UNRISD will continue to refine their alternative development discourse. Although Cowen and Shenton (1996), along with Storey (2000), note that the use of trusteeships and sponsorships blur the distinction of the ostensibly non-economistic alternative development paradigm from an economistic approach toward development, they fail to factor in the conditions related to systemic crisis. Systemic crisis conditions mandate a leadership contingent, but one which is intimately linked to the constituents it aims to assist, and not only to technocratic elites disconnected from the demotic stratum. And it is when geopolitical conditions are favorable that higher level trusteeships can forge linkages with localized polities and NGOs.

Insofar as Karen refugees in Thailand are concerned, *when* geopolitical conditions are favorable is hard to define. As discussed in Chapter 5, complicating the ambiguity is that the United Nations High Commission for Refugees (UNHCR) does not have a direct role in assisting Karen refugees, or any other ethnic refugees from Burma. Bangkok does not want to risk angering Rangoon by allowing a prominent humanitarian organization to shed light on the consequences of Burma's ethnic cleansing. As a result, all Karen refugee camps are "unofficial" and not formally recognized by the Thai Government or the UNHCR. The management and administration of all refugee camps are thus left to NGOs as well as whatever arrangements can be worked out between Karen refugee leaders, local Thai villagers, Thai border officials, as well as the Thai Ministry of the Interior.

Due to the ambiguity in the status of Karen and other ethnic minority refugees from Burma, the camps are not "closed camps." Camp protection from the Thai Army is often tokenistic. According to a Human Rights Watch/Asia 1998 report, the UNHCR "has been less forceful than it might have been in trying to challenge Thai government actions" (HRW/A 1998, 9). Despite having been stationed in Thailand since 1977, with its first regional office established in Bangkok, the Thai government has since 1998 insisted that the UNHCR mandate "was limited to work on behalf of the Cambodians, Vietnamese, and Laotians who flooded into Thailand in the aftermath of the Vietnam War" (HRW/A 1998, 9). The Thai government has successfully prevented the UNHCR from carrying out its "mandate" for Burmese refugees in spite of the fact that the UNHCR has three branches in Thailand's smaller towns of Mae Sot, Mae Hong Son, and Kanchanaburi, cities that are across the border from Kawthoolei (HRW/A 1997, 7).

> As far as much of the rest of the world is concerned, there is no such thing as a Karen refugee. Those who flee the front line but remain in Kawthoolei are regarded by the UN High Commission for Refugees as 'displaced person' within their own country: Burma. Those who cross into Thailand become illegal immigrants. Nowhere do they qualify for refugee status and consequently they get little official

assistance. What help they do receive all comes from private charity (Falla 1991, 194).

Karen Liberation Ethnodevelopment as a Form of Nationalism

The processes of liberation ethnodevelopment can enhance the large body of literature on nationalism. Yet there has not been an explicit nor clear attempt to configure nationalism as containing its own dialectic, namely between fascism (oppressive nationalism from above) and agency nationalism (nationalism based on liberation from fascism). As a result even scholars of nationalism and ethnicity such as Hobsbawm, Smith, Hechter, Brass, Van Den Berghe, and Cohen fail to pit one form of nationalism in constant tension with the other. By ignoring this important juxtaposition, distinct structurally opposed institutions and distinct transcommunal trajectories are thus rendered virtually invisible to analyses.

This oversight is damaging for the formulation of development strategy since agency nationalisms will continue to be the mainstay of twentieth first century geopolitics, flowing transnationally through the memories of its peoples, diasporas, and on the information highway. In the last decade, not only has nationalism shown no signs of abating, it has flourished more widely and with more intensity than any period since the Second World War II (Smith 1998, Gurr 1993). Indeed Gurr noted in his 1993 seminal and data-rich work *Minorities at Risk* that "every form of ethnopolitical conflict has increased sharply since the 1950s" (ibid., 316) and groups whose members have experienced systematic discrimination continue to take political action to assert their collective interests against the states that claim to govern them.

Following the Cold War minority peoples have become the principal victims of human rights violations. By the 1970s, there were increases in global indigenous rights movements. During 1990, Gurr noted that over 233 ethnies, or more than one-sixth of the global population (17.3 percent or 915 million people) qualified as minorities at risk (ibid., 315). By early 1992, over 20 million refugees were suffering from communal conflicts, including 3 percent of sub-Saharan Africa (ibid., 314). The case of peoples like the Karen are even more severe as they are "threatened by great ecological pressures on their traditional lands and resources as well" (ibid., 315).

The protagonists in the most persistent communal rebellions of the postwar era have been ethnonationalists such as the Karen and Kachin in Burma, Tibetans, the Nagas and Tripuras in India, the Eritreans and southern Sudanese, the Palestinians and Kurds, and the Basques. Eighty guerilla and civil wars were fought by these and other communal rebels between 1945 and 1989...twenty-six were in

Asia, twenty-five in Africa south of the Sahara, twenty-two in the Middle East and North Africa, and only six elsewhere (Gurr 1993, 318).

It is thus important to acknowledge that colonization has not ended, but instead, has shifted toward an internally colonizing context. In this regard ethnic conflict via nationalisms will continue to intensify. According to Gurr, ethnonationalist civil wars are the most protracted and deadly conflicts of the late twentieth century. For Gurr the acute intensity of ethnonationalist civil wars is due the fact that all parties involved are aware that communal demands for independence "imply the breakup of existing states" (ibid., 319). Pertaining to this point, mainstream development discourses and strategies continue to support an overarching nation-state project because it is believed that ethnic conflict can be resolved through centralized economic and technocratic development (Yagcioglu 1996). The establishment of freer markets through industrialization is thus idealized as a means to break down racial and ethnic barriers. The logical and "rational" process of economic development will mute the "irrationality" of ethnic identity as all groups gain social and class mobility (Yagcioglu 1996). If one adopts this classic neoliberal position, then liberation ethnodevelopment of the Karen becomes an oxymoronic endeavor.

The oxymoron, however, is quickly negated by the fact that Burma is not a multicultural democracy, but an ethnocratic and totalitarian society. Moreover, Castells is correct to note that a "totally different situation arises when identities and interests dominating in local institutions reject the notion of integration" (1997, 274). As such a free market dynamic will not be able to contest the fact that Burma's ethnocracy will play gatekeeper and hoard resources, that is, resources will only benefit the pro-Burman military regime. There will not be a trickle-down effect that will benefit the Karen. The oxymoron, then, is to continue to pitch neoliberal development with the current arrangement in Burma. With Aung San Suu Kyi and her democratic forces immobilized, liberation ethnodevelopment is the only democratic alternative for developing Burma.

Despite the staying power of ethnicity, the material consequences of ethnicity remain a virtually unexplored area of development studies. This is because most development scholars have not treated ethnicity as an organic phenomenon, that is, organic in the sense that one's ethnic identity is not always activated. If a region is multiethnic and its administration is experiencing systemic crisis, ethnic identity will be activated as a means generating ethnic cohesion and survival, and in the case of the Karen, self-determination. When systemic crisis activates ethnic identity, its accompanying material consequences rob its social articulation of class dynamics, relegating class interests to a secondary role. New social relationships are thus formed and configured. As Seers noted:

The roots of an independent strategy may lie not so much in the country's particular productive structure or military capability, important though these are, as in a culture strong and homogenous enough to avoid...dependence on an imported way of perceiving the nation's own needs (1983, 72).

A. Democratic Politics or Ethnodemocratic Politics?

What must be asked, then, is to what degree the international community, predominantly the democratic voices emanating from the West, will continue to relegate Burma's ethnopolitics behind the country's democratic politics. Development orientation that subsumes the former under the latter will do so at great peril for peoples like the Karen. Many in the KNU believe that the West has also given too much weight to Aung San Suu Kyi and the NLD as the bearer of democracy in Burma. The tendency manifests itself when international observers and analysts subsume self-determination politics espoused by the KNU under the NLD's aim for democracy. This highly skewed international approach means that the acknowledgement of KNU achievements and setbacks are frequently ignored or articulated through the lens of Burman democratic nationalists/activists. One consequence of this is that references to the suffering of Burma's ethnic nationalities and ethnopolitics continue to be addressed as a secondary issue. Another consequence is that this pattern only reinforces a failed process in the construction of a Burmese union.

Much of the international community rarely questions the sovereignty of an overarching nation-state and views ethnic self-determination politics as belonging in the country's internal affairs. In an age where the global is local, no bigger myth exists than a political position that argues that intra-state affairs belong to the "internal" jurisdiction of a particular country. As demonstrated in Chapter 7, the military regimes of Burma have always sought assistance from regional and major powers that can provide for its military oligarchy. Thailand, China, Germany, India, Singapore, and Israel, to name but a few, continue to sustain the militarists in Rangoon. The KNU counters this by harnessing its own capacity to transcommunalize and engage in international diplomacy with governments and international organizations that are sympathetic to the Karen cause.

What needs to be remembered is that the KNU is an autonomous organization that administers the construction project of a Karen nation. As Colonel Nerdah Mya reminded a misinformed journalist during National Day 2004, the leader of the Karen is not Aung San Suu Kyi. Similarly, neither is Aung San Suu Kyi the leader of other ethnic nationality groups, as Kachin, Shan or Wa leaders, in spite of their agreed upon ceasefires with Rangoon, will quickly point out (the KNU acknowledges her leadership role via the Mae Tha Waw Hta Agreement of 1997 but did not subsume their leadership under the NLD). The vast majority of leaders of Burma's ethnic nationality groups, regardless of their ceasefire status, insist that ethnopolitics and issues should take precedent in the political discourse of Burma.

Moreover, because the NLD does not possess arms nor control a military wing, its non-violence stance has exacted a price on the organization as a whole. As a result, the Tatmadaw has repeatedly made house arrests, harassed, intimidated, and launched periodic crackdowns on democracy-oriented constituents. Without a military wing to protect the interests of the NLD, the SPDC sets the agenda in its interactions with the organization. Although economic sanctions and vocal denunciations by the West have undoubtedly spared Suu Kyi's life, it has not succeeded in dislodging the dictatorship. Although the 1991 Nobel Peace Prize winner and iconic figure certainly deserves much reverence for her accomplishments, the fact remains that the Tatmadaw has rendered Aung San Suu Kyi and her cadres in the NLD politically immobilized for close to twenty years.

Although the need for a federal Burma is supported by the NLD, the articulation of the ethnic nationalities issue in the NLD political discourse has been relegated until after "a democratic system is successfully adopted in the country" (Fredholm 1993, 239). This trajectory implies that "at the time [it] was a typical reflection of exactly the type of 'Burman chauvinism' so often condemned by minority leaders" (Fredholm 1993, 239). Moreover:

> Aung San Suu Kyi's privileged youth never enabled her to fully realize the magnitude of the nationalities problem within her country. Also unlike her father, she never came into close physical contact with war between the different nationalities. In a book first published in 1985, Aung San Suu Kyi for instance remarked: "Some Burmese attitudes have been responsible for the distrust of the Karen."[89] This description of the BIA's massacres of Karen villagers was…quite an understatement. In her biography of her father, Aung Suu Kyi mentions the execution of the Muslim headman but treats it as a legally sanctioned political act. She fails to mention that the…man's widow later filed a murder charge against Aung San (Fredholm 1993, 239).

The sad fact is none of the strategies provided by Aung San Suu Kyi and the NLD have ever been implemented in Burma due to SPDC control. Colonel San Htay emphatically told me on National Day 2004, "It's been close to fifteen years with no results, and people need change now."

---

[89] Fredholm is referring to Aung San Suu Kyi's book *Freedom from Fear.*

The SPDC continues to utilize one of Asia's largest armies to establish a death grip on the country. With the 2004 purge of the SPDC's relatively reform-minded Khin Nyunt, the hardline military death grip on the country has grown even stronger. This is why all the efforts by the international community to democratize Burma via Aung San Suu Kyi and the NLD have been unsuccessful to date. Moreover, with the military dictatorship in power future efforts at humanitarian relief for Burma's ethnic nationalities will continue to be unsatisfactory.

With the current political arrangement Aung San Suu Kyi cannot free Burma from the center radiating outward, unless of course, the regime relinquishes power on its own. Since this will not happen any time soon, considering the growing hardline stance of the SPDC, the future of a free democratic Burma will need to come from its periphery and the international community, that is, from the non-ceasefire groups such as the KNU, transcommunalities, international governments, and NGOs. In other words, the liberation of the Karen will have to be based on promoting liberation ethnodevelopment through self-determination, agency nationalism and transcommunality.

I have met many Karen who passionately and consistently argue that the political problems of Burma are ethnic problems, first and foremost. There is concrete historical validity to this claim for even under U Nu's "democratic" government in the 1950s Burmanization continued unabated. If development strategists continue to focus on democratic politics in Burma as a panacea to its social problems, without acknowledging the protracted problem of ethnic oppression by a totalitarian ethnocracy, their policies will miss the bullseye of Burma's problems. My aim of presenting the Karen struggle, along with the mention of the struggles of other ethnic nationalities, is based on reinforcing the argument that cleavages in Burma have always been due not to class, but to ethnicity, "between those seen as foreign and those seen as native, and between the native races themselves" (Myint-U 2001, 243). Pastor Lah Thaw personally shared with me an appropriate analogy: "You can't bring in new furniture without first removing the old furniture."

Burma's ethnic nationalisms have always intersected its democratic politics. Indeed, I share Southalan's sentiments that self-determination has been an integral part of Burma's tortuous political and military development since British colonial times (Southalan 2000, 14). However, one of the arguments I put forth at the beginning of my work is that the Western view on nationalist self-determination is rather negative. Even Seers acknowledged, "like many of those educated in the Anglo-Saxon cultural tradition, I saw nationalism as fundamentally irrational…and a menace in the second half of the twentieth century, getting in the way of the creation of a just, peaceful and prosperous world society" (Seers 1983, 10).[90] My response to this concern was to construct Karen agency nationalism (bottom-to-top nationalism) as a liberatory ethnodevelopment that is in structural opposition to Burman fascism. By incorporating the former trajectory into development analyses the instrumentalist, primordialist, and rational choice cues that characterize the Karen Revolution are made visible.

Southalan argues that self-determination can mean much more than the right to secede, which "is often politically virtually impossible for minorities within a state, or spread across several states, such as the Kurds and several of Burma's ethnies" (2000, 7). The KNU realizes this and has maintained that their current platform of self-determination is to be based on attaining a federalized Burma. Nevertheless, it is important to note that varying degrees of self-determinations exist which have the potential to dramatically improve the lives of the people involved, without necessarily threatening the territorial integrity of the state or states concerned.

Nevertheless, an ethnodevelopment that advocates self-determination generates fear among multicultural powers that ethnies within their own countries will be inspired to aim for their own self-determinations. One must bear in mind that the geopolitical and strategic interests of regional powers largely determines whether and how the "self-determination" process develops (Southalan 2000). That is, geopolitical interests and alliances may mean that political will may not exist to recognize the claim to self-determination of even the best qualified ethnie because the implications are potentially destabilizing to the current geopolitical arrangements of state boundaries. The post-World War II privileging of states has thus manifested itself through diplomatic discourses that rarely question the sovereignty and premise of the state (Khosla 1999).

Heraclides identified this pattern and argued that international respect for currently configured territorial boundaries and state sovereignty has restrained outside support for autonomy-seeking groups (Heraclides 1990). As Saideman noted, "ethnic groups with such aims are greater threats to other states and to international norms governing boundaries because they seek to revise existing boundaries" (Saideman 2002, 30). Because the vast majority of states around the world are multi-ethnic, supporting the Karen cause (or any ethnic nationalist cause around the world), may set off neo-liberation ethnodevelopment movements that are unprecedented in recorded history (Heraclides 1990, Suhrke and Nobel 1977).

Around the world, many states have unresolved ethnic tensions percolating under its political surface—China has restless Muslim Uighurs in

---

[90] Yet after Seers worked in different parts of the world, he noted: "I came...to see that nationalism is neither trivial nor in decay [and] this had made me reflect on the strength of nationalism" (10-11). Seers also noted, "cultural dependence is, indeed, more fundamental than economics as a determinant of the room to manoeuvre" (Seers 1983, 72).

the Xinjiang Autonomous Region, hoping that they do not fall under the Sinofication that Tibetans are currently experiencing, the Aymara construction of nation has already challenged Bolivian and Peruvian attempts at assimilating them into the mainstream of their state projects, Indonesia has to now contend with self-determination politics in Aceh since the liberation of East Timor, while India has to contend with its autonomy seeking groups within the Kashmiri, Sikh, Naga, Assam, and Muslim populations. The answer to Burma's self-determination dilemma will be extremely complex and will require flexibility, compromise and goodwill. Yet one must bear in mind that if one lesson can be learned from Burma's history, it is that any solution sought to be imposed by one group upon the others will fail (Southalan 2000, 15).

B. *The Future of Military-rule in Burma*

Castells argued eloquently in his important work *The Power of Identity* (1997) that a state experiencing a legitimation crisis will respond by shifting its power and resources to local and regional governments (that is, ethnodevelopment along Stavenhagen's lines). Yet by doing so the state may ultimately fail to "equalize the interests of various identities and social groups represented in the nation-state at large" (1997, 275). In the case of SPDC-ruled Burma, the polity has done the opposite: it has retreated into its own top-heavy bureaucracy, and for decades, ignored the demands placed by the ethnic nationalities like the Karen as well as those made by its own Burman population since 1988 for an end to military rule.

One geopolitical reason, albeit an oversimplified one, of how the Tatmadaw is able to remain unscathed, is due to China's patronage. It is clear that Beijing prefers to utilize rogue states in Asia as buffer zones, and Burma is part and parcel of what I call the Beijing triad: Pakistan, Burma, and North Korea. This political configuration allows Beijing to create a "pincer" geopolitical configuration against Western policy in the region. North Korea and Burma allow Beijing to attend to Japan and Taiwan, while India is surrounded by Pakistan in the West and Burma in the east. Thailand, America's staunchest ally in the Southeast Asian region, also falls under Beijing's observation via Burma.

Unless Beijing can be steered away from its support of the SPDC, the future of military-ruled Burma will remain unchallenged from the international sphere. In purely strategic terms the Tatmadaw is willing to make allowances in its grip on power in exchange for being in the orbit of a powerful ally. Had the attempted acquisition of California-based UNOCAL by Hong Kong-based Chinese National Offshore Oil Company (CNOOC) during spring 2005 been successful, China would possess the infamous UNOCAL rigs in the Gulf of Martaban as well as its business arrangements with Thailand. As demonstrated in Chapters 5 and 6, this would likely mean that Beijing would have intimate administration of the shipping of natural gas through Kawthoolei (where forced labor and excessive logging occurs), into Thailand. The Tatmadaw would then serve as a corporate militia, much like its role in protecting UNOCAL and Total workers.

As a result, Thailand's policy toward Burma is as much based on its fear of angering Beijing as it is based on seizing whatever natural resources are available to them from Burma. Additionally, India's Singh is too much of a technocrat to dabble with the emotively charged "internal" affairs of SPDC Burma. If Beijing's influence can be tempered, Bangkok will placate to international calls for democratic reforms and New Delhi will rise to the occasion by living up to its reputation of being the world's largest democracy. Most importantly, if Beijing severs ties with the Tatmadaw unfolding domestic events can topple the regime. With Beijing mated to Burma as the SPDC's largest arms supplier, it will be up to the pro-democracy Burman population and remaining self-determination groups like the Karen to continue the fight against the SPDC on their own. Maldevelopment of Kawthoolei will continue to worsen.

Implications of the Karen Struggle for Understanding a Materialist Ethnicity

An ethnodevelopment view of the Karen struggle points to an alternative way to understand ethnicity because the observer can leave what Bell (1975) describes as a "diffused" arena where an ethnie's culture is characterized by aesthetics. By departing from a social constructionist view the material consequences of ethnicity can be observed through the lived experiences of the ethnie. It is in this regard that the experiences of the Karen ethnie can be directly framed within a development context. Whereas a cultural treatment of ethnicity may not place an ethnie to a specific site, the material aspects of ethnicity: the lived experiences of the Karen, the territory of the Karen, the Karen informal economy and infrastructures that sustain their construction of nation, all can now be situated objectively. Therefore the implications for future development analyses of a materialized ethnicity will require a historical examination into three areas of the ethnie's collective experiences: (1) disentanglement from class dynamics, (2) experiences with systemic crisis, and (3) the political maneuverings that facilitate their ethnodevelopment.

A. Ethnicity Disentangled from Class Dynamics

To read ethnicity and its ethnopolitical trajectory, ethnicity will need to be disentangled from class analyses. At the end of Chapter 3, I included discussions by scholars such as Stavenhagen (1996), Ryan (1995), and Seers (1983) regarding the historical tentativeness of class identification, and how class "consciousness" is abandoned during times of heightened nationalist sentiment. Here I reintroduce Daniel Bell (1975) back into our discussion. Bell noted that the organizational momentum of ethnicity is much stronger given that class movements in advanced industrial societies no longer have a revolutionary purpose. As such Bell argues that actors no longer feel a "strong affective tie" to class interests, and class politics has lost its sense of purpose. For Bell, class politics contains unresolved contradictions, "on the one end, they have been part of a 'social movement' which seeks to transform society; on the other, a 'trade union' seeking a place within it" (Bell 1975, 160-171).

> The 'social movement' aspect of labor, with all the attendant aspects that the ideology sought to stimulate—fraternal organizations, cooperatives, theater and cultural groups—is no longer a 'way of life' for its members. The union has focused on the job, and little more (ibid., 160-171).

Bell's thought-provoking arguments beg the question: what alternatives does one have in a non class-based critique of imperialism?

> Imperialism has been overlooked largely in economic and political terms, but clearly it had a cultural component which emphasized the superiority of the older nations and which had extraordinary psychological effects on the personalities of those who lived under imperialist rule (ibid., 160-170).

Frantz Fannon (1963) and Albert Memmi (1965) would have certainly agreed with Bell's assessment. Indeed, the resistances to imperialism can be very cultural, as can resistances to a globally-imposed class order. For Bell, localized and indigenized nationalisms have and are continuing to harness ethnicity as a mode of "personal self-assertion" that challenges this hyper and global class structure.

Whether my attempt to disentangle class dynamics from ethnic dynamics was successful is for readers to judge. I do believe however, that I may have found a resolution not from the tedious analytical process of resolving the class versus ethnicity tensions, but from a dynamic far larger than both: the forces generated by the social system that frames an ethnie's experiences, and in the case of the Karen ethnie, a social system in the state of systemic crisis. Systemic crisis is thus the pivot that transforms class interests into ethnic interests: it dramatically changes economic, political, and social relationships and configurations.

B. Ethnicity during Systemic Crisis

In my analysis, the social system that sustained the Karen struggle has been mauled by fifty-nine years of war. As such the Karen continue to experience systemic crisis, or what Leach would refer to as systemic "disequilibria," their material and symbolic institutions are subjected to the continuing onslaught of an internally colonizing force. With Gordon's (1969) implication that a people's historical identification is activated during a shared crisis, the implication of systemic crisis in my work lies in how it creates a political trajectory that pushes ethnicity to the forefront of nation-construction. Indeed, the unique processes of historical identification are its frequent ability to occur across class lines as well as freezing ethnic identification in place. In the case of Karen nation-building, the freezing of ethnic identification serves as a collective coping mechanism for dealing with the systemic and humanitarian crises that frame their lives. For the Karen, nation-construction during times of systemic crisis exemplifies what Bell described as "historical energies" that drive a people forward to seek a place on the stage of history:

> Economic competition is dispersed between interests and occupations... For this obvious reason, where there has been a strong, aggressive nationalism, class and ethnic rivalries have been subdued or muted. As World War I and other wars have shown, country rather than class has the overriding appeal, even among workers (Bell 1975, 160-161).

An important alternative understanding of ethnicity should contribute to a discourse that unites ethnicity to its material consequences. Future research into ethnicity should distinguish between how social stability and instability function to materialize ethnicity in different ways. Moreover, by making a clear distinction regarding when actors chose ethnic identification over class identification, ethnicity and systemic crisis become heuristic devices for disentangling the intersections of class and ethnopolitics.

C. Ethnicity during Political Maneuverings

There is yet another context based on the political maneuverings of an ethnie. My preferred reading of the Karen struggle is derived from its political articulation, one which harnesses primordial sentiments for nation construction. But this articulation also has tangible outcomes as constituents compete for the "chief values of the society" (Bell 1975, 139).

An interesting feature of Karen multicultural political maneuverings is the simultaneity of horizontal and vertical trajectories. Framing both trajectories are geopolitical influences surrounding Burma and Kawthoolei. The horizontal process is exemplified by the KNU's transcommunal, NGO, and diasporic links. For over fifty-nine years the KNU has established ties with Burma's other ethnic nationalities to counter military aggression from Rangoon. The vertical process is exemplified by the vacillating ties between the KNU and the BSPP/SLORC/SPDC. Decades ago Cady already pointed to the complex interplay between the KNU and the Tatmadaw. In *A History of Modern Burma* (1958):

> The apparent Burmese policy of dispensing economic and political favors to break the unity of the Karen National Union was measurably effective, but it was not calculated to dispel Karen distrust which was itself the basis of the obdurate and, from the Burman point of view, unreasonable Karen demands for independence (Cady 1958, 551).

The geopolitical dimension of political maneuverings is exemplified by the KNU's responses not only to the Tatmadaw, but the Tatmadaw' international allies, as well as the Karen's own international allies, the NGOs, and the overt and covert support for both parties from the international community. Future examinations of an ethnie's political maneuverings during self-determination should include analyses of its horizontal and vertical geopolitical trajectories. Only then can we assess when and why some states in the international community are extremely reluctant to recognize claims to self-determination by minorities within a state. Southalan claims that overall international law has not greatly advanced the claims of such minorities since the establishment of the United Nations, and it would not seem prudent to expect otherwise from the "nations united" (Southalan 2000).

> The reason why international law has made so little contribution to the reduction of ethnic strife is because of its positivist composition: it constructs its rules as a synthesis of what states in fact do, rather than by reference to what they should do according to principles of fairness and justice (ibid., 7)

Sociological Implications of Ethnodevelopment for Development Studies

One of the most important lessons that Karen self-determination can teach us is that an ethnie's struggle for a greater autonomy, within the context of experiencing ethnic cleansing, is a development process. The Karen self-determination struggle, part of a global resurgence of ethnic self-determination activity, thus should not be ignored as it is typical of a broader historical resistance against continuing internal colonization dynamics. In the case of Burma, the avoidance by global finance institutions such as the World Bank, the Asian Development Bank, and the IMF to address the ethnic strife in the country further reproduces a blind spot in development analyses (Brunner et al. 1998). Because neoliberal policies and scrutiny cannot fully explain nor remedy what is actually occurring in military-ruled Burma, current and future application of development policy for Karen self-determination cannot be situated in an economistic context where development is simply about establishing a functioning free market.

Development strategists supportive of the alternative development paradigm such as Stavenhagen, Hettne, and Brown, possess a unique advantage: they are in the position to spotlight the human condition generated by a failed state that has yet to resolve its ethnic/racial strife and establish stable social systems for all of its multicultural constituents. Indeed, the alternative development paradigm, of which ethnodevelopment is part and parcel, is a culturally and politically expedient orientation in that its scrutiny upon multicultural states behooves us to attend to the contradictions within them. In the case of military-ruled and multicultural Burma, the primary contradiction within the state includes the interplay between an ethnocratic antagonist and a myriad of ethnie protagonists, led by the Karen. This makes ethnodevelopment a very useful and important perspective for analyzing how multicultural asymmetry affects the human condition.

Yet it is important to answer Cowen and Shenton's question as to whether alternative development really constitutes a departure from mainstream development. In light of how alternative development also utilizes trusteeships to manage their goals, and in my case via Karen elites and its supporting transcommunalities and NGOs, can the discourse avoid its similarity to a mainstream development trajectory which is also guided by the intent of trusteeships (Cowen and Shenton 1996, 453)? That is, to what extent does alternative development simply transfer notions of development and trusteeship to other mechanisms beyond the World Bank or IMF? And do these alternative mechanisms, for example, the role of local and international NGOs, actually represent people-centered initiatives?

As noted earlier in my work, I share Pieterse's (1998) view that alternative development is more of a critique of mainstream development planning that provides a "loosely connected series of alternative proposals and methodologies" rather than a "theoretical break with mainstream development" (Pieterse 1998, 345). Ethnodevelopment and mainstream development strategies are not mutually exclusive but symbiotic and temporal, that is, social stability may entail the use of mainstream development while social instability might entail the use of alternative development approaches. To adopt one doctrine in a mutually exclusive manner only partially reads the development or maldevelopment of a people.

The utility of an ethnodevelopment strategy lies in its ability to be specifically catered for analyzing oppressive multicultural states ruled by an undemocratic ethnocracy. In my work, the degree to which this ethnocracy oppresses its ethnic nationalities was used as an indicator for how much a state has failed. Once the Karen are rid of its ethnocratic nemesis, non-ethnodevelopment strategies, be it based on protectionism, state capitalism, or a free market, can thus make its entrance. In this regard ethnodevelopment is temporal because it forces strategists to historically scrutinize ethnic contradictions in a multicultural context as a prelude to analyzing the development of a functioning state as a whole.

My argument that ethnodevelopment can be a temporal strategy that functions as a prelude to other development strategies, was conceptualized by my talks with Karen. When the Karen look west they see a totalitarian wasteland, where close to sixty years, a brutal military dictatorship rules and represses its peoples. When they glance east they see Thailand and its dramatically more opulent and democratic way of life. When they look further east in Southeast Asia, they are aware of the birth of East Timor following the UN-sponsored act of self-determination in 1999 that forced a the Indonesian government to relinquish control of the territory, allowing the East Timorese to achieve full independence on May 20, 2002. When Karen activists and laborers work in Thailand, many dream of returning to a Karen homeland where amenities such as basic household goods can be purchased in a formal market, where airports can be built, where universities can spring, where there is peace.

When these Karen dream of their future the future is that of achieving modernity on par with much of Southeast Asia. As a result, the transfer of trusteeship to various transcommunalities, or supporting NGOs, should not be conceptualized as a problematic scenario. Indeed it compliments the instrumentalist approach of Karen elites. Although ethnodevelopment dynamics do not literally emanate from the intent of the people as it is idealized by the alternative development paradigm, it does emanate from elites who are obligated and accountable to its constituents, a relationship solidified and further heightened by the exigencies of war. Moreover Cowen and Shenton have never scrutinized the social distances between trusteeships and their constituents, which in the case of the KNU and the Karen, is close due to their shared history, circumstances of war, and a dwindling Karen territorial base.

But it is crucial to remember that Karen liberation ethnodevelopment is based on agency nationalism, the latter of which is the polar opposite of fascism. Ethnodevelopment strategists should not hesitate to forgo negotiations with a central government if it is demonstrated to be corrupt and totalitarian; that is, the latter need not be the main conduit for seeking a political solution. If liberation ethnodevelopment is "intentional practice" as conceptualized by Cowen and Shenton (1996), then it is a practice that will need to be situated in Kawthoolei before Naypidaw, or conversely with the KNU before the SPDC.

Liberation ethnodevelopment is more radical than ethnodevelopment because it urges the breaking up of, and as a point of clarification—failed—multicultural states, into new countries. The process of birthing new countries should not be viewed as an anomalous political trajectory if there exists a consensus by development strategists, technocrats, and scholars that failing states exhibit internally colonizing dynamics. In my work, I attempted to make visible that processes in the Tatmadaw's implementation of the *Four Cuts* constitute military-ruled Burma as a failed state. Moreover, as Gurr (1996) has demonstrated empirically, breaking up of states—as unpleasant as the proposition may sound—frequently leads to a cessation of large-scale conflict.

Even though a number of ethnies have in recent years successfully demarcated their claims in the language of self-determination the obstacles that remain in their paths are formidable. Moreover, international law is obviously prejudiced to such a process given global institutions like the United Nations are, as aforementioned, nothing more than clubs for member states.

> If the effect of international law were to assist in the destruction of states it would be a revolutionary tool, almost the obverse of a legal rule. It is not surprising, then that, rather than the principle of self-determination, it is the principle of national unity that has been almost universally followed by the international community—which, after all, is composed of states whose interest is to maintain themselves (Southalan 2000, 6).

Where does this leave the future of ethnodevelopment? Ethnodevelopment currently remains on the periphery of development studies due to its relatively provocative prescriptions that challenge the premise of the nation-state (Stavenhagen 1986). Although in principle, self-determination can garner universal sympathy, the support "rarely translates into encouragement from the international community for the break-up of states" (Southalan 2000, 1). Because ethnodevelopment is also a Barthian approach that desires to reconstruct the state system so that territorial boundaries correspond more closely to the social and cultural boundaries among peoples, Gurr notes that this is a "most radical proposal for resolving conflicts between states and peoples" (1996, 323). However, I believe that its variant, liberation ethnodevelopment, will be of great utility as a development strategy for failed multicultural states suffering from perennial ethnic conflict. Moreover:

Since the late 1980s...governments across the region have made greater efforts to acknowledge the distinct identities of both ethnic minorities and indigenous peoples, while donors have begun to fund projects to address their needs. In many cases, these initiatives have brought tangible benefits to the groups concerned. Yet in other respects progress to date has been modest and ethnodevelopment... remains confined to a limited number of initiatives in the context of a broader pattern of disadvantage and domination (Clarke 2001, 413).

Clarke nevertheless stresses the importance of applying ethnodevelopment in Southeast Asia simply because so many of Southeast Asia's ethnies have frequently been and continue to be exploited and victimized by their governments. Since nine out of ten Southeast Asian states have achieved their independence only after World War II, their ethnocracies continue to favor the nation-state project where there is a romanticized quest for national unity in spite of differences (Clarke 2001, 420).

Although any ethnopolitical wars in Southeast Asia may be winding down, others are sure to intensify (Gurr 1996).[91] This is why it is important for scholars to be suspicious of nation-state projects espoused by a totalitarian polity, especially when they are achieved by violence, as in the case of military-ruled Burma. The prescience of such a caveat goes as far back as 1970s when Connor (1972), in his article "Nation-building or nation-destroying," reminds scholars not to treat ethnicity as an "ephemeral nuisance" as well as warning against the promises of nation-state builders.

---

[91] Thailand escaped colonization during the 19th century by positioning itself as a buffer state between French colonial interests in the east (France had secured southern Vietnam) and British colonial interests in the west (Great Britain had incorporated Burma as a province of India). Prior to 1939 the country was known as Siam, and it included substantial Laotian, Cambodian and Malaya territories. Siam later ceded Malaya territory to the British while substantial Laotian and Cambodian territories were ceded to the French (the population of northeast Thailand, also known as "Isan" still speak a primarily Laotian-based dialect). It was a pyrrhic strategy designed to placate the expansionism of the colonials. The few Muslim provinces once administered by Siam are today rebelling against Thai hegemony.

Epilogue

The burden of international assistance and conflict resolution for genocide will need to begin by supporting the premise that some multicultural countries have failed in their construction of an overarching nation-state. From this observation, the international community should question the premise of the state given the specificities of their failures. Burma, in its current form, is such a failed state. On this point I subscribe to the position noted by Bryant who bluntly argued that "for Kawthoolei to be born, the old Burma would have to die" (1997, 7). Although there are no perfect options or solutions to quickly eliminate the Tatmadaw at this point, there are, according to Yagcioglu, "clearly wrong options":

> Oppression is wrong; ethnic cleansing and genocide are wrong; assimilation, if forced, is wrong. Unfortunately, despite the global changes and the new worldwide trends, many governments still consider such brutal strategies and policies within their range of choices. Let us hope that some day governments will realize that these are not solutions, but the very core of the problem (Yagcioglu 1993, 11).

The KNU has long been regarded as the "backbone" of the ethnic and democratic movement in Burma, so its future will have great implications for all groups fighting for self-determination and democracy. By having held their ground since 1949 and also during the 1990s when many of its most powerful allies have signed ceasefires with the regime, the KNU continues on with the construction of a Karen nation that can exist in a federalized Burma.

Karen civilians continue to bear the brunt of human rights violations from perennial Tatmadaw incursions into their country as well as live in abject poverty as IDPs and/or refugees. From Stavenhagen's ethnodevelopment that also emphasizes what Childs (2003) terms as *free determination*, and what Sen emphasizes development should be: *freedom*, my main position is that it is very important to support a *politicized* Karen self-determination platform if we want the Karen people to survive genocidal policies designed to obliterate them. That is, assessing the Karen human condition must include our understanding of how the ethnies like the Karen "decide whether and to what degree integration and separation from the...state should take place" (Childs 2003, 28). Let us hope that the self-determination of the Karen seeking freedom from oppression, will soon grant them peace and what Sen describes as a "momentous engagement with freedom's possibilities" (1999, 298).

References

Andersen, Margaret L. and Patricia Hill Collins (eds). 2001. *Race, Class and Gender.* Australia: Wadsworth.

Anderson, Benedict. 1991. *Imagined Communities.* London, New York: Verso.

Allen, T. & A. Thomas (eds). 1992. *Poverty and Development in the 1990s.* Oxford: Oxford University Press.

Amann, E. & W. Baer. 2002. "Neoliberalism and its Consequences in Brazil." *Journal of Latin American Studies.* 34, pp. 945-959.

Apple, Betsy and Veronika Martin. 2003. "No Safe Place: Burma's Army and the Rape of Ethnic Women." *Refugees International.* April. New York: Refugees International.

Armstrong, John. 1982. *Nations Before Nationalism.* Chapel Hill: University of North Carolina Press.

Ashton, William. 2004. "The arms keep coming--but who pays? *The Irrawaddy On-line Edition.* June 2004. Retrieved July 29, 2004. (http://www.irrawaddy.org/article.php?art_id=3759)

Bachoe, Ralph. 1996. "United We Stand, Divided We Fall--Reunification." *Bangkok Post.* October 6.

_____. 1996. "Bo Mya--ASEAN Should Not Admit Burma." *Bangkok Post.* December 8.

_____. 1997. "It's Not Over Till It's Over, Keeping up the Fight." *Bangkok Post.* March 2.

_____. 1998. "Concern over Karen Refugee Repatriation." *Bangkok Post.* January 18.

Balassa, B. 1988. "The Lessons of East Asian Development: An Overview." *Economic Development and Cultural Change.* 36 (3): S237-S290.

Bangkok Post. 1996. "No Progress in KNU-Junta Peace Talks." November, 28.

Bangkok Post. 1997. "Army on Alert as Burmese Close in on Rebel Base-- Intruders to be Repelled by Force." February 18.

Bangkok Post. 1997. "Mass Surrender of Rebel KNU fighters: Burmese force meets 'negligible' opposition." February 19.

Bangkok Post. 1998. "Raiders Burn Karen Refugee Camp, Leaving 9,000 Homeless." March 11.

Bangkok Post. 1998. "UNHCR Slams Burma over Raid on Refugee Camp." March 13.

Banton, Michael. 1983. *Racial and Ethnic Competition.* Cambridge: Cambridge University Press.

_____. 1994. "Modeling Ethnic and National Relations." *Ethnic and Racial Studies.* 17 (1): 2-10.

Banton, Michael and Mohd-Noor Mansor. 1992. "The Study of Ethnic Alignment: A New Technique and an Application in Malaysia." *Ethnic and Racial Studies.* 15 (4): 599-613.

Baran, Paul. 1957. *The Political Economy of Growth.* New York: Monthly Review Press.

Bates, Robert H. 1974. "Ethnic Competition and Modernization in Contemporary Africa." *Comparative Political Studies,* 4, January 4: 457-484.

Bernstein, H. 1971. "Modernization Theory and the Sociological Study of Development." *Journal of Development Studies* 7: 141-60.

Billet, B. 1993. *Modernization Theory and Economic Development.* Praeger, Westport.

Birsel, Robert. 1995. "Burmese Said to Prepare New Assault on Karen Base." Burmanet News. February 8. Retrieved March 3, 2004. (http://www.burmalibrary.org/reg.burma/archives/199502/msg000 54.html)

Brass, Paul R. 1991. *Ethnicity and Nationalism.* New Delhi, Newbury Park, London: Sage Publications.

British Broadcasting Corporation. 2004. Television news report on United Nations reforms, PBS, Channel 28, Los Angeles, 5:00 PM broadcast. December 1.

Brohman, J. 1996. *Popular Development: Rethinking the Theory and Practice of Development.* Oxford: Oxford University Press.

_____. 1995. Universalism, Eurocentrism, and Ideological Bias in Development Studies: From Modernisation to Neoliberalism. *Third World Quarterly.* 16 (1): 121-140.

_____. 1995. Economism and Critical Silences in Developmental Studies: A Theoretical Critique of Neoliberalism. *Third World Quarterly.* 16 (2): 297-316.

Brown, David. 1994. *State and Ethnic Politics in South-East Asia.* New York: Routledge.

Brenner, N. & T N. Theodore. 2002. "Cities and the Geographies of 'Actually Existing Neoliberalism.'" *Antipode.* 34 (3): 349-379.

Brunner, Jake, Kirk Talbott, and Chantal Elkin. 1998. "Logging Burma's Frontier Forests: Resources and the Regime." *World Resources Institute.* August 1998.

Bryant, Raymond L. 1997. "Kawthoolei and Teak: Karen Forest Management on the Thai-Burmese Border." *Watershed.* July-October. Vol. 3 (1).

Buergin, Reiner. 2000. "'Hill Tribes' and Forests: Minority Policies and Resource Conflict in Thailand." *Socio-economics of Forest Use in the Tropics and Subtropics.* July 2000.

Burma Ethnic Research Group (BERG) and Friedrich Naumann Foundation. 2004. "Forgotten Victims of a Hidden War: Internally Displaced Karen in Burma." Bangkok, Thailand. April.

Burmanet News. 1995. "Guerrillas Report Heavy Burmese Troop Losses." February 8. Retrieved March 3, 2004. (http://www.burmalibrary.org/reg.burma/archives/199502/msg000 54.html)

Burmese Border Consortium. 2002. *Internally Displaced People and Relocation Sites in Eastern Burma*. September. Retrieved on June 7, 2004. (http://www.ibiblio.org/obl/docs/BBC_Relocation_Site_Report_(1 1-9-02).htm)

Burawoy, Michael, Joseph A. Blum, Sheba George, Zsuzsa Gille, Teresa Gowan, Lynne Haney, Maren Klawiter, Steven H. Lopez, Sean O Riain, Millie Thayer. 2000. *Global Ethnography: Forces, Connections, and Imaginations in a Postmodern World*. Berkeley: University of California Press.

Buzan, B. 1983. *People, States and Fear: The National Security Problem in International Relations*. Brighton: Wheatsheaf.

Cady, J. 1958. *A History of Modern Burma*. Ithaca: Cornell University Press.

Castles, S. and M. J. Miller. 1998. *The Age of Migration: International Population Movements in the Modern World*. New York: The Guilford Press.

Chambers, R. 1983 *Rural Development: Putting the Last First*. London: Longman.

Chapman, Malcolm, Elizabeth Tonkin and Maryon McDonald (eds). 1989. *History and Ethnicity*. London, New York : Routledge.

Childs, John B. 2003. *Transcommunality: From the Politics of Conversion to the Ethics of Respect*. Philadelphia, PA: Temple University Press.

Childs, P. and R. J. P. Williams. 1997. *An Introduction to Post-colonial Theory*. London, United Kingdom: Prentice Hall.

Clarke, Gerard. 2001. "From Ethnocide to Ethnodevelopment? Ethnic Minorities and Indigenous Peoples in Southeast Asia." *Third World Quarterly*. 22 (3): 413-436.

Cohen, Abner. 1969. *Customs and Politics in Urban Africa*. Berkeley: University of California Press.

Connor, W. 1972. "Nation-building or Nation-destroying." *World Politics*. 24 (3): 319-355.

_____. 1994. *Ethno-nationalism: The Quest for Understanding*. Princeton: Princeton University Press.

Cowen, Michael and Robert W. Shenton. 1996. *Doctrines of Development.* Routledge.

Delang, Claudio O. (ed). 2000. *Suffering in Silence: The Human Rights Nightmare of the Karen people of Burma.* Parkland. USA: Universal Publishers.

Desai, A. 2003. "Neoliberalism and Resistance in South Africa." *Monthly Review.* Jan 2003.

DeMartino, G. 1999. "Global Neoliberalism, Policy Autonomy, and International Competitive Dynamics." *Journal of Economic Issues.* XXXIII (2): 343-349.

Dictatorwatch. 2004. Official Website. Retrieved June 21, 2004. (http://www.dictatorwatch.org/karenclinic.html)

Dowley, Kathleen M. and Brian D. Silver. 1999. "Subnational and National Loyalty: Cross-national Comparisons." *International Journal of Public Opinion Research.* 12 (4): 357-371.

Earth Rights International and Southeast Asian Information Network. 1996. *Total Denial: a Report on the Yadana Pipeline Project in Burma.* July 10. Retrieved on September 26, 2004 (http://www.ibiblio.org/freeburma/docs/totaldenial/td.html)

Economist. 2004. "Fighting for Survival." November 20: 25-27.

Edwards, M. 1989. "The Irrelevance of Development Studies," *Third World Quarterly.* 11 (1): 116-135.

Eller, Jack and Reed Coughlan. 1993. "The Poverty of Primordialism: the Demystification of Ethnic Attachments." *Ethnic and Racial Studies.* 16 (2): 187-201.

Enloe, C. 1973. *Ethnic Conflict and Political Development.* Boston: Little Brown.

Eriksen, Thomas H. 1993. *Ethnicity and Nationalism.* London: Pluto Press.

Erlich, Richard. 2004. "A Road Map to Mockery." *Bangkok Post,* May 22.

Esteva. G. 1992. *Development.* Pp. 6-25 in Sachs, W. (ed) *The Development Dictionary: A Guide to Knowledge as Power.* London: Zed Books.

Evans, Gareth. 2004. "When is it Right to Fight?" *Survival.* 40 (3), Autumn: 59-82.

Fahn, James David. 2003. *A Land on Fire: The Environmental Consequences of the Southeast Asian Boom.* Westview Press.

Falla, Jonathan. 1991. *True Love and Bartholomew: Rebels on the Burmese Border.* Cambridge, MA: Cambridge University Press.

Fanon, Frantz. 1963. *The Wretched of the Earth.* New York: Grove Press.

Fink, Christina. 2001. *Living in Silence: Burma under Military Rule.* Bangkok, Thailand: White Lotus.

Fishman, Joshua. 1980. "Social Theory and Ethnography." In Peter Sugar (ed). *Ethnic Diversity and Conflict in Eastern Europe.* Santa Barbara: ABC-Clio.

_____. 1989. *Language and Ethnicity in Minority Sociolinguistic Perspective.* Multilingual Matters Limited.

Frank, Andre G. 1969a. *Capitalism and Underdevelopment in Latin America.* New York: Monthly Review Press.

_____. 1969b. *Latin America: Underdevelopment or Revolution.* New York: Monthly Review Press.

Fredholm, Michael. 1993. *Burma: Ethnicity and Insurgency.* Westport, CT: Praeger.

Free Burma Rangers (FBR). 2004. Official Website. Retrieved February 22, 2004. (http://www.freeburmarangers.org/About_Us/)

Geertz, Clifford. 1963. *Old Societies and New States: The Quest for Modernity in Asia and Africa.* New York: Free Press of Glencoe.

_____. 1973. *The Interpretation of Cultures.* London: Fontana.

George, Susan. 1990. *A Fate Worse Than Debt.* New York: Grove Weidenfeld.

Glazer, Nathan and Daniel Moynihan (eds). 1975. *Ethnicity: Theory and Experience.* Cambridge: Harvard University Press.

Gordon, Milton M. 1964. *Assimilation in American Life: The Role of Race, Religion, and National Origins*. New York: Oxford University Press.

Gould, Stephen Jay. 1994. "The Geometer of Race." *Discover*. November 1994: 65-69.

Guha, R. 1982. On Some Aspects of the Historiography of Colonial India. In Guha (ed) *Subaltern Studies*, Vol. I.

Grosby, Steven. 1996. "The Inexpungeable Tie of Primordiality." Pp. 51-56 in Hutchinson, John and Anthony D. Smith (eds). *Ethnicity*. Oxford: Oxford University Press.

_____. 1994. "The Verdict of History: the Inexpungeable Tie of Primordiality—An Reply to Eller and Coughlan." *Ethnic and Racial Studies*. 17 (1): 164-71.

Gurr, Ted Robert. 1996. *Minorities at Risk: A Global View of Ethnopolitical Conflict*. Washington, D.C.: United States Institute of Peace Press.

Gyaw, Htun Aung. 1995. "Kawmoora offensive." *BurmaNet News*, Saturday, February 18. Retrieved on April 23, 2004: (http://www.hartford-hwp.com/archives/54/033.html)

Habermas, Jurgen. 1973. *Legitimation Crisis*. Boston: Beacon Press.

Hah, Chong-do and Jeffrey Martin. 1975. "Towards a Theory of Synthesis of Conflict and Integration Theories of Nationalism." *World Politics*. 27 (3): 373-379.

Hall, Stuart. 1992. "The New Ethnicities." In J. Donald and A. Rattansi (eds), *Race, Culture and Difference*, London: Sage Publications.

Halliday, F. 1979. *Iran: Dictatorship and Development*. Harmondsworth: Penguin.

Hanson, M. & J. Hentz. 1999. "Neocolonialism and Neoliberalism in South Africa and Zambia." *Political Science Quarterly*. Fall 1999 114 (3): 479-502.

Hart, G. 2001. Development Critiques in the 1990s: Cul de sac and Promising Paths. *Progress in Human Geography*. 25(4): 649-658.

Hechter, Michael. 1971. "Towards a Theory of Ethnic Change. *"Politics and Society*, 2 (1): 21-45.

Hechter, Michael. 1973. "The Persistence of Regionalism in the British Isles, 1885-1966." *The American Journal of Sociology*, 79 (2): 319-342.

_____. 1975. *Internal Colonialism. The Celtic Fringe in British National Development*. Berkeley: University of California Press.

_____. 1986. "A Rational Choice Approach to Race and Ethnic Relations." In Mason, D. and J. Rex (eds). *Theories of Race and Ethnic Relations*. Cambridge: Cambridge University Press: 268-277.

_____. 1996. "Ethnicity and Rational Choice Theory." In Hutchinson, John and Anthony D. Smith (eds). *Ethnicity*. Oxford: Oxford University Press: 90-98.

Heraclides, Alexis. 1990. "Secessionist Minorities and External Involvement." *International Organization*. 44 (3): 341-378.

Hettne, Bjorn. 1990. *Development Theory and the Three Worlds*. New York: Longman Scientific and Technical.

_____. 1996. "Ethnicity and Development: An Elusive Relationship." in D. Dwyer and D. Drakakais-Smith (eds), *Ethnicity and Development: Geographical Perspectives*, Chichester: John Wiley.

Hewitt, T. 1992. "Developing Countries: 1945 to 1990." In *Poverty and Development in the 1990s*. T. Allen & A. Thomas (eds). Oxford: Oxford University Press: 221-237.

Hobsbawm, Eric. 1990. *Nations and Nationalism since 1780*. Cambridge: Cambridge University Press.

Hobsbawm, Eric and Terence Ranger. 1983. *The Inventions of Tradition*. Cambridge: Cambridge University Press.

Hodgson, G. M. 2001. *How Economics Forgot History: The Problem of Historical Specificity in Social Science*. London and New York: Routledge.

Hom, R. 2002. "The puppet master of Burma." *Time Asia*, December 9, 2002. Retrieved December 2, 2003: (http://www.time.com/time/asia/covers/1101021216/newin.html)

Horowitz, Donald. 1985. *Ethnic Groups in Conflict*. Berkeley: University of California Press.

Human Rights Watch. 1995. "Abuses Linked to the Fall of Manerplaw." Vol. 7, No.5, [A] - March 1995.

Human Rights Watch. 1997. "Burma/Thailand: No Safety in Burma, No Sanctuary in Thailand." Vol. 9, No. 6, [C] - July 1997.

Human Rights Watch. 1998. "Unwanted and Unprotected: Burmese Refugees in Thailand." Vol. 10, No. 6, [C] October 1998.

Hunt, Diana. 1989. *Economic Theories of Development: An Analysis of Competing Paradigms*. New York, NY: Harvester Wheatsheaf.

Hutchinson, John and Anthony D. Smith (eds). 1996. *Ethnicity*. Oxford: Oxford University Press.

International Criminal Tribunal for the former Yugoslavia (ICTY). 1996. *The prosecutor of the tribunal against Zejnil Delalic Zdravko Mucic, also known as "Pavo", Hazim Delic Esad Landzo, also known as "Zenga."* March 19. Retrieved on July 2, 2004.
(http://www.un.org/icty/indictment/english/cel-ii960321e.htm)

International Crisis Group Asia Report (ICG). 2003. "Myanmar Backgrounder: Ethnic Minority Politics." No. 52, May 7: 1-38.

International Labour Organization (ILO). 2004. "Report of the Committee Set up to Consider the Representation Made by the International Confederation of Free Trade Unions under Article 24 of the ILO Constitution Alleging Non-observance by Myanmar of the Forced Labour Convention, 1930 (No.29)." (Geneva: ILO), November 1994.

The Irrawaddy On-line Edition. 2004. "Foreign investment in Burma: Foreign investment of permitted enterprises up to November 1999." Retrieved March August 3, 2004.
(http://www.irrawaddy.org/res/invest.html)

The Irrawaddy On-line Edition. 2004. "An Interview with Desmond Ball: Desmond Ball unbound." Retrieved June 23, 2004.
(http://www.irrawaddy.org/interview_show.php?art_id=3763)

The Irrawaddy On-line Edition. 2004. "Chronology of meetings between the Karen National Union and Burma's military government." Retrieved June 30, 2004. (http://www.irrawaddy.org/res/ceasefireKNU.html)

The Irrawaddy On-line Edition. 2004. "Universities Opened and Closed: Updated on January 2003." Retrieved July 28, 2004. (http://www.irrawaddy.org/res/uniopen.html)

The Irrawaddy On-Line Edition. 2008. "KNU Call on Ethnic Ceasefire Groups to Support Uprising." Retrieved September 28, 2008. (http://www.irrawaddy.org/article.php?art_id=8782)

Jinakul, Surath. 2004. "Tall in the saddle." *Bangkok Post.* May 16.

Joseph, G. G., V. Reddy & M. Searle-Chatterjee. "Eurocentrism in the Social Sciences." *Race and Class,* 32 (1): 1-26.

Kawthoolei Education Fund. 2004. "Distribution Report: Updated on June 6, 2003." Retrieved May 13, 2004. (http://members.cscoms.com/~teaching/background.html)

Kaosa-ard, Apichari. 1989. "Teak: It's Natural Distribution and Related Factors." *Natural History Bulletin of the Siam Society.* Vol. 29: 55-74.

Kardlarp, Somsak. 1995. "Myanmar Gas for Ratchburi Power Plant: The Good Impact on Salween Dam." *Bangkok Post,* April 17.

Kaopatumtip, Songpol and Maxmilian Wechsler. 2004. "In the Midst of a New Revolution.'" *Bangkok Post:* Sunday, January 4.

Karen Women's Organization. 2004. *Shattering Silences: Karen Women Speak Out about the Burmese Military Regime's use of Rape as a Strategy of War in Karen State.* Mae Hong Son Province, Thailand: KWO Central. Please visit: (http://www.karenwomen.org/)

Karen Human Rights Group. 1995. "SLORC's Northern Karen offensive." March 29. Retrieved on March 1, 2004. (http://www.khrg.org/khrg95/khrg9510.html)

_____. "1997. Attacks on Karen Refugee Camps." March 18. Retrieved March 7, 2004. (http://ibiblio.net/obl/reg.burma/archives/199704/msg00282.html)

Kasem, Supamart. 1997. "Karens Change Military Tactics in war against Burmese Forces: Leaders put Emphasis on Guerrilla Warfare. *Bangkok Post.* April 27.

Kawthoolei Education Fund (KEF). 2004. Official website: Retrieved May 2, 2004. Please visit (http://www.ktwg.org/) http://members.cscoms.com/~teaching/Districts/dooplaya.html)

Keyes, Charles F (ed). 1979. *Ethnic Adaptation and Identity: The Karen on the Thai Frontier with Burma.* Philadelphia, PA: Ishi

Khosla, Deepa. 1999. "Third World States as Intervenors in Ethnic Conflicts: Implications for Regional and International Security." *Third World Quarterly.* 20 (6): 1143-1156.

Kiely, R. 1995. *Sociology and Development: The Impasse and Beyond.* London, United Kingdom: UCL Press.

Kiely, R. 1998. *Industrialization and Development: A Comparative Analysis.* London, United Kingdom: UCL Press.

Kitching, Gavin. 1982. *Development and Underdevelopment in Historical Perspective.* London: Methuen.

Klak, T & G. Myers. 1997. "The Discursive Tactics of Neoliberal Development in Small Third World Countries." *Geoforum* 28 (2): 133-49.

Klinghoffer, A. J. 1969. *Soviet Perspectives on African Socialism.* Rutherford/Fairleigh Dickinson University Press, Cranbury, N. J.

Korten D. 1990 *Getting to the 21st Century: Voluntary Action and the Global Agenda.* West Hartford: Kumarian Press.

Kumekawa, E. (1993). "Sansei Ethnic Identity and the Consequences of Perceived Unshared Suffering for Third Generation Japanese Americans." *American Mosaic: Selected Readings on America's Multicultural Heritage.* New Jersey, NJ: Prentice Hall.

Kuttner, R. (1985). "The Poverty of Economics." *Atlantic Monthly*, February: 74-84.

Latimer, Wyatt, Naris Bhumpakkaphan and Clemens Fehr. 1992. "Report and Proposal for Kaserdoh Wildlife Sanctuary." *Regional Community Forestry Training Center* (RECOFTC): Bangkok, Thailand.

Leach, E. R. 1954. *Political Systems of Highland Burma.* London: The Athlone Press.

Lehman, F. K. (ed). 1981. *Military Rule in Burma Since 1962*. Maruzen Asia PTE. LTD.

Lertcharoenchok, Yindee. 1995. "KNU claim SLORC Inciting Religious Split in Thailand." *Nation*. January 14.

Lintner, Bertril. 1994. *Burma in Revolt: Opium and Insurgency since 1948*. Boulder, CO: Westview Press.

Lummis, Douglas C. 1992. "Equality." Pp. 38-52 in Wolfgang Sachs (ed), *The Development Dictionary: A Guide to Knowledge as Power*. London, United Kingdom: Zed Books.

Mander, J. and E. Goldsmith (eds). 1996. *The Case Against the Global Economy: and for a Turn Toward the Local*. San Francisco: Sierra Club Books.

McGarry, John and Brenden O'Leary. 1993. *The Politics of Ethnic Antagonism*. London: Routledge.

McMichael, P. 1996. *Development and Social change*. Thousand Oaks, CA: Pine Forge Press.

Melson, Robert and Howard Wolpe. 1970. "Modernization and the Politics of Communalism: a Theoretical Perspective." *American Political Science Review*. 64 (4): 1112-1130.

Memmi, Albert. 1965. *The Colonizer and the Colonized*. Boston: Beacon Press.

Merril, Kay. 1999. "Burma Looks to Reject the Lessons of History." *Jane's Intelligence Review*. 1 August 1999.

Moerman, Michael. 1968. "Being Lue: Uses and Abuses of Ethnic Identification." June. 1968. *Essays on the Problem of Tribe*, Proceedings of the 1967 Annual spring meeting of the American Ethnological Society. Seattle: University of Washington Press, pp: 153-169.

Mizzima. 2004. "Mizzima interview with Karen leader General Saw Bo Mya." *Mizzima.com*. March 15. Retrieved July 23, 2004. (http://www.mizzima.com/mizzimanews/Interview/21-Nov-2006-05.html).

Myint-U, Thant. 2001. *The Making of Modern Burma*. Cambridge, MA: Cambridge University Press.

Nairn, Tom. 1975. "The Modern Janus." *New Left Review*. 94 (November-December).

Nairn, Tom. 1977. *The Break-up of Britain*. London: New Left Books.

Naw, Rebecca. 1989. "Karen education: Children on the front line." *Cultural Survival*. Retrieved June 27, 2004. (http://www.cs.org/publications/Csq/csq-article.cfm?id=827).

Nerfin, M. 1977. *Another Development: Approaches and Strategies*. The Dag Hammarskjold Foundation, Uppsala.

Nielsson, G. P. 1985. "States and Nation-groups: A Global Taxonomy." In Tiryakian, E. A. and Ragowski, R., (eds), *New Nationalisms of the Developed West*. Boston, MA: Allen and Unwin.

Nyerere, J. K. 1968. *Ujamaa: Essays on Socialism*. Dar Es Salaam.

Palgrave, Supamart Kasem Gifford. 1997. "Retreating Karens burn headquarters: 3,000 Refugees Move Deeper Inland." *Bangkok Post*: February 14.

Patterson, O. 1983. "The Nature, Causes, and Implications of Ethnic Identification." Pp. 25-50 in C. Fried (ed). 1983. *Minorities: Community and Identity*. Verlin: Springer-Verlag.

Paung, Shah. 2004. "KNU to resume ceasefire talks with junta." *The Irrawaddy On-line Edition*. August 3. Retrieved August 3, 2004. (http://www.irrawaddy.org/article.php?art_id=3754)

Peck, Grant. 2004. "Karen discuss laying down arms." *Bangkok Post*: January 23.

Phongpaichit, P., Sungsidh Piriyarangsan, Nualnoi Treerat. 1998. *Guns, Girls, Gambling, Ganja: Thailand's Illegal Economy and Public Policy*. Chiang Mai, Thailand: Silkworm Books.

Pieterse, J.N. 1998. "My Paradigm or Yours? Alternative Development, Post-Development, Reflexive development," *Development and Change* 29 (2): 343-373.

Rajah, Ananda. 2002. "A 'Nation of Intent' in Burma: Karen Ethno-nationalism, Nationalism and Narrations of Nation." *Pacific Review*. 15 (4): 517-537

Rerkasem, Kanok. 1996. "Population pressure and agrodiversity in marginal areas of northern Thailand." *Population, land management, and environmental change: NU Global Environmental Forum IV*, ed. J. I. Uitto and A. Ono. Retrieved on July 9, 2004: (http://www.unu.edu/unupress/unupbooks/uu03pe/uu03pe0a.htm)

Roberts, K. M. & M. Arce. 1998. "Neoliberalism and Lower Class Voting Behavior in Peru." *Comparative Political Studies*. April-May 31 (2): 217-246.

Rogers, Benedict. 2004. *A Land Without Evil: Stopping the Genocide of Burma's Karen People*. Oxford: Monarch Books.

Ryan, Stephen. 1995. *Ethnic Conflict and International Relations*. Dartmouth, UK: Antony Rowe Ltd.

Sachs, W. (ed). 1992. *The Development Dictionary: A Guide to Knowledge as Power*. London, United Kingdom: Zed Books.

Said, Edward W. 1979. *Orientalism*. Vintage Books

Saideman, Stephan M. 2002. "Discrimination in International Relations: Analyzing External Support for Ethnic Groups." *Journal of Peace Research*. 39 (1): 27-50.

Sassen, Saskia. 1998. *Globalization and its Discontents: Essays on the New Mobility of People and Money*. New York: The New Press.

Seers, D. 1979. "The birth, life and death of development economics." *Development and Change*. 10 (4) October 1979.

Seers, D. 1983. *The political Economy of Nationalism*. Oxford: Oxford University Press.

Selth, Andrew. 2000. "Burma's Secret Partners." *Canberra Papers on Strategy and Defence*. No. 136. Strategic and Defence Studies Centre: The Australian National University, Canberra, 2000.

Selth, Andrew. 1995. "The Burmese Army." *Jane's Intelligence Review*, November 1, 1995, vol 7, no. 11.

Sen, Amartya. 1999. *Development as Freedom*. New York, NY: Random House.

Sharansky, Natan and Ron Dermer. 2004. *The Case for Democracy: The Power of Freedom to Overcome Tyranny and Terror.* Public Affairs.

Sharp, R. 1995. "Organizing for Change: People Power and the Role of Institutions." Pp. 309-330 in J. Kirkby, P. O'Keefe and L. Timberlake (eds) *The Earthscan Reader in Sustainable Development.* London: Earthscan.

Shils, E. 1957. "Primordial, Personal, Sacred and Civil Ties." *British Journal of Sociology*, 8: 130-145.

Sidanius, J., Feshbach, S., Levin, S. and F. Pratto. 1997. "The Interface Between Ethnic and National Attachment: Ethnic Pluralism or Ethnic Dominance Revisited." *Public Opinion Quarterly.* 61(1): 102-133.

Silverstein, Josef. 1980. *Burmese Politics: The Dilemma of National Unity.* New Brunswick: Rutgers University Press.

_____. 1981. "Minority Problems in Burma since 1962." In Lehman (ed). *Military Rule in Burma since 1962: A Kaleidoscope of Views.* Singapore: Maruzen Asia PTE. LTD.

Smith, Anthony. 1998. *Nationalism and Modernism.* New York: Routledge.

Smith, Martin. 1999. *Burma: Insurgency and the Politics of Ethnicity.* Dhaka: The University Press.

_____. 1994. "Paradise lost? The Suppression of Environmental Rights and Freedom of Expression in Burma." September 1994, Article 19, ISBN 1 87079837 6, Retrieved June 13, 2004: (http://www.unhcr.org/cgi-bin/texis/vtx/refworld/rwmain?docid=4754182e131d)

Smith, N. 1997. "The Satanic Geographies of Globalization." *Public Culture* 10 (1): 169-89.

Smith, P. 1992. "Industrialization and Environment." In *Industrialization and Development.* P. 281 in T. Hewitt, H. Johnson, and D. Wield (eds). Oxford: Oxford University Press.

Southalan, Louise. 2000. "Issues of Self-determination in Burma." *Legal Issues on Burma Journal.*, no. 5, April.

Stavenhagen, R. 1986. "Ethnodevelopment: A neglected Dimension in Development Thinking." Pp. 71-94 in Anthorpe, Raymond and Krahl Andras (eds). *Development Studies: Critique and Renewal.* Leiden: E. J. Brill.

_____. 1993. "Self-determination: Right or Demon?" *Stanford Journal of International Affairs* II (2): Summer.

_____. 1996. *Ethnic Conflicts and the Nation-state.* New York: St. Martin's Press.

Steinburg, D. J. 1990. *The Future of Burma: Crisis and Choice in Myanmar.* Lanham: University Press of America.

Storey, Donovan. 2000. "Human Development Strategies and Human Development Reports on the Pacific: A Viable Alternative or Just Another Development?" Paper presented at *DevNet Conference 2000 - Poverty, Prosperity and Progress*, in Wellington, New Zealand.

Suhrke, Astri and Lela Garner Nobel (eds). 1977. *Ethnic Conflict in International Relations.* New York: Praeger.

Suu Kyi, Aung San. 1995. *Freedom from Fear.* London, England: Penguin Books.

Tharckabaw, David and Roland Watson. 2003. "The Karen People of Burma and the Karen National Union." *Dictatorwatch.org*, Retrieved February 12, 2004. (http://www.dictatorwatch.org/articles/karenintro.html)

Thomas, A. 1992. Introduction. *Poverty and Development in the 1990s.* Pp. 1-9 in T. Allen and A. Thomas (eds). 1-9. Oxford: Oxford University Press.

Thomas, A and D. Potter. 1992. "Development, Capitalism and the Nation-state." Pp. 116-144 in *Poverty and Development in the 1990s.* T. Allen and A. Thomas (eds). Oxford: Oxford University Press.

Thompson, B. R. and D. Ronen. 1986. *Ethnicity, Politics and Development.* Boulder: Lynn Rienner.

Toye, J. 1987. *Dilemmas of Development.* Oxford: Blackwell.

UNDP. 1994. *Pacific Human Development Report: Putting People First.* Suva: UNDP.

UNDP. 1999. *Pacific Human Development Report: Creating Opportunities*. Suva: UNDP

Van Den Berghe, Pierre. 1978. "Race and Ethnicity: a Sociobiological Perspective." *Ethnic and Racial Studies*, 1 (4): 401-411.

_____. 1979. The ethnic phenomenon. New York: Elsevier.

_____. (ed). 1990. *State Violence and Ethnicity*. Niwot: University Press of Colorado.

_____. 1996. "Does Race Matter?" Pp. 57-62 in Hutchinson, John and Anthony D. Smith (eds). *Ethnicity*. Oxford: Oxford University Press.

Van Schendel, Willem. 1992. "The Invention of the 'Jummas': State Formation and Ethnicity in Southeastern Bangladesh." *Modern Asian Studies*. 26 (1): 95-128.

_____. 2002. "Stateless in South Asia: The Making of the India-Bangladesh Enclaves." *The Journal of Asian Studies*. 61 (1): 115-147.

Varese, Stefano. 2002. *Salt of the Mountains: Campa Ashaninka - History and Resistance in the Peruvian Jungle*. University of Oklahoma Press.

Wade, R. 1990. *Governing the Market: Economic Theory and the Role of Government in East Asian Industrialization*. Princeton: Princeton University Press.

Walzer, M. 1983. "States and Minorities." Pp. 219-227 in C. Fried (ed). 1983. *Minorities: Community and Identity*. Verlin: Springer-Verlag.

Watson, Roland. 2004. "KNU Ceasefire with the SPDC." *Mizzima.Com*, Retrieved on July 12, 2004. (http://www.mizzima.com/Solidarity/July/12-July04-01.htm).

Weber, Max. 1996. "The Origins of Ethnic Groups." Pp. 35-39 in Hutchinson, John and Anthony D. Smith (eds). *Ethnicity*. Oxford: Oxford University Press.

Wechsler, Maxmilian. 2003. "Burma's opposition." *Bangkok Post*: October 12.

_____. 2004a. "Deadly harvest will continue." *Bangkok Post*: Sunday, February 1.

Wechsler, Maxmilian. 2004b. "Uncertainty over Pang Sang." *Bangkok Post*. Sunday, February 1.

_____. 2004c. "Demilitarisation is key to transition." *Bangkok Post*. Sunday, May 16.

Wee, Vivienne. 2002. "Ethno-Nationalism in Process: Ethnicity, Atavism and Indigenism in Riau, Indonesia." *The Pacific Review*. 15 (4): 497-516.

Weiner, M. 1987. "Political change: Asia, Africa and the Middle East." Pp. 33-64 in M. Weiner and S. P. Huntington (eds). *Understanding Political Development*. Boston: Little Brown.

Wyatt, David K. 1982. *Thailand: A Short History*. New Haven, CT: Yale University Press.

World Bank. 1985. *Research News*, 6, 1, Summer.

Yagcioglu, Dimostenis. 1996. "Nation-states vis-à-vis ethno cultural minorities: Oppression and assimilation versus integration and accommodation." Yagioglu home page. Retrieved August 3, 2004: (http://www.geocities.com/Athens/8945/minor.html)

Yeni. 2004. "Karen refugees have 'window on the world', conference told." *The Irrawaddy On-line Edition*. November 17. Retrieved November 17, 2004: (http://www.burmanet.org/news/2004/11/17/irrawaddy-karen-refugees-have-window-on-the-world-conference-told-yeni/)